Led Zeppelin

ALSO BY BARNEY HOSKYNS

Hotel California: The True-Life Adventures of Crosby, Stills, Nash, Young, Mitchell, Taylor, Browne, Ronstadt, Geffen, the Eagles, and Their Many Friends

Across the Great Divide: The Band and America

Waiting for the Sun: A Rock and Roll History of Los Angeles

Lowside of the Road: A Life of Tom Waits

Glam!: (David) Bowie, (Marc) Bolan and the Glitter Rock Revolution

Led Zeppelin

The Oral History of the World's Greatest Rock Band

BARNEY HOSKYNS

John Wiley & Sons, Inc.

Copyright © 2012 by Barney Hoskyns. All rights reserved

Cover Design: Susan Olinsky
Cover Image: © Pictorial Press/Alamy

Published by John Wiley & Sons, Inc., Hoboken, New Jersey
Published simultaneously in Canada

For general information about our other products and services, please contact our Customer Care Department within the United States at (800) 762-2974, outside the United States at (317) 572-3993 or fax (317) 572-4002.

Wiley also publishes its books in a variety of electronic formats and by print-on-demand. Some content that appears in standard print versions of this book may not be available in other formats. For more information about Wiley products, visit us at www.wiley.com.

Library of Congress Cataloging-in-Publication Data:

Hoskyns, Barney.
   Led Zeppelin : the oral history of the world's greatest rock band/Barney Hoskyns.
     p. cm.
   Includes bibliographical references and index.
   ISBN 978-0-470-89432-3 (cloth); ISBN 978-1-118-22111-2 (ebk);
ISBN 978-1-118-23490-7 (ebk); ISBN 978-1-118-25955-9 (ebk)
  1. Led Zeppelin (Musical group) 2. Rock musicians–England–Biography. I. Title.
  ML421.L4H66 2012
  782.42166092'2–dc23
  [B]
                                2012016374

Printed in the United States of America

10 9 8 7 6 5 4 3 2 1

For Mat Snow

What did Led Zeppelin prove? That great music is always the best excuse for bad behavior.

—Kim Fowley

CONTENTS

PREFACE

In Through the Out Door: "The Biggest Unknown Group in the World . . ."

> Led Zeppelin was unobtainable and unattainable, and
> we very seldom talked about it. Basically, the myth
> propagated itself.
>
> —Robert Plant to the author, May 2003

On a white-hot morning in Twentynine Palms—the Mojave desert town name-checked on Robert Plant's 1993 album *Fate of Nations*—I can see a number of the strangely shaped Joshua trees that lend their name to the nearby national park, the same place where, on Cap Rock in 1969, Gram Parsons dropped acid with Keith Richards and Anita Pallenberg.

Ever since Parsons OD'd and died in Joshua Tree itself—twenty-five miles east along Route 62—the whole area has become one of California's holy rock sites. So it's fitting that as I fill up my rental compact at a Twentynine Palms gas station, I hear the booming strains of a rock song approaching. Within seconds, I know it as a staple of classic-rock radio—an evergreen of easy-riding highway rock—and the pop snob in me groans. Pulling up next to me is a mirror-shaded dude astride a black beast of a motorcycle, its wheels flanked by vast speaker bins that punch out the song I know so well:

"Babe babe babe babe babe babe 'm bayeebee I'm gonna LEEEEAVE you . . ."

The owner of the song's strangulated male voice *ain't joking, woman*, he's *really got to ramble*—rather like this man in his sunglasses. The voice soundtracks the guy's chrome-horse freedom on a song recorded almost four decades ago, and he is making sure we all know it. I look at him and want to dismiss him as an idiot. He's at least as old as the song, and if he took the shades off, he might be old enough to have seen Led Zeppelin in their pomp, maybe at the L.A. Forum, possibly at the Long Beach Arena or the San Diego Sports Arena—the huge venues where the West was won. Perhaps he saw Zep's last, occluded U.S. show at the Oakland Coliseum in the summer of '77. Or he may only have seen the band in his mind, back when he was a beer-chuggin' adolescent spellbound by their satanic limey majesty, one of the vast legion of disciples who worshipped them as "your overlords."

It doesn't really matter which it is, because I understand the mythic potency of the music that's blasting from his speakers. And slowly I start to see him, in all his delusions, as oddly heroic. Like Robert Plant on "Babe, I'm Gonna Leave You," he's gotta keep moving, hitting the highway again, on to the next town and the next chick. Maybe he's heading east, farther into the empty Mojave, where he can "feel the heat of your desert heart" ("Twentynine Palms"), and then on to Arizona or New Mexico or just someplace where he can hole up and be free. Alternatively, he could be heading west to gaze out on the infinite Pacific and leave *terra firma* behind him. He could be a gung-ho libertarian, a man for whom "Babe, I'm Gonna Leave You" says, simply, "I have no responsibility to anyone except *me*." Or he could just be a weekend warrior, escaping the deep dreariness of his nine-to-five life.

As the song's frenzied descending chords fade over Plant's frayed larynx, I silently bond with Mr. "Get the Led Out," as I recall my own first exposure to the second track on Zeppelin's astounding debut album. (When I asked John Paul Jones which album he would play to someone who'd never heard the band, he said, "The first one. . . . It's all there, right from the word go." I'm not sure he wasn't right.) I understand why this and other songs became battle cries for a lost generation of disowned teenagers searching for dark magic in their suburban shopping-mall lives. I understand how Zeppelin became a new Fab Four for the younger siblings who missed out on Beatlemania—and for whom the Rolling Stones were just too Côte d'Azur for their own good.

For what you hear on "Babe, I'm Gonna Leave You" and every great Zeppelin track is not just power—amplified aggression matched by priapic swagger—but yearning, journeying, questing for an ideal.

"There is a point in your life," Chuck Klosterman wrote in *Killing Yourself to Live*, "when you hear songs like 'The Ocean' and 'Out on the Tiles' and 'Kashmir,' and you suddenly find yourself feeling like these songs are actively making you into the person you want to be. It does not matter if you've heard those songs a hundred times and felt nothing in the past, and it does not matter if you don't normally like rock 'n' roll and just happened to overhear it in somebody else's dorm room. We all still meet at the same vortex: for whatever the reason, there is a point in the male maturation process when the music of Led Zeppelin sounds like the perfect actualisation of the perfectly cool you." For the scurrilous Svengali Kim Fowley, who consorted with them in their Hyatt House heyday, Led Zeppelin were both "dangerous" and "spiritual"—and you couldn't have one without the other. Another way of saying that is to resort to hoary metaphors of light and dark, good and evil. Certainly, it's difficult to talk of Zeppelin and *not* speak of evil; many of those interviewed for this oral history do just that. And while it's too easy to identify Robert Plant and John Paul Jones with "the light" and Jimmy Page and John Bonham (and Peter Grant and Richard Cole, et al.) with "the dark," the occult appeal of Page as a guitar magus steeped in the nefarious teachings of Aleister Crowley remains central to Zeppelin's appeal to adolescents as they strive to create identities for themselves in a world that never recovered from the failure of America's hippie dream.

"Led Zeppelin always drew a difficult element," reflected the late Bill Graham, the pugnacious San Francisco promoter who became their inadvertent nemesis in Oakland. "A lot of male aggression came along with their shows. This was during the warp of the '70s, which was a very strange era. It was anarchy *without* a cause." "By 1975, *ZoSo* was painted or carved on every static thing rocker kids could find," wrote the sociologist Dr. Donna Gaines. "It had become a unifying symbol for America's suburban adolescents. The children of *ZoSo* are Zep's legacy. Mostly white males, nonaffluent American kids mixing up the old-school prole(tariat) values of their parents, mass culture, pagan yearnings and '60s hedonism." Yet the resonance of Zeppelin's music goes way beyond acne'd initiation rites; otherwise we'd be talking about them today as we talk about (or *don't* talk about) Kiss or Peter Frampton or Grand Funk Railroad. The reason my biker in Twentynine Palms is blasting "Babe, I'm Gonna Leave You" from his roadhog bins after all those years is because Led Zeppelin still speaks to him of danger and spirituality, darkness and light, power and beauty; because their albums—at least, up to and including 1975's *Physical Graffiti*—still sound so mighty and so sensual. Because they locked together tighter than any other rock unit in history. Because Jimmy Page wrote the most crunchingly powerful riffs ever fashioned by an electric guitarist. Because encoded within their metal blitzkrieg lies a deep funk that gives even James Brown a run for his money. Because their beauteous acoustic music is as sublime as their amplified anthems. Because live—as the countless Zep bootlegs attest—they took "How Many More Times," "Dazed and Confused," "No Quarter," and "In My Time of Dying" into new dimensions of giddy improvisation. Because John Bonham did things on his drum kit that confound the ear to this day. Because—even when his lyrics smacked of ethereal piffle—Robert Plant possessed the most frighteningly exciting hard-rock voice ever captured on tape, a bloodcurdling fusion of Janis Joplin and Family's Roger Chapman.

Also because of the dizzying diversity of styles and moods the band mastered: dense Chicago blues ("You Shook Me," "I Can't Quit You, Baby," "The Lemon Song," "The Girl I Love She Got Long Black Wavy

Hair"); metallic funk ("Whole Lotta Love," "Bring It on Home," "Immigrant Song," "The Ocean," "Custard Pie," "The Wanton Song," "Nobody's Fault but Mine," "For Your Life"); kinetic folk-rock ("Babe, I'm Gonna Leave You," "Ramble On," "Gallows Pole," "The Battle of Evermore," "Over the Hills and Far Away," "Poor Tom"); hyper-prog bombast ("The Song Remains the Same," "No Quarter," "In the Light," "Ten Years Gone," "Achilles' Last Stand," "Carouselambra"); unplugged pastoral ("That's the Way," "Bron-yr-Aur," "Going to California," "Black Country Woman," the first half of "Stairway to Heaven"); headbanger raunch ("Heartbreaker," "Sick Again"); trebly Big Star swagger ("Dancing Days," "Houses of the Holy"); swampy Delta dread ("Hats Off to Harper," "Black Dog," "When the Levee Breaks," "In My Time of Dying"); Motor City protopunk ("Communication Breakdown"); eerie Orientalism ("Friends," "Four Sticks," "Kashmir"); searing blues balladry ("Since I've Been Loving You," "Tea for One"); and retro rock 'n' roll ("Rock and Roll," "Boogie with Stu," the numerous live covers of Elvis, Eddie Cochran, et al.) . . . almost all of which I'd put up there with the best of Elvis/Dylan/Beatles/Stones/Hendrix/Young/Nirvana/Radiohead and any other rock act from the last half-century.

Oh, and because all those dumb rock critics just didn't get it.

"It's remarkable that we kept it going for as many records as we did," Plant told Steven Rosen in 1986. "Really, there wasn't one record that had anything to do with the one before it. And that's a great credit when there are so many artists who will unconsciously rest on their laurels and say, 'This is it, this is the way it must be.' Complacent? No." Beyond this is the mythology itself, the shaping of Zeppelin by not just its members but by Grant and Cole and Atlantic Records and lawyer Steve Weiss and agent Frank Barsalona and all of the underage groupies and grizzled roadies who served the band. Many of these people finally get to have their say in this book. All contribute to a narrative—a rise-and-fall-and-resurrection—the scale of which we will never experience again in our lifetimes.

"As the years go on, it's become a little easier to talk about this group," says Sam Aizer, who worked for Zeppelin's Swan Song label in

New York. "For a long time they had such a hold on the people they worked with that no one ever wanted to say anything. It was almost like a secret society."

. . .

"Those were the days," Robert Plant says with a big wry smile, "but these *are* the days . . ."

I am standing backstage at the Anselmo Valencia Amphitheater in Tucson, Arizona, when the lion-maned, tennis-muscled frontman of the Band of Joy beckons me over to join the gaggle of friends that invariably surrounds him after shows.

Plant knows why I am here: he knows I haven't flown from L.A. to Tucson simply to see him perform with Buddy Miller, Patty Griffin— soon to become the latest of his many inamoratas—and the other Nashville-based players who helped him make *Band of Joy*, the follow-up to the three-million-selling *Raising Sand*.

"How on earth did you find *John Crutchley?!*" Robert says in the semigentrified Black Country tones that have barely changed since he did his first interviews as the nineteen-year-old frontman of Jimmy Page's new band in 1968. Crutchley, one of the sweetest people on God's earth, played guitar in Listen, the mod-era R&B band that provided Plant with his first recording opportunity. Like many from Robert's past, he remains in touch with his former bandmate and still talks of him as if he were just another chum from the old Black Country days.

Plant may publicly disparage retromania—specifically, the unending classic-rock fixation with Zeppelin stories and tropes—but secretly he's as nostalgic as the next man. Holding court on his tour bus and then in Tucson's venerable Mission-style Arizona Inn, he is screamingly funny about the Black Country customs that have brought him so much joy during his sixty-three years. (As he remarked to me in Birmingham in 2003, "The whole deal was that I *didn't* go to L.A. or Virginia Water or wherever it might be . . .")

Regaling the assembled company—which includes Miller, Griffin, his Welsh personal assistant Nicola Powell, and former Ensign Records boss Nigel Grainge—with descriptions of the old Bull and Bladder in Brierley Hill, a pub "where the women played darts with six-inch nails," he has us all convulsed with laughter. And the more we howl, the more he warms to his themes, telling tales of John Bonham that sorely tempt me to reach inside my shoulder bag and surreptitiously press the "on" button of my Olympus digital recorder.

"Bonzo and I used to called John Paul 'Stanley,'" he informs us at one point. "Of course, he didn't think it was funny, because Capricorns don't have any sense of humor." The line is spoken like the true Leo that Plant is—and like a man who knows full well that there were *two* Capricorns in Led Zeppelin.

After interspersing two hours of Zep-related tales—one about the fundamentalist Christian owner of a Texas ranch where the band had decided to entertain the infamous "Butter Queen" and her attendant groupies in the swimming pool; another about driving up the Pacific Coast Highway at fifteen miles per hour, so wired on cocaine he thought he was doing seventy and wondered why he was being overtaken by blue-rinsed septuagenarians—with discursions on everything from Joe Meek B-sides to Edward the First's imposition of English rule on Wales in the thirteenth century, Plant decides to hit the hay.

"Night-night," he says as he grasps my hand with a leonine paw. "See you in the Bull and Bladder!"

• • •

I catch sight of Led Zeppelin's other Capricorn across the crowded launch party for his friend Gary Kemp's autobiography in London. By one of those odd but meaningless coincidences, I have this very afternoon finished a proposal for a new book about Jimmy Page's old band and can't resist telling him as much. He is friendly enough, twinkly smiles lighting up his flat, almost oriental face. The undyed hair is so much better than the shoe-polish look he was sporting when I interviewed him in Covent Garden six years ago. I seize the moment and ask whether he himself is currently contemplating any kind of autobiography. Might he be interested in collaborating on such a book?

I know enough about Page to realize it's a nonstarter, but he surprises me by extracting an ancient Nokia phone from his pocket and taking 'my number. He surprises me even more by calling the next day and summoning me to the Tower House, his fantastical residence in Holland Park.

For any Zeppelin fan out there thinking, "This story cannot have a happy ending," prepare not to be disappointed. A few weeks later, after a rambling and inconclusive conversation with Page in the nondescript antechamber that sits above the Tower House's garage-cum-granny-flat, his friend the photographer Ross Halfin tells me in a faintly sneering voice, "You ain't got a hope in hell of doing a book with Jimmy. And if you're wondering why he agreed to meet with you, it was for one reason only: to get all the information he could possibly get out of you."

Was I crestfallen by Halfin's candor? No. Brusque though Ross is, he wasn't trying to be unkind. Would it have been worth ghosting Page's memoirs? Almost certainly not: Halfin himself told me that when he helped with captions for the guitarist's limited-edition coffee-table book of photographs (which Page had failed to even mention to me), its subject snapped at him when asked for the time and place of one particular image. Apparently, his exact words were: "Why do you need to *know*?"

"Pagey liked the idea of being considered a man of mystery," Robert Plant told Mat Snow in 1985. "He really should have been a San Francisco version of Simon Templar, hiding in shadows and peeping round corners. He got some kind of enjoyment out of people having the wrong impression of him. He's a very meek guy, shy to the point where sometimes it's uncomfortable. But he let it all go on, and it's his choice whether it all continues. It's not up to me to start saying the guy plays cricket."

The many who've fallen foul of Page over the years—usually through mildly paranoid misunderstandings—will be unsurprised

"Rock on and thanks . . ." The fourth Zeppelin album,
signed by Page on April 17, 2003.

to learn that subsequent mention of my name propelled him into minor furies, reportedly because he believed I was telling prospective interviewees that he'd given my book his blessing, something that would have been as stupid as it was dishonest. I never heard from Jimmy again and so set out on the trail of the truth about Led Zeppelin, once described by the late Ahmet Ertegun—their great champion and mentor at Atlantic Records—as "the biggest unknown group in the world." I was determined to get away from glorifying tales of mudsharks and Riot House mayhem (though you will find plenty of hair-raising stories in these pages). I was more interested in the context from which Zeppelin sprung and in the apparatus around them: the "power" they wielded and how it synced with the might of the music they made. As Erik Davis wrote in his erudite $33\frac{1}{3}$ study of their untitled fourth album, "The enjoyment that Led Zeppelin has given to many of us is partly a function of our fantasies about their own engorged enjoyment of the world."

To that extent, *Led Zeppelin* is as much about Peter Grant, Richard Cole, and others as it is about Zeppelin themselves. The more one learns about the band, the more symbiotic the relationship between Zep and their henchmen becomes. Is it conceivable that Grant himself was the giant inflatable airship that gave the group its name? His own personal tragedy of intimidation, greed, and self-destruction—part Falstaff, part Charles Foster Kane—closely parallels the triumph and tragedy of Zeppelin itself, a morality tale that starts with thrilling promise, climaxes with intoxicating splendor, and declines into pitiful addiction and violence.

It's an old story, you might say, but one rarely told on such a scale of success or excess. For the better part of a decade, Led Zeppelin was the greatest group on the planet, greater than the Stones or anyone else, and eclipsing records set by Elvis and the Beatles. Artistically and financially, they were the apex of the genus Hard Rock in all its—to use Page's preferred term—"light and shade."

Light and shade, good and evil: with Zeppelin, it all seems to circle back to that central dialectic. How did something born of such potent kismet in a basement rehearsal room in Soho turn into something so colossally callous—not to mention *Spinal-Tap*-esque?

And should it even matter when we have such astonishing music to remember them by?

—*Barney Hoskyns, London*

PERSONAE GRATAE:
VOICES IN THIS BOOK

JUSTIN ADAMS World music–steeped guitarist and Plant's principal '90s sideman

SAM AIZER Worked at Swan Song's New York office, mainly with Bad Company

STEVE ALBINI Produced the 1998 Page and Plant album *Walking into Clarksdale*

KEITH ALTHAM Interviewed Jimmy Page, the Yardbirds, and Led Zeppelin for *NME*, *Record Mirror*, and other publications

KENNETH ANGER Black Arts–dabbling director of *Lucifer Rising*, for which Jimmy Page supposedly failed to complete a soundtrack

MIKE APPLETON Producer of BBC2's *Old Grey Whistle Test* and mate of Zeppelin's

DICK ASHER Epic Records chief in the late '60s, snubbed by Page and Peter Grant in favor of Atlantic

JANE AYER Publicist at Atlantic Records' L.A. office and Zeppelin confidante

LONG JOHN BALDRY Singer with Blues Incorporated and other '60s R&B groups in London

FRANK BARSALONA Founder of the Premier Talent booking agency, which represented Zeppelin until 1972; once described by Ahmet Ertegun as "the most powerful man in the record industry"

JUNE HARRIS BARSALONA Former U.S. correspondent of *New Musical Express* and wife of Frank Barsalona

PETER BARSOTTI Worked for promoter Bill Graham at the time of the Oakland incident in 1977

DAVID BATES A&R man for Robert Plant and for Page and Plant's *No Quarter* album

JEFF BECK Childhood acquaintance of Jimmy Page's and guitarist in the Yardbirds; client of Peter Grant's

MAGGIE BELL Managed by Peter Grant as the singer in Stone the Crows; signed to Zeppelin's Swan Song label

JOHN "JB" BETTIE With his brother Paul ("PB"), worked at Horse-lunges in Peter Grant's twilight years

BEV BEVAN Drummer in the Move and the Electric Light Orchestra and friend of John Bonham's

ED BICKNELL Former manager of Dire Straits and friend of Peter Grant's

RODNEY BINGENHEIMER L.A. scenester, DJ, and owner in the '70s of the English Disco club on Sunset Boulevard

CHRIS BLACKWELL Founder of Island Records, who nearly signed Zeppelin

ROBBIE BLUNT Black Country guitarist and Robert Plant sideman in the '80s; former member of Silverhead and Bronco

DEBBIE BONHAM R&B singer and John Bonham's younger sister

BILL BONHAM Organist in Robert Plant's pre-Zeppelin band Obs-Tweedle, no relation to John

JASON BONHAM John Bonham's son; drummer with reunited Zeppelin at the O2 show and the Atlantic 40th Anniversary show

JOHN BONHAM Led Zeppelin's drummer; died in 1980

MICK BONHAM John Bonham's younger brother; died in 2000

CAROLINE BOUCHER *Disc and Music Echo* writer; interviewed Zeppelin several times

LORAINE ALTERMAN BOYLE As Loraine Alterman, toured with and interviewed Zeppelin several times for *Melody Maker* and other publications

RUSTY BRUTSCHE Cofounder with Jack Calmes of ShowCo sound and lighting in Dallas; worked with Zeppelin from 1971 to 1980

BEBE BUELL Celebrated rock consort; girlfriend of Jimmy Page's for a brief period in the mid-'70s

TREVOR BURTON Original rhythm guitarist in Birmingham band the Move

ALAN CALLAN President of Swan Song in the UK from 1977 to 1979

JACK CALMES Cofounder and head of Showco sound and lighting company in Dallas; worked with Zeppelin on all of their '70s tours

JULIE CARLO Wife of Phil Carlo

PHIL CARLO Roadie for Bad Company, tour manager on the last Zeppelin tour, and Page's right-hand man for most of the '80s

GARY CARNES Showco lighting director on 1977 tour

ROY CARR Interviewed Zeppelin several times for *NME*, friend of John Bonham's

PHIL CARSON Head of Atlantic Records UK and close confidant of Zeppelin's

CLEM CATTINI Leading drummer on London session scene of the '60s, played regularly with Page and Jones

CHRIS CHARLESWORTH Journalist—and sometime New York correspondent—who interviewed Led Zeppelin several times for *Melody Maker*

NICKY CHINN Cowriter with Mike Chapman of countless glam-rock hits (by Sweet, Suzi Quatro, and Mud) for Mickie Most's RAK label

ROBERT CHRISTGAU Music editor of the *Village Voice*, 1974–2006

PETER CLIFTON Film director who completed *The Song Remains the Same* and shot all of the band's fantasy sequences

BILL COLE Bass player in skiffle and R&B era

MARILYN COLE First wife of Zeppelin tour manager Richard Cole

RICHARD COLE Zeppelin's tour manager from 1968 to 1979

PHIL COLLINS Genesis drummer; played with Robert Plant in the early '80s and performed with Zeppelin at Live Aid

JOHN COMBE Author of the Kidderminster rock history *Get Your Kicks on the A456*

GYL CORRIGAN-DEVLIN Zeppelin friend who traveled on the 1973 tour

CLIVE COULSON Zeppelin roadie who became Bad Company's tour manager; died in 2006

CAMERON CROWE Interviewed Zeppelin for the *L.A. Times* and *Rolling Stone* before becoming a film director; based scenes in *Almost Famous* on his Zeppelin experiences

JOHN CRUTCHLEY Guitarist with Plant's pre-Zeppelin band Listen

BILL CURBISHLEY Manager of the Who and later of Jimmy Page and Robert Plant

DAVID DALTON Biographer of Janis Joplin and cowriter of autobiographies by Marianne Faithfull, Steven Tyler, and others

RAY DAVIES Leader of the Kinks; Page played on some of his early Pye sides

MALCOLM DENT Caretaker of Boleskine House, the sometime Aleister Crowley residence in Scotland, bought by Page in 1970

MICHAEL DES BARRES Friend of Zeppelin's; singer with Silverhead and with Swan Song band Detective

PAMELA DES BARRES L.A. groupie and girlfriend of Page's in 1969–1970; married (and divorced) Michael Des Barres

JACKIE DeSHANNON L.A. pop/folk singer-songwriter; worked and had relationship with Page in London and America in 1964–1965

MARIE DIXON Widow of Chicago bluesman Willie Dixon, who sued Zeppelin for copyright breach on "Whole Lotta Love" and other songs

DONOVAN Scottish folk-pop-rock star for whom John Paul Jones arranged "Sunshine Superman" and others

CHRIS DREJA Bassist with Page's pre-Zep band the Yardbirds

DAVE EDMUNDS Swan Song artist from 1977 to 1982

MARK ELLEN Presenter of *The Old Grey Whistle Test*; interviewed Page and Roy Harper in 1984

BOB EMMER Publicity director, Atlantic West Coast office

AHMET ERTEGUN Cofounder of Atlantic Records; mentor and inspiration to Zeppelin

MARIANNE FAITHFULL Immediate Records singer; covered songs written by Page and Jackie DeShannon

BP FALLON UK press officer for Zeppelin, 1972–1976

MICK FARREN Singer with the Deviants; writer for the underground press and *NME*

BILL FORD Bassist in Bonham's early '60s Brum band the Senators

KIM FOWLEY L.A. producer and scenester

MITCHELL FOX Swan Song U.S. staffer, 1977–1980

PAUL FRANCIS Drummer with Maggie Bell in the mid-'70s

TONY FRANKLIN Bassist in Page's post-Zeppelin band the Firm

TOM FRY Worked for promoter Freddy Bannister at the time of Zeppelin's Knebworth shows

KEVYN GAMMOND Guitarist in Plant's pre-Zeppelin group the Band of Joy and post-Zeppelin group Priory of Brion

STEFAN GATES The naked boy on the cover of *Houses of the Holy*

VANESSA GILBERT L.A. scenester and Zeppelin friend on the 1973 U.S. tour

DANNY GOLDBERG U.S. press officer for Zeppelin and president of Swan Song in New York

HARVEY GOLDSMITH Promoter of Zeppelin's O2 show in 2007

LORD JOHN GOULD West Sussex vintage car enthusiast who be-friended Peter Grant in the last years of his life

BILL GRAHAM Rock promoter who opened the Fillmore in San Fran-cisco and the Fillmore East in New York; promoted Zeppelin's ill-fated final shows on U.S. soil; died in 1991

GLORIA GRANT Wife of Peter Grant

HELEN GRANT Daughter of Peter Grant

PETER GRANT Manager of the Yardbirds, Led Zeppelin, Maggie Bell, and Bad Company; died in 1995

WARREN GRANT Son of Peter Grant

JERRY GREENBERG General manager of Atlantic Records, 1969–1980

GEOFF GRIMES Plugger for Atlantic Records UK, 1972–1978

ROSS HALFIN Doyen of hard-rock photographers and close friend of Page's; compiled *The Photographers' Led Zeppelin*

CONNIE HAMZY AKA "SWEET CONNIE FROM LITTLE ROCK" Arkansas groupie of wide renown

BOB HARRIS Presenter of *The Old Grey Whistle Test*, 1972–1978

ROY HARPER Maverick British folkie; friend of, and inspiration to, Page and Plant

BILL HARRY Zeppelin's first UK press officer

BILL HARVEY Black Country jazz drummer who gave the young Bon-ham early tutorials

ANDREW HEWKIN Black Country–born painter and friend of Plant's

DAVE HILL Guitarist in the 'N-Betweens and Slade

MICK HINTON Bonham's roadie-cum-dogsbody; died in 2007

ABE HOCH Ran Swan Song's UK office, 1975–1977

GLENN HUGHES Black Country singer and bassist with Trapeze, Deep Purple, and (with Jason Bonham) Black Country Commu-nion

CHRIS HUSTON Owner of Mystic Sound studios in L.A.

ELIZABETH "BETTY" IANNACI Receptionist and Zeppelin point person in Atlantic's West Coast office, 1975–1977

TONY IOMMI   Black Sabbath guitarist and close friend of John Bonham's

ANNI IVIL   Press officer at the Atlantic UK office, late '60s–early '70s

CATHERINE JAMES   Hollywood groupie, an early squeeze of Page's

ANDY JOHNS   Younger brother of Glyn; engineer on *Led Zeppelin II, III*, and the untitled fourth

GLYN JOHNS   Engineer/producer on early Page and Jones sessions; engineer on *Led Zeppelin*

PHIL JOHNSTONE   Keyboard player and Plant collaborator on *Now and Zen, Manic Nirvana*, and *Fate of Nations*

JOHN PAUL JONES   Bassist and keyboard player with Led Zeppelin

REG JONES   Singer and guitarist with Bonham's pre-Zeppelin band A Way of Life

JOHN KALODNER   '80s A&R kingpin who signed Coverdale/Page to Geffen Records

SHELLEY KAYE   Assistant to Steve Weiss in U.S. office of Swan Song

NICK KENT   Legendary *NME* journalist; interviewed Led Zeppelin and the solo Page on several occasions

DESIREE KIRKE   Ex-wife of Bad Company drummer Simon Kirke and close friend of Led Zeppelin

SIMON KIRKE   Drummer with Free and Bad Company

ALEXIS KORNER   Sang and recorded with Plant in 1967, shortly before the latter joined Obs-Tweedle

EDDIE KRAMER   Engineer on *Houses of the Holy*, most of *Led Zeppelin II*, and some of *Physical Graffiti*

ALISON KRAUSS   Plant's partner on 2007's Grammy-scooping and multi-million-selling *Raising Sand*

HARVEY KUBERNIK   L.A. correspondent for *Melody Maker* in the '70s; author of *Canyon of Dreams*

DENNY LAINE   Singer with Birmingham's Moody Blues, friend of Bonham's

DON LAW   Boston rock promoter

BENJI LeFEVRE   Zeppelin sound technician from 1973 to 1980; Plant's right-hand man from 1975 to 1986

DAVE LEWIS   Founder and editor of Zeppelin fanzine *Tight But Loose*; traveled on the 1980 tour

HARVEY LISBERG   Manager of Herman's Hermits and '60s associate of Mickie Most's and Peter Grant's

PAUL LOCKEY   Bassist in Plant's pre-Zep Band of Joy

MARK LONDON   Comanager with Peter Grant of Stone the Crows and Maggie Bell

LULU   Close friend of John and Pat Bonham's

JOHN LYDON   Former lead singer with the Sex Pistols

UNITY MacLEAN   Managed Swan Song's London office from 1976 to 1980

MIKEAL MAGLIERI   Son of Mario, proprietor of the Whisky a Go Go and the Rainbow Bar & Grill on L.A.'s Sunset Strip

TONY MANDICH   Artist relations manager at Atlantic's West Coast office, 1972–1997

TERRY MANNING   Engineered tracks on *Led Zeppelin III*; owner of Compass Point studios, Nassau

DANNY MARKUS   Artist relations manager in Atlantic's Midwest office; later comanaged Luther Vandross and others

STEVE MARRIOTT   Lead singer and guitarist in the band Small Faces; later formed Humble Pie

JOE MASSOT   Original director of *The Song Remains the Same*; died in 2002

LORI "LIGHTNING" MATTIX   Teenage groupie who became Page's main L.A. squeeze in 1973

JIM MATZORKIS   The Bill Graham security guard severely beaten in Oakland by Peter Grant and John Bindon

MALCOLM McLAREN   Manager of the Sex Pistols; spent months researching a biopic of Peter Grant

MARIO MEDIOUS   Atlantic Records promotion man, 1965–1972

MARTIN MEISSONNIER Parisian world-music producer; prepared African tape loops for *No Quarter: Page and Plant Unledded*

JOHN MENDELSSOHN Reviewed the first two Zeppelin albums for *Rolling Stone*

JONI MITCHELL High priestess of the L.A. singer-songwriter community and inspiration for Zeppelin's "Going to California"

MICKIE MOST Producer of the Animals and Herman's Hermits; partner with Peter Grant in RAK Records and Management; died in 2003

DON MURFET Head of security for Zeppelin in the late '70s; died in 2005

CHARLES SHAAR MURRAY Famed journalist and blues writer who interviewed Zeppelin for *NME* and other publications

LAURENCE MYERS Accountant who partnered with Mickie Most and Peter Grant in RAK Records and Management in the mid-'60s.

HOWARD MYLETT Author of *Led Zeppelin* (1976) and renowned Zeppelin collector and expert; died in 2011

SIMON NAPIER-BELL Second manager of the Yardbirds

RON NEVISON Engineer on Headley Grange sessions for *Physical Graffiti*

DAVE NORTHOVER Nominally John Paul Jones's assistant on Zeppelin's 1975 and 1977 U.S. tours

JEFF OCHELTREE Drum tech who advised and assisted Bonham on 1977 U.S. tour

JOHN OGDEN Pop music writer on the *Birmingham Express and Star* newspaper from the early '60s to the '90s

ANDREW LOOG OLDHAM Manager of the Rolling Stones and founder of Immediate Records; hired Page and Jones to play on sessions

JIMMY PAGE Led Zeppelin's founder and guitarist

DAVE PEGG Played bass in Bonham's pre-Zep band A Way of Life; close friend of the Zeppelin drummer's

ROBERT PLANT Led Zeppelin's lead singer and lyricist

MAC POOLE   Midlands drummer; replaced Bonham in A Way of Life

IGGY POP   Lead singer of the Stooges; habitué of Rodney's English Disco

AUBREY POWELL   Cofounder of Hipgnosis Design; created sleeves for all Zeppelin albums from *Houses of the Holy* to *In through the Out Door*

GUY PRATT   Bassist in Coverdale/Page; played on Olympics version of "Whole Lotta Love"

PERRY PRESS   London estate agent to the stars; found homes for Led Zeppelin and Peter Grant

DOMENIC PRIORE   L.A. music historian; author of *Riot on Sunset Strip*

HOSSAM RAMZY   Egyptian arranger on *No Quarter: Page and Plant Unledded* album and tour

TERRY REID   Singer originally considered for Zeppelin before Plant; managed by Mickie Most

BARRY JAY REISS   Worked with Steve Weiss before and during the Swan Song era

JOHN RENBOURN   Folk guitarist on the Kingston/Richmond circuit and founder member of Pentangle

KEITH RICHARDS   Guitarist and coleader of the Rolling Stones

RICHARD RIEGEL   Rock critic and contributor to *Creem*

JAKE RIVIERA   Managed Dave Edmunds and signed him to Swan Song

WILLIE ROBERTSON   Provided insurance coverage to Zeppelin and numerous other rock bands; died in 2011

LISA ROBINSON   New York rock writer; interviewed Zeppelin for *Disc*, *NME*, and *Creem*

PAUL RODGERS   Lead singer of Free, Bad Company, and the Firm

STEVEN ROSEN   Interviewed Page and Jones for *Guitar Player*; traveled on the Zeppelin plane on the 1977 U.S. tour

CYNTHIA SACH   Worked in Swan Song's UK office, 1977–1981

JANINE SAFER WHITNEY   As Janine Safer, worked closely with Zeppelin and other Swan Song acts in the label's New York office; main press liaison officer on the 1977 U.S. tour

EDWARD ST. AUBYN   Author of *Mother's Milk* and other acclaimed novels

ELLEN SANDER   Traveled with Zeppelin in 1969 and published her account of the experience in the 1973 book *Trips*

RAT SCABIES   Drummer with the Damned, whom Zeppelin came to see at London's Roxy in 1977; auditioned for the Firm in 1984

TONY SECUNDA   Manager of Birmingham bands the Move and the Moody Blues; died in 1995

HARRY SHAPIRO   Biographer of Alexis Korner

DENNIS SHEEHAN   Assistant to Robert Plant on the 1977 U.S. tour; subsequently, road manager for U2

BURKE SHELLEY   Bassist and singer in the '70s Welsh power trio Budgie

PAUL SIMONON   Bassist with the Clash

JIM SIMPSON   Founder of Big Bear Records and mainstay of Birmingham music scene; hired Bonham to play in Locomotive

DIGBY SMITH   Tape-operator/engineer at Island Studios on sessions for *Led Zeppelin III* and the untitled fourth album

HENRY "THE HORSE" SMITH   Roadie for the Yardbirds and Led Zeppelin, 1966–1972; subsequently worked for Aerosmith

STEVE SMITH   Producer of Robert Palmer and other artists; was asked to produce Maggie Bell for Swan Song

BARNABY SNOW   Director of a TV documentary about the Black Country

MAT SNOW   Former editor of *MOJO*; interviewed all three surviving Zeppelin members several times for *MOJO* and *Q*

DON SNOWDEN   Author of the Willie Dixon biography *I Am the Blues* (1995)

DENNY SOMACH   Creator and producer of the "Get the Led Out" segment on many U.S. classic rock radio stations

SABLE STARR Queen of the L.A. ultravixens; Lori Mattix's coconspirator and chief rival; died in 2009

ROD STEWART Singer in the Jeff Beck Group, managed by Peter Grant and road-managed by Richard Cole

MARTIN STONE Guitarist in the Action and Mighty Baby; later sold rare occult books to Page

BIG JIM SULLIVAN Leading session guitarist on the '60s London studio scene and mentor to "Little" Jimmy Page

RAY THOMAS Flautist and singer with the Moody Blues

BRAD TOLINSKI Editor-in-Chief of *Guitar World*

DAN TREACY Singer and guitarist with the Television Personalities; worked in Swan Song's UK office

STEVEN TYLER Lead singer of Aerosmith; tried out as Plant's replacement in London after the O2 show

JAAN UHELSZKI Interviewed Zeppelin for *Creem*; traveled with the band on 1975 and 1977 U.S. tours

STEVE VAN ZANDT Guitarist in Bruce Springsteen's E Street Band; inducted Frank Barsalona into the Rock and Roll Hall of Fame in 2005

CHARLIE WATTS Drummer with the Rolling Stones

JON WEALLEANS Architect who drew up plans for Page's Equinox bookshop in Kensington

STEVE WEISS New York entertainment lawyer who negotiated Zeppelin's Atlantic deal and subsequently took care of all Swan Song legal affairs; died in 2008

CHRIS WELCH *Melody Maker* staffer who interviewed Zeppelin several times in the '70s and Page and Plant in the subsequent decade

MORGANA WELCH L.A. groupie, Zeppelin friend, and author of *The Hollywood Diaries*

JERRY WEXLER Atlantic Record producer and executive; signed Led Zeppelin in 1968; died in 2008

JACK WHITE   White Stripes singer, writer, and guitarist, influenced by Zeppelin; costar with Page and U2's the Edge in 2009 documentary *It Might Get Loud*

DAVID WILLIAMS   Boyhood friend—and fellow blues and rock 'n' roll fanatic—of Page's in Epsom

RICHARD WILLIAMS   *Melody Maker* writer and editor; interviewed Plant in early '70s

ROY WILLIAMS   Black Country veteran and live engineer for Robert Plant

SALLY WILLIAMS   Ex-girlfriend of Bonham roadie Mick Hinton

MICHAEL WINNER   Director of *Death Wish II*, for which Page supplied the soundtrack music

JOE "JAMMER" WRIGHT   Chicago blues guitarist and Zeppelin roadie; later played with Maggie Bell

PART 1

All Shook Up

Before there was Led Zeppelin, there was a plethora of pre-Zeppelin bands, only one of which could be said in any meaningful sense to have made it. That was the Yardbirds, a blues boot camp for three legendary axmen who came out of the so-dubbed Surrey Delta southwest of London: Eric Clapton, Jeff Beck, and Jimmy Page, the latter pair overlapping in the lineup for a few electrifying months between 1966 and 1967.

Page (born in Heston, Middlesex, on January 9, 1944) had served an earlier apprenticeship in the rock-'n'-rolling Redcaps and in Neil Christian & the Crusaders. Then this slight, shy only child from sedate Epsom wearied of the road and set himself up as the most in-demand guitarist on the London session scene. He played on hundreds of early '60s singles—hits and misses alike—by the Kinks, Lulu, Them, and Val Doonican (not forgetting the Primitives, the First

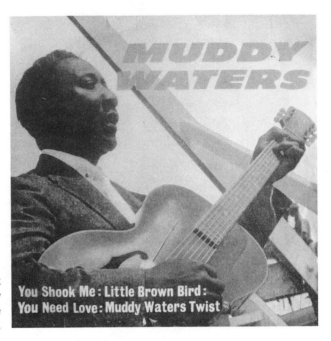

He shook them: Muddy Waters EP, Pye Records, 1962.

Gear, the Lancastrians, and Les Fleurs de Lys) before sussing out that the twilight life of a guitar-toting gunslinger-for-hire was sapping his soul.

Coming to a similar conclusion was fellow gunslinger John Paul Jones (born in Sidcup, Kent, on January 3, 1946), who'd gone by the rather less sexy name of "John Baldwin" before Rolling Stones manager Andrew Loog Oldham affixed the new moniker to him. If Page was the hottest six-string player in town, Jones was the lad you hired when you required a fat, Staxy bass line to underpin your pop productions. It didn't hurt that the guy was a virtuoso keyboard player and a deft string arranger in the bargain. Between 1963 and 1966, Jones and Page frequently played together on sessions at Decca, Regent Sound, and Olympic Studios.

Meanwhile, in the West Midlands—the smoke-belching "Black Country" that was England's industrial heartland—a very different pair of schemers were plying their trade together, not on sessions but in a raw blues band called the Crawling King Snakes. Robert Plant (born in West Bromwich, Staffordshire, on August 20, 1948) was cut from the same blue-eyed-soul cloth that produced local hero Stevie Winwood; John Bonham (born in Redditch, Worcestershire, on May 31, 1948) was the roughest, toughest, and certainly the loudest drummer on the "Ma Regan" circuit that dominated the satellite towns around Birmingham.

Come summer '68, while Jones was still arranging Donovan tracks for producer Mickie Most, Jimmy Page was co-fronting the Yardbirds on a last go-round of America's new hippie ballrooms. Plant and "Bonzo," on the other hand, were slogging their way 'round the U.K. in the psychedelicized Band of Joy, Plant combining the distant spirit of his new Haight-Ashbury heroes with the hard rock 'n' soul of his principal vocal influences, Winwood and Steve Marriott.

Cue manager Peter Grant, man-mountain facilitator of Page's musical dreams and the catalyst for bringing these four young men under one umbrella. From the ashes of the Yardbirds rose a phoenix of a supergroup. The "New" Yardbirds were stitched together as a London-Birmingham amalgam and, lo, Led Zeppelin was born.

1

Surbigloom Blues

> They come from quiet towns and near suburbs, terraced
> houses thrown up in the aftermath of German bombs.
> Places you don't see until you leave them, and why would
> you want to leave them, the same roses on the same
> trellises?
>
> —Zachary Lazar, *Sway* (2008)

ALAN CALLAN (president of Led Zeppelin's Swan Song label in the U.K., 1977–1979)   In 1977, I was at the Plaza Hotel in New York with Jimmy Page, and we were going out somewhere. It was absolutely pissing down as we walked out through the side door of the hotel to where the limo was waiting.

As the doorman takes us to the car, a woman standing in the doorway in a fur coat says, "What do I have to do to get some attention here? Look at these two with their jeans and long hair—how come they get a car immediately?"

The doorman says, "Well, ma'am, it's like this: the first guy there, he's been practicing what he's good at since he was six years old. If you went home and did the same, *you'd* probably get a limo when it rained."

JIMMY PAGE I remember going onto the playing fields one day and seeing this great throng crowded around this figure playing guitar and singing some skiffle song of the time, and I wondered how he did it. He showed me how to tune it, and it went on from there: going to guitar shops, hanging around watching what people were doing, until in the end it was going the other way, and people were watching *you*.

ROY HARPER (maverick folk singer and friend of Zeppelin's) Skiffle was derived from both Southern country and Northern urban blues. We didn't really discriminate, though I have to say I thought the more authentic brand was the Southern country blues. Any self-respecting eleven- to fourteen-year-old with an ear was doing the same thing in the mid-'50s.

KEITH ALTHAM (reporter for *New Musical Express* in the '60s and early '70s) What spun out from Elvis was skiffle, which had at its heart folk and Leadbelly and Big Bill Broonzy, so the links started to point toward blues. When you went and bought your Lonnie Donegan album, you saw "New words and music by L. Donegan," but the song was actually attributed to Leadbelly or Broonzy. So you went in search of those names.

CHRIS WELCH (reporter for *Melody Maker* from 1964 to the mid-'80s) Hearing Lonnie Donegan's "Rock Island Line" on the radio was such a shock. We'd never heard anything as ethnic or authentic. That was our introduction to American folk and blues, if you like. It was very much a school craze. We might once have collected stamps, and now we were out collecting blues records. My friend Mike bought a 10" Leadbelly LP and we'd sit listening to that for hours. Then we set about copying it and forming a skiffle group.

CHRIS DREJA (rhythm and bass guitarist in the Yardbirds) Jimmy Page was involved in skiffle because it was accessible. It was cheap. It was something you could do at a school concert.

JIMMY PAGE It was a process of accessing what was going on in skiffle, and then, bit by bit, your tastes changed and matured as you accessed more. There was the blues, there was Leadbelly material in Donegan, but we weren't at all aware of it in those days. Then it came to the point where Elvis was coming through, and he was making no secret of the fact that he was singing stuff by Arthur "Big Boy" Crudup and Sleepy John Estes.

KEITH ALTHAM   Someone knew Jimmy's mother and knew that he was in a skiffle group that was appearing at the Tolworth Co-op Hall. So I went along to watch them with a couple of mates from school, and on comes this kid about three foot nothing with a guitar about four foot and proceeds to play the arse off it. It was extraordinary, a *twelve-year-old*. There I am at sixteen struggling with four chords. And that was it, as far as I was concerned: "If some twelve-year-old punk can play guitar like that, I may as well give up."

CHRIS DREJA   I grew up in Surbiton, which one wag nicknamed "Surbigloom." Life was all about the unbelievable driving banality of the suburbs for anybody who had an ounce of energy and intelligence. It's amazing that Eric Clapton came from Ripley—under daunted circumstances, according to him—but he still frequented all the places I did.

KEITH ALTHAM   Epsom was a quiet suburban racing town. The only time it was really buzzing was Derby Day. Lester Bowden's was the big store where everyone bought their clothes.

JIMMY PAGE   It was still those somber postwar days of rationing in Epsom. Then this explosion came through your radio speaker when you were eleven or twelve. There were some good programs on TV, too, like *Oh! Boy* with Cliff Richard and Tony Sheridan. But Lonnie Donegan was the first person who was really giving it some passion that we related to.

GLYN JOHNS (engineer on the first Zeppelin album)   Jimmy lived at one end of Epsom, and I lived at the other. The first time I ever met him was at the youth club at St. Martin's Parish Church. We had a talent competition. He was probably about twelve or thirteen. I'll never forget, he sat on the edge of the stage with his legs hanging over, playing acoustic guitar. And I thought he was fantastic *then*. Maybe there was something in the water, I don't know. It *was* strange, the three best British rock guitarists—Clapton, Beck, and Page—all coming out of this one little area.

CHRIS DREJA   How ridiculous that white blues developed in this gen-teel area of southern England. What is a howlin' wolf when you live in *Surbiton?*

AHMET ERTEGUN (cofounder of Atlantic Records, Zeppelin's label) When I used to go to Keith Richards's house, that's all you'd hear all day long, the blues. Go to Eric Clapton's house, all you hear is the blues. It was a much more conscious effort to digest that music than Americans seem to have made, because Americans took it for granted and figured, "Well, the blues is here, it's part of our country."

ELIZABETH "BETTY" IANNACI (worked in Atlantic's West Coast office, 1975–1977)   I never heard "race music," I never got those 45s. I heard Bo Diddley through the Rolling Stones. These boys got those records from the underground black market in England, and that was how I experienced blues first—through the Stones, through Alexis Korner, through Led Zeppelin.

MARILYN COLE (first wife of Zeppelin tour manager Richard Cole)   Jimmy and his mother, Pat, were very close. Richard always said she had influenced him greatly.

DAVID WILLIAMS (boyhood friend of Page's)   I am certain that Jim's mother was the initial driving force behind his musical progression. She was a petite, dark-haired woman with a strong personality, a glint in her eye, and a wicked sense of humor.

NICK KENT (*New Musical Express* journalist in the '70s and the '80s)   Jimmy was very, very middle-class. When everyone else would say, "Fuck!" he would say, "Gosh!" It was the same with me—we both wanted to be wild and dangerous, but we didn't want our parents to know. Whereas working-class guys don't give a shit *what* their parents think.

For almost twenty years, 34 Miles Road, Epsom, was home to James Patrick Page.

DAVID WILLIAMS That small front room at Jim's house became the center of our world. Jim must have had equally tolerant neighbors, for we did make a racket in that tiny space. . . . We started to buy the *Melody Maker* . . . and soon found that there were a few more interesting examples of the new music available than those [that] made the hit parade and the radio.

CHRIS DREJA I first met Jimmy outside the Tolworth Arcade with a rare goldfish in a plastic bag. He was very sweet. You could relate to him immediately. Eric Clapton was hiding secrets, so he tended to be a bit more of an enigmatic personality, but Jimmy was a very well-adjusted young kid from round our way and had all the right credentials. He adored his mother but wasn't so fond of his father, as I understood it from various conversations I had.

DAVID WILLIAMS Apart from his brief flirtation with skiffle, Jim had not really reached the stage where he was playing with other musicians, and it was about this time that he made his first solo appearance on a children's television talent show called *All Your Own*. I reckon his mother must have been instrumental in setting it up.

MARILYN COLE   Even at thirteen, in that famous TV clip, Jimmy had a determination about him. He talked eloquently to Huw Wheldon. I thought he stood out even then—sure of himself, ambitious.

UNITY MacLEAN (manager of Swan Song's London office, 1976–1980) Jimmy was small and feminine and a little bit of a crybaby from time to time. Very, very creative and very inquisitive. He wanted to explore every sound and every instrument and every nuance of music, largely because he was brought up as an only child and his mother was a bit of a social climber. He was always looking for another high to stimulate his interest, hence the interest in black magic.

JIMMY PAGE   My interest in the occult started when I was about fifteen.

GLYN JOHNS   I don't know that Jimmy was ever angelic, though he was always as tight as a duck's ass. I bet he's got the first two bob his mum ever gave him.

JIMMY PAGE   The record that made me want to play guitar was "Baby, Let's Play House" by Presley. I just heard two guitars and a bass and thought, "Yeah, that's it." I want to be part of this.

MICHAEL DES BARRES (lead singer of Swan Song band Detective)   Jimmy is epitomized in that scene in the *It Might Get Loud* documentary where he's listening to Link Wray's "Rumble," and he's a child, and he's so excited and enthralled by the magic of that record.

JEFF BECK (Eric Clapton's replacement in the Yardbirds)   [My sister] was just getting settled into—where was it?—Epsom Art School, and she came back and said, "There was a bloke at school with a funny-shaped guitar like yours." I went, "Where is he? Take me to him!" She said, "I'll fix it up. His name's Jim, Jimmy Page." I couldn't believe that there was another human being in Surrey interested in strange-shaped solid guitars. We came on the bus, and [Jimmy] played for us. [He] played "Not Fade Away." I never forgot it.

JIMMY PAGE It was more like, "Can you play Ricky Nelson's 'My Babe'?" And we'd both have a go at trying to play the solo, because that was the key James Burton solo.

JOHN PAUL JONES I was an only child. A spoiled brat. It's interesting because I was reading something about only children, and you have a different view on life. It comes out of a certain insecurity.

I had a ukulele banjo, a little one, and I had that strung up like a bass. Actually, my father, because I was very young, had to sign a guarantee, and he said to me, "Don't bother with a bass guitar. Take up the tenor saxophone. It'll take two years, and the bass guitar will never be heard of again." But I really wanted a bass guitar.

CHRIS WELCH We were torn between skiffle and rock 'n' roll. But in our eyes, it was all wonderful music that we liked for different reasons. We went to see the famous rock 'n' roll movies, and there was all *that* excitement.

JOHN PAUL JONES My dad bought a record player and let me go out and buy records by Jerry Lee Lewis and the Everly Brothers, Little Richard, Ray Charles. Ray Charles got me into organs. I listened to a lot of Jimmy Smith in those days, but my dad didn't like Jimmy Smith: "Nothing to it, just running up and down the keyboard!"

ROY CARR (writer for *New Musical Express* from the '60s to the '80s) It was all matching-tie-and-hanky and Hank Marvin. When Johnny Kidd and the Pirates came along, they offered a different take on it all. In their own way, they were quite threatening.

CLEM CATTINI (leading drummer on London session scene of the '60s) It became a sort of turn from skiffle to rock 'n' roll, basically. I was touring with Johnny Kidd and the Pirates. We used to play this place in Aylesbury, and Jimmy was in Neil Christian and the Crusaders, which was the support band. He was only fifteen, and he was already a phenomenal player.

JOHN PAUL JONES I remember him having a reputation almost before I turned professional, when he was with Neil Christian and the Crusaders. It was always, "You've got to hear this guy."

Page playing with Red E. Lewis and the Redcaps, 1960. Left to right: John "Jumbo" Spicer, Red E. Lewis, and Little Jim on the Grazioso. (Courtesy of David Williams/Music Mentor Books)

JIMMY PAGE   This was before the Stones happened, so we were doing Chuck Berry, Gene Vincent, and Bo Diddley things, mainly. At the time, public taste was more engineered toward Top 10 records, so it was a bit of a struggle. But there'd always be a small section of the audience into what we were doing.

CHRIS WELCH   We learned about the roots of rock 'n' roll through people like Chris Barber and Alexis Korner.

KEITH ALTHAM   As trad jazz got a bit tired, there were little breakaways by people like Chris Barber, who really was the godfather figure of British blues. And the father was obviously Alexis Korner, who I saw with Cyril Davies at the Thames Hotel in Hampton Court.

BILL WYMAN (bass guitarist with the Rolling Stones)   By providing a base first for skiffle and then for the blues, Chris was virtually a founding father of what came next—a British rock scene.

JEFF BECK   The thing that shook me was an EP by Muddy Waters. . . . One of the tracks was "You Shook Me," which both Led Zeppelin and I ripped off on our first albums.

JIMMY PAGE   There were guitarists who could play really well acoustic, but they couldn't make that transition. It just didn't work on electric for them. But Muddy managed to come up with this style that really crystallized his whole thing. As a kid, as a teenager listening to that music, I was really just shaken to the core by it.

GLYN JOHNS   I had a band I managed called the Presidents, and the bass player Colin Goulding knew Jimmy. Colin and I were in a coffee shop on Cheam High Street, and Ian Stewart went by on his bicycle. Colin said, "See that guy there? He's got the most amazing collection of blues records." So I sought Ian out. He told me he was putting this band together with a guy called Brian Jones.

JEFF BECK   Stu was definitely the cornerstone of that Surrey-Richmond thing. He was Mr. Blues. He made you feel guilty about liking any other kind of music.

GLYN JOHNS   When I heard the Stones, it was like whoopee time. Popular music of the day was pretty banal and pretty naff, so we were all a bit frustrated. I remember this guy up the road played me a Snooks Eaglin record, and it was so raw and rough and gutsy. There was nothing prissy about it.

LONG JOHN BALDRY (singer with Blues Incorporated and other '60s R&B groups in London)   We thought of blues as being strictly acoustic music, and Muddy came over to Britain with this electric guitar and a big amplifier, and a lot of people said, "Ooh, sacrilegious, dreadful, dreadful, he's selling out the blues," and all that. But Cyril Davies, Alexis Korner, and I looked at this and thought, "Hmm, this is interesting," and we started trying it ourselves.

JOHN RENBOURN (folk guitarist on Kingston scene and founder member of Pentangle)   The R&B craze had replaced skiffle, and the best band was considered to be Blues Incorporated.

ALEXIS KORNER (singer-guitarist with Blues Incorporated) Blues Incorporated was basically a reaction against trad. Most of us had been through trad jazz, and for various reasons we wanted to play something that was the complete antithesis of trad jazz, which by then had got very finicky and very kitsch altogether. You couldn't have found anything more fundamentally opposed to the concept of trad jazz than Muddy Waters.

BILL COLE (bass player in skiffle and R&B era) Alexis had a band [at Studio 51 in Soho]—a sort of mainstay band that included the late Cyril Davies on harmonica, who sadly died of leukemia very early. But we all liked that stuff, you know—the country blues, the Delta blues, the Chicago electrified blues. We were all listening to that stuff long before the general members of the public. None of us could have foreseen that it would take off in the way that it has done today. I used to sit in with [the Rolling Stones] at the 51 Club. They were the Sunday afternoon group.

BILL WYMAN On March 3rd, 1963, we played . . . an afternoon session at Studio 51. It was ironic that we were given a great welcome by the ladies, Vi and Pat, who ran this stronghold of New Orleans style jazz— whereas the jazz snobs at the Marquee and elsewhere saw us as upstarts who should not be encouraged.

KEITH RICHARDS (guitarist with the Rolling Stones) At this time, there was a huge strain between what we were doing and traditional jazz, which basically represented the whole London club scene. All the clubs and pubs were locked up within a few promoters' hands, and suddenly I guess they felt the chill winter coming in and realized there would be no more "Midnight in Moscow" or "Petite Fleur" for them.

CHRIS DREJA It started to happen because we all had a lot to do with Alexis and Cyril and Blues Incorporated. It was a time when we had the absolutely ridiculous idea that we could play music and form bands. We were looking for venues, and the Melody Maker had little ads in the back, and that was another way we used to communicate. You started to get promoters who had places, and then you realized that people were paying and kids were coming to hear blues, much more so than trad jazz. We knew about Alexis because the Stones played the Ealing club, which was a pivotal hole-in-the-ground in 1962.

JIMMY PAGE   When I was still at school, the amount of records about was so thin on the ground. One of your pals would be a rock collector, another would be a blues collector. Then this rumor went round on the grapevine that one of the guys had actually found a *girl* who liked Howlin' Wolf.

CHRIS DREJA   You had to go to this import shop in Streatham. It was a fucking long journey, and in the winter we all got chilblains because it was damp and horrible, and the buses were open with no doors. It was a hard blues life!

MARTIN STONE (blues guitarist and friend of Page's)   Dave Kelly's Swing Shop was a pretty important psychogeographical landmark in the blues boom. The South London blues mafia congregated there, and Dave worked behind the counter on Saturdays. It was one of the only places you could buy American blues records. Eric Clapton bought *Freddie King Sings* there, and I later stole it from his girlfriend.

CHRIS DREJA   Communication was very difficult. You often saw people on the platform of the station with a record, and then there was the slow grapevine of the arts school system. L'Auberge, the coffee shop in Richmond, was where we all hung out. In Café Nero, you've got twenty million choices, but in those days you had two. And as a down-and-out student or musician, you could make that coffee last four hours. All of us—Eric, myself, other players—started to drift there. These were very gentle days. The furthest-out you got were suede shoes.

CHRIS WELCH   The original Jazz & Blues Festival in 1961 was how I became aware of all this going on in Richmond. But the crucial year was 1963. I managed to get tickets as a reporter for the *Bexleyheath and Welling Observer*, and we were all watching Acker Bilk when an announcement came over the P.A. that the Rolling Stones were playing in the tent across the field. The whole audience turned round and ran toward this tent. We were all stuck in this marquee, and they were quite aggressive, and it was like seeing the Sex Pistols years later.

JIMMY PAGE   I came across Mick and Keith, curiously enough, on a pilgrimage to see the Folk Festival of the Blues in Manchester. We all went up in a van, all the guys from the Epsom area and the record collectors. I remember them vividly, because Keith said he played guitar and Mick said he played harp.

MARIE DIXON (widow of Chess Records legend Willie Dixon)   Willie went over to Europe because he felt like the blues was dying in the United States. He said to me, "I'm going overseas to see if I can't drum up some more business for my music." He wanted to make the blues more widespread in England and Europe. He had no problem with these young skinny English boys learning his music.

CHRIS DREJA   The Stones came down the grapevine pretty fast. On a Friday or Saturday night, Top Topham and I used to go the Station Hotel in Richmond, and at the back they had a hall that was crammed. Seeing the Stones a couple of times made Top and I even more obsessive about doing our own band.

JIMMY PAGE   I was involved in the old Richmond and Eel Pie Island sets—well, I used to play at those jazz clubs where the Kinks played, and I'd always been in groups around the Kingston area. Kingston and Richmond were the two key places, really, but by that time I was well into the Marquee. It was a good scene then, because everyone had this same upbringing and had been locked away with their records, and there was something really new to offer. It just exploded from there.

ROY CARR   I used to buy import Chess albums from Impulse on New Oxford Street. I remember going in one day to pick up something, and Brian Jones was looking at it and wanted it. The guy said, "I'm sorry, it's already sold to this gentleman." And I went down to the Marquee that night, and it was one of the Stones' first gigs there. Brian was very sullen when he saw me.

JIMMY PAGE Cyril Davies, who had just broken away from Alexis Korner and was the one who turned everybody on to the electric harmonica, asked me to join his band [and] I did in fact play with them a bit, and the band was basically the nucleus of Screaming Lord Sutch's band. I think Neil Christian felt I wanted to go with Cyril Davies, but I was being perfectly honest in telling him that I couldn't carry on—I couldn't understand why I was getting ill all the time.

LORI MATTIX (L.A. groupie and principal Page squeeze in America, 1973–1974) Jimmy went to art school and dropped out. He told me that he started in art school and then decided he wanted to become a session musician.

CHRIS DREJA One of the great things the British government did was start this arts stream for selective children—and it wasn't hard to get in. Kingston was terribly relaxed, run by a guy called Dyson and a younger arts master whom we completely wrapped around our finger. It all came out of that art school semi-intelligentsia—that's where the Southern blues thing kicked off. I mean, we weren't that intelligent, but we were given a chance in that system.

MARTIN STONE I was playing in a Shadows-type band, like most guitarists, but when you listened to R&B records, you would hear this guitar that was *not like* Bert Weedon. It was overloaded, there was sustain on it. It had what Jake Riviera calls "the fuck beat." And I leaped on it. It was like, "Now I've got this thing, and *you don't know what it is.*"

CHRIS DREJA Eric Clapton used to turn up at L' Auberge with a guitar and long thumbnails; he was very Robert Johnson. He jumped at the Yardbirds because he came to a rehearsal and saw that we were attempting to play the music that he was obsessed with. He wasn't God then. He was just the only guy we knew.

CHRIS WELCH The very first band I was asked to interview when I started at *Melody Maker* in 1964 was the Yardbirds. We went out to a coffee bar in Fleet Street called the Kardoma. They seemed like the most exciting rock band around—much more wired-up than the Stones, who were looser. It was frantic nervous energy, like schoolboys going mad.

GEOFF GRIMES (plugger for Atlantic Records U.K., 1972–1978)   There was a series of clubs we all used to go to: the Ricky Tick, the Marquee, the Scene. We'd spend almost two days completely out of it—the evening session, the late night, then we'd sleep somewhere and get up and do it all again. And in among this, the Crawdaddy opened, and the first band we saw there was the Stones. Then, when it moved to a better ground across the road, we met the Yardbirds. I saw all the guitarists in the Yardbirds: Eric Clapton first of all, and I was there when Jeff Beck played. I used to go every Sunday to the Crawdaddy. It was a religion. You had to go.

JOHN PAUL JONES   There was this whole little white R&B movement [that] grew up quite separately and would evolve into the Stones and the Yardbirds. . . . They were all into Chuck Berry and the Chess people—blues twits, really. As a musical scene, they just didn't rate, really.

   None of those people did: the Yardbirds, it was like, "Oh dear," it was more punk than R&B. Oh, it was great for that, but when you heard them play "Little Red Rooster," you'd go, "Oh, no, please don't."

2

The Impenetrable Brotherhood

The artists were the least important people, because they didn't write the songs. You would much rather have the session singers and the session musicians than the guys who'd just about learned their three chords.

—Laurence Myers

GLYN JOHNS (engineer on the first Zeppelin album)   I decided the only way to get any experience as an engineer was to get downtime in the studio and invite musicians in, so I started doing Sunday sessions at IBC studios in Portland Place. The Stones were the very first act that came in under that agreement. The older guys at the studio didn't get it, and they didn't like it, so I created an opportunity, and it gobbled me up. I think Jimmy turned up at one of those sessions.

JIMMY PAGE   I sort of stopped playing and went to art college for about two years. I was concentrating more on blues playing than on my own, and from the art college there was the Marquee club and Cyril Davies, and by this time it had just started happening, and stuff had come around again, so I used to go up and jam on a Thursday night with the interlude band.

CHARLIE WATTS (drummer with the Rolling Stones)   Within about a month of Alexis starting on those Thursday nights, Harold Pendleton had 950 people packed in there; he wasn't allowed to admit any more.

JIMMY PAGE   Somebody came up to me at the Marquee and said, "Would you like to play on a record?" I said, "Why not?" That was my first proper session, which was for Carter-Lewis & the Southerners. And that record, which was called "Your Mama's Out of Town," made a dent in the charts.

GLYN JOHNS   Jimmy rang me and said the art school had found out he was earning money and he was going to lose his grant, so he wasn't going to do any more sessions. Well, that lasted two minutes. The phone started ringing, and all of a sudden he was doing three sessions a day for everybody and their mother—and quite right, too.

I would get Jimmy in whenever I could. He was a very ordinary, nice, quiet young guy and obviously immensely talented. As things progressed with both of us, we became more friendly, and I would always give him a lift home from sessions in my convertible E-Type. We'd go to the pie stall on Battersea Bridge and have something to eat. In the back, I had one of the Stones's first Vox P.A. columns sawn in half and a four-track cassette deck. And I'd drive back down the A3 with the roof down, Jimmy sitting next to me, with the objective of getting the engine note to alter with the chord sequence of whatever was playing. Good fun.

JIMMY PAGE   Big Jim Sullivan was carrying the whole weight on his shoulders—he was the only other young face there.

CHRIS DREJA (rhythm and bass guitarist in the Yardbirds)   We all knew about Big Jim. I suspect that initially, Jimmy was playing rhythm parts and second guitar work, but it didn't matter. To do session work, you needed to be focused, professional, and able to deliver it in ten minutes. Big Jim took Jimmy under his wing. He sorted him out because there weren't that many good guitar players around.

BIG JIM SULLIVAN (leading session guitarist on the London studio scene of the '60s)   We said hello, sat down, started chatting. Had a blow. He was great, obviously. He covered parts that I hadn't covered. That was the thing about what Jimmy did—certain phrases, mostly James Burton phrases. He used to called me Big Jim and I'd call him Little Jim. I taught Jim to read, basically. If it was country, I'd do it; if it was rock, *he'd* do it. That was the general rule.

JIMMY PAGE   I was in on a lot of sessions for Decca artists at the start, and some were hits, although not because of the guitar playing. Nevertheless, I'd been allowed into the whole sort of impenetrable brotherhood.

DAVID WILLIAMS (boyhood friend of Page's in Epsom)   Eventually, the recordings would be released commercially, and Jim would have to go to the local store and purchase a record in order to hear what his work sounded like. . . . He would play me the records and occasionally express disappointment when he felt his best efforts had been lost or buried in the mix.

JOHN PAUL JONES   I had been in various small bands and done all the American bases. Jet Harris was with the Jet Blacks; I walked up to him on Archer Street and asked him if he needed a bass player. He said, "No, I don't, but they do," pointing me toward the Jet Blacks. He was leaving them, so I auditioned and joined up. Later he heard about me, swapped his bass player for me, and I went on the road with *them*. I was seventeen and earning £30 a week with Jet and Tony Meehan . . . that's when I first met Peter Grant. He was tour-managing Gene Vincent for Don Arden.

RICHARD COLE (Zeppelin's road manager, 1968–1980)   I left Herbie Goins and the Night-Timers as road manager around about June 1965, which was when John Paul *joined* them. Mick Eve, the sax player, told me, "He's really a bass player, but he also plays fantastic keyboards."

GLYN JOHNS   I worked with John Paul almost every day. First of all, one of the nicest blokes you'll meet. Second, I went to his flat in town once, and there was a bloody Hammond B3 in his living room—I'd had no idea he played anything other than the bass.

ANDREW LOOG OLDHAM (manager of the Rolling Stones and founder of Immediate Records)   There was a young arranger I knew named John Baldwin. The thing was, I wanted my arranger to have a more artistic surname than Baldwin, particularly as I'd be recording a single with him. There was a new Robert Stack movie going the rounds, called *John Paul Jones*. I had no idea what, or who, it was all about, but the name had the kind of ring to it that I'd always liked. I called up John and told him the news: "No more answering to the name of Baldwin. From now on, you're John Paul Jones."

JOHN PAUL JONES   I was very grateful, because [Andrew] trusted me with these sessions and all these musicians. His sessions were always fun: everybody used to enjoy going to them, he was always funny on the talk-back mic. So many sessions were run-of-the-mill, banal, mundane, very boring, you couldn't wait to get out of them.

BP FALLON (U.K. press officer for Zeppelin, 1972–1976)   John Paul I met in 1965, when he was one of Andrew Oldham's bright young kids and came over to Dublin to produce Rosemary and Howard's "Broken Promises," a Del Shannon song on Tony Boland's Tempo label. He was very cool, very chilled.

JOHN PAUL JONES   Somebody came up to me and said, "Can you arrange?" I said, "Sure. What do you want?" "Well, we've got this horn section and . . . " "Okay, don't worry." I rushed out and bought Forsythe's book of orchestration to find out where to write the instruments. Oh, it was appalling. I had it all too low and muddy.

EDDIE KRAMER (Zeppelin engineer, 1969–1972)   My clearest memory is of John Paul walking into Olympic Studios through the double doors carrying his bass on one shoulder and the charts under his arm, while he wheeled in his amp. It's a sixty-piece orchestra, and he sets up all the charts and does all the arrangements—and wonderful

John Paul Jones in session at Olympic Studios, 1967. (Eddie Kramer Archives)

arrangements, too. He would plug in, and we'd section off a little area because nobody played very loudly on those sessions. Then he would get the orchestra together and stand up on the conductor's rostrum with the score open and—literally with the bass in his hand—stand there and conduct the whole bloody orchestra with the bass waving around. He was so cool.

JOHN PAUL JONES I can't remember what the session was, but it was probably about 1964, and [Jimmy and I] were booked on the same date. Decca or somewhere like that, up in Broadhurst Gardens in West Hampstead. I was just really happy to see another young face. I think he was the youngest session musician until I came along.

CLEM CATTINI (leading drummer on the London session scene of the '60s) The thing with us was that we all came from a rock 'n' roll background, whereas most of our peers came from the jazz world.

Suddenly, you've got these hooligans like myself and Jim who had come in from the rock 'n' roll era from groups.

JOHN PAUL JONES It was always Big Jim and Little Jim—Big Jim Sullivan and Little Jim and myself and the drummer, either Bobby Graham or Clem Cattini. Apart from group sessions, where he'd play solos and stuff like that, Page always ended up on rhythm guitar because he couldn't read too well.

BIG JIM SULLIVAN John Paul, surprisingly, could read. The three of us plus Bobby Graham were *the* rhythm section. Bobby had good rhythm, good time. It was terrible pressure, but you learn to live with it after a while; it became second nature. Time was of the essence.

BOBBY GRAHAM (leading session drummer on London '60s scene) Charlie Katz . . . was the fixer for everybody. He was like God, very tough and very touchy. He'd ring up and say, "Bob, I'd like you to be at Decca studios tomorrow morning at ten o'clock until one o'clock." "Charlie, who's the musical director on it?" "Bob, do not ask the names of the higher-ups."

Jimmy wasn't one of the most way-out and weirdest characters I ever met; he was very quiet, very shy. He had a slightly dirtier sound than Big Jim Sullivan.

BIG JIM SULLIVAN You had to be a special breed of person to do sessions, almost insensitive. Some of the producers were assholes, they didn't know what they're doing. There were a few who allowed us our rein, where we could do more what we liked, people like Mike Vernon. The worst ones were when Charlie Katz booked us at Decca 3, the big studio at the back, and you knew it would be an orchestra, a Muzak act.

CLEM CATTINI I remember during one session at Decca, Charlie was saying to the string section, "It's the fifteenth for that session." To which one of the guys replied, "I can't, it's my wedding anniversary." And he knew that if he said no, he would be put on holiday, depending on how long Charlie decided he wanted to put you on holiday. They had a lot of power that time until us lot came in, the Jimmy Pages and the John Paul Joneses, the guys people were asking for.

JOHN PAUL JONES [Jimmy] was always very interested in recording. We were kind of geeks in those days, in a way. At the end of a session, most of the musicians would sit back and read their golf magazines, but we would always go into the control room to listen to playbacks and watch the engineers, watch the producers.

EDDIE KRAMER In 1963, I was working at Pye in London recording the Kinks. I was an assistant engineer, and my memory tells me that Page came in and did an overdub. It was for Shel Talmy, who was half blind and a fantastic producer.

The next time I'm aware of Page is at Olympic in 1967. The studio has just opened, and we're very busy, and Mickie Most books a session for Donovan, and I'm the engineer on it. Concurrently with Jimmy being in the studio doing overdubs, John Paul Jones was a huge participant in the session-musician entrée into the studio. He was always in, always out, always coming in.

JIMMY PAGE Sessions with staff producers could be fairly impersonal. It comes down to costs again. Someone like Shel Talmy was just producing groups, and you'd be there to strengthen the weak links if the drummer wasn't tight enough or the guitarist not up to scratch.

RAY DAVIES (lead singer and songwriter with the Kinks) The recording of "All Day and All of the Night" was a frantic affair, with the Kinks arriving in London late at night from a gig up north to record the song the following morning at Pye Studios, where the first album had been recorded. . . .

When we went upstairs to hear the playback in the tiny control room, we found it crowded with onlookers and assorted musicians. Among them was Jimmy Page, who cringed as it came to Dave [Davies's] guitar solo. Perhaps he was put out about not being asked to play on the track, and we were slightly embarrassed by the amount of jealousy shown by such an eminent guitarist.

KIM FOWLEY (L.A. producer and scenester) Jimmy was the session genius that everybody sought out. When I showed up in London in 1964 as P.J. Proby's publicist-cheerleader, Jimmy was just a tremendous one-take wonder. He was a great musician because he could *listen*, and a lot of musicians don't listen.

A few months later, I found myself at Regent Sound with Andrew Loog Oldham, and there are Jimmy and John Paul Jones and a forgotten genius engineer named Bill Farley. This is the first time I have ever been recorded as a singer, and my backing band features Jimmy Page and John Paul Jones! Both of them were very patient and didn't laugh or throw their guitars down in disgust.

HARVEY LISBERG (manager of Herman's Hermits)   John Paul was Mickie Most's right-hand man, really. All the early Herman's Hermits stuff was arranged by him, so I got to know him quite well, but there was also Lulu and Donovan. He was terribly quiet, very introverted and serious. You hardly noticed him.

MICKIE MOST (producer of Herman's Hermits and founder of RAK Records)   John Paul did a lot of bass playing and arrangements for me, and Jimmy used to play on my sessions. If you get the best people, it's much easier, and I don't think it's anything to do with the musicians in the band feeling hurt.

ANDY JOHNS (brother of Glyn; Zeppelin engineer, 1969–1971)   Glyn was doing some sessions at IBC, and Jimmy comes in with this fuzzbox and says, "This is a fuzzbox." It was held together with bits of Sellotape and string, very homemade, and he plugged it into a Vox and went, "Bloody hell!"

Before you know it, I'm at Glyn's bungalow in south Epsom, where he was living with Ian Stewart. Suddenly, there's a knock at the door, and it's Pagey, and he's got a bloody lip. Glyn goes, "What happened, man?" Jimmy says, "I was just getting off the train, you see, and these three chaps jumped me." Glyn said, "Don Arden, right?" "Well, I disparaged Don last week to somebody, and they didn't like it much." So that's why Pagey later got Peter Grant. Because he'd been duffed up.

MARTIN STONE (guitarist in '60s bands the Action and Mighty Baby)   I was working on the *Croydon Advertiser*, and they farmed me out to the *Sutton and Cheam Advertiser*. They didn't quite know what I could usefully do, so they gave me the "Youth" page. Once a week I had to seek out local youths who were doing interesting stuff.

I found out there was this boy-genius guitar player living in Epsom, so I went out to 34 Miles Road and interviewed him for the *Sutton and Cheam Advertiser.* He was already doing sessions, and that was the thrust of the piece. The skiffle Jimmy was long gone, because he certainly didn't look like that when *I* met him. I guess I saw him as a kind of fellow spirit or outlaw. He'd probably come to Aleister Crowley the same way I did, through liking supernatural fiction and horror stories—Arthur Machen and so on. From there, you get interested in the true occult, which leads you to the Tarot and Crowley.

CHRIS DREJA   Jimmy started to get a bit of a reputation on the grapevine of being a little off-center. He quite liked schoolgirls. The thing about him in a way is that in many respects he's quite effeminate. Maybe those amazing unbelievable riffs come about as a counterpunch to sounding a little bit, you know, "I want to be a medicine man when I grow up and do good things in Africa." You know which devil panned out in the end.

ANDREW LOOG OLDHAM   He didn't suddenly come in and say, "Look, I'm fucking brilliant." I more recall him working his way in slyly. We offered him the job as in-house producer, based really on an affinity of purpose. We were so fed up with old farts that you would gravitate toward people your own age. It was all in the nod, the look in the eye. And I saw that in Jimmy.

JIMMY PAGE   I got involved with Immediate [Records], producing various things, including John Mayall's "Witchdoctor" and "Telephone Blues" around late '65. Eric [Clapton] and I got friendly, and he came down, and we did some recording at home. Immediate found out I had tapes and said they belonged to them, because I was employed by them. I argued that they couldn't put them out because they were just variations on blues structures, but in the end we dubbed some other instruments over them and they came out—with liner notes attributed to me, though I didn't have anything to do with writing them. Stu was on piano, Mick Jagger did some harp, Bill Wyman played bass, and Charlie Watts was on drums.

ALAN CALLAN (president of Zeppelin's Swan Song label in the U.K., 1977–1979)   Most great guitarists are either great on electric or great on acoustic. But Jim is equally great on both, because he is always faithful to the nature of the instrument. He told me that quite early on, he'd gone to a session, and the producer had said, "Can you do it on acoustic, rather than electric?" And he said he came out of that session thinking he hadn't nailed it, so he went home and practiced acoustic for two months.

JACKIE DeSHANNON (L.A. pop-folk singer-songwriter)   I wanted to record at EMI Studios in Abbey Road—a singles date, four sides. I took the songs with me: "Don't Turn Your Back on Me, Babe" and a bunch of others. I wasn't really familiar with the musicians—who might be the best to work with. I wrote on acoustic guitar, so those riffs were really the backbone of my records. I asked them who the best acoustic guitarist was. They suggested Jimmy Page. They said he was one of the best session guitar players in town, and he'd played on a lot of hit records—he could play any style. I said, "Great, let's get him!"

The call went out, and we found out that my session was scheduled for when he was in art school, so we would have to wait for him to get out of school. I said, "He'd better be really good." I played Jimmy the songs. He listened and played them back so perfectly, with so much soul and technique, that I could tell instantly what a brilliant artist he was. He could play anything, even at his young age. He was a big part of those records.

MARIANNE FAITHFULL (Immediate Records singer and girlfriend of Mick Jagger)   In the hotel room next to mine, Jimmy and Jackie were having a very hot romance. He played on almost all my sessions in the '60s, but he was very dull in those days. This was before he went away and became interesting. I guess what he was doing in that hotel room was getting interesting.

Tony Calder said to them, "As soon as you two are finished in that room fucking each other's brains out, why don't you write Marianne a song as well?"

JIMMY PAGE   We wrote a few songs together, and they ended up getting done by Marianne, P.J. Proby, and Esther Phillips or one of those colored artists. . . . I started receiving royalty statements, which was very unusual for me at the time, seeing the names of different people who'd covered your songs.

KIM FOWLEY   One morning at the beginning of 1965, I'm having breakfast by myself at the Continental Hyatt House in Hollywood, and in staggers Jimmy. I said, "What happened to you?" He said, "Jackie invited me to spend some time with her. And she restrained me." So I said, "What exactly did she do?" And he wouldn't answer, but whatever it was, it appeared that he'd been held against his wishes.

Up to this point, Jimmy was like a Jonas Brother, a very gentle Yes-Sir–No-Ma'am kind of guy, and here he was as some kind of boy-toy captive of Jackie DeShannon. Possibly it was in his own mind, but he seemed to *think* he had gone through some kind of restraint that was rather traumatizing. Possibly Jimmy was naïve. Or possibly he was the best actor who ever lived.

•   •   •

CLEM CATTINI   I wasn't getting frustrated, but I was getting fed up with sessions. People don't realize the pressure we were under.

KEITH ALTHAM (writer for *New Musical Express, Record Mirror,* and other publications)   I'd see Jimmy on the platform at Epsom. It struck me even then that he was frustrated that other people—like Eric Clapton—were getting further down the line. I think he was quite envious of the idea of being in a group situation and wanted something that would propel him in that direction, rather than just being the guy that everybody called to play the more complicated guitar parts.

CHRIS DREJA   I don't know what Jimmy was paid in those days—it was probably quite a lot of money. But he must have got to a point where he found the studio a bit too claustrophobic, and he saw the way bands were going, and I think he wanted a bit of it. I think he thought, "I could die and nobody would know who I was. I want to be out there onstage."

JIMMY PAGE   "She Just Satisfies" and "Keep Moving" were a joke. Should anyone hear [them] now and have a good laugh, the only justification I can offer is that I played all the instruments myself, except the drums.

JAKE RIVIERA (founder of Stiff Records and manager of Swan Song artist Dave Edmunds)   I've got a copy of *Beat Instrumental* from the '60s that has an interview with Page in it. He was pushing himself when no one knew what Jim Sullivan or Vic Flick even looked like.

JIMMY PAGE   A point came where Stax Records started influencing music to have more brass and orchestral stuff. The guitar started to take a back trend, and there was just the occasional riff. I didn't realise how rusty I was going to get until a rock 'n' roll session turned up in France, and I couldn't play. I thought it was time to get out, and I did.

CLEM CATTINI   I remember Charlie Katz saying to Jim, "Silly boy, you're giving up a good career."

3

Walking into Stourbridge

> Liverpool started the ball rolling. Now the Midlands is ready
> to take over.
>
> —Dennis Detheridge, in the first issue of *Midland Beat*,
> October 1963

ROBERT PLANT I feel an affinity with the Black Country. I'm fascinated by local history, and I love the humor. It's very locked into the spirit of the region, that little circle to the west of Birmingham.

BARNABY SNOW (director of a documentary film about the Black Country) They have a certain cultural identity in the Black Country, but they don't like to blow their own trumpet about it. They see themselves as people who were at the core of the Industrial Revolution in Britain, because it's all based on a coal seam that was mined out in the nineteenth century. They regard themselves as really more of a rural community that became industrialized but never became like Birmingham, which they don't like to be confused with.

MAC POOLE (Midlands drummer and friend of John Bonham's) The Black Country is where all the *shit* was. If I didn't start my dinner by

31

a particular time, the plate would bounce across the table because of the stampings not far away. There were places we would walk past as kids, and we wouldn't look in because we thought the devil was there—great big ovens with all this fire, blokes handling great big lumps of steel and chucking them under hammers. And this was going on twenty-four hours a day. Furnaces everywhere, all open, white molten metal, men with no teeth, wearing leather aprons. At thirty-five, they looked like they were sixty.

ANDREW HEWKIN (painter and friend of Plant's)   There was an old local joke about your parents being in the iron and steel industry—"My mother irons, my father steals."

GLENN HUGHES (singer and bassist with Trapeze, Deep Purple, and Black Country Communion)   In the Midlands you had half of Zeppelin, a couple of guys in Purple, Judas Priest, Roy Wood, and Jeff Lynne. I really think there was a defining Black Country sound, a Brummie Midlands sound, whether it's Winwood, Plant, myself, Rob Halford as singers, or Bonham as a definitive industrial massive-sounding drummer with a bricklayer vibe going on.

TREVOR BURTON (rhythm guitarist in the Move)   Birmingham was a different place back then. It was a very industrial city, and we were pretty tough people. You were factory fodder. And an amazing load of bands came out of that. It was a way out of going into a factory. I was making £15 a week, and that was twice as much as my dad was making in a factory.

BILL BONHAM (organist in Robert Plant's pre-Zeppelin band Obs-Tweedle)   In the Midlands, a lot of people couldn't climb out of it because all we had to play there were the pubs. The musicianship was incredible. We were a really tight little society. But you still had to go down to London and pay to play or play for nothing. It was very hard to get people to come up and listen to you.

NICK KENT (writer for *New Musical Express*)   Look at Manchester in the '60s, and you've got Herman's Hermits and the Hollies. You look at Birmingham, and you've got Steve Winwood, Denny Laine, the

Moody Blues, and so many more. If you'd seen the Move in 1967, they were one of the best groups that ever existed. Ironically, the band probably most identified with Birmingham—as the supposed birthplace of heavy metal—was Black Sabbath, the least musically talented of *all* of them.

JIM SIMPSON (founder of Big Bear Records and veteran of the Birmingham music scene)   People don't remember what came out of this place. Maybe they could scoot down to London too quickly. We were always told that London knew best, so quite a few bands went down there and made very cheesy records. Birmingham hasn't proved the most elegant place to live. Musicians who were successful here very quickly seemed to get out of town. But the fact is, we produced a lot of really great players and bands, more than our fair share. The bands we had were tough and rough, and they didn't aim at the charts as neatly as those silly Liverpudlians with fringey haircuts and stupid collars on

Jim Simpson, the unofficial godfather of Brum Beat, Birmingham, April 2010. (Art Sperl)

their jackets. There's a kind of false modesty in this part of the world: "Let's go onstage and play some more rubbish." Secretly, we expect somebody to go, "No, it's great!" But nobody ever does.

ROY WILLIAMS (engineer for Robert Plant)   It's the accent. There's no getting around that. It's not as simple as that, but it's a big part of it.

RAY THOMAS (flutist and singer in the Moody Blues)   There were about 250 groups. Half thought they were Cliff and the Shadows, and the other half thought they were the Beatles.

TONY IOMMI (guitarist in Black Sabbath)   You'd see all the local bands at Alex's pie stand, the Fleur de Lys. There'd be five or six bands with all their equipment, and you'd all end up chatting at two o'clock in the morning.

DAVE HILL (guitarist with Slade)   There was always a Johnny and the Somebodies kind of group. Or it was the Montanas or the Californians, who were like the Beach Boys of Wolverhampton.

GLENN HUGHES (singer and bassist with Trapeze, Deep Purple, and Black Country Communion)   There were so many bands breaking out of the cabaret circuit, playing the working men's clubs up and down the country, especially in the north and northeast, five sets a night. The Montanas were the biggest band in the Midlands that had a Top 50 hit in the charts in America. To me, they were like the first real local pop stars, the singer with the dark glasses. That whole Midlands scene was five sets a night, playing whatever was in the charts.

MAC POOLE   The first band that kicked through the dust clouds was the Applejacks in 1964. And they did it by pure fluke, diverting the record company from going to see other bands and instead going to Solihull Civic Centre to see *them*. One day Al Jackson of the Applejacks is cutting our hair in Birmingham, and he says they've got a record deal. Five heads all turn round and go, "I guess you won't be cutting hair much longer."

JIM SIMPSON   There must have been three or four hundred pubs in the area that put music on. The lower-level gigs were in the suburbs, where you cut your teeth, but there were four or five big ones, like the Queen's Head in Erdlington. If you weren't doing doubles on Saturdays, your agent wasn't doing his job right. There were five just on the Ma Regan circuit, and they'd probably use six bands on a night and certainly four. If you played two of them on one night, you got £25.

JOHN CRUTCHLEY (guitarist with Plant's pre-Zeppelin band Listen) Ma Regan looked after the Handsworth Plaza, the Oldhill Plaza, the Ritz at King's Heath, and later the Brum Cavern, which was the last one. If you passed the audition, you could turn professional, because you were playing four to five nights a week at three different venues. It was nice steady work. You'd start off at, say, the Handsworth Plaza, then go to the Ritz at King's Heath, and finally nip over to Oldhill after that. All the bands loved Oldhill, because it had a revolving stage, and that gave you a little more time to set up your equipment.

Rufus Thomas—and Robert Plant's Listen—at Ma Regan's Ritz Dance and Social Club, July 1966. (Courtesy of John Crutchley)

TONY IOMMI   On the Ma Regan circuit, you very rarely came up with your own stuff. If you started playing something nobody knew, you were out very quickly.

DAVE HILL   I remember turning professional and growing my hair long and doing the Regan circuit. We were semiprofessional, and then we turned professional. When you packed up your job, you had to go farther afield than Wolverhampton. You had to go up north and down south on the odd occasion—same as the Beatles. They went to Germany, and we went there and all.

ROBBIE BLUNT (Kidderminster guitarist and Plant sideman in the '80s)   Everybody wanted to be in a band. If you had a drum kit, you were automatically in, even if you couldn't play. Every village hall had a band playing in it. It was when the Mod thing started, which was its own musical revolution, and we all got into the blues.

DAVE PEGG (bass player with Fairport Convention)   The Shadows were gods, and we all learned to play from listening to their records, but the transition from the Shadows to, say, Buddy Guy happened very quickly. All of a sudden, you didn't play any of that shit anymore. All of a sudden, you were fifteen, and you were into R&B and the blues, and that was it. It happened so quickly.

ROBERT PLANT   With the blues, you could actually express yourself, rather than just copy; you could get your piece in there. Only when I began singing blues was I able to use the medium to express what was inside me, my hopes and my fears.

ED BICKNELL (former manager of Dire Straits)   Robert has the greatest knowledge of black blues of any white person I've ever met. I once took part in a blues quiz with him that culminated in a competition to come up with the name of the archetypal blues singer, and he came up with "Blind Peg-Leg Loser." At which point we decided to retire for the night.

ROBERT PLANT   My love was always that whole "Devil Got My Woman" thing—the *accidental* blues heroes. For me, the way to start the day is to listen to Son House with no guidance, no nothing at all.

ROY WILLIAMS Robert's first gig was playing washboard with Perry Foster in the Delta Blues Band.

KEVYN GAMMOND (guitarist in Plant's pre-Zeppelin group the Band of Joy) Perry was a local guy. He would chauffeur Howlin' Wolf around and take him to a tailor's like Burton's and say, "Mr. Burnett would like a new shirt," and they could never find a collar big enough.

ROBERT PLANT Perry came from not far away, and he was an incredible eight-string guitarist. Instead of playing it the normal way, he used to play it like Big Joe Williams, with [the guitar] half on his lap. He was a horrible bloke at times, but he was a real white bluesman, and when I was fifteen, I immediately fell under his spell. My dad used to drop me off at the Seven Stars in Stourbridge, and we used to wail away on "Got My Mojo Working." That was really the initiation. I was at school at the time, and it was really hard to combine the two and keep a compatible relationship with schoolmasters and parents at the same time as doing what I really wanted to do.

PHIL CARSON (head of Atlantic Records in the U.K.) Sorry to blow this for Robert—and he certainly is a man of the people—but his father was a civil engineer, and they lived in a nice house.

KEVYN GAMMOND Robert's dad was a lovely man, but he wasn't happy about his son not going down the conventional career path.

ANDREW HEWKIN We used to go to parties at Stourbridge Arts College with the Winwood brothers and all that lot. There was always this big bloke in the corner with a harmonica about two inches long, playing the blues. We would say, "Who *is* he? All he does is sit in the corner and play the harmonica." He had the corkscrew hair, and you couldn't see his face. In the Midlands, there was definitely a lack of good-looking guys, so if you were reasonably good-looking, you did alright. Robert fell into that category, as did all the guys who ended up in Traffic. There were all these bands playing at Stourbridge Town Hall—five shillings on a Wednesday night—and Robert was itching to join one of them. All this stuff was coming over from America. It was mainly soul, but Robert was seriously into the blues.

PAUL LOCKEY (bassist in Plant's pre-Zep Band of Joy) Robert, you know, even in those days, at eighteen or nineteen years old, people were taken aback. He'd walk into a party, and all the women would be just standing there, going, "Ahhh." They were always really taken with Robert—even my wife! All the girls were just fascinated, and the guys were, too, in a different sort of way.

ROY WILLIAMS Nobody particularly liked him round here. It was, "That bloody Planty, cocky bastard." He was very up-there and witty but also very grounded. If he hadn't been that kind of character, he wouldn't have been able to grab hold of his gig with Zeppelin.

ANDREW HEWKIN I took a room at 1 Hill Road, Lye, and then Robert took a room there. He just sort of hung around with everybody at Stourbridge Art College. I don't know what he did for work. Nobody ever asked him; nobody ever asked anybody *anything*.

KEVYN GAMMOND Fresh ideas and new approaches happened even in little towns like Kidderminster and Stourbridge, all within a sort of ten-to-fifteen-mile radius. Roger Laverne was the keyboard player on "Telstar," but everyone else was a nameless nobody. He was the only one who'd ever made it from Kiddy.

JOHN COMBE (Kidderminster music historian) Robert used to have a scooter, and he used to hang around with the Mods in Stourbridge.

ROBBIE BLUNT One of the greatest things round here was the Thursday night "Big Beat Sessions" gigs at Kidderminster Town Hall. You had all the biggest bands coming through, and my dad used to drop me off with five bob.

STEVE MARRIOTT (lead singer with the Small Faces) Percy Plant was a big fan. He used to come to the gigs whenever we played in Kidderminster or Stourbridge. He was always saying he was going to get this group together. He was another nuisance. He kept coming into the dressing room, just another little Mod kid. We used to say, "That kid's here again."

ROBERT PLANT In England, there was much more of a blue-eyed soul thing than there was in America. There was Rod Stewart, Steve

Marriott. Stevie Winwood was amazing, and coming from the same area as me, he was probably the most eloquent and stylish and tasteful of all of us.

DAVE PEGG   It was the Spencer Davis Group, really, that did it, because they had so many hits. You couldn't see Steve Winwood without going, "Wow!"

TONY SECUNDA (manager of the Move and the Moody Blues)   You knew that group was going to make it, the first time you saw them. Everyone knew it. So when they did, there was an entire city full of earwigs walking round saying "Told you so" to each other.

DAVE PEGG   It was very difficult to be a band that could make it in Birmingham. The Move did it, for sure, and the Spencer Davis Group. The Spencer Davis Group had Steve's unique talent, so it was only a matter of time before somebody of that age cracked it, but the Move had the benefit of Tony Secunda. Most of the other Midlands groups didn't really happen, so you'd get somebody together with a band, and then he'd go because he got a chance of playing with a big London group.

BILL BONHAM   If Robert had moved down to London, I think it would have happened for him earlier. But his parents were dead against him doing music and refused to help him in any way. So he had no money and no support system, and he had to stay with people.

JOHN COMBE   The famous story is that Robert had a huge bust-up with his mum and dad, and he slept in a transit van that he parked in a lay-by here in Kidderminster.

ROBERT PLANT   Blues gave me my first band titles—my first band was the Black Snake Moan, after Blind Lemon Jefferson, and the second was the Crawling King Snakes, after a brilliant John Lee Hooker track. [The King Snakes] . . . was a little bit more of the commercial sound then—a bit more "Daddy Rolling Stone" and hopping about the stage with the mic stand in the air.

ROBBIE BLUNT   I was watching *Fireball-XL5* on the TV, having me beans on toast, and Robert came and dragged me off to do a gig up at one of the Ma Regan venues. It may have been the Crawling King Snakes. The usual guitarist was a real cool dude called Maverick, but he used to go missing. I really didn't know what I was doing. Robert said, "Just look good and move about a bit."

ROBERT PLANT   I was sixteen years old and singing at the Plaza Ballroom in Oldhill. There was a guy with quite an arrogant air to himself, very cocky, standing [and] watching me. He said, "You're pretty good, but you'd be a lot better if you had a drummer like me." I thought, "Nobody says that sort of thing to *me*. Don't they know who I might one day end up being?" That was the first moment that [John Bonham and I] ever communicated at all. We tried it out, and he joined the Crawling King Snakes for a while. And it was the beginning of a fantastic exchange of energies between us over the years—not always particularly smooth but always pretty dynamic. . . .

MICK BONHAM (younger brother of John Bonham)   Me and John were very much alike. Somebody would only have to look at you or say something wrong, and then we wanted to fight the world.

DEBBIE BONHAM (younger sister of John Bonham)   John got his influence from Gene Krupa and Buddy Rich, because my mum and dad used to play those bands all the time. They loved the Tommy Dorsey band and Glenn Miller and Harry James and Frank Sinatra. And that's what John used to play to, in the shed, till the neighbors would come round and start banging on the door to my mum: "Tell him to turn it down!"

ROY CARR (writer for *New Musical Express*)   He liked those powerhouse jazz drummers. The same with Keith Moon, who was a big fan of Gene Krupa and even used to mimic the way Krupa leaned over his drums when he played. Bonzo wanted to get sounds out of his drums, as opposed to just bashing them.

JOHN BONHAM   In *The Benny Goodman Story*, Krupa came right out into the front. He played drums much louder than they'd ever been played before—and much better. People hadn't taken much notice of drums until Krupa came along.

BILL HARVEY (drummer replaced by Bonham in the Blue Star Trio in late 1962)   [John] was very adaptable. On top of that, he was self-taught, which made a heck of a difference because you could pick things up—you didn't have to rehearse too much. The one thing that marked him out at that stage was his kick-drum technique, which absolutely flabbergasted all of us, the way he could do these triplets with the bass drum. I asked him once how he did it, and he said, "Oh, no, I'm not gonna tell ya, but I'll tell you what I *have* done: I've took the leather strap off the bass-drum pedal, and I've put a bike chain on instead." And of course, all the bass-drum pedals now are chain-driven. To my mind, he was the first one that ever did it.

BILL FORD (bass player with the Senators)   At this stage in 1963, the Senators still had an unreliable drummer and were let down by him on a number of occasions. [He] let us down again one night when we had a double gig. [He] played drums on the first set at the first gig at Perry Hall, Bromsgrove. During the break, he shot off in his car to fetch his mate, who he said could play the drums. He came back twenty minutes later with this lad named John Bonham. We started the second half, and it was as if someone had stuck rocket fuel in our drinks. John joined us as our drummer there and then. With this final lineup, we played regularly at many of the Birmingham venues and pubs.

JOHN BONHAM (speaking in 1975)   We used to have *so* many clubs we could play around Birmingham in those days. Lots of ballrooms, too. All those places have gone to the dogs—or bingo.

ROY CARR   There was a certain style of drummer in the Midlands: Bonzo, Bev Bevan, Don Powell, Carl Palmer, Bill Ward—they all seemed to be very aggressive. I mean, Bevan was really a monster drummer.

MAC POOLE   As a drummer, you were having to get louder to compete with the guitarists turning up with bigger amps. Most of the Midlands drummers were attacking the guitarists, they weren't sitting back. We were determined to be heard, and it was that attitude John took through Zeppelin to the rest of the world.

BEV BEVAN (drummer with the Move)   My first recollection of John was him coming to see me when I was with Denny Laine and [the] Diplomats back in 1963, and [then] Carl Wayne and the Vikings in 1964, just before we started the Move. I was the loudest drummer in the area at the time.

DENNY LAINE (singer with the Diplomats and the Moody Blues)   John used to watch me and the Diplomats at the Wednesbury Youth Centre. Years later, he stayed at my house, and though I couldn't remember any of the original material the Diplomats did to save my life, *he* could. We got a bit drunk, and he started singing "Why Cry," "A Piece of Your Mind," and others we did. He knew all the words and everything.

JIM SIMPSON   In Locomotive, we called John "Bonnie," though we may have called him Bonzo as well. He could have walked into any band in the world and felt comfortable. He'd have smiled and said, "Who's gonna count me in?" He was very calm, nothing would faze him. I had to sack him two or three times. We all loved him, but he was utterly outrageous—or maybe just boisterous. We got banned from several places because of him. He took his shirt off and stood on his drum kit at Frank Freeman's School of Dancing in Kidderminster. Frank said to me, "You were very good tonight, Jim, but we're never going to book you again with *that* drummer." John could always sense when he was near to getting the bullet, because he would bring things from his mother's store to cheer the band up—packs of cigarettes or a bottle of whisky. We'd all go, "Oh, we can't sack him *now*."

DAVE PEGG   John lived in a caravan in the garden of his parents' shop, the general store at Astwood Bank. He was always very generous with the Benson and Hedges, which I hope Mrs. Bonham never finds out about.

ROBERT PLANT   John was so good, everyone wanted him in their bands. You knew your relationship with John was going to change when he decided to get the drums out of the van to clean them. Because you'd never see him again: "I just wanna clean me drums, mate," and that would be the end of that—he'd be off with somebody else for a couple of months.

TONY IOMMI He used to be in a different band every other bloody week. We used to play at the Midland Red Club in Birmingham, and he would be in one band. The next week we'd play there again, and he'd be in *another* band.

He had the names of the groups on his drum case, and the last one would be crossed out and the new one written in. He must have had fifteen names on that case.

4

The Freakout Zone

The groups come from all over England, and if they make it
at the Marquee, that's the big break. The management here
has recording studios and can help and promote a favoured
group. The hipless boys from Birmingham have gone over
about seventy per cent this evening.

—Jane Wilson, "Teenagers," from
Len Deighton's London Dossier (1967)

JOHN CRUTCHLEY (guitarist in Plant's pre-Zeppelin band Listen)   One
Monday night in 1965, there was a DJ playing records at Oldhill Plaza.
Things like "Land of a Thousand Dances," some Stax and Motown
stuff. After we'd nearly finished our set, he asked if he could come up
and sing with us. It was Robert. So we started to look forward to Oldhill on a Monday. He'd jump up and do "Everybody Needs Somebody"
or "Smokestack Lightning." So we said, "D'ya wanna come in as the
singer?" He was a breath of fresh air.

BILL BONHAM (organist in Robert Plant's pre-Zeppelin band Obs-
Tweedle, no relation to John)   I saw Listen at Walsall Town Hall.

Listen at the Bull Ring, Birmingham, 1966 (left to right: Robert "Lee" Plant, John Crutchley, Geoff Thompson. (Courtesy of John Crutchley)

Robert was on another level, very dynamic. I'd never seen anything like him. Very misunderstood in the working men's clubs, where they thought he just wailed. He always had a tremendous girl following.

JOHN CRUTCHLEY My dad used to call him "The Rubber Man" because he was so flexible when he danced onstage. We'd start off with "Hold On, I'm Coming," me playing through a fuzzbox. At the beginning, it was one number after another, very fast and tight, but after a while we got looser, and Rob would talk to the audience, telling them where the numbers came from. He introduced *us* to a lot of stuff. He was the first to really introduce me to the blues. There was a live album called *Folk Festival of the Blues* with Muddy Waters, Howlin' Wolf, and Buddy Guy, and Rob played me that when he was living on Trinity Road in West Brom. Rob lived there with Maureen—he met her when he was in Listen, when *I* was going out with her sister Shirley. The four of us used to go about together.

ROBERT PLANT   When I was seventeen, I began dating the consequent mother of my children. She lived in an East Indian area, so I was constantly surrounded by Indian film music. To a conservative ear, the swirling strings and the way the vocals came out of the instrumental sections wouldn't have been attractive at all. But to me, it was all very sensual and alluring. And five blocks from that was the Jamaican neighborhood, where I used to hang out when I wasn't working, eating goat stew and listening to ska records.

KEVYN GAMMOND (guitarist in Plant's pre-Zeppelin group the Band of Joy)   Maureen had grown up in quite a large Indian family, with a local mentality—beautiful girl, she hipped Robert to curries and spices from an early age. That bonding with that family—which is still part of his life—is still very important to him. So already from eighteen, nineteen, they'd gone into quite a settled way of life.

JOHN OGDEN (reporter for the *Birmingham Express and Star*)   Robert's mum, Annie, rang up to ask if I thought he was any good or if he stood any chance. Of course, I said yes, but I don't think it reassured her much. I know his dad wasn't happy till he saw a report in the *Financial Times* about how much Led Zeppelin were making. And you can understand, because Robert really had a brain on him.

JOHN CRUTCHLEY   It was getting a little bit frustrating, so we thought, "Let's try and be a pop band." We got a manager, a chap called Mike Dolan, and he got in touch with some London agents. We used to go down to London, where the Malcolm Rose Agency would book us into the 100 Club, the Bag o' Nails, and farther down south on the Astra circuit—the 400 Ballroom in Torquay, places like that.

It wasn't a great deal of money. It was the Mod era, so it was slowly changing to smart dress and short hair. We got these secondhand gangster suits from shops in Aston. I used to love dressing up, and Rob used to love dressing up, and it went down well on the Regan circuit.

ROBERT PLANT   The day England won the World Cup [July 30, 1966], I was seventeen, and we were opening for the Troggs at the Boston Gliderdrome in Lincolnshire. I watched the World Cup Final through the window of a TV rental company called DER Rentals.

JOHN CRUTCHLEY We made a demo of three tracks in London and Mike Dolan got Danny Kessler at CBS interested. Danny said Rob's voice stuck out but to do things fast he wanted to use session guys and augment the sound with brass and backing singers. We were upset about it but we were trying to get an instant hit so we went along with it.

DAVE HILL (guitarist with the 'N Betweens) We must have both been listening to the Young Rascals when we first brought out "You'd Better Run." And then it was like, "Oh, Rob Plant's got one of them, too." Coming from the same area, it wasn't so odd, really, and they're both good versions. Ours is more rock. I don't think it made a difference, in that neither of them did anything. It was just nice to have a record out.

ROBERT PLANT Those were my first tricky moments in the studio, with a roomful of session guys eating sandwiches between takes. It was a daunting experience for me. I was quite pleased with myself up there in the Black Country when I was sixteen or seventeen, and I'd bludgeoned them into believing that I had something to offer. I went into the room and I was faced with Clem Cattini and Lesley Duncan and Kiki Dee and I looked at them thinking, "Geez, I must have come to the wrong place." So to squawk my way through these things was an absolute pleasure, but also the tension and fear and will to do it right [were] magnificent, really.

CLEM CATTINI (London session drummer) The session was down at the new Regent Sound in Warren Street. I always remember after the session the singer saying, "Nice playing." But I didn't realize who it was until some time later, when I went to Lulu's wedding. Robert came up to me and said, "D'you realize you played on my first record?"

ROBERT PLANT Coming out of that studio at the end of that session, I've never ever been so relieved in all my life. It was like, "Christ, I did it!" Then it came out and had a label and you could see it and it had a dust sleeve and it was a record with me on it. That was the beginning.

JOHN CRUTCHLEY Rob says it went suspiciously into the charts for one week. But it didn't make the Top 30, which might have got us on

Listen's 1966 near-hit "You'd Better Run." (Courtesy of John Crutchley)

Top of the Pops. When it didn't, things started disintegrating. We were completely broke at the end of thirteen, fourteen months. So we petered out in the end. But the thing about the CBS contract was that we didn't sign it, *Robert* did. So he was signed for two more singles.

DAVE PEGG (bass in Bonham's pre-Zeppelin band A Way of Life)   I remember bumping into Robert once outside opposite Yates's Wine Lodge in Corporation Street. He had these postcard publicity pictures, and I said, "How are you doing?" He said, "I'm thinking of doing cabaret stuff." I went, "Really?" He went, "Yeah, I know, but I'm giving it a go." It was like a Tom Jones–type picture. It all comes back to that Midlands thing of having to get out there and make it.

KEVYN GAMMOND   With "Our Song," I think it got to about ninety-eight takes, because Robert was not that kind of singer. He told me he was in tears because he couldn't crack it.

JOHN CRUTCHLEY   And then Robert went on to form one stage of the Band of Joy. He said he wanted to do more meaningful numbers like

Mr. Plant blossoms out as a ballad singer

ANY FANS of Listen who have not yet heard vocalist Robert Plant's first solo disc are in for a big surprise. Gone is the familiar soulful voice, the churning beat and the wild sound with which he was associated for so long.

In its place is the voice of a ballad singer of the old school, singing a love song of the old school.

On the C.B.S. label, it's called "Our Song," and the original version was a No. 1 hit in Italy and it's obvious that the song is highly thought of in the pop world. There are other cover versions of the song by Rita Pavone and Julie Rogers.

The fact that these two artists are also cutting the song gives an indication of what it's like. But Bob's version does manage to avoid extreme sentimentality, even though I think it's completely the wrong song for him.

I asked him how he felt about it the other day, and he admitted that at first he didn't like the song either, although he's now changed his mind.

He thinks that R and B and the Tamla-style music is becoming more and more discredited by being associated with "the

Robert Plant . . . already the new style has earned him the tag "The Tom Jones of the Midlands."

POPPETTS

WATCH OUT for Denny Laine's new single. Without having yet heard it I'd say it could well be a hit for him.

TOP 20

"I'm thinking of doing cabaret stuff." Plant the balladeer in the *Birmingham Express and Star*, March 1967. (Courtesy of John Ogden)

* * *

"Season of the Witch" and "Hey Joe," things with a little more edge to them. He said, "Come along if you want to." I said, "Well, let me try and make a bit of money first."

* * *

MICK BONHAM   [John] met Pat Phillips when he was sixteen, and his love for her didn't diminish at all, through all their years together. Pat went with him everywhere.

MAC POOLE (Midlands drummer and Bonham's replacement in A Way of Life)   I was there when Bonzo started dancing with Pat at the Oldhill Plaza. I knew Patty and her sister Beryl, because they were girls on the circuit who liked music. They were both lovely girls.

JASON BONHAM (son of John Bonham)   When I was born [in 1966], they didn't have anywhere to live, really. Mum had gone back home to her parents, and Dad would then come over and visit on the bus.

DAVE PEGG It was a very close-knit community, that whole Birmingham thing, and when I got involved with John, it was in a group called A Way of Life that had two brothers, Reg and Chris Jones. It was quite short-lived: our first gig was on September 17, 1967, at the Crown and Cushion at Perry Bar, and our last was the 23rd of October at the Queen's Head.

REG JONES (singer and guitarist with A Way of Life) We were holding auditions on a Sunday afternoon at the Cedar Club in Birmingham, and we had about twenty drummers turn up for this audition. John came along and said, "What gigs we got, then?" And I thought, "Blimey, *he's* cocky. . . ."

DAVE PEGG We didn't do much original material. We'd do cover versions of Vanilla Fudge, and we did some Hendrix things. We played everywhere you could play on the Midlands circuit. You've never heard a drum kit sound that way. The bass drum was an annihilator. Reg and Chris used to write a couple of songs, but it never really developed. It was about playing music that we all liked at the time, mainly stuff from America. Bonzo was very much a Vanilla Fudge fan. The first gig we did with A Way of Life was in Aberystwyth at the King's Hall. We had to siphon fuel on the way back. It was Bonzo's idea. He was like, "Well, if we do that, we can split the money up." That was his logic.

MAC POOLE Reg and Chris Jones were slightly off the wall. Chris was a great guitarist, but they always had an agenda, and Bonham and I suffered from it. If he got a bit pissed, they'd sack him, and if *I* got too loud they'd sling me out and get someone else in the band. Reg was very keen on contemporary soul stuff—he wasn't into experimental things—but A Way of Life was more West Coast rock.

DAVE PEGG I remember going to the Top Spot in Ross-on-Wye with Bonham, where they had a traffic-light system for the noise level. When it went red, they cut the mains off. When we set the gear up, John hit the bass drum, and it turned the electric straight off.

ROBERT PLANT The early Band of Joy was an Otis Clay tribute band playing stuff like Vernon Garrett. Some of the guys in the band had been playing with the Stringbeats, which was a West Indian band that I think in the end became Steel Pulse.

PAUL LOCKEY (bassist in Plant's pre-Zeppelin Band of Joy) Chris Brown invented the name. Someone said, "What shall we call ourselves?" and he said, "Robert Plant and the Band of Joy." It sounded a bit comical.

ANDREW HEWKIN (Midlands-born painter and acquaintance of Plant's) They used to practice in the cellar at Lye. It was like a mini-cavern. This was the early days, and they were playing at Mother's in Edgbaston. Stourbridge and Kidderminster were the two main places. Stourbridge was Wednesday night, and Kidderminster was Thursday.

ROBBIE BLUNT Frank Freeman's Ballroom was a very strange thing to have in Kidderminster—this old chap and his wife opening their doors to us. It was just this little place upstairs that I remember with incredible affection. Every Sunday they'd have a show, and John Peel would come up and spin the records. I was there when Peel brought Captain Beefheart up.

KEVYN GAMMOND Beefheart was sitting there rolling joints while Frank and his wife were making him and the band cups of tea.

ROBBIE BLUNT I saw A Way of Life at Frank Freeman's. People would say, "You've gotta come and see this band with this drummer." Bonzo already had those chops down, and he was just so loud.

ROBERT PLANT I was sacked because [Pop Brown, the father of Chris] told me I couldn't sing: "I'm sorry, Robert, there's just something about you." So I formed another Band of Joy, still with Mike Dolan. I'd gone back to him out of desperation.

KEVYN GAMMOND It was Mike who set up the whole "Legalize Pot" publicity stunt for Robert.

JOHN OGDEN The "Legalize Pot" march was a ridiculously bad publicity stunt, but Robert went for it wholeheartedly. He even conducted

Plant arriving at Wednesbury Court on August 10, 1967, to demand the legalization of pot. (Courtesy of John Crutchley)

his own defense at eighteen years old—and *got off.* He was pretty full of himself. Nothing was really happening for him, so people thought, "What's *he* got to brag about?" He was quite impatient. If he thought something wasn't working, he'd move on it from pretty quickly. He was desperate to make it.

ROBERT PLANT   I did as many spoof things as I could to get a bit of publicity. I joined the Noise Abatement Society and invited them to my gig and then played as loud as possible. I was the only guy to be accepted and rejected within one day. But I was seventeen, and it didn't seem to matter then. It was just a hoot.

BEV BEVAN (drummer in the Move and the Electric Light Orchestra)   Audiences found Robert was being a bit too experimental. With Denny Laine and Carl Wayne, our bands were just playing the hits and what people wanted to hear. . . but [the Band of Joy] weren't playing Top 40 stuff, and they didn't always go down that well with audiences.

ROBERT PLANT The second Band of Joy decided to have painted faces—a little bit before Arthur Brown. It frightened everybody to death, and there was this big fat bass player who'd come running on and dive straight off the stage, wearing [bells and a] kaftan . . . billowing into the audience.

ROY HARPER (maverick folk singer and friend of Zeppelin's) I was playing at Mother's, a lovely free sort of place with a lot of young people milling around with quite a buzz in the air. I was sitting on the floor, chewing the fat with the promoter and some fans, and the room was pretty full. A tallish young man came through with at least a couple of women on his arm and another couple following. It was a *team*.

He was a striking individual, and I can remember saying, "Who's that?" The reply, in a broad Black Country accent was, "That's Bob Plant. He's got a group called the Band of Joy, and they're really good." I remember them walking through and thinking, "Tall blond teenager with four women, looks like a star. . . . I wonder what the Band of Joy is?"

GLENN HUGHES (singer and bassist with Trapeze, Deep Purple, and Black Country Communion) I used to see Robert hanging out, and he was aloof, and he had the kaftan and the cool look. And I thought, "Oh, that's kind of a rock star."

ROBERT PLANT The third and final Band of Joy was when Bonham came up to me wearing an orange ostrich-skin bomber jacket, which he'd nicked off Ace Kefford. He used to squint at me and say, "You're all right, but you're no good without me." I said, "But you live too far away. I can't come all the way." He said, "Don't worry, I'll get some fags from me mum's shop and we'll sell 'em to buy the gas."

KEVYN GAMMOND Rob and John were quite devious. When they heard Paul Lockey's dad had a van, they went and approached Paul to be the bass player. We got dressed up in suits like we were going to get a bloody bank loan and went to see the Lockey family to persuade them to let Paul join the group. And, of course, we ran that van into the ground.

The Band of Joy (Mk. 3) in the snowy grounds of Holland Park School, London, January 1968: (left to right) Kevyn Gammond, Robert Plant, John Bonham, Chris Brown, Paul Lockey. (Ron Howard/Getty Images)

PAUL LOCKEY Robert and John were ambitious, because they were probably the best in the West Midlands. But we never had any arguments, it was always a laugh. We had in mind that one day we would try and write our own material, but we never seemed to have the time. "Memory Lane" and "Adriatic Seaview" were just put together one afternoon in a boardinghouse somewhere up north before a gig: sitting around in the lounge with a couple of guitars, a nice sunny afternoon with the sun coming through. Pop Brown lived in Dagger Lane, so that's what we were singing about. It was a real good live number, a vehicle to build excitement.

KEVYN GAMMOND "Memory Lane" was, I think, the first song Plant and Bonham ever wrote. Dagger Lane was where the Jamaicans lived in West Brom. There was a coffee bar near there called the Kasbah, which was another watering hole where Robert hung out around the time of that "Legalize Pot" publicity stunt.

ROBERT PLANT With Bonzo, the Band of Joy became a total freakout. We started playing with Mick Farren and moved away from the blue-eyed soul circuit onto what was the underground blues movement.

MICK FARREN (singer with the Deviants and writer for the underground press) The Band of Joy opened for my band the Deviants. We'd driven from Carlisle or somewhere, and we were sitting on the edge of the stage while they were having a kind of full rehearsal. They said, "Oh, do you want to sound check?" and we were like, "Nah, don't worry, we're tired and hungry and miserable."

So they go back to what they do, which appeared to be Plant and the keyboard player fighting over who was the star of the show and rehearsing this terrible fucking tune, something about "Auntie Jane comes down the lane. . . ." One of those horrible flower-power songs. I mean, Robert was really good, but we fucking hated it. Rock 'n' roll *bel canto* with a keyboard player: it was really fucking obnoxious, as far as I was concerned.

JOHN CRUTCHLEY Kevyn Gammond had a very unorthodox guitar style. He used to stick out like a sore thumb, in the nicest possible way. Played a nice 335 Gibson.

KEVYN GAMMOND We'd go from the most ridiculous hyper-blues like "Evil Woman" into something really sensitive like Tim Hardin's "How Can We Hang on to a Dream?" With Bonzo's drumming, it sometimes sounded like he was trying to get out of a cupboard. If a dog had wandered onstage, it would have died from the volume.

PAUL LOCKEY At the Speakeasy in London, people would come in, look at us for about a minute, and then go through to the bar. Nobody took any notice 'cause many of them were pop stars. Little did they realize who they were looking at. We saw all the hippies doing acid at the Middle Earth, but our scene was much more a pint of bitter. Or two pints.

JOHN OGDEN I was running a blues club in Wolverhampton called the Blue Horizon, and I got people like Champion Jack Dupree in. Robert rang up and asked if the Band of Joy could play there, so I said, "Yeah, sure." But by then, he'd got into West Coast stuff, which didn't really go down too well with the blues fans. He thought people would be ready for this revolutionary music, and they really weren't. One of the top gigs was at the Ship and Rainbow, and it was run by a woman whose husband was a police sergeant. When the Band of Joy played there, they did "Spoonful," and Robert sang a line about "a spoonful of sugar laced with LSD." The sergeant threw them all out of the pub.

PAUL LOCKEY There was a lot of improvisation. We'd start off, we'd have an ending, and what happened in the middle was . . . anything goes! You never worried about the arrangement. There was so much energy that it would spill over into everything. But I think we were a bit ahead of the curve, if anything.

ROBERT PLANT Mike Dolan accidentally booked us out as the Joy Strings, who were a Salvation Army band that had a hit in 1964 with "It's an Open Secret." He put us into working man's clubs in Newcastle, and by the time we got halfway through "Omaha" by Moby Grape, they'd closed the curtains and taken us off with not so much as a thank-you.

KEVYN GAMMOND When we played the college up the road here in Kidderminster, Mr. Cotterell the principal yanked the plug halfway through "Killing Floor" and called the police. John had to phone Pat to say he wasn't coming home because they'd found some Purple Hearts [amphetamines] on him.

PAUL LOCKEY They booked us into Regent Sound in London. I can't remember if it was one or two days. We had a break, so we walked down Wardour Street to the Marquee. We walked in the back way for some reason, and it was absolutely jammed, and there was a band called Free on the stage. I thought they were tremendous—a little like us, but a bit tighter.

KEVYN GAMMOND There was a record shop near Regent Sound, and as we were browsing through the records, we overhead all this talk about the political topics of the day. We were kind of country bumpkins, learning about the whole upheaval of the '67–'68 period. Rob really went, in his head, to California and all the hippie bullshit of the search for truth and experience. We were recording things like "For What It's Worth," which we thought was about Vietnam, when in fact it was about the Sunset Strip.

ROBERT PLANT I really just wanted to get to San Francisco and join up. I wanted to be with Jack Casady and Janis Joplin. I found the projection of English rock to be built on a proficiency and a skill factor that didn't exist in L.A. and [on] the West Coast. There was some kind of fable being created there and a social change that was taking place, and the music was the catalyst in it all. With Neil Young, things like "On the Way Home" and "Expecting to Fly" were so spacey and yet so ambiguous. Because I come from the Black Country and I'm not a tormented Canadian Scorpio, I didn't get any of that. But I tried to join in here and there.

KEVYN GAMMOND From the Ma Regan circuit, where there were loads of gigs, it all kind of slowed down a bit.

ROBERT PLANT For a long time, there were duff promoters and agents trying to keep groups down—only booking them to play Kinks numbers or chart stuff all night. The Band of Joy only managed to get about two gigs a week. It was only through Maureen working that we kept going, or we'd have ended up a Belsen case.

PAUL LOCKEY Things were coming to a head. We were all a bit down. Mike Dolan hadn't managed to get us a deal. We were driving north, and the engine dropped out of the van. We all looked at each other and thought, "Hmmm, that's probably the end of the band." There was no bad blood. We all stayed mates.

KEVYN GAMMOND We were on our way up to Dunfermline, and one of the doors was missing. I said, "I just can't do this anymore." I think that was the end of the Band of Joy. From there, Mike Dolan got me a gig with Jimmy Witherspoon, and Rob did some recordings with Alexis Korner. Alexis said to Rob, "That guy's not the right drummer for what you're trying to do. It's like World War III coming at you."

DAVE PEGG John got a gig with Tim Rose, and I played with him behind Tim for one day, when he'd got an extra gig before his tour started. John phoned me up and said, "We'll have to go to London to rehearse, and there's two gigs: the American Air Force Base at Upper Heyford and RAF Bicester." I said, "Yeah, great, mate."

We drove down to London to Ken Colyer's club, Studio 51. Tim Rose came in and rehearsed for two or three hours, and we got the set list together. We did "Hey Joe," but he didn't like the walking bass thing I'd copied off the Hendrix record. We packed the gear up and went off to Upper Heyford, which was like being in America. John dropped me back off about four-thirty in the morning, and we got £15 each. Which was a lot of money in those days.

Rich returns in September

on vocals, trumpet, slide whistle and drums, the other members being Lynn Dobson (tnr, sop, flt), Chris Spedding (gtr), "Butch" (bass), Charlie Hart (organ), Jamie Muir (drs), Pete Baily (congo, bongoes, talking drum).

The group appear at an open-air happening in Trafalgar Square on Saturday.

SHACK MAY TOUR

CHICKEN SHACK and Savoy Brown Blues Band expect to tour the States later this year. The groups' agent, Harry Simmonds, flies to America next month to finalise negotiations for the tours.

Decca Records have shipped 5,000 copies of Savoy Brown's album, "Getting To The Point," to America for release at the end of August.

PAPER DOLLS GUEST

PAPER DOLLS will feature "My Life (Is In Your Hands)" on this Saturday's Time For Blackburn TV show. They also guest on Saturday Club the same day.

Girls play a week's cabaret at New Cavendish Club, Sheffield, from August 4 and holiday in Spain from 17 to 24.

They record their next single when they return.

TIM ROSE TOUR

TIM ROSE will tour European major cities in August returning for a Royal Festival Hall concert at the end of September.

Tim returns to an eight-week tour of the USA in November and will take with him his two British backing musicians, drummer John Bonham and bassist Steve Dolan.

TREMELOES STAR

THE Tremeloes and their former singer Brian Poole

DUSTY: Sunday concert

Cilla in Mo

CILLA BLACK flies to the South of France on July 26 for a cabaret appearance at a Grand Gala at Monte Carlo's Sporting Club.

She will also appear on French TV during the trip.

She is currently working on a new album.

"Tim Rose Tour,"
Melody Maker, July
20, 1968.

JOHN OGDEN   Bonzo actually sang backing vocals on some of the Tim Rose numbers, and he'd have this grin on his face as he sang. I don't think he *wanted* to sing, but you couldn't refuse Tim, I suppose.

HARRY SHAPIRO (biographer of Alexis Korner)   Alexis Korner took Robert out with him in a duo during the early part of 1968 because Planty was getting pissed off that his career was going nowhere. He told Alexis that if he hadn't made it by the time he was twenty—his birthday was coming up in August—he would quit.

ROBERT PLANT   I used to sleep at Alexis's place on Queensway. "Goodnight, Robert," he'd say. "You'll have to sleep on the couch tonight—oh, by the way, it's the same couch that Muddy used to sleep on when he stayed here." This was fabulous—I'm from Wolver-hampton, you know?

BILL BONHAM   My band was trying to get a really cool-sounding name—something like Procol Harum—so that we could get into this new wave of things where bands no longer had the word *The* before the name. My dad had a dictionary and just started shouting out names. We settled on Obs-Tweedle.

Robert and Maureen came to see us play at Dudley Zoo, and Robert asked if he could join. He'd just been working with Alexis Korner. A lot of the early gigs were done as the Band of Joy, because they were dates Robert had already booked before they broke up. It was Robert who got us to do things by the Buffalo Springfield and Moby Grape. Around May of 1968, a guy called Terry Rowley produced demos of songs like "Mr. Soul" and "Rock 'n' Roll Woman."

ROBERT PLANT   I joined them for about three months because I'd got nowhere to live, and Billy Bonham lived in an apartment just opposite Noddy Holder, who became our roadie because his dad had a window-cleaning firm and he had a van.

JOHN OGDEN   Robert was ambitious, and he was scuffling a bit. He did try everything to succeed. I think with Obs-Tweedle, he was just marking time till Jimmy Page rescued him.

5

Happenings Fifty Years' Time Ago

> The English, I think, have always had a better idea of the
> multi-voiced nature of performance than Americans. They
> were able to view the blues as theatre, which it was and
> still is.
>
> —Mike Spies, slate.com, March 2011

CHRIS DREJA (bassist with Page's pre-Zeppelin band the Yard-birds)   When Eric Clapton left the Yardbirds, I was upset because—being a junior member—I didn't really have a decision in that. He did us a favor, ironically, because he'd become very blinkered at that point, in terms of music. I was sorry to see him go as a friend, but there was no more "I'm not doing that," and we now became totally free to be eclectic with Jeff Beck.

SIMON NAPIER-BELL (second manager of the Yardbirds) Paul Samwell-Smith left, and Jeff said, "I want Jimmy Page in the group." I didn't know much about rock musicians, but I had enough instinct to know it was a crazy idea. I told Jeff, "You're the genius guitarist in the group; to bring in someone as good as you is crazy." But Beck absolutely insisted—and besides, Page would supposedly be playing bass.

BIG JIM SULLIVAN (leading London session guitarist in the '60s)   Jim and I talked quite a bit when he was trying out for the Yardbirds. I think he was quite happy to get out of the session world. I wouldn't give up sessions at that moment. I thought, "I've got two cars, I've got a gardener, who needs any more than that?" I suppose it was a risk to start a band.

JIMMY PAGE (speaking in 1966)   I was drying up as a guitarist. I played a lot of rhythm guitar, which was very dull and left me no time to practice. Most of the musicians I know think I did the right thing in joining the Yardbirds. I want to contribute a great deal more to the Yardbirds than just standing there looking glum. Just because you play bass does not mean you have no presence.

Page on bass in the Yardbirds, with Jeff Beck, June 1966. (Howard Mylett collection)

JEFF BECK   Jimmy was not a bass player, as we all know. But the only way I could get him involved was by insisting it would be okay for him to take over on bass. And gradually—within a week, I think—we were talking about doing dueling guitar leads. We switched Chris Dreja onto bass in order to get Jimmy on guitar.

JIMMY PAGE   We had to play this gig in San Francisco—at the Carousel Ballroom, I believe—and Jeff couldn't make it. So I took over lead that night, and Chris played bass. It was really nerve-racking because this was at the height of the Yardbirds' reputation, and I wasn't exactly ready to roar off on lead guitar. But it went off all right, and after that we stayed that way—so when Jeff recovered, it was two lead guitars from that point on.

CHRIS DREJA   Jimmy and Jeff were like a couple of gunslingers, really. Jeff had been on the road more than Jimmy. He'd discovered California. He'd discovered blond women. He'd got divorced. He'd got away from his flat and was getting a reputation. He had his big ego. So it didn't really work, but it did work on "Happenings Ten Years' Time Ago." I think we encapsulated the whole bloody scene within two and a half minutes on that song.

CHRIS WELCH (writer for *Melody Maker* in the '60s and '70s)   I saw them at the Marquee. It was a stereo guitar duel, the two of them battling it out. I felt a bit sorry for Keith Relf, who was drowned out. It was deafening. I suppose we were witnessing the birth of hard rock.

HENRY "THE HORSE" SMITH (roadie for the Yardbirds and Zeppelin, 1966–1972)   There was always something electrifying going on when Jeff and Jimmy played live together. Even though they both played bluesy guitar, they played totally different. Jeff was like the Eddie Haskell of guitar players; he was the guy saying, "Oh, hello, Mrs. Cleaver, you look very nice today," and then he turns around and plays something back that's really snide.

Competition between Jimmy and Jeff was healthy. It wasn't a love-hate relationship, because they both respected each other. They could egg each other on a little bit and take it to the brink, but if you had to pick a winner every time, it would probably be Jeff.

JIMMY PAGE We had something that could have been really special when we were doing the dual-lead thing together. But we'd rehearse hard on certain things—working out sections where we'd play harmonies like a stereo guitar effect—and then onstage Jeff was just uncontrollable.

MICK FARREN (singer with the Deviants and writer for the underground press) The Yardbirds didn't make any sense at all. You'd go and see them, and they'd be playing blues, and then they'd come out with "Over Under Sideways Down." Keith Relf was so kind of transparent that you couldn't really take him seriously. So the Yardbirds were essentially a medium for guitar players.

Page wasn't really what we were going to see. He was a good lad, but I could never quite pin it down. Page back then didn't have the apparent Beck ego. Beck once walked onstage at the Roundhouse, looked at the assembled crowd, and said, "Bollocks to this"—and there was no *show*! I said, "What? We didn't come all this way for Arthur Brown!"

JEFF BECK Simon Napier-Bell got us *Blow-Up*, a real feather in his cap. "Okay, pal, you're the new manager, what've you got?" "How about three grand for doing an Antonioni movie?" I had a great time smashing up Hofner guitars for three days.

BP FALLON (U.K. press officer for Zeppelin, 1972–1976) I was an extra in *Blow-Up*, ten quid a day to look stoned and watch the Yardbirds. You couldn't meet Jimmy then and not be conscious that the cat was cool in the same way that Miles Davis or Serge Gainsbourg was cool. During the filming, he was sitting there being very quiet while Jeff Beck was mouthing off about what a bad singer Mick Jagger was. It was like, "Your time is gonna come . . ."

JIMMY PAGE When I joined the band, Jeff wasn't going to walk off anymore and stuff. Well, he did a couple of times. If he'd had a bad day, he used to take it out on the audience, which was a bit weird.

JUNE HARRIS BARSALONA (wife of talent agent Frank Barsalona) Frank and I were once in Detroit for a Yardbirds show, and we're waiting for Jeff to come on at the Grande Ballroom, and suddenly we're told that he is not going on—he's going home, or at least back to Mary Hughes in California. It was hysterical at the time. Jeff couldn't take the success.

JEFF BECK I went back to L.A. and hung around there by the pool for a while and then went home, expecting the Yardbirds to fold, but Page was on form, and people started freaking over him, so they were alright.

CHRIS DREJA Jimmy wanted it to succeed, and when we pulled off that Dick Clark tour, it was him saying, "Let's go on as a four-piece." He was the only one who wanted to go on in that form. He liked the life, and he had all sorts of advantages and not just musically. He had the freaks that he liked.

RICHARD COLE (road manager for the Yardbirds and Led Zeppelin) The Yardbirds knew all the groupies in New York, and all the groupies knew them. These were the core American girls—Devon, Emeretta, and a few more we can't mention since they're happily married now to famous rock stars. They knew the bands' itineraries as well as I did, God knows how.

I'd been to L.A., but I'd never met these girls that the Yardbirds knew. We would go up to Frank Zappa's house, the old Tom Mix cabin, and Captain Beefheart would come round. Those girls were known as groupies, but they were nothing in comparison to what came later.

JIMMY PAGE Simon Napier-Bell called up with the news that he was selling his stake in the Yardbirds to Mickie Most. I think they must have cooked it up, actually, the three of them: Napier-Bell, Most, and Beck. This way Beck could have a solo career, which he had already begun in a way with the recording of "Beck's Bolero."

MICKIE MOST (record producer and partner with Peter Grant in RAK Management) Jeff decided halfway through a tour that he didn't want to be in the Yardbirds anymore. For fifteen minutes, he wanted to be a pop star. And he came back from Los Angeles in pop star gear. I'd just come back from New York, and I had this song called "Hi Ho

Silver Lining" and I played it to him. And the next thing we know, we were in the studio and it was a hit. John Paul Jones did those lovely cello arrangements.

ANDY JOHNS (engineer on Led Zeppelin *II*, *III*, and the untitled fourth album) John Paul was a trained, studied sight reader. He was as quick as greased lightning. I used to have a deal with him where I would polish his Fender Jazz bass and say, "Seeing as I've polished your bass, could you show me how that goes?" And he would.

He said to me, "I'm tired of doing these sessions." So I got him a Corn Flakes ad, and he went, "Thanks a fucking lot! Kellogg's Corn Flakes!" He was going to be an arranger, or he was going to join a band. He did the arrangements for the Stones on *Their Satanic Majesties Request*. He said, "I'm going to make so much money in the next two or three years, you're not even going to recognize me." I said, "Yeah, right." Sure enough, within two years he'd made a million pounds.

. . .

MALCOLM McLAREN (manager of the Sex Pistols) Peter Grant was an extraordinary underling, a character who came from the back streets of London and sought to change his life. And entering into the world of rock 'n' roll was the best way to do that.

PETER GRANT (manager of the Yardbirds, the Jeff Beck Group, and Led Zeppelin) I'm proud of myself —especially for my dear old mum. I mean, I was born illegitimate, and in the late '30s that must have been horrendous. I never knew my father, and I'm proud for my mum and for my own children that I've done what I did.

GLORIA GRANT (ex-wife of Peter Grant) Peter always clammed up about his childhood. He would say, "Well, I'm an illegitimate child, end of subject." He never once said, "I want to find out more about my dad." Probably his mother never said much to him either, and I didn't feel I could ask her myself. I think he was upset about it, really, and yet in another way he was *cross* about it. But we don't know the full story. Things were completely different in 1935. The only thing he ever told me was that his dad's surname was Underwood, though I don't think he was even completely certain about *that.*

HELEN GRANT (daughter of Peter Grant)   Dad's way of dealing with those sort of things would be to just shut them out, really. You know, he wouldn't want to think about anything like that.

PHIL CARSON (head of Atlantic Records U.K. and close confidant of Zeppelin's)   Peter and I grew up in a very similar area of south London. I went to St. Joseph's College, which was the Catholic school for the sons of gentlemen, whereas Peter went to Ingram Road School. You can tell from the name that the school is going to be rough and tough. And we laughed about it, because there was a lot of jealousy between the two schools.

One day there was an inter-school fight arranged on Streatham Common, and the boys from our 1st XI football team showed up with about six fifteen-year-olds from Ingram Road, who proceeded to beat the shit out of them. Apparently, Peter was one of the six or seven.

MALCOLM McLAREN   He was the guy who hung around fairgrounds in the '50s, because that's where all gypsies and outlaws hung.

PETER GRANT   All I know is that if I hadn't been a fucking stagehand at the Croydon Empire for 15 bob a show, and if I hadn't done all the things I have—like being a film extra and on the road with Gene Vincent and the rest—there's no way I could have coped with the events of the past five or six years.

KEITH ALTHAM (writer for *NME, Record Mirror,* and other publications)   The first time I ever ran into Peter was at the Flamingo on Wardour Street, and he was on the door. He was an ex-wrestler who'd come up through Paul Lincoln at the 2i's club. My first *close* encounter, though, was when I was on *Teen* magazine, and he was taking Gene Vincent on tour.

We're on the coach with them, going to a doubleheader in Aylesbury, and Peter's main task is to stop Gene [from] drinking. After the first gig, Peter's having a little trouble negotiating the money outside the coach, and suddenly there's this banging noise coming from inside the coach. Gene's got hold of his wife by the hair and is thumping her head against the window. So Peter jumps on the coach and comes down and separates them with the words, "Listen, I'm trying to sort out the fuckin' readies!" He goes back out, and it starts up again. Except this time, it's the wife who's banging *Gene's* head against the window.

Before the second show, Gene decides it would be a good idea to down half a bottle of vodka. And he stands up and slips, and his good leg gets wedged between an upright bar and one of the seats. So Peter wanders down like Samson, gets hold of the bar, and pulls it apart so he can extract the leg, which has swollen horribly, so that Gene can barely stand and may not be able to do the show.

It transpires Peter has worked out that as long as Gene is onstage when the curtain opens, he'll get the money. So the curtains open, and Peter has inserted a microphone stand through Gene's leather jacket to hold him upright. We hear the opening bars of "Be Bop a-Lula," and Gene falls forward flat on his face. Peter walks on and carries him off like a pig on a spit. And he gets the money.

MICKIE MOST   He always made sure a contract was honored . . . and he had a very good head for figures.

KEITH ALTHAM   Peter was sufficiently savvy to pick up the percentages, and the profits added up. He was not what I would call an intelligent man, but he'd picked up the rudiments of the music business, and he was a formidable figure to deal with in terms of his physical presence and also in terms of his attitude. He wasn't scared of *anybody*.

GLORIA GRANT   In late 1961, I was in a singing act with my sisters Sue and Jean, and we were working for the Noel Gay agency. There was a tour coming up where we'd be working for Cadet cigarettes. So we went to rehearsals in Denmark Street, and this man came in to talk about the show we were going to do. It was Peter, and we sort of said hello to each other.

It transpired that he had a big van, and the agency wanted him to drive us around the miners' clubs in South Wales. It was a really good show, and we all got on well together, all of us staying in digs. Peter even joined in when we sang "We'll Keep a Welcome in the Hillside"— though he couldn't hold a tune to save his life.

He would often say to the three of us, "*I'll* be your manager." And I'd say, "How do *you* know how to manage anybody?" By the end of the tour, which was about March or April of 1962, we were engaged to be married. We didn't have much money, but we had a lot of laughs. We moved in with his mum in South Norwood. Dorothy wasn't quite ready for me. She was very Victorian in her ways, and I *wasn't*. I was twenty-three, and I'd been working in the theater since I was eighteen. We didn't quite gel, but we got on *alright*. There were times when Peter had to stick up for me.

Then I found out I was pregnant with Helen, so we rented a little flat a bit farther up the hill at Dorrington Court, and that's when Peter started working for Don Arden.

ED BICKNELL (former manager of Dire Straits and friend of Peter Grant's)   I think Don gave him £50 a week, out of which he had to pay for the petrol. Through that, he started driving for the other tours Don was promoting, like Little Richard and Bo Diddley. Famously, Don called Peter into his office one day and said, "I want you to go to America and get Chuck Berry."

ALAN CALLAN (president of Swan Song in the U.K., 1977–1979)   Don Arden thought the artists worked for *him*, and Peter thought he worked for the artists. I think what really brought that about was Peter's involvement with Chuck Berry. He went to America to try and bring Chuck to England, and I believe Chuck drove him from the airport to the Chess offices. Peter couldn't believe that Chuck was actually his *chauffeur*. [Peter] asked him how many records he'd sold, and Chuck said, "I don't know." And Peter thought, "My God, this is *wrong*."

ROY CARR (writer for *New Musical Express*)   Don Arden was an asshole. He thought he was Al Capone. He was just a working-class Jewish boy who got it into his brain that he wanted to be Edward G. Robinson.

ED BICKNELL   Occasionally, Peter would be dispatched by Don to sort out an irksome issue, like Robert Stigwood trying to steal a band from him. I once asked Peter if it was true he'd dangled Stiggy out of a window by his ankles. He said, "No, I merely introduced him to the view."

LAURENCE MYERS (music-business accountant and partner in RAK Records)   I think the Don Arden effect—"I am the Don, I am a gangster"—impressed Peter to the point where he used his physicality in the same way: "I'm a big guy, and you don't want to fuck with me." But I never actually heard of him hitting anybody.

MICKIE MOST   I admit, we did use a bit of the old-fashioned scare tactics. But nobody had any guns. It was handbags at ten paces, really. I don't think Peter was involved with gangsters. He was a sweetheart, really. All that stuff about being a muscle man and beating people up . . . it was all nonsense, really. It was more bravado.

ROY CARR   I knew Peter as someone you'd see up at the bar in the Marquee or round the drinking clubs. He was massive, and he had that sort of Fu Manchu facial hair.

CHRIS DREJA   Mickie Most was a very polite guy, and then there was this monster of a man who sat opposite him who looked like he could crush you with one hand.

Peter Grant in America with the New Vaudeville Band, May 1967. (Richard Cole Collection)

LAURENCE MYERS My first impression of Peter was of this huge mountain of a man, clearly not educated and definitely conscious of it. You'd be in meetings, and you could feel that he was uncomfortable if people started to talk about anything cultured or about world affairs. It didn't occur to me that he could run a management company successfully, just because of his background. But his practical knowledge was immense, as was his knowledge of dealing with bands.

GLORIA GRANT Don and Peter were very similar in their makeup, and Peter learned from him by being with him all the time. Peter would come back with these extraordinary tales of being on the road with Little Richard and Bo Diddley. There was always plenty to talk about.

RICHARD COLE I think Gloria was quite in awe of Peter, and he could always make her laugh.

LAURENCE MYERS My first-ever meeting in the music business, after I'd first got Mickie Most as a client, was with Don Arden. The Animals were managed at the time by Mike Jeffrey, and they were driving him mad that they hadn't been paid about six and a half thousand pounds for a tour Don had organized, and that Peter had been the road manager on. Mickie said, "Don't worry, I'll get the money out of Don." So I got the accounting together, put on my best suit, and the three of us went over to Don's offices on Hay Hill.

We're sitting in reception, and I can hear through the doorway this voice ranting and raving, saying, "Listen, you Christian *schmuck*, are you fucking *mad*?!" And then the phone is slammed down. So we go into the office, and Don is sitting there, beaming. Mickie starts in on him and bangs the desk. Peter stands up, towers over Don, and says, "Listen, you asshole, pay up!!" I then try to make my mark in the world by saying, "Gentlemen, gentlemen, let me handle this."

Don goes, "Who the fuck are *you*?" I said I was a chartered accountant and that I was authorized by the Animals to speak on their behalf, and I brought out my beautifully produced piece of paper showing that he owed them whatever it was. I said, "Are you going to pay them?" And he said, "No." I said, "Oh."

Peter starts banging the desk and says, "I'm going to turn this desk over, Don." I start up again in a very smug voice: "Will you *please* let me deal with this? Mr. Arden, do you know what will happen if you *don't* pay this? We will issue a writ against you." Don goes, "Will you?" He opens a drawer full of writs, takes them out, and chucks them out the window. He goes, "Listen, you *putz*, if you don't get out of my office, you're gonna follow them out the window." At which point Peter starts bouncing the desk up and down, and eventually we walk out. I don't think the Animals ever got paid.

HARVEY LISBERG (manager of Herman's Hermits)   Mickie and Peter were a bit of a comedy act, a bit like Laurel and Hardy. Mickie was a very strong character, very opinionated, had an answer for everything. Peter was a sweetie, really, nothing like the way he looked.

HELEN GRANT The good thing about Dad and Mickie was that they saw each other outside of the work thing. We used to see Mickie in the south of France a lot. We used to go to Monaco, to the Grand Prix. Dad always spoke very highly of Mickie.

LAURENCE MYERS We decided to set up three companies under the RAK umbrella: records, publishing, and management. There were three desks. Mickie's brother Dave looked after publishing, so he was at one desk. Then there was Mickie, who looked after records, and then Peter, who was going to run the management side. I had a client named Geoff Stephens, who'd written and produced a record called "Winchester Cathedral." The record became a huge hit, and we put together the New Vaudeville Band to go on *Top of the Pops*. I said, "Let's get Peter to manage them." That was RAK Management's first-ever client.

GLORIA GRANT Helen came up to me one morning at our house in Shepherd's Bush and said, "Mummy, there's a man at the door in a long black coat." I went to the door, and it was Richard Cole. I can still see him in that long black sort of Crombie coat. He was a real Jack-the-lad.

RICHARD COLE In the middle of 1966, I was driving back from Nottingham with Keith Moon and John Entwistle, and this record called "Winchester Cathedral" comes on the radio. Moonie says, "What the fuck is that old piece of shit?" And what happened was that Geoff Stephens, who'd made the record, approached Peter and said, "Look, the record is No. 1 all over the place, but there's no band. Can you put a band together for me?"

I was recommended as tour manager for the New Vaudeville Band, so I went to see Peter in their new office at 155 Oxford Street. In those days, Peter managed Ray Cameron—Michael McIntyre's dad— and a girl trio called the She-Trinity. And then came the New Vaudeville Band. I said to Peter, "I want thirty pounds a week, take it or leave it." Years later, he told me, "I thought, if you're that cheeky to *me*, you'll be alright getting the money off those promoters." He also said, "If I hear you've been telling tales out of this office, I'll bite yer fuckin' ears off."

MARK LONDON (comanager with Peter Grant of Stone the Crows and Maggie Bell)   I first met Peter in 1965, when he and Mickie already

155 Oxford Street, London: RAK's offices were on the top floor. (Art Sperl)

had the office on Oxford Street. Then I got into management with Peter when we set up a company called Colour Me Gone. I said I'd go look for acts, and we'd manage them together. I took a band called Cartoone to Ahmet Ertegun and Jerry Wexler, and they liked it, and we did two albums for Atlantic. I hired Les Harvey to play guitar with them, and I said I'd come back and look at Power, the band Les had with Maggie Bell in Glasgow. Peter and I went up to see them, and he renamed them Stone the Crows.

MAGGIE BELL (singer with Stone the Crows and Swan Song solo artist) 155 Oxford Street had a tiny little lift that only took two people or one Peter Grant. I used to take the chance and get in there with him. They would all be in that office at one time, and there was standing room only because you couldn't sit down anywhere.

RICHARD COLE Mickie sat on the right-hand side behind a big desk, and Peter sat on the *left*-hand side behind a big desk. There were no seats, so you had to stand up when you talked to them. And while you were talking to one of them, the other would be making V-signs behind your back. Mickie was always dressed impeccably—as were his wife and son, who would come in on a Friday afternoon because they were flying down to Cannes, where Mickie kept his yacht.

JOHN PAUL JONES [The office] was like fifty-foot long, and Peter was up one end and Mickie was down the other. I was the musical director for Mickie, so that was how I met Peter. He was a very sensitive man. He was a very, very smart man. People just think of his size and his reputation, but actually he never had to use his size. He could out-talk anybody.

6

Turning to Gold

I'd been an apprentice for years, and I'd discovered
something that someone like Mickie didn't have a clue even
existed.

—Jimmy Page to Nick Kent, 1973

JIMMY PAGE Peter was working with Mickie and was offered the
[Yardbirds'] management when Most was offered the recording. I'd
known Peter from way back in the days of Immediate [Records]
because our offices were next door to Mickie, and Peter was working
for him. The first thing we did with Peter was a tour of Australia, and
we found that suddenly there was some money being made after all
this time.

CHRIS DREJA (bassist with the Yardbirds) The last year, when Peter
was with the band, was the only year we ever made any money. He
dealt with very stroppy promoters and started to turn the tables on
them. He fought. It was through Peter I learned that if you want to
make money on tour in America, don't order room service—it all gets
charged to your account.

JEFF BECK   I was beginning to think about forgetting it all. Then Peter Grant saw that there was more in it and, rather than lose the whole thing, said he'd fix up an American tour [for the Jeff Beck Group], and that was just the one thread left that we were hanging onto. Anyway, we made it to New York and blew the town apart completely, smashed it wide open with one performance, and we had an identity as a band right there, and that cemented it all for eighteen months.

ED BICKNELL (former manager of Dire Straits)   Up until the mid-'60s, the music business people were the tail end of the variety industry. They were either gay blokes or hard-nosed East End geezers. Then came the first wave of people who'd got degrees, people like Chris Wright and Terry Ellis of Chrysalis, who were at Manchester and Newcastle, respectively. There was a shift away from people who thought in terms of variety and, most important, a shift away from people who thought pop music was going to be over in two years. Although Peter was not an educated man in the academic sense, he was moving away from the Don Arden approach toward the idea that the act was everything and that everything *flowed* from that. He was quite passionate about that.

CHRIS DREJA   I think Mickie and Peter were both very lucky to have the Yardbirds, because we gave both of them kudos and credibility, plus some real serious practical experience.

ANNI IVIL (press officer with Atlantic U.K., late '60s–early '70s)   Peter realized that you had to tour in America. Frank Barsalona at Premier Talent knew that that was how to break a group. To me, Frank *was* rock 'n' roll. He was absolutely the first guy who really saw what the underground was going to become.

FRANK BARSALONA (founder of Premier Talent agency, speaking in 1974)   I realized that all these people I'd thought so much of were pretty stupid, and the way they wanted to handle my acts was pretty stupid. I wanted to guide their careers, rather than exploit their suc- cess. . . . I realized then that rock might really have potential, and I remembered all that business about all of the war babies growing up at the same time, and I decided then to start my own business.

JUNE HARRIS BARSALONA   I met Frank right after I moved to New York from London in 1964. He was young, and nobody was concentrating on rock. He started something new, and I was able to help him because I knew a lot of the English acts. I had done a deal with the *Mirror* group to write about anything English that was happening here. I would see the bands, and he would get them.

STEVE VAN ZANDT (guitarist with Bruce Springsteen's E Street Band)   Against the family's recommendation, Frank opens the first rock 'n' roll agency, called Premier Talent. He divides the country up into territories—sounds familiar, doesn't it?—and divides it up to these hungry new guys: Larry Magid in Philly, Jack Boller in Washington, Don Law up in Boston, you know, Bill Graham over there in Frisco, the Belkers in Cleveland, and Ronnie Delsener here in New York. In other words, he threw out all the old thieves and replaced them with a bunch of new young thieves.

ANNI IVIL   The promoters made their money on it—*everybody* made money on it. As Frank used to say, "There's only one pot, and everyone's got to be paid out of it."

LORAINE ALTERMAN BOYLE (writer for *Rolling Stone* and *Melody Maker* in the late '60s and '70s)   Premier was *the* major rock booking agency in the country, and every big act really went through them. Frank and June's first apartment was on West 57th Street, and people would hang out there. Frank just seemed to control the whole scene.

JUNE HARRIS BARSALONA   Frank said, "This is it, this is the future." When he signed an act, he said, "No more of the belief that you're only as big as your last record. You've got to go out and perform. You've got to give them something for their money if you want longevity in this business." So it was great for him to see how the acts developed. They looked at him as a kind of mentor, even though they were on the same level and the same plane.

Frank Barsalona
with writer Loraine
Alterman,
New York, 1967.
(Courtesy of Loraine
Alterman Boyle)

Frank would sit in his office in a pair of jeans, his feet on the desk, a shirt that probably had ink stains or spaghetti stains on it, and his Indian jewelry. When he said, "Let's go eat," it meant bringing people back to the apartment and hanging out. I once came back from picking my mother up from the airport, and there were thirteen people in the apartment expecting dinner—four of whom were the Who.

What started out as the underground and hard rock, that's where you've got Peter with the Yardbirds and with Jeff Beck. And you've got rock stations that were beginning to form and that were only interested in contemporary rock, everything that happened at Monterey and then Woodstock. There was this peer group of people who saw what was happening in the industry and who encouraged it and were able to go along with it—who were able to go to a blues club in Chicago and know where the music was coming from and were able to *talk to musicians*.

SAM AIZER (artist relations man at Swan Song in the United States)   People like Frank and Steve Weiss were the first ones in. Steve was a very sharp entertainment lawyer who'd had Jack Paar, and that's how he'd made his name. Once you get one successful band, you get ten bands, and all of a sudden you're important. This guy had the power that Peter didn't: he had the Rascals, Herman's Hermits, Jimi Hendrix, all these bands.

DANNY GOLDBERG (Zeppelin's U.S. press officer and subsequently president of Swan Song)   Steve was a gruff tough. He was a certain type of a character that had obviously been good enough at law school and everything. He was definitely new to entertainment law and must have had a background of legitimate law, but he stumbled into rock 'n' roll and became permanently changed by it. By the time I met him, he had longish gray hair and would wear these odd clothes that were halfway between him and normal and he strutted around with a tremendous sense of himself. Always had a quick temper and flattered himself on having a quick temper. He'd been Herman's Hermits' lawyer. He knew Harvey Lisberg, who was the warmest, sweetest guy.

HARVEY LISBERG (manager of Herman's Hermits)   Steve was a very charismatic figure, beautifully dressed, a ladies' man. My wife had to accompany his mistress around town, and then the next evening we're back at his home having dinner with him and his wife. It was like something out of *Mad Men*.

JANINE SAFER (press officer at Swan Song in the United States)   Steve had two households. He did finally marry Marie, the mistress, who was one of the loveliest people you'd ever want to meet in your life—*déclassé* in every conceivable way, from an Italian family in Queens, a beautiful woman with dyed-blond hair and makeup three inches thick.

SHELLEY KAYE (assistant to Steve Weiss and office manager at Swan Song in the United States)   I was twenty-three when I started working for Steve in 1968. I was a young kid, I didn't know anything. I walk in, and here's a guy wearing a gray pinstripe suit with a white shirt with purple flowers down the front. And I went, "Oh my gosh!" That was my introduction to the music business. Within six months to a year, I became his secretary.

RICHARD COLE (Zeppelin's road manager) Peter told me he'd been involved in a court case in America, and Steve had been the opposing lawyer and had wiped the floor with whoever Peter's lawyer was. So Peter then hired Steve, who'd done stuff for Herman's Hermits and the Young Rascals and Jimi Hendrix, a host of acts. Steve was the lawyer for Vanilla Fudge when I was their road manager. I knew their manager Phil Basile very well, and Philly was connected. Lovely guy, but you wouldn't cross him. At some conference in America—it wasn't a roast, but something like that—Joe Smith of Warner Brothers once said, "Of course, we can't forget our dear friend Steve Weiss, who's always got a kind word . . . *and a gun.*" What we heard was that Steve's dad had worked for Meyer Lansky.

JACK CALMES (cofounder of Showco sound and lighting company) Steve was the attorney for Jimi Hendrix and later for the estate. His father and family were associated and consiglieore for the mafia.

ABE HOCH (president of Swan Song, 1975–1977) There was always the intimation that Steve was connected, but we never knew what he was connected to. The thing about Peter is, when he sanctioned somebody, you basically just went along with it.

HENRY SMITH (roadie for the Yardbirds and Led Zeppelin) There was a time with the Yardbirds when we were staying at a hotel in New York, and the truck was parked out front with all the gear in it. I wake up around eight in the morning, and the truck's not in front of the door. I panic and call Barry Jay Reiss, Steve's right-hand man, and tell him the truck is missing with all of the gear in it. Before noontime, the truck is returned with all the gear. That shows you the power of Steve Weiss.

BARRY JAY REISS (attorney who worked with Zeppelin's U.S. lawyer Steve Weiss) Steve had a reputation as a very, very tough and vigorous negotiator. He was a real fighter. Sometimes he was a violent person, in the sense that a lot of telephones got yelled into. But he was also a wonderful teacher and mentor. After we worked with Lulu, who had a U.S. tax problem that we sorted out, we wound up representing quite a number of British artists in that period. Then the managers for Jimi Hendrix found us, so we started working with him. The first time Steve and I saw Jimi was at a high school gym out in Queens or on Long Island. The first twenty minutes, the kids had no idea what they were looking at. By the time he'd finished, they were on their feet.

SHELLEY KAYE   The first rock concert I went to was Hendrix, which Steve promoted with Ron Delsener. I mean, I was a very conservative little girl from Brooklyn, I didn't know about any of this stuff. I was amazed by it, and it changed my whole life.

BARRY JAY REISS (lawyer and associate of Steve Weiss)   It was a very exciting time. Music was king. It was a whole new industry. When I went to law school, we didn't *have* any courses in entertainment law. We were really inventing as we went along.

SHELLEY KAYE   Everything was turning to gold. There were so many phenomenally talented artists around. It seemed that all you needed to do was come from the U.K. to America, and you'd get a record deal. I was and still am a real Anglophile, so I just thought it was fantastic. It was important to know the British terms; otherwise, you wouldn't know what people were talking about. I had no idea what a "loo" was.

EDDIE KRAMER (engineer on *Led Zeppelin II* and *Houses of the Holy*)   When you look at the history of American pop music, you note carefully where the Brits come in, first with the Beatles and all of the subsequent bands that followed them. Then the next wave is about three to four years later, which would be Jimi coming over in 1967 and showing the Americans what they've been missing. And then following that in early '68, Traffic came over to the U.S. and a whole bunch of bands came over—and that went over into 1969 and 1970, and from that point on, the floodgates were open. There must have been twenty, thirty English bands that all did very well in the U.S.

HARVEY GOLDSMITH (U.K. promoter)   The two people that introduced me to America were Ahmet Ertegun and Frank Barsalona. All the English acts that Frank signed, I promoted. So we were very, very close. I watched how he built the whole American territorial system up.

TERRY MANNING (engineer on Memphis sessions for *Led Zeppelin III*; founder of Compass Point studios)   I was in a regional band in Memphis called Lawson and Four More, and we were the support band on a Dick Clark Caravan of Stars tour. They had several international acts on these tours, and I was very excited because the Yardbirds were one of them.

I made sure to introduce myself to Jimmy, and we just became friends. He was erudite, thoroughly together, very gentle and very unassuming—and obviously a musical genius. I just loved the guy immediately. He even told me about a couple of records that he had played on that weren't common knowledge then—and some that still aren't, where he was the *secret* guitarist.

The next tour was just the Yardbirds, and we weren't playing on it. I went to a few shows that were nearby. Jeff had *just* left the band, so there was some consternation about whether Jimmy could pull off the full lead/rhythm thing.

HENRY SMITH   When Jeff left the Yardbirds, there was a different focus on what was going on: they knew from the very beginning that it was the last Yardbirds tour, but it was also introducing Jimmy to the world as a single musician. It was a coming-out party for Jimmy Page, the session guy that a lot of people didn't know in the States.

At the same time, the Yardbirds became two camps. McCarty and Relf and Dreja were one camp, and Jimmy and Richard Cole and Peter Grant were another camp. I remember sitting on the tour bus, and Keith Relf and Jim McCarty came up to me and said, "We're starting a new band after the Yardbirds are over, and would you like to come with us?" And then Pagey came to me and said, "*I'm* starting a new band after this, and I'd like you to work with *me*."

By that time, Jimmy knew that he had a bass player, John Paul Jones. I think he had talked to Mo, John Paul's wife, to get that solidified even before he talked to Jonesy. I think she said, "Yes, he'll do it," even before *he* did.

CHRIS DREJA (bassist with the Yardbirds) That last American tour was bloody great, because we knew we were going to finish. Ricardo Cole was always up to pranks. The trouble was that you had to be very careful with him because if you suggested something, he would go and do it. Anything—prankster stuff. He was a fixer. Especially in America, when a lot of the music business was run by the mafia.

I saw Peter with a gun in his belly on a bus after we played a State Fair in Canada. The promoter says, "I ain't paying you." Peter gets up at the back of the bus, pushes his stomach out, and bumps the guy all the way to the steps, where they all fall about laughing. He says, "You're going to kill me for a thousand bucks?" I was on the bus. I saw it.

JIMMY PAGE After the San Francisco bit and it was down to four of us, the Yardbirds were doing really well in a live situation, but recording-wise we were working with Mickie Most, and he was really interested in singles, and we were interested in albums, and I know Keith and Jimmy McCarty lost the enthusiasm. They just didn't even want to be in a band called the Yardbirds anymore.

JEFF BECK [Mickie] didn't understand what the hell was going on with progressive rock, because he'd never meddled with it—it was all chunk-chunk stuff, Lulu and Donovan, easy stuff, where he could walk into the session and take over and say, "That's too loud, I want more acoustic guitar, Donovan louder and you softer."

CHRIS DREJA The Yardbirds missed that wonderful moment when albums became king, and you weren't only as good as your last single. The only credible thing that came out of those sessions with Mickie was the one that Jimmy pretty much produced, because Mickie was not interested in albums, and he left us alone to do *Little Games*.

MICKIE MOST The Yardbirds were on the point of breaking up and becoming the first version of Led Zeppelin, but before they could do that, they had a commitment to finish another album, so I went into the studio with them, and we just made it willy-nilly. It was one of those things where I probably spent more time making bean soup than I did making the album, because nobody was really interested.

CHRIS DREJA   Mickie never got it, but he didn't *need* to get it, because he was so successful with singles. He had a great eye for what was catchy, because a pop single never goes away. What he didn't have an eye for were bands like Crosby, Stills and Nash and Led Zeppelin. He didn't relate to musicians. He could only relate to session guys and that way of packaging it.

MICKIE MOST   Jimmy really had his thoughts on his own thing. I'd already done the *Truth* album with Jeff Beck and Rod Stewart, and that turned out to be a very, very successful album in America . . . a seriously underground kind of album breaking out. Jimmy saw the marketplace, and Peter Grant, Jimmy, and I all contributed to putting together Led Zeppelin.

JIMMY PAGE   In the Yardbirds I remember playing the Fillmore, and there was one song that we had called "Glimpses," and I had tapes going of the Staten Island ferry and all manner of things, which was quite avant-garde at the time. As far as the power of it went, it never had the power of the rhythm section, but as far as the subtleties and the ideas, we had those areas within the Yardbirds. The Yardbirds [were] quite powerful within [their] own right, no doubt about it.

CHRIS DREJA   There was all that funny business about Jimmy pulling the live album we did at the Anderson Theatre in New York. It was badly wired up, and they did a dreadful job with the audience sound, but a lot of people say to this day that it was the most exciting concert they ever went to.

JIMMY PAGE   Epic said to us, "Can we do a live LP?" And they sent down the head of their light music department to do it. It was just awful, so they had to shelve it. They must have dragged it out of the vaults a few years later when they realized they had some unreleased Jimmy Page stuff, and out it came.

NICK KENT   Jimmy always says, "I'm a musician, don't talk to me about anything else." But he also had an extremely canny and very instinctual sense of rock image—of how to present himself and how to look. He was always checking out the way people like Keith Richards were dressing.

CHRIS DREJA   He had great dress sense. When we toured America, he got us into trouble for wearing the Iron Cross and the Civil War cap and things like that. He was very provocative: although it may have been flower power, America was still run by the establishment. When we were in America, we got spat on by businessmen and basically treated like we were dirt on the floor.

MARTIN STONE (guitarist with the Action and Mighty Baby)   I was walking down the King's Road, and I bumped into Jimmy with a mate. He was wearing the military jacket that all true South London blues guitarists wore at the time. But his friend was wearing a kaftan, and they both had beads round their necks. Jimmy said he'd just got back from San Francisco with the Yardbirds. He said, "There's a thing happening over there. It's called *psychedelia*."

PART 2

In the Light

Led Zeppelin's first rehearsal in Soho was instant karma and instant camaraderie. The four men tore through Johnny Burnette and the Rock and Roll Trio's "Train Kept a-Rollin'" and Garnet Mimms's "As Long as I Have You" and then grinned at one another in delight.

Funded by the savings of Page, Jones, and Peter Grant, the band fulfilled old Yardbirds commitments in Scandinavia and then recorded a devastatingly powerful album of the blues ("You Shook Me") and proto-heavy-metal songs ("Dazed and Confused") they'd worked up on the road. Grant—also managing the similarly proto-metal Jeff Beck Group—flew to New York with his golden boy Page and secured an unprecedentedly generous deal with legendary Atlantic Records.

By mid-1969, Led Zeppelin were routinely blowing heavy headliners off the stage with their unholy fusion of funk, guitar riffology, and hair-raising emotion. Grant focused almost exclusively on North America and soon had his charges topping bills from Texas to California, a state that became their U.S. home away from home. Despite a remorseless touring schedule, they squeezed in enough sessions to make the steamroller album that was *Led Zeppelin II* (1969), kicked off by the chest-pummeling single "Whole Lotta Love"

Record Mirror, April 12, 1969.

but also boasting the beauteous, Tolkien-inspired "Ramble On."
Critics scented a hype and condemned Zeppelin as proponents of
mere power, but young boys understood and quickly adopted the
band as their preferred British import.

To prove their versatility, Zeppelin in 1970 made a third album that
was equal parts electric thunder ("Immigrant Song") and strumming
folkiness infused with the spirit of Plant's beloved Welsh mountains
("That's the Way"). Wonderful as it was, *Led Zeppelin III* only confused matters for critics and fans, who took more warmly to the
untitled 1971 fourth album, Zeppelin's best-ever seller. Even *Rolling
Stone* gave a thumbs-up to the pile-driving "Black Dog" and the
medieval prog-rock epic "Stairway to Heaven."

By *Houses of the Holy* (1973)—the group's most diverse, most
carefully arranged, and most underrated album—Zeppelin were on
top of the world. A show in Tampa, Florida, drew a record-breaking
rabble of more than fifty-five thousand delirious disciples, eclipsing
the Beatles' 1966 show at Shea Stadium.

7

Whatever Jimmy Wants

I've always said Led Zeppelin was the space in between us all.
—John Paul Jones, December 1997

MARILYN COLE (wife of Richard Cole) Peter Grant had the utmost respect for Jimmy. Jimmy was his real special boy, the chosen one. Jimmy was God.

ABE HOCH (president of Swan Song in the U.K., 1975–1977) I think Peter had a love affair with Jimmy all his life. Jimmy was almost like an adopted child for him, and I think that Jimmy out of all of them was the most Machiavellian. The way Jimmy went was the way everything else went.

HELEN GRANT (daughter of Zeppelin manager Peter Grant) I can't ever recall Dad saying a bad word about Jimmy, really. He was absolutely devoted to him. I think it was, "Whatever Jimmy wants."

MICHAEL DES BARRES (singer with Swan Song band Detective) Peter loved Jimmy with all his heart and would never accept anything Jimmy didn't want. Out of that came the idea that Led Zeppelin should be unapproachable. But it was an organic thing, it wasn't a strategy.

PETER GRANT   What I can remember distinctly is driving Jimmy around Shaftesbury Avenue near the Saville Theatre after the split. We were in a traffic jam, and I said, "What are you going to do? Do you want to go back to sessions or what?" And he said, "Well, I've got some ideas." I said, "What about a producer?" He said, "I'd like to do that, too."

RICHARD COLE (Zeppelin's road manager)   Jimmy was going to take the Yardbirds' name, and he was talking about getting people of the caliber of Steve Marriott or John Entwistle on bass and Keith Moon on drums. The idea was that it was going to be heavier than the Yardbirds had been. It's possible that he looked at the Jeff Beck Group as a template, but you could also say he was looking at the Who or Hendrix. What they all had was a great guitarist, a great bass player, and a great drummer. They had power. And then you had to find a singer to fit in there. When the Yardbirds were coming to an end, the guy he was thinking of was Danny Hutton.

JIMMY PAGE   I was trying to build a band. I knew which way it was going to go. I'd been out to the States with the Yardbirds, and I knew exactly the way things were in place. I had a good idea of what style of vocalist I was looking for, too. The personality aspect—of course, that does come into it, but initially, if you've got a bond musically and everyone has that mutual respect for each other, well, that's going to give it the momentum.

AUBREY "PO" POWELL (designer of Zeppelin album covers, 1973–1980)   It was Jimmy and Peter who started Led Zeppelin. Right at the beginning, there was a serious bonding of right time, right place, and right individuals. Peter had the clout, and Jimmy had the talent and the foresight to create Zeppelin. Jimmy and Peter were very close, and I don't think anybody to this day—not even Robert—knows exactly what that relationship was about, financially or otherwise.

CHRIS DREJA (bassist with the Yardbirds)   I think Peter saw there was room for a band that wasn't pop but that delivered a great show that was really heavy. The Yardbirds were never going to be as heavy as Zeppelin, even as a four-piece, and there really weren't that many bands that encompassed the blues, the riff-making, the heaviness with a white singer. Jim was going to do the songs and the recordings, and Peter was going to take care of the business. And boy, did he take care of it.

RICHARD COLE   Jimmy already had it in his mind that he was going to own the publishing. Whatever facet there was, he wanted to own it or part-own it. He'd written songs, so he knew a bit about the publishing side of it. He knew where all the money was.

CHRIS DREJA   Jimmy really wanted to prove to people that he was going to end up with more money than them. That was one of his big motivations. I could see that very early on in his personality: "You may look down on me now, but one day I'll show you." And he did. Eric wanted to be the penultimate bluesman, but Jimmy just wanted to be incredibly successful so he could tell everybody to fuck off.

RICHARD COLE   Peter had two top guitarists, Beck and Page, but Jimmy was far more driven than Jeff. Jeff was a brilliant guitarist, but in those days he was a little unreliable. You could get him to the water, but you couldn't make him drink. If he decided he wasn't going to do a show, then he wasn't going to do it. And there were a few too many of those for my liking.

ROD STEWART (singer with the Jeff Beck Group)   Beck needed a singer, and I was his singer; that was it. Everything was geared to his own playing. He used all of us. That's why he's had so much trouble keeping a group together.

NICK KENT (writer for *New Musical Express*)   Rod had these horror stories about Peter Grant. He told me he'd started mentioning that he wanted the band to be billed as "The Jeff Beck Group with Rod Stewart," and Grant got wind of this and said to him, "Listen, you're just a worthless little poof. Mickie warned me about you. He didn't want you in the group in the first place. It's only Jeff that wants you in the group, you and that other talentless cunt Ronnie Wood."

BILL BONHAM (organist in Robert Plant's pre-Zeppelin band Obs-Tweedle)   Peter told me that with the Beck Group, people were just raving about Rod. And they're getting ready to do this tour in

America, and Peter gets a phone call from Jeff. Peter says, "Where are you?" And Jeff says, "I'm in London, and I've quit the band."

MARK LONDON (comanager with Peter Grant of Stone the Crows and Maggie Bell)   When Peter started with Zeppelin, Jeff Beck was making $7,500 a night in America. If he hadn't left Peter, I think he would have done a lot better.

ALAN CALLAN (president of Swan Song in the U.K., 1977–1979)   Jeff could always get to what he heard in his head, but he had absolutely no vision of how he was affecting the culture. He was a pure guitar player, whereas Jimmy learned to express himself with a depth and clarity and purpose that just overtook everybody else. He had a completely different mind-set [than] Jeff: as a session player, he completely understood that he had three hours to go in and figure out a number; deliver something solid, focused, and commercial; and get out. There was no *drama* in that. And he brought that attitude to his writing and his stage playing.

RICHARD COLE   Why Jeff didn't want to be a leader was because he didn't want to be responsible for anyone else. Jimmy was completely different. Peter knew that, with Jimmy, "This is what we're gonna do, and we'll get on and we'll do it." It was more self-contained. Between Peter and Jimmy, they didn't have to rely on anyone else.

TERRY REID (singer with Peter Jay and the Jaywalkers, signed to a solo deal by Mickie Most)   Jimmy was only in the Yardbirds for five minutes, but he wasn't going to allow a repeat of the album with Mickie. Nobody was going to produce the new group but Jimmy. He saw a big hole in the scene. Cream was gone. The Jeff Beck Group was never going to last. Jimmy knew the sort of band to fill that gap.

ROBERT PLANT   I'd met up with Terry a year after the Listen single. There was a kind of package that went round England with Aynsley Dunbar's Retaliation, and there was Terry Reid and the Band of Joy. The three bands seemed to end up everywhere together.

TERRY REID   Jimmy wanted to put this group together, and he said he wanted me to be the singer. I said, "What's the band?" But there *was* no band. Jimmy was just formulating what he might be doing. He asked Steve Winwood, he asked Steve Marriott; he wanted a certain type of singer.

NICK KENT There were a number of great white male singers—Paul Rodgers, Steve Marriott—but Terry, to my mind, was the best. I'm not sure it would have worked with Page, though. He wouldn't have been into something like "Dazed and Confused."

TERRY REID I was very flattered, and I said, "Let's have a go when I come back off the Stones' tour." But Jimmy said, "No, I want to put something together *now*." I remembered seeing Robert and John in the Band of Joy, so I went tearing into the office to see Peter Grant, and I said, "You've got to hear these two guys"—not just Robert but the two of them.

ROBERT PLANT Terry said, "You've got to meet this guy who lives in Pangbourne and who's a great guitarist."

BILL BONHAM Robert invited Jimmy and Peter to come up and see Obs-Tweedle play in Walsall. I was really happy for him because he was a friend. I said, "Jump on it!" I mean, *I* would have taken it. But the Yardbirds at that time were considered has-beens, so he wasn't sure if it was the right move. He felt really bad about quitting Obs-Tweedle, and it was partly for that reason that he helped me get a job with Terry Reid.

JIMMY PAGE Obs-Tweedle . . . were playing at a teachers' training college outside of Birmingham—to an audience of about twelve people . . . you know, a typical student setup where drinking is the prime consideration, and the group is only of secondary importance. Robert was fantastic, and having heard him that night and having listened to a demo he had given me, I realized that without a doubt his voice had an exceptional and very distinctive quality.

ROBERT PLANT There was a time where—in another day at another juncture in my life and everybody else's in this game—if you were a man and you couldn't sing a D above top C, you couldn't cut it. That whole idea of being a high-powered, high-octave singer was incredibly important, and often the whole critical analysis of your ability was based on just that. I was marooned in that place and still am to a large degree.

CHRIS DREJA   I remember coming back in the car from Walsall and the discussion we had about Robert—because he was a hell of a shrieker and a little uncouth, and I'd been used to working with a singer who was not a shrieker but a songsmith.

ROBERT PLANT (speaking in 1969)   I knew [the Yardbirds] had done a lot of work in America—which to me meant audiences who *did* want to know what I'd got to offer—so naturally I was very interested. I went down to Pangbourne. It was [a] real desperation scene, man, like I had nowhere else to go.

JIMMY PAGE   He came down to my house. I think he was tarmac'ing roads at the time, and he came in and I had this quite sassy American girlfriend, and he must have thought, "*This* is alright." I started going through material with him. I tried to size him up, because he'd had a solo career and two or three records. I thought, "Let's see what he's about."

ROBERT PLANT   I got so enthusiastic after staying down there for a week, I hitched back from Oxford and chased after John, got him on the side, and said, "Mate, you've *got* to join the Yardbirds." I had nothing to convince him with, except a name that had got lost in American pop history.

BILL BONHAM   I went with Robert over to John's flat in Eve Hill. Pat was not happy to see Robert, because John had a good job with Tim Rose. Every time John went with Robert, the money stopped coming in. So John took some persuading to join this new group.

MAC POOLE (Midlands drummer and friend of Bonham's)   We were in the Black Horse in Kidderminster, and I saw Rob with Maureen. He told me about the New Yardbirds. He said, "We just need a drummer." I said, "What about Bonham?" He said John was sticking with Tim Rose. John had serious bills to pay; he was living in the caravan with the old man breathing down his neck. Why leave Tim and join Planty after doing all those gigs with the Band of Joy when no one was interested in the band?

JOHN BONHAM   I had to consider so much. It wasn't a question of who had the best prospects, but which was going to be the right kind of stuff.

MAC POOLE   The only way to convince John was to take Grant and Page to see him and to talk him round. And, of course, they offered him more money. So he went back to Pat, and she said okay. I think Robert really wanted another Black Country boy in the band. He didn't want to be the only Midlands guy in a London band.

JOHN BONHAM   Chris Farlowe was fairly established, and I knew [Joe] Cocker was going to make it, but I already knew from playing in the Band of Joy with Robert what he liked, and I knew what Jimmy was into, and I decided I liked their sort of music better, and it paid off.

MAC POOLE   I saw the pair of them only a few weeks later in the Rum Runner, and I said to John, "Don't tell me, you're in the band." And he said yes. I said, "Oh, here we go again." That's when he told me they'd got an advance. And it was a lot of fucking money, three grand each! And from there, it was really a move into a different dimension, because nobody had ever got that sort of money. All of a sudden, John's got the Jag and the latest stereo system. For Pat, it was like winning the pools, though she was very philosophical about it. She thought it wouldn't last long.

• • •

JOHN PAUL JONES   The first rehearsal was pure magic. I suddenly realized there was no dead weight in this band, and it was an exciting thing to find out. It wasn't like, "The drummer's dad owns the van, so we'll just have to put up with him." I'd worked with a lot of really good drummers, but I was younger than all of them—except for possibly Clem Cattini, and he wasn't actually on the session scene when I first started. There were only two young guys on the scene at that time, and that was me and Jim. And I'm younger than Jim. So to find a drummer of my age group, at that professional level, and to find him *that good*, was revelatory. I knew immediately, "This is what I want to do."

39 Gerrard Street,
Soho: possible site of
the first New Yardbirds
rehearsal. (Art Sperl)

JOHN BONHAM   I was pretty shy. I thought the best thing was not to say much but suss it all out. We had a play, and it went quite well.

JOHN PAUL JONES   I'd worked with Jimmy, but never in that sort of situation. We'd always been scattered at the back of *Manuel and His Music of the Mountains* or something. In fact, I'd never been in a band like that, at that professional level. With Jet [Harris] and Tony [Meehan], it was a good band and it was great for me, but I never felt it was *my* music. Whereas with Zeppelin, obviously, the music came from all four of us.

ROBERT PLANT   I didn't even know what we had. I was nineteen when I heard the tapes of our first rehearsal. I mean, it really wasn't a pretty thing. It wasn't *supposed* to be a pretty thing. It was just an unleashing of energy. But it felt like it was something I'd always wanted.

CHRIS DREJA   The heaviness was creeping in. I wasn't John Paul Jones, and Jimmy McCarty was not John Bonham. These were the pivotal players who created that sound. I knew about John Paul, and I thought, "You're not going to top that, Jimmy. You're a lucky man there!" At that point, he was a better bass player than Jimmy was a guitar player—and, of course, he understood music. There was no way I was going to interface myself between him joining the band. And you couldn't have met a nicer guy. What a real ace gentleman he was.

HENRY SMITH (roadie for the Yardbirds and Led Zeppelin) Jonesy, out of all the musicians in Led Zeppelin, is probably the one that's most overlooked. He gave Page the ability to do what he wanted to do, without having to worry about the rest of the song. There was a set path: we know where we're starting, and we know where we're going to end up, but in between they could go any place they wanted to go.

GLYN JOHNS (engineer on the first Zeppelin album) John Paul was as responsible for the success of Led Zeppelin as the other three, though it's only the other three that people ever talk about. Why? Because nobody ever talks about the bass player. Though, of course, he was also a great keyboard player.

ALAN CALLAN At the beginning, they were going to use Keith Emerson as a keyboard player. And Jonesy said, "No, I'll play keyboards." So the others said, "In that case, you have to play every other instrument, too." I think he even learned the violin.

MAGGIE BELL (singer with Stone the Crows, later signed to Swan Song as a solo artist) Jimmy wanted this to work, and Peter loved his conviction that it was *going* to work. Jimmy could quite easily have gone for the rest of his life and made great records with people and been a session guy. Peter said to me, "This is quite frightening, Mags, but I think it's going to work because Jimmy's made *sure* it's going to work." I was in the office when Peter said to him, "Jimmy, you're the one. You play the instrument. You've got the music in your head. I can keep all the shit away from you, and I can steer the band in the right direction."

HENRY SMITH It was Jimmy's band. He put it together like you would put together a boy band. He was the leader of the pack. When he said, "Everybody go left," everybody went left.

PAMELA DES BARRES (L.A. groupie and girlfriend of Page's in 1969–1970)   It was really subtle leadership. I saw Jimmy's puppeteering control in an almost disguised way, but it was there. He pulled all those invisible fairylike strings. And I know Robert felt sort of under his . . . I don't know if *control* is the right word, because it was very subtle.

Good-natured Page: *Melody Maker*, October 12, 1968.

PHIL CARSON (head of Atlantic U.K. and confidant of Zeppelin's) Robert was a walking compendium of music. He knew more about blues music and the roots of rock 'n' roll than John Paul did—and certainly as much as Jimmy did—so he could absolutely hold his own intellectually when it came to working on the music.

JOHN PAUL JONES My father, who was a jazz musician, had turned me on to things like Big Bill Broonzy and Sonny Terry and Brownie McGhee, but beyond them, I didn't really know much about blues. I didn't know a lot about Delta blues; it was more urban blues, Muddy Waters. It was through joining Zeppelin that I found out more about the older guys.

BP FALLON (U.K. press officer for Zeppelin, 1972–1976) Everyone wants to have this picture that it was Jimmy, with the others sort of several steps behind and maybe Peter Grant in front of the rest of the band. Led Zeppelin was a *band*, and every band has a leader. Some have *two* leaders. To be a successful leader, you don't blow your leadership trumpet all the time. And that allows something to be cooperative, even when it would appear not to be. Does that mean everyone has parity? No. Does it mean everyone is a star? Yes.

GLYN JOHNS Jimmy never had a superior attitude with the others at all. They would have listened to him anyway, so he didn't *need* an attitude.

HENRY SMITH He was very centered, very quiet. He knew himself. And I think that had a lot to do with the chemistry of the band, because those were the types of people that he sought out when he went to start his band. Jeff Beck was like the high school bully, and Jimmy wasn't that way.

BRAD TOLINKSI (U.S. music journalist and friend of Page's) As much as everyone wants to depict him as controlling or Machiavellian, I've never heard Jimmy say a bad thing musically about any of the other guys . . . and I've talked to him a lot. He always talks about the chemistry and the alchemy in the most glowing terms. He may say he groomed and shaped them, but he won't say he could have done it without them.

JIMMY PAGE We still had some Yardbirds concerts to fulfill in Scandinavia, so we did some Yardbirds material, as well as some new numbers. We knew we just had something that other people didn't have. All four of us in the room knew this was beyond anything that anybody else was doing. Everyone was a musical equal, which was superb. We just knew that we had it there.

PETER GRANT I remember everything about that first show in Copenhagen. I remember everything Jimmy had told me about Bonzo, and the whole performance. It was so . . . exciting! Just to be part of it was fantastic. There was never a thought of, "God, this is going to sell X amount of records." I thought they could be the best band ever. Remember that I'd been to America a lot of times, with the Animals, the Yardbirds, and different other bands. I just knew that Jimmy would come through. I knew it would be the best.

RICHARD COLE Jimmy once said to me, "The difference between Peter and most managers was he genuinely loved his bands. He loved Maggie, he loved Terry Reid, he loved Rod and Jeff, and he loved us." It wasn't just a moneymaking machine for Peter, and they must have felt that.

ROBERT PLANT In Scandinavia, we were pretty green; it was very early days, and we were tiptoeing with each other. We didn't have half the recklessness that became, for me, the whole joy of Led Zeppelin.

JOHN PAUL JONES There was the North-South divide and a lot of friendly teasing going on. I think Robert was slightly in awe of us. To him, session men were pipe-smoking, *Angling Times*–reading, shadowy figures. He never knew what to make of me and to an extent still doesn't.

ROBERT PLANT Page and Jones obviously became friends [with me], but they were never *mates* like Bonzo was, because he and I started out with that age and experience gap that was never totally bridged.

JOHN PAUL JONES All four of us were middle-class lads; there wasn't that much difference between the way we were all brought up.

JIMMY PAGE   I wanted artistic control in a vise grip, because I knew exactly what I wanted to do with these fellows. In fact, I financed and completely recorded the first album before going to Atlantic. We recorded the whole first album in a matter of thirty hours. That's the truth. I know because I paid the bill.

GLYN JOHNS   Jimmy rang me up and asked me to engineer. I asked if there was a producer, and he said no. So I said, "Well, if I'm the only one in the control room, I'm going to end up producing it." So he said, "Okay, you have to go and see Peter." This all happened very quickly, within a matter of days. I went to see Peter in Oxford Street and said I needed to get an agreement, and he said no problem. We agreed on a percentage of the retail price, which was normal. And we shook hands. I wouldn't normally have gone into the studio without a contract, but because I'd known Jimmy and John Paul since we were virtually kids, it never entered my mind that there would be anything amiss.

ROBERT PLANT   *Led Zeppelin* was created in a very crisp businesslike fashion. Nobody really knew each other. The record and the jamming that developed was what it was, and it was a very swift session. There were songs that began and ended cut-and-dried, like "Communication Breakdown" and "Good Times, Bad Times." But the real thing about the group was the extension of instrumental parts, which was in full swing even before we made our first record.

GLYN JOHNS   Led Zeppelin for me was so different from anyone else that it was like a completely new chapter. When I heard them on that first day, I can't ever remember being quite so excited. Blew my fucking socks off. Cream was nothing like it, because of the sophistication of Zeppelin's arrangements. That was the key. There was very little free-form *anything*; it was all very carefully arranged, by some pretty shit-hot arrangers. They were very hard-working: the Stones would take nine months to make a record, and these guys took nine days—including mixing. Were they trying to save money in the studio? More than likely.

Olympic Studios, Barnes, southwest London, a year after the studios closed in 2009. (Art Sperl)

PHIL CARSON Zeppelin were more *explosive* than the Who or Cream or Hendrix. Taking absolutely nothing away from Cream, they were a little one-dimensional. Neither the Beck Group nor Cream had the ability to explode in the way Zeppelin did. Cream didn't have a Robert Plant on vocals, and the Jeff Beck Group didn't have a John Bonham or a John Paul Jones.

MAC POOLE Zeppelin was really an airplane. It was dead simple: Plant was at the front, Bonham was at the back, and the wings were Jimmy and John Paul. And it balanced out because those two knew each other, just like Robert and Bonzo knew each other. It was a London-Birmingham weld.

NICK KENT What gave Led Zeppelin its power was the mixture of Black Country muscle and the more kind of analytical southern ability to step back and see the big picture. There's an alchemy there.

GLYN JOHNS   I didn't produce that band—in the sense that I had nothing to do with them until they walked into the studio. They were really well rehearsed, they'd picked all the material, and they knew exactly what they were doing. So half that job had already been done by them, and probably by Jimmy—who would certainly take the credit for it. However, once they were in the studio, I very much contributed to the production of that record, without any question at all—because that's what I thought I was doing and what I thought we'd agreed.

JAAN UHELSZKI (U.S. music journalist; traveled with the band on the 1975 and 1977 U.S. tours)   Jimmy, to this day, thinks his greatest achievement was how he recorded Bonham's drums. It's like he made Bonzo who he was mythically, so it's really symbiotic.

BRAD TOLINSKI (editor-in-chief of *Guitar World*)   Page's production of Bonham's drums is probably one of the biggest musical events of the past fifty or sixty years. It's had as much impact on popular music as Louis Armstrong or Miles Davis. The notion of putting the drums right up there with the guitar and the vocals is huge, as simple as it is. It's still being felt in hip-hop and in all contemporary music.

GLYN JOHNS   Everyone always asks about the Bonham drum sound. And the fact of the matter is, *they* got the fucking sound. I'd recorded Jimmy and John Paul nine million times, but I hadn't recorded the other two. The sound from Bonham's kit was phenomenal because he knew how to tune it, and not many rock 'n' roll drummers know how to do that.

I only used to use three mics: the idea was to capture the sound the guy was giving you and not fuck with it. I did put Bonham on a riser, however, to try and get the maximum out of his kit. On those sessions I stumbled, by accident, across stereo drum mic'ing, and it made him sound even bigger. Your jaw was on the floor from the minute he counted off. It was like the meeting of the gods: Jimmy and John Paul found these guys who were as good as *them* at what they did.

MAC POOLE   John told Jimmy, "Don't put me in one of those egg-box studios." And, of course, Jimmy knew all the studios and knew which one would be best for drums. When I heard the album, I was surprised by how simple the drumming was. Bonzo told me, "I couldn't do anything, man." I said, "Why not?" He said, "Coz Pagey wanted it really simple." He told me Granty came up to him and said, "If you wanna stay in this band, do what you're fuckin' told . . . or *leave by any window.*"

LAURENCE MYERS Peter once famously said, after John Bonham got a bit lippy, "Could you play drums in a wheelchair?" It was a story that went around all the time.

MAC POOLE Bonzo said, "I wasn't taking *him* on, he was twenty-four fucking stone!" And I still say that that was the reason Zeppelin made it, because Bonham had somebody to control him. In Birmingham, nobody could do that.

GLYN JOHNS Bonham, being the phenomenal drummer he was, would not have been the easiest guy for any bass player to work with. But because John Paul had such a history of playing with every drummer under the sun, he knew how to listen—intricately and probably subliminally.

JOHN PAUL JONES I immediately recognized the musicality of it. John kept a really straight beat on slow numbers like "You Shook Me"— mainly because he *could*, and there aren't many that can. Lots of people can play fast, but to play slow and groove is one of the hardest things in the world. And we could *both* do it, and we both recognized it in each other. It was a joy to sit back on a beat like that and just ride it. It required intense concentration but intense relaxation at the same.

Within the same rhythm, we always had a choice as to how we would play it. That's what makes it musically interesting and musically exciting. And to the listener who doesn't know what you're doing, it sounds as if it's got texture and color and movement . . . and *life*!

GLENN HUGHES John was *the* most musical drummer I ever heard or had the opportunity to be friends with. He was a huge *arranger* for the band. People talk about Entwistle and Moon, but the subtle aspect of Zeppelin was the way John and Jonesy played together.

JOHN PAUL JONES   You could *dance* to Led Zeppelin. Blues wasn't our only experience of black music. John and I were both into soul and funk, and I was into jazz as well. As a session musician, I did all the Motown covers because I was the only one who knew how to play in that style.

EDDIE KRAMER (engineer on *Led Zeppelin II* and *Houses of the Holy*)   I think Jonesy led the parade there, in the sense that he'd really absorbed what the Detroit bass players were doing and what the Philly bass players were doing.

CHRIS DREJA   On a good night Cream were great, but they were terribly raggedy at times. With Zeppelin, you had this sense of *construction*.

ALAN CALLAN   John Paul—who to this day I think is probably the greatest musician I've ever met—orchestrated everything *behind* Jimmy.

MAC POOLE   Musically, out of all four of them, I would put John Paul Jones as being *the* fucking man. He may play a very simple line on "Dazed and Confused," but the guy's thinking for the mood is so musical, and that makes it work. Jimmy's a great guitarist, but without Jones in that band—without that *fundamental*—it would be nothing.

JOHN PAUL JONES   In all honesty, I'd say that I probably should have paid much more attention to the writing credits in the earlier days of Zeppelin. In those days, I'd just say, "Well, I wrote that, but it's part of the arrangement," or something like that, and I'd just let it go. Not realizing at the time that that part of the arrangement had more to do with the writing than just arranging something. I always thought that John Bonham's contribution was always much more than he ever received credit for. In fact, I know it was.

HENRY SMITH   Most of the magic of the songs is between Jimmy and Jonesy. Jimmy would feel things out, come in with little riffs, and Jonesy would add his magic to it. Bonham could fill in any way you needed him to, and Robert adding vocals and words to it made it even more special. But the down-and-dirty part of it was Jimmy and Jonesy.

JOHN PAUL JONES Zeppelin was really a partnership between four people, and sometimes when you see songs with "Page-Plant" on everything, it makes it seem like it was a "Lennon-McCartney" situation, where they wrote everything and John and I just kind of learned the songs that Jimmy and Robert taught to us. That's so far from the truth it's ridiculous.

8

Atlantic Crossing

> Ahmet used to say to me, "Only sign a band if there's at
> least one virtuoso musician in there. I don't care if it's the
> drummer or the keyboard player." Led Zeppelin had four.
>
> —Phil Carson, November 2010

JERRY WEXLER (president of Atlantic Records, 1953–1975)   The main
reason that Atlantic Records became a power in white rock 'n' roll—
especially with English rock—is because we took the black thing as
far as it could go. Atlantic made music for black adults, while Motown
made music for white teenagers. Of course, we left Motown in the
lurch, but how? With Zeppelin and Yes and Crosby, Stills, and Nash!
We couldn't get black music to cross over. People have romantic delusions, remembering what never happened. Ray Charles and Aretha
Franklin never really *happened.*

JERRY GREENBERG (general manager of Atlantic, 1969–1980)   When
I first came to Atlantic in 1967, I thought Jerry was the president of
Atlantic and Ahmet Ertegun was the president of Atco. Because Jerry
was signing all the Wilson Picketts and Ahmet was signing all the
white rock acts.

AHMET ERTEGUN (cofounder of Atlantic Records)   The British Invasion had tremendous repercussions. The Beatles and the Stones changed everything. Jerry considered the music derivative. Most of it surely was; some of it, however, was original.

JIMMY PAGE   I had already worked with one of Atlantic's producers, and I visited their offices in America back in 1964, when I met Jerry Wexler and Leiber and Stoller.

AHMET ERTEGUN   In the '60s, we had started to make records in England, as well as here, and one of our legendary producers, Bert Berns, was raving about these session players Jimmy Page and John Paul Jones. In those crazy days of London madness, Carnaby Street, the angry young men, the nightclubs, the Speakeasy, and the Revolution, I had run across and met both Jimmy and John Paul. When Peter Grant and Steve Weiss came to see us about a new group formed by Jimmy, we were very excited about the prospect of this new group, the New Yardbirds.

JERRY WEXLER   Ahmet's gift for acquiring talent was remarkable. Whether in London or in L.A., his timing was impeccable; he was always in the right venue at the right time. His cool was irresistible to managers and artists alike.

DANNY GOLDBERG (U.S. press officer for Zeppelin and president of Swan Song in New York)   Culturally, there's no question that Zeppelin benefited from the breakup of Cream. It created a vacuum. The quirk of the signing of Zeppelin was that Ahmet didn't sign them, Jerry did. Dusty Springfield had told Wexler about John Paul Jones, so it actually was a Wexler signing. But within a year or so, it became Ahmet's band, and Wexler stopped paying attention to them.

JERRY WEXLER   I signed Led Zeppelin, and then I had nothing to do with them. Absolutely nothing. Ahmet took over their care and cleaning. I don't think I could have tolerated them. I got along fine with Peter Grant. But I knew he was an animal.

ROBERT PLANT   Ahmet was a friend and [a] sidekick. He was yet another member of the Zeppelin entourage who came to us to fulfill his dreams of craziness or whatever. He was doing that as well with John Coltrane and Ray Charles, you know, which is even more amazing. He was a fucking incredible character and personality, with great wit and humor.

JUNE HARRIS BARSALONA (U.S. correspondent for *New Musical Express* and wife of Frank Barsalona)   Ahmet was the one who could hang out on that very high, sophisticated level, so for anybody who wanted celebrity status, that was perfect: if you were seen with Ahmet, you were there. That was the ticket to the stars. If you were more interested in the music, you'd hang out with Jerry.

JERRY GREENBERG   We didn't know Robert, we didn't know Bonzo. It was based on Jimmy and on Dusty saying how Jonesy was the most incredible musician. But why *wouldn't* you want to sign with Atlantic? It was the same with Mick Jagger. It was the heritage of Atlantic that caught the English people who were raised on that music, raised on blues, and made them say, "Man, I want to be a part of this."

RICHARD COLE (Zeppelin road manager)   I think Jimmy and Peter felt Atlantic was more bona fide than Atco, which was a subsidiary. Atlantic was the powerhouse.

AHMET ERTEGUN   Signing Zeppelin was the result of our signing the Young Rascals. Steve Weiss represented the Rascals in the contract, and he was one of the toughest lawyers I had ever encountered. He made a terrific deal for them. Having done that, he liked us; we became very good friends. When Peter Grant came to America to make a deal for "The New Yardbirds," Weiss was Grant's lawyer. So the man we complained about bitterly—because of the tough deal we'd had to make for the Rascals—became our friend. He became the man who brought us one of the greatest groups in the history of music.

JANINE SAFER (Swan Song press officer, 1975–1977)   Zeppelin was certainly the first band to get the deal they got, and that was all Steve—maybe not all Steve's *idea*, but certainly all Steve's execution. Peter posturing and bullying would never have worked with Ahmet and Jerry. Steve being an incredibly good negotiator, it *did* work.

TERRY MANNING (engineer on *Led Zeppelin III* tracks)   Chris Blackwell was right on the verge of signing Zeppelin to Island, and he had offered them autonomy and production, because that was his ethos. Peter then took that as leverage to Atlantic and got more money for the same deal: "Island is giving us all this, and you'll have to match that and give us more money, or we're going there."

CHRIS BLACKWELL (founder of Island Records)   It was a handshake deal, but I was dealing with Peter Grant, so it wasn't a deal until it was really a deal. And to tell you the truth, I'm glad I didn't get them because it wouldn't have worked for us at Island. Too dark. I couldn't have dealt with it.

JERRY WEXLER   Clive Davis and Mo Ostin were also in the horse race, but I prevailed by offering Zeppelin a five-year contract with a $75,000 advance for the first year and four one-year options. Steve Weiss said that for another $35,000, we could have world rights. I called Polydor, our English distributors, and suggested they chip in $20,000, but they passed.

DICK ASHER (head of Epic Records in the late '60s)   Grant and Steve Weiss arrived in Clive Davis's office, and we all sat down. It was Clive's first meeting with Peter, and we talked and talked about all sorts of things. Finally, Clive said, "Well, aren't we going to talk about Jimmy Page?" Grant replied, "Oh no, we've already signed them to Atlantic." We were all stunned, especially after all we'd done for [the Yardbirds].

JERRY GREENBERG   Steve told me, "You know how you got this band? It was because Clive Davis slammed the door in my face. And I never forgot it. I wanted to give it to him, and I gave it to him, boy. I snatched Jimmy up and brought him to Atlantic." Steve was a sensitive guy, and people don't forget.

RICHARD COLE   Steve got five percent of anything Peter made, but then there were no lawyers' fees. He used to drive us fucking mad because he was always writing memos and notes. I once heard Peter say, "Thank fuck I haven't got to pay him by the sheet of paper."

BARRY JAY REISS (lawyer and colleague of Steve Weiss) Steve and Peter got along famously. Both of them were volatile personalities, so I think they felt at times like soul brothers. There were some screaming matches, but nothing out of the ordinary.

GLYN JOHNS (engineer on first Zeppelin album) Peter went to New York and got the deal with Atlantic, came back, and had a meeting with the band. I can only assume he told them what the money was and how it would be divvied up, and how the royalty situation would work out. And again, I can only assume that it came to me and my bit, and Jimmy said, "Oh no, he didn't produce it, and he's not going to get a royalty." I think it was all right for me to have a royalty before the deal was done, but once there was a large amount of money involved, they changed their minds. I got a call from Peter, and I was told that I had no arrangement. I had been shafted royally.

JIMMY PAGE [Glyn] tried to hustle in on a producer's credit. I said, "No way, I put this band together, I brought them in and directed the whole recording process, I got my own guitar sound—I'll tell you, you haven't got a hope in hell."

GLYN JOHNS Jimmy, since then, has been proved to have the most extraordinary attitude to anything he's involved with, which is that he will take credit for pretty much everything and never allow anyone else to have credit for *anything*. I never spoke to John Paul, who was a friend. I knew it was nothing to do with him. I don't even think it was Peter. I knew it was Jimmy, and it was Peter doing Jimmy's bidding.

CHRIS DREJA (bassist with the Yardbirds, photographer) I did the first photo session for Zeppelin in my studio before I moved to New York. I think the fee was 21 guineas. I have a theory that they commissioned me because they wanted to keep me sweet and not be funny about them using the Yardbirds' name. Years later, Jimmy, for some weird reason, informed me he had a piece of paper proving he owned the name. I think it was because at that point—along with his ambition to be the wealthiest man in rock and open up the Olympic Games—he liked the whole control thing.

• • •

EDDIE KRAMER (engineer on *Led Zeppelin II* and *Houses of the Holy*)   I was finishing off some Hendrix stuff, and John Paul called and said, "I've got something I want to play you. Come over to the house." So I went over, and he played me the first Zeppelin record. I said, "What the fuck *is* this? This is an incredible record!" He said, "It's the new band I'm working with." So I said, "What's it called?" He said, "Led Zeppelin." I said, "That's the stupidest fucking name I ever heard."

JIM SIMPSON (mainstay of Midlands music scene)   We didn't think the Yardbirds were that great: there were tougher and better in Birmingham. So when Bonnie told us about Led Zeppelin, we all got a fit of the giggles. "How could a band ever make it with a name like that? They've got *no* chance." We all thought they'd gone off to join the London softies. We thought it was a really silly move. For about ten minutes.

TERRY MANNING   The first album was revolutionary. It was fresh, it was powerful, and it still had pop sensibilities. It was really just an amazing recording, a shot out of the dark. There was a heft to it. They were recording in the same place as several of the other big bands, with some of the same technical and production staff, so the difference had to be the players. And those four just had a copacetic mingling of all their sensibilities and tones. It was overwhelming and undeniable.

ELIZABETH IANNACI (artist relations in Atlantic's L.A. office, 1975–1977)   There's a purity and a spareness about that first record that the later records don't have. I remember putting the stylus onto that vinyl and playing "Communication Breakdown." And the world changed in that moment. It was like reading Gertrude Stein for the first time or seeing the first Cubist painting. The world was never to be the same again.

ROBERT PLANT   I'd only written one song prior to meeting Jimmy, and that was "Memory Lane." So from writing nothing to cowriting "Communication Breakdown" was quite a move.

GLENN HUGHES (singer and bassist with Trapeze, Deep Purple and Black Country Communion)   "Good Times, Bad Times" was the first time I really heard Robert. I thought, "Oh shit, *that's* what it's about, is it? We've had Cream, and now we've got *this*." I didn't even know what they looked like, but just listening to that song, I thought, "Ooh, I bet they look good and all." You could see it and smell it.

MICK FARREN (singer with the Deviants and writer for underground press) The whole Cream thing had happened, and to us it was like, "Here comes another one." In other words, somebody on high picks their dream band and puts it all together, but who the fuck's the singer—or the bass player and the drummer, for that matter? There was the same kind of vibe about it.

DAVE PEGG (bassist in Bonham's pre-Zeppelin band A Way of Life) Bonzo turned up one day in his mother's estate [station wagon] with a copy of the album just out of the blue and said, "You've got to hear this." It was fantastic. The following week, he turned up in a gold S-type Jag. They obviously took off really quickly and became huge, because Robert bought a similar gold S-type Jag. The two of them had identical cars for a while.

ROBERT PLANT We had no idea of success. You couldn't really say to people, "We're doing really well." Because it was like an existentialist thing—one minute we were doing gigs and people were going nuts, and the next minute I was back in the industrial Midlands of England, trying to justify having a Jaguar.

ROY WILLIAMS (live engineer for Robert Plant) Robert and Bonzo used to go to the Plough and Harrow in Kinver. They'd go in Bonzo's Jag, and on the way back—so they didn't get stopped by the police—Bonzo would put on a chauffeur's cap, and Robert would sit in the back.

DAVE PEGG John still lived in a council flat in Eve Hill, which was quite fascinating. The way the flat was done up was all nouveau riche. It was like being a pools winner, I suppose. A chap from the Midlands, and all of a sudden he's got all this dosh. In the couple of months from when he got the flat to when he left it, he'd transformed it, and it'd got an oak-paneled sitting room and gold chandeliers, and all the taps were gold. It was like he'd bought up Rackhams department store, which was the posh shop in Birmingham.

ED BICKNELL (former manager of Dire Straits)   I was the social secretary at Hull University. I came to London in late 1968, and during that trip, I went to the Chrysalis booking agency at 155 Oxford Street. While I was in there, this huge figure entered the room, and I was briefly introduced to Peter, who was trying to get the agents at Chrysalis to go see the New Yardbirds at the Marquee. Being agents, they all studiously ignored him, but I toddled down to Wardour Street and found myself in a queue that stretched all the way round the corner into Old Compton Street.

PETER GRANT When I saw that queue in Wardour Street, that convinced me. I thought, "That's it—no singles, no television." Because if the people believe in the band, they're going to come and see them.

ED BICKNELL I thought they were the absolute dog's bollocks. They didn't know a lot of songs, and the guitar solos went on a bit, but the energy of the band, and particularly the rhythm section, you were just thrown back by it. And I left thinking, "I've got to book this group," which I duly did for £100, supporting Jethro Tull, who got £400. In between the time I booked the New Yardbirds and the time they were due to play, they

Dave Pegg and John Bonzo in Barmouth, Wales, summer 1968. (Courtesy of Dave Pegg)

became Led Zeppelin. In the contract, Peter crossed out "New Yardbirds" and put "Lead Zeppelin," spelled L-E-A-D, and signed it "Jimmy Page." They never played the show because they went off to the States instead.

ROY CARR (writer for *New Musical Express*)   Most people had written the Yardbirds off, as they had Manfred Mann and people like that. Somebody told me the Yardbirds were changing their name, and Peter Grant was running around the Fishmonger's Arms and all those places. And that was it, they went to the States, and it happened much faster than anybody imagined.

CHRIS WELCH (writer for *Melody Maker*)   I got this phone call from Jimmy, who'd been tipped off by Neil Christian that I was okay—a journalist he could trust. He just appeared in the *Melody Maker* office and told me about his new band. I said, "Well, what happened to the Yardbirds?" He said the band had got a bit slack toward the end. He used a very Home Counties expression—something like, "Come on, chaps, we're not putting enough effort into this!"

He never ever used Americanisms, Jimmy. It was all very English, whereas everyone else was trying desperately to adopt American rock slang, and he never did. He was his own man and stood apart—very self-assured in that respect, and checking people out in the way he checked *me* out. I wrote down the new name of the band, and he corrected my spelling: "It's L-E-D, not L-E-A-D."

REG JONES (singer and guitarist with Bonham's pre-Zeppelin band A Way of Life)   I drove John and Robert to their first engagement as Led Zeppelin in my Jaguar. It was at Surrey University. There was a huge banner hanging outside that read—in big letters—"Tonight! The Ex-Yardbirds." Underneath, in small lettering, it said, "Led Zeppelin." After the gig, I couldn't start the Jaguar and we all came home on the train.

JOHN PAUL JONES   Originally, I think I probably went into the band thinking, "Give it a couple of years." Was touring with Zeppelin more tiring than session work? Probably not, at the rate I was working as a studio musician. The music I was doing on the session scene was just . . . I was basically dying in any creative area. I was literally just working. And Zeppelin was total release.

ROBERT PLANT   Did I know it was going to be special? It just seemed to be the way I'd always wanted it to be in the Band of Joy. Of course, with Jimmy and Jonesy there was a seniority. They were mature and more worldly wise, while Bonzo and I were a pair of chancers, really, nicking the hubcaps off the cars of people who'd invited us in for dinner. We learned a few graces, and it was great. It felt unbelievably powerful and unashamedly so.

KEITH ALTHAM (writer for *NME*, *Record Mirror*, and other publications)   Peter phoned me at the *NME* and said, "Come and see my band, Keef. They're playing in Elephant 'n' Castle." I got there about seven-thirty, and I could hear them about three blocks away. I'd never heard, in a confined space, a band playing so deafeningly loud. I stood it for about three numbers, and my ears started bleeding.

It sounds like heresy, but they weren't that good. They were obviously good musicians, but they weren't playing like a band. I decided it was one of those supergroups that just wasn't going to work, and I left. Peter phoned me the following day and asked what I thought. I told him. Of course, thereafter he never ceased to remind me of what I'd said: "Whatchoo fink of my band *now*, Keef?"

MICK FARREN   A few months after the Band of Joy opened for the Deviants, it all turned around. Now we were opening for *Led Zeppelin*. There is some dispute about this—Russell [Hunter] swears it was Bristol; I think it was Exeter Civic Hall—but when we turn up, there's this big truck outside. And it was like, "Who's paying for *this* nonsense?"

We all came in, and the stage was full of their equipment. Then the lads show up, and Jimmy and Robert are perfectly friendly. Even then, John Paul seemed to be nine paces apart from everybody else. And then there was the loathsome Bonham: Keith Moon with all of the dynamite and none of the charm.

The gig was a violent mess, a culture clash with a bunch of ignorant fucking farmers. When we came offstage, we said to Zeppelin, "They almost killed us out there." Robert said, "Wow, you must have been terrible." I said, "Try it." And it just got worse. They hated him even more than they'd hated *me*.

JEFF BECK I could see the potential. It was just amazing, blew the house down, blew everybody away. . . . I was blind jealous, although maybe jealousy is the wrong word, because it's a negative emotion.

ED BICKNELL Peter had a street wisdom. He understood what musicians were about, and he understood the audience, which a lot of people in the business don't. He understood that if you can get fifty people going mad in a tiny club, it's not a huge leap to getting half a million people going mad in a stadium. He always said to me that the most important thing was the word-of-mouth.

JIMMY PAGE When our first album came out, the way you had to promote it was on the television and the radio, and at the time you'd fit into somebody's show and do three or four numbers, and eventually there was a John Peel show. That was the one avenue you had. The other was television, and we weren't going to mime. We were playing live, but quite honestly we didn't fit into the format of TV at that time.

KEVYN GAMMOND (guitarist in Plant's pre-Zeppelin group the Band of Joy) The first time I saw Zep, they'd already got the whole showmanship sorted out. It was almost like the time I saw T-Bone Walker in Birmingham, with the guitar behind his back and doing splits. Jim had that same kind of persona, where he could make it work away from just a semi-pro thing, which I guess we were. But Robert and John also took the Band of Joy framework into Zeppelin.

ROBERT PLANT Jimmy brought his mastery and technique and an extension of the Yardbirds signature to the proceedings. But Bonzo and I were already in this freakout zone with the Band of Joy. It was quite natural for us to go into long solos and pauses and crescendos. I listen to it now, and it swings, it has all those '60s bits and pieces [that] could have come off the *Nuggets* album.

So for Jimmy it was an extension of what he did, and for us it was an extension of what *we* did. The only difference—and it was the crucial thing—was that there was such quality playing. John Paul had found a place so way down in that pocket that Bonzo just fell into it.

9

Like a Freight Train on Steroids

> Nineteen years old and never been kissed, I remember it well. It's been a long time.
>
> —Robert Plant, March 1975

PETER GRANT I sat down with them in October 1968 and said, "Listen, you start on Boxing Day for ten or twelve dates in America with Vanilla Fudge, which means you've got to go on Christmas Eve." And I was shitting myself having to tell them, "Incidentally, fellas, I'm not going." It was one of the few times I never went, and I regretted it so much that I thought, "I'm never going to not go with them again."

RICHARD COLE (Zeppelin's road manager) The first tour was paid for by Jimmy and Peter and John Paul out of their own money. My first introduction to them as a band was when they flew into LAX with Kenny Pickett on the 23rd of December, and I went out to the airport to meet them. I already had Terry Reid and his band at the Château Marmont.

BILL HARRY (Zeppelin's first U.K. press officer)   Richard Cole stuck to them like glue. He was the equivalent of a fifth Beatle, in a way, in that he was always there. He looked after everything. He was always doing things. If Bonzo ripped his trousers onstage, Richard fixed them.

CHRIS WELCH (writer for *Melody Maker*)   Richard was a breed of real tough Londoner who could be incredibly charming at the same time. He would be very polite to girls and then turn around and swing a punch. Zeppelin was a strangely small entourage, like a little family. It always amazed people how few of them there were. At the start, anyway, it was just the band and Peter and Richard.

MICHAEL DES BARRES (singer with Swan Song band Detective)   Cole was their rottweiler pimp. You did not want to fuck with him. He's the gentlest, sweetest man today, but back then, he would shove a coat hanger up your ass and hang you out the window. All of the Zeppelin road incidents were in essence choreographed by Ricardo.

RICHARD COLE   They were both very sweet, Bonham and Plant. I was twenty-two, only two years older than them. Jimmy and I had shared

No entry: Ricardo closes the door on Jimmy Page, 1969. (Chuck Boyd)

a room in the Yardbirds days, so I had a two-bedroom suite ready for him and me. Bonzo and Robert had a bungalow or a suite on that first tour, and then there were John Paul and Kenny Pickett.

ROBERT PLANT   We ended up in the suite Burl Ives had just vacated. Down the corridor were the GTOs, Wild Man Fischer, and all those Sunset Strip characters of the time. Rodney Bingenheimer was making coffee . . . [and] all that dour Englishness swiftly disappeared into the powder-blue, post-Summer-of-Love California sunshine. I was teleported.

RICHARD COLE   On Christmas Day, I went to see a girl up in Laurel Canyon, so the band had Christmas dinner together. I think Bonzo cooked the turkey.

CHRIS WELCH   Robert was always gently taking the mickey out of Bonzo, and Bonzo would get irate about it. But you could tell they were very fond of each other.

RICHARD COLE   The ones that used to row were Bonham and Plant. It was never about the music, it was usually about one of them not wanting to pay for the petrol when they were driving back to Birmingham—things that were so amusing to us because their arguments were like arguments between two brothers. Because they both came into the band at the same time as outsiders, I suppose, and I'm sure must have felt that in their own conversations.

ROBERT PLANT   It was much easier for John to connect with me in my changes than it was for the other two guys. Because we were from the same place and because we'd played together before, he could tap into parts of me that Jimmy and Jonesy either didn't know about or didn't bother to connect with.

PAMELA DES BARRES (groupie and girlfriend of Page's in 1969–1970)   Unlike a lot of bands, Led Zeppelin did actually hang out at clubs and restaurants together. They really did like one another.

JOHN PAUL JONES   There was that whole sort of hippie hangover, where all the bands used to live together, yet by the time they got on the road they were at each other's throats. Whereas we were always really pleased to see each other at the airport on the first day of the tour, and I'm sure that had something to do with the longevity of the band.

There weren't any *camps* in Led Zeppelin. People think it was like Jimmy and Robert were always together, so that would leave the rhythm section. But then it was always the Midlanders and the Southerners—lots of good-natured banter. We'd take the piss out of them, and they'd take the piss out of us: "You poncey Southern so-and-sos. . . . " But we were all very protective of Led Zeppelin. Any member attacked by the press, we would all rally round . . . and probably still do. There's still that defensiveness.

BILL HARRY   Robert was absolutely loads of fun. He was the joker in the pack. When you were in his company, you felt completely relaxed and there were no tensions.

CHRIS WELCH   Robert had an extraordinary boyish exuberance. I once saw him come into a hotel foyer and do a forward roll across the floor. In the hotel bars, all the girls gravitated toward him; he would never be sitting there alone. A lot of rock musicians would be very crudely on the pull, and Robert would never do that, he was just magnetically drawing girls toward him. He would never go for any groupie who happened to throw herself at him.

KIM FOWLEY (L.A. producer and scenester)   Led Zeppelin fell in love with Los Angeles because there are certain places where everybody says yes, instead of being stuck in Grimsby or Belgium. The physical Englishmen liked L.A., while the cerebral ones liked New York. L.A. fell in love with Led Zeppelin because we're connected to England. When a new English band came over, we wanted to be the first people on our block to welcome them at the club. It was, "Let's go down and steal their essence and consume their magic."

ROBERT PLANT   We couldn't believe we were in the States. Everything was new to us. Meanwhile, Pagey was walking around like a king, the King of the Yardbirds, with all these chicks.

KIM FOWLEY   Jimmy came up to my room at the Château Marmont and said, "Hey, take a look at my new bullwhip." And he showed me this whip that Aleister Crowley would have drooled over—a spectacular item. He had the dark clothes on and the velvet cuffs. He was decked out, and this was three in the afternoon. He wasn't about to go onstage. The shy boy I'd met in 1965 was suddenly a very confident young man; he was the Jimmy Page who is the subject of folklore. Still polite, but with some edge on him that he hadn't exhibited before.

PAMELA DES BARRES   When I first met Jimmy, he wasn't taking drugs at all. He was very in control of himself and liked to have the girls a little *out* of control. I never minded it. I enjoyed it and felt totally safe. I know a lot of people talked about his whips and the things he did, and maybe he did those things, but he was very respectful of me and never harmed me. Apart from breaking my heart, of course.

RICHARD COLE   The first show, in Denver, was in the round, and you really couldn't get a good idea of a concert when it was in the round. They were supporting the Vanilla Fudge, who were friends of mine because I'd tour-managed them. Bonham and Jones had this mutual respect between them and Tim Bogert and Carmine Appice.

ROBERT PLANT   Colorado was so beautiful and gentle compared to L.A., but I was petrified by the hugeness of the venue.

RICHARD COLE   It was maybe during the fourth show, in Portland, that they started to gel. I remember watching Bonham's solo with John Paul Jones and saying to him, "Fucking hell, this guy's really something." Jimmy was an old hand at America, but the others were relatively new to working there, and I think they had to feel the audiences out and get comfortable with them. They'd never played to thousands of people before, and I'm sure it was very intimidating.

JIMMY PAGE   Led Zeppelin's live performance was so important as to the sum of the parts and how we would go on stage. If all four of us were really on top of it, it would take on this fifth dimension. That fifth dimension could go in any direction in any way. Sometimes you'd do one number, and it would be really quite slow and dirgey, and the next day it would be quite fast. We stuck to the set list quite a lot, but the reason was that we were changing the numbers so much within that; the improvisation and spontaneity were happening all the time, and that was the beauty of it.

GUY PRATT (bassist with Page's post-Zeppelin band Coverdale/Page) When I played with Jimmy in the late '80s, he would listen to all the Zeppelin bootlegs. He was always interested in how they played things at certain gigs. Because everything was different every night, so they would just hit on a new arrangement. Jimmy would say, "Oh yeah, that's when we started doing *that*."

ROBERT PLANT   I was just so pleased to *be* there. I didn't even know what to do with my *arms*. Now I understand why Joe Cocker did that thing for a while, because what are you going to *do*? There are so many *solos*. But it was such an amazing time, and things moved at such a rate of knots. On 80 percent of the nights, it was an absolute extravaganza for me to be around it.

If you look at all the sort of bits and pieces I used to throw in for my own enjoyment—I mean, it's a bit corny now, because it's referring to Eddie Cochran or Elvis—it was the previous generation of rock 'n' roll. It was what we feasted on to get riffs, to get organized, to become a big band with big riffs. So I was kind of *visiting* most of the time in Led Zep. On that aspect of the British rock-blues thing, on "How Many More Times" and "Dazed and Confused," those extensions had me . . . *interestingly foxed* for a while.

CATHERINE JAMES (L.A. groupie and girlfriend of Page's)   The Led Zeppelin debut at the Whisky a Go Go wasn't that big of a deal—they were complete unknowns. But when they played, Wow! That was when things really changed. That was a turnaround for music in Los Angeles. . . . After the Zeppelin gig, you saw the beginnings of a whole different lifestyle. That's when the groupies started coming out of the woodwork. They started coming in from the Valley.

MIKAEL MAGLIERI (son of Whisky a Go Go founder Mario Maglieri) The Whisky was the place where groups hung to see other groups.

Zeppelin make their L.A. debut at the Whisky, January 1969.

That really was the basis of the Whisky: whoever was in town, even if they weren't playing, they all hung out together.

RODNEY BINGENHEIMER (L.A. scenester and DJ)   I remember being backstage, and Jimmy had the flu. He was green. He was very ill, and they went and did the show. They were just really cool, but Jimmy was real sick, so he wasn't very talkative.

PAMELA DES BARRES   Richard Cole carried Jimmy off the stage. It was so dramatic. He had on red patent leather slippers, and they dropped off his feet as he was being carried out. Afterward, I said to myself, "Okay, that was pretty amazing, but I'm not sure I want to get to know those people."

JIMMY PAGE   We went to California and caused a bit of a fuss there, especially at the Fillmore in San Francisco, and all of a sudden, the name of the band traveled like wildfire.

ROBERT PLANT   Bonzo and I looked at each other during the set and thought, "Christ, we've got something." That was the first time we realized Led Zeppelin might mean something; there was so much intimacy with the audience, and if you could crack San Francisco at the height of the Airplane, Grateful Dead period, then it meant something.

JIMMY PAGE   There were bands and we were supporting them, but they weren't turning up, and that was happening on the West Coast and the East Coast. So we were really quite an intimidating force.

JOE "JAMMER" WRIGHT (Chicago blues guitarist and Zeppelin roadie) Zeppelin was like a freight train on steroids, a huge machine coming at you. And it had a lot of funk to it. I went, "Holy fuck!"

JAAN UHELSZKI (writer for *Creem* magazine) I used to work at the Grande Ballroom in Detroit, and since I worked there, I saw all the bands free. I saw from the schedule that Led Zeppelin was coming through, and I knew that Page was in it. I already had this Page obsession from the Yardbirds, whom I'd seen the year before.

That first gig, they weren't as foppish and beautiful and refined as they became with all the brocade and outfits. I think they were just wearing jeans and T-shirts and leather jackets, very meat-and-potatoes dressing. Pam Grant reviewed that first Detroit show for *Creem*, and I think she called them "capable" or something ridiculous. The first show was maybe only half-full, but everybody who was there told everybody they knew, and by the third show it was full. That's how good they were.

I'd seen Cream that summer, and they were really prosaic compared to Zeppelin. Clapton had that imperious, lording-it-over-the-crowd thing, but there was something much more intricate and musical and exciting about Zeppelin. And it was very sexualized from the first album onward: they really *were* trying to get in your pants and didn't make any bones about it.

BEBE BUELL (celebrated rock consort and girlfriend of Page's) One of the reasons people feel there is something satanic about the lure of their music is because it was very primal—what it did to your head and the way it captured you. With the Stones, I thought about sex; with Zeppelin, you felt . . . *danger.*

MARIO MEDIOUS (Atlantic Records promo man, 1965–1972) When I heard them singing about the killing floor and squeezing the lemon till the juice ran down your legs, it freaked me out because I was raised up on that music. But it was more exciting the way they did it. I had grown up with Muddy Waters and Buddy Guy, but I had grown bored with it. It didn't mean shit to me anymore. When these cats came along with their electric shit and putting all that energy into it and taking solos an hour long, it knocked me out. It made me appreciate my heritage even more so.

JOHN PAUL JONES   We played four nights at the Boston Tea Party, and by then we had an hour and a half's music to play. We played *four* and a half hours on the last night—we played the act twice, and then did everybody else's act with Who, Rolling Stones, and Beatles numbers.

MARIO MEDIOUS   They got about ten encores at the Tea Party. People would not even let them leave, so they just kept playing. You could hear the whole building moving and shaking. It ended up with just blues jams and Jonesy moving back and forth between bass and keyboards.

PETER GRANT   [Zeppelin] absolutely *pulverized* them . . . people in the audience used to tell me it was like a *force*. It was in their heads for three or four days. I thought, "There's no holding them back now."

JOHN PAUL JONES   Peter hugged us at the end of the gig, picked all four of us up at once. We knew we were actually going to make it.

AHMET ERTEGUN (cofounder of Atlantic Records)   Peter defended the band as though they were his only children in life. He was a sensational manager: he built an aura of mystique around that group that still exists.

BILL HARRY   Peter wanted me to do their publicity, but really it was *non*-publicity. It was to keep the press off their backs. They didn't want to do interviews, and he didn't want them to do interviews, so it was basically to filter them out.

JOHN PAUL JONES   We allowed ourselves to be guided by Peter, and we trusted his decisions. . . . His idea was to be everywhere—and then nowhere. Just at the point where everyone was going to get fed up with seeing us, we were gone! He was just right, all the time. A lot of Americans helped us, like Frank Barsalona. The bright ones could see what [Peter] was doing and could understand what he was getting at. . . . He was a very smart man, which wrong-footed them. They just saw a big guy and thought if they could move quickly they could get round him.

DENNIS SHEEHAN (assistant to Robert Plant on the 1977 U.S. tour; subsequently tour manager for U2)   Peter didn't get where he was by being a nice guy. Could he have managed U2? I don't think so. But could Paul McGuinness have managed Led Zeppelin? I certainly don't think so, either. Very different management techniques for their times.

PETER GRANT It's what I call verbal violence. You don't actually say, "I'm gonna do this to you," but you intimidate them. That's the game, intimidating them verbally. And I realized that if you were British, you could really do it, because you could always out-verbal them any time you wanted to. They had a great thing of calling you "Pal," and I'm like, "I'm not your pal. How dare you address me like that! I hardly know you, you wretched little man." And they'd think, "Fucking hell, what's *that* all about?" [They'd] never heard anything like it before.

EDDIE KRAMER (engineer on *Led Zeppelin II* and *Houses of the Holy*) I remember Peter laughing at me and saying, "Not bad for an old gypsy, am I?" He was a tough boy. You didn't mess with him. If you're going into a record company or an agency or a venue, it's nice to know you've got Peter Grant there. He was like a walking mountain, but he was also very smart.

LAURENCE MYERS (partner with Mickie Most and Peter Grant in RAK Records) Peter realized what he had, which was that Zeppelin were really, really important. If you are unquestionably a huge star, you can push and push and push, and people will stand for it.

LISA ROBINSON (New York correspondent for *Disc, New Musical Express*, and *Creem*) Ahmet always knew where the power was, and so his focus was always slightly more on Peter and Jimmy than on Robert.

MALCOLM McLAREN (manager of the Sex Pistols) Jimmy was the artist Grant most admired—the only character he ever compromised with, because he believed artists had a gift from God. Theirs was a meeting of the physical and [the] cerebral. Grant played the ugly Igor to Page's irresistible Dracula.

SHELLEY KAYE (assistant to Steve Weiss) Peter was not the most handsome guy in the world, but he was actually quite dazzling as far as personality went. He was our protector. He was the one we were making sure everything was good for.

HENRY SMITH (roadie for the Yardbirds and Led Zeppelin)   I've heard many people say he was a big bully and a mean type of person, but to me, he wasn't. He was almost like a father figure.

JUNE HARRIS BARSALONA   Regardless of how other people perceived Peter, I always had a soft spot for him. He could be a baby. When you got on a plane with him, he was terrified of flying. He'd sit there and grab your hand and not let go until that plane landed. We spent a lot of time with him—down time, personal time, which was how we knew Gloria and the kids. Gloria came to New York at least once or twice. I remember her coming up to the apartment and having dinner. They were a regular husband and wife.

GLORIA GRANT (wife of Peter Grant)   I didn't really know what Peter was doing, even though we were in the same house. It wasn't easy when he was away a lot of the time. And when he *wasn't* away, he was on the phone sorting things out. He was *always* on the phone with Steve Weiss. He found it very difficult to switch off. I think when we moved from Beulah Hill to Rose Walk in Purley, that was when I realized that he was making lots of money. The first time I met Zeppelin, we stayed in the penthouse suite at the Fontainebleau in Miami, and I said to Peter, "How much is this *costing?*" And he said, "Seventy-one pounds a night." I said, *"Seventy-one pounds?"*

HOWARD MYLETT (author of the first book on Zeppelin)   Peter and Richard together had really sussed out the whole American underground and also the youth and universities—what was selling and why albums were selling.

ED BICKNELL (former manager of Dire Straits)   Because Peter had managed the Yardbirds and the Beck Group—and gone to America with them—he realized there was this underground scene in the States, and you didn't need pop radio play to access it. In fact, in some ways pop radio was a *dis*advantage because it had no street cred.

HARVEY KUBERNIK (L.A. correspondent for *Melody Maker* in the '70s)   Our friends in Led Zeppelin walked into the glorious world of FM radio and free-form unrestricted format. These little things were even migrating through pop magazines or papers across the United States in a pre-Internet world where J.J. Jackson at WBCN in Boston knew the son of promoter Don Law.

ANNI IVIL (press officer for Atlantic in the U.K. office, late '60s–early '70s) They had Peter Grant, Frank Barsalona, Atlantic Records, and every major promoter working to make them succeed because it was in everybody's interest. All they had to do was deliver.

JUNE HARRIS BARSALONA There were so many groups being formed at that time. The difference with this one was that, from the get-go, it had all the elements to make it happen. If Peter got involved with something, it was going to succeed. And it was reflecting what was going on in the late '60s: 65 percent of the American population was under thirty-five, and there was a big revolution going on in San Francisco. England still had a prominent position in what was going on in the development of rock, so you were more likely to listen.

DON LAW (Boston rock promoter) English bands? Straight ahead. They were consistently better focused and prepared to play that market. There was an energy and intelligence that wasn't there from the West Coast bands.

EDDIE KRAMER Zeppelin had a deal with Concerts East and Concerts West, and we all know who those geezers were. They split up the country into two sections, and it was very clever the way they put it together. If that's what it takes to move ahead, go for it. But it all contributed to this feeling that they were invulnerable.

ELLEN SANDER (U.S. journalist who profiled Zeppelin for *Life* magazine in 1969) They were considered one of the most interesting of the new blues-based bands: one to watch, a powerhouse. By then, the British Invasion was a fait accompli, and British bands were not alien at all. There was already a sense of legacy, and Jimmy Page was a part of that. They came over to my place after a lunch, and we listened to Elvis records. They behaved perfectly. Their publicist, Diane Gardiner, told me they thought we got on very well.

JERRY GREENBERG (general manager of Atlantic, 1969–1980)   Mario Medious—the Big M—was an accountant at Atlantic, but he would talk trash to me about these bands. So when I came up of the idea of somebody going on the road to start promoting to FM stations, I went to Mario.

MARIO MEDIOUS   All these college and hippie stations started up. All of a sudden, they're playing esoteric music—blues, jazz, rock, pop, folk—but they're playing it from an album, not a two-and-a-half-minute single like on AM. I had a white-label test pressing of the first Zeppelin album, and I started promoting that to FM radio.

The first place I got the record played was New York City, on WNEW on Alison Steele's nighttime show. I took a test pressing in there and told her it was the new Yardbirds album. I had her play the whole album. I left New York and went to Boston and did the same thing at WBCN, and they went crazy over it. The distributor up there told me he'd only ordered two thousand, so I said, "Man, they're playing the hell out of the test pressing on BCN, maybe you should think about ordering some more!" I think they ended up selling about fifty thousand there.

DANNY GOLDBERG (U.S. press officer for Zeppelin, president of Swan Song in the U.S.)   In the United States, there was a tremendous shift once rock radio became established. The power of critics was reduced by 50 percent overnight because people could hear music themselves, played by DJs who couldn't write and weren't so intellectual and weren't part of any group.

Zeppelin was the first big radio superstar in the rock world, which coincided with WBCN in Boston. They said they owed everything to J.J. Jackson. They didn't say, "We owe everything to *Rolling Stone*." Whereas a couple of years earlier, the Jefferson Airplane would have said, "Thank God for *Rolling Stone!*"

JOHN PAUL JONES   The first *Rolling Stone* review really *did* hurt, because it seemed spiteful. If we were crap and they said we were crap, well, fair enough. But we were really good, and we couldn't understand what the agenda was. *Why* didn't they like us? They could have said, "It's early days, and they'll do better next year." But that review was total damning stuff, and we thought, "What's the problem?" It was galling, but at the same time you felt it was a shame that they didn't get it—that something was getting in the way of them getting it. So you had to have a defensive shield, and unfortunately a good defensive shield defends you against the good stuff as well as the bad stuff.

JOHN MENDELSOHN (reviewer of Led Zeppelin for Rolling Stone)   I don't think anybody paid any particular attention to what I said. My review was a terrible piece of writing and a terrible piece of criticism— I thought Fusion's was very much better than my own. I'd never been a big fan of the blues. It was absolutely devoid of all the things I liked: melody, wit, vocal harmony. At the end of the first song when Robert Plant sang, "I know what it's like to be alone," I thought to myself, "No, he doesn't." He sounded sarcastic and glib, and it just really annoyed me. And that was the best song on the album.

MARIO MEDIOUS   The moment they became successful, all the writers wanted to put down every fucking thing they did. That's what hurt Jimmy's ego. He would say, "Fuck those guys, they don't even play, they can't even write a note, so what the fuck does that mean?" I always said to him, "You can't read your reviews and worry about them—the fans are the most important thing."

DANNY GOLDBERG   Jimmy, particularly, was stung by Mendelsohn's review. There was this generational gap opening up. You had critics who were twenty-three to twenty-five years old, and suddenly they were feeling their mortality. There were these teenagers who were experiencing music in different ways and didn't care so much about what had been cool in 1965. Personally, I never identified with the most opinionated Rolling Stone critics. I was always a bit of a populist. I didn't have the rigid critical ideology.

RICHARD RIEGEL ('70s writer for Creem magazine)   A lot of us really got involved in the blues that the English bands had taught us in the '60s, and—like the way the Animals taught it—we thought the blues should get more bluesy and more black all the time. And Zeppelin come along and not only steal the blues musicians blind but erect this super-blues skyscraper that's as *white* as possible.

ROY CARR (writer for *New Musical Express*)   Led Zeppelin made it without anyone saying, "I've just seen the future of rock 'n' roll, and its name is . . . " The American writers then were totally different than the ones over here. They thought they owned the bands.

JOHN MENDELSOHN   My understanding is that my *Los Angeles Times* review of their live performance at the Rose Palace in Pasadena was more upsetting to them. It was one of those things where the audience was going crazy, and I thought it was excruciating. So they objected to the fact that, in my review, I didn't acknowledge how much the audience loved it. Which I don't think is necessarily the job of a review.

Robert Plant famously threatened me from the stage of the Anaheim Convention Center. I was told by several people that they announced one song by saying that if they got hold of me, they were going to make cauliflower out of my ears.

JIMMY PAGE   Before they saw us in America, there was a blast of publicity, and they heard all about the money being advanced to us by the record company. So the reaction was, "Ah, a capitalist group."

JUNE HARRIS BARSALONA   I think maybe some people felt that the group was selling out. Looking back, it was sour grapes and resentment. You're not playing music so that you can't afford to get on a plane to go to your next gig; you're playing music so that you have a million-selling album. Come on! It *was* all about money, it was just that it was very unchic to *say* so. Bill Graham used to say, "It's not about the money; it's about the money."

BILL GRAHAM (San Francisco rock promoter)   Woodstock told industrial America, "Ah *ha*!" [It] said, "What is that tidal wave? Big business! My God, look at the *money* there."

PAMELA DES BARRES   It might have been very different had they got good reviews in the beginning. They might have been more open to the press and more open to everybody else. But then it wouldn't have become such a strangely dark and enigmatic band.

ROBERT PLANT   The press themselves were a completely different animal. They were beer-swilling, monosyllabic guys who reviewed gigs from the beer tent. I don't think Nick Kent had surfaced, and Lester Bangs and those guys in America—the real poets, if you like—weren't involved in what we're talking about here.

MICHAEL DES BARRES   I always think of David Lee Roth's remark that the reason critics loved Elvis Costello was that they all looked like him. A great metaphysical observation.

PHIL CARSON   The band never had an issue with the British fans. The British journalists were a different story. That was the war that developed, because the journalists never got it. Almost as one, they started a campaign against Zeppelin. You know, "They're big in America, so what?" It was the self-aggrandizement of journalists who wanted to knock something down so they could look good, but they were manifestly wrong.

BRAD TOLINSKI (editor-in-chief of *Guitar World*)   I don't think the critics understood them then, and I don't think they understand them now. There are people so caught up in the Zeppelin myth that they haven't taken time to understand the music.

DAVE LEWIS (publisher of Zeppelin fanzine *Tight But Loose*)   I remember Charlie Gillett once inadvertently took on the might of Peter Grant. He wrote a piece in the *NME* about singles and Led Zep's resistance to them. Grant misread this as criticism of his boys and wrote a complaining letter in the following week's issue. With typical candor, Charlie replied, "Perhaps Led Zeppelin would like to tell me what they would like written about them."

MICK FARREN (singer with the Deviants and writer for the underground press)   The whole intimidating thing with Zeppelin was like something out of *Performance*. It was like the romance between the Krays and rock 'n' roll. Jonathan Green wrote a bad review of *Led Zeppelin II* in *Frendz*, and Grant calls up and says, "I expect you use your fingers for typing, doncha?" He's obviously sitting around in his office with nothing better to do that afternoon, so he calls up and hassles this poor overweight Jewish underground writer. Give me a fucking break.

CHRIS WELCH   Word didn't filter back from the States as quickly as it would do now, so I wasn't as aware of the hostility of American critics toward the band. But I used to wonder why Zeppelin were so anti the American press. The critics over there probably didn't realize they'd paid their dues and come up through the pubs and clubs. It was as if the music was a fait accompli, somehow.

CHRIS CHARLESWORTH (writer and New York correspondent for *Melody Maker* in the '70s)   They were nicer to Chris Welch than to anybody else, so they got him inside from the very beginning and took him to America to see them play at Carnegie Hall.

CHRIS WELCH   We were in the Hilton on Sixth Avenue, and when I woke up the next morning, Jimmy asked if I'd had a good night. I told him I'd just sat in my room and watched television. Turned out they'd arranged to have some hookers and porn films and whips delivered to my room, but the girls had been stopped by the house detective before they got up to my floor. I mean, I barely knew what the word *hooker* meant. Jimmy looked very disappointed.

CAROLINE BOUCHER (writer for *Disc and Music Echo*)   Personally I always looked forward to interviewing them. They were easy, and they were approachable, amenable. I would have a nice meal with them, and they would seem gentlemanly, lovely, nice. We used to hang out at the Golden Egg on Fleet Street. It was the only place you could eat, a terrible old dump.

I remember one interview with Plant. We must have come out of 155 Oxford Street and gone down Carnaby Street for a coffee. And he saw this beautiful sort of see-through shirt. So we went into the shop, and he didn't have any money on him. He said, "Can I have this, please? I can pay you by check." And the shop assistant said, "We don't take checks. Have you got any ID?" So he went and got the first Zeppelin album and took it to the front of the shop.

10

Every Inch of My Love

> He's like a huge golden lion conquering me. My legs cling
> around his waist as we rise and grind into each other.
>
> —Lucille's fantasy about Robert Plant, in Fred and Judy
> Vermorel, *Starlust: The Secret Fantasies of Fans* (1985)

BP FALLON (U.K. press officer for Zeppelin, 1972–1976)   A lot of
bands sing about sex, but Led Zeppelin made sexy, horny music. It *is*
sex. But it's never crass, it's always tasteful.

BILL CURBISHLEY (manager of the Who and later of Jimmy Page and
Robert Plant)   Zeppelin was really about sex, and the Who was more
about intellectual frustration and aggression.

MICHAEL DES BARRES (singer with Swan Song band Detective)   Jimmy
leaves the Yardbirds and hooks up with this blond teenager who just
epitomizes Viking Tolkienesque elfish mythology, all that Celtic
magic—a high priest of the blues singing about Mordor in velvet
pants. Fuck me! It was an incredible potpourri of influences and so
sexy. Jimmy cast that band like a good director.

MARIO MEDIOUS (Atlantic Records promo man, 1965–1972)   After Zeppelin played the Fillmore East, Iron Butterfly had to wait two hours to let the people cool out. Led Zeppelin was a motherfucker on that first show, man. They killed me, Jimmy pulling out that fucking bow and shit. Robert rocking around and screaming and carrying on, with his big old balls down there showing in his tight jeans, all the little chicks around him with their mouths wide open. I went back to Ahmet and said, "Man, they blew the fucking place away."

BEBE BUELL (groupie and girlfriend of Jimmy Page's)   You didn't hear Led Zeppelin on the radio; you heard *about* them from the boys in your class. Usually, it was the little girls who understood first, but in this case, it was not like when you came to school and asked your girlfriends which Beatle they liked best. It was driven by testosterone. I don't know if the music was designed to give boys power and sexual prowess, but I do know that when boys listened to it, they would become extremely cocky and full of themselves.

JAAN UHELSZKI (writer for *Creem* magazine)   They became these proto-alpha types. Men aspired to be them, and women aspired to be *with* them. They used to say that Hendrix onstage would make every woman feel like she'd been raped—and had liked it, which is such a misogynistic thing to say—and Zeppelin made misogyny work for them. It was sex, but it was beyond sex.

To this day, I still feel emotional about Led Zeppelin's sound. When you think about the equation of sex plus drugs plus rock and roll, the drugs were the least interesting part of it. In fact, they didn't *need* the drugs because the other stuff was in place. And then when they had that dark stain of the bad things happening, that only added to it, which was the whole occult part.

BEBE BUELL   Nobody in my group paid much attention to Plant; it was all about Page and Bonham. Even though we'd had Hendrix and Clapton thrust at us, Page and Bonham had an extreme and unique musicianship that had not been seen by too many people.

JAAN UHELSZKI   There was something fragile and almost china doll–like about Page. I mean, you think about him later, and to even imagine that he was unthreatening is pretty naïve. But I guess it harkens back to that whole doe-eyed English masculinity that we all responded to. Back then, he was like the template for English male beauty for teenagers. With Page, it was that mystery, whereas Robert was bigger and in a way more like an American man—he was more *obvious.* You were either a Jimmy girl or a Robert girl; it was almost polarized along Lennon and McCartney lines.

PAMELA DES BARRES   Jimmy was the perfect British rock star, with the red lips and the pale skin. For a woman, androgyny is like embracing *yourself.* There's a safety there, even though the danger comes along with it. They understand you. You can share lip gloss. You can primp with the same hair products and wear the same clothes. Jimmy would leave town and give me his clothes that he'd been wearing, and they'd fit. And he created romance in his relationships. He was totally all encompassing in his lovemaking, so that you were absolutely lost in him. He knew exactly what he was doing. Incredible manipulator of the senses, the emotions, all that stuff. It's pretty sadistic, when you think about it now, but he wanted us to believe the fairytale. I remember Bonzo backstage, saying, "I wouldn't be surprised if I see you in Pangbourne"—Jimmy's actual English world.

MARILYN COLE (wife of Richard Cole)   In Italian, they call it *affascinante*—it's a word that mixes "fascinating" and "charming," and that's what Jimmy was. When you were with him, he was never one to look over his shoulder. His whole attention was on you. For that half an hour or whatever, you were enveloped, you were wrapped in gossamer.

MICHAEL DES BARRES   Robert was Marilyn Monroe, and Jimmy was Hedy Lamarr with a Les Paul.

MAC POOLE (Midlands drummer and friend of Bonham's)   Bonzo used to take the piss out of Percy. He'd say, "It's alright for you, you big fairy, running around getting all the glory; I'm the one doing the fucking work."

PAMELA DES BARRES   They were still men and loaded with testosterone, whether or not they wore lip gloss. They're still doing their manly thing, which is wanting more women than they could possibly copulate with.

GYL CORRIGAN-DEVLIN (friend of Page's and Plant's; traveled on Zeppelin's 1973 U.S. tour)   When Charlotte Martin came along, in our minds it was a little bit like the Yoko-and-John thing. As beautiful as she was, she sort of took Jimmy away from us, and we didn't like that. We felt we were a family at that point.

PAMELA DES BARRES   Jimmy met Charlotte literally on his birthday one week after Christmas 1969, and I heard about it and thought, "This can't be true." But he stopped calling, and when they came to town, he invited me up to his room at the Hyatt House to tell me about it. It was the most gentle explanation of how he'd fallen in love and was going to settle down. He just wanted to let me down easy, which I think was incredibly rare in the world at that time.

• • •

RICHARD COLE (Zeppelin's road manager)   They'd played all the major starting venues in America, but the response wasn't covered in England. And then when we came back, we did a whole range of small venues like Klook's Kleek and Cook's Ferry Inn, and they were sold out within minutes.

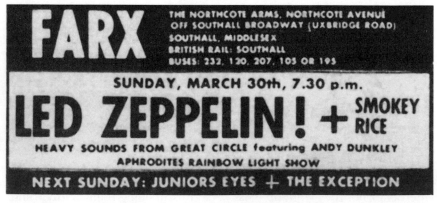

At the Farx Club, Southall, March 1969.

MAC POOLE   John called me and said, "We're down at the Farx Club in Southall," which was a pub where all the blues boys used to get together. Zeppelin had just done the first tour in America, and here they were back in England in a pub.

JIMMY PAGE   When we did shows in England, they were always the shows that the press would come to and your family would come to, and there was that worry about dropping a note, and it was silly, but you go through that. We discussed those aspects of it. But when we went out to the States, we didn't give a fuck and became total showoffs.

ROBERT PLANT   *Led Zeppelin II* was recorded and written mostly on the road, with the idea of using acoustics and developing much more of the textural part of the Led Zeppelin thing. Because if we weren't careful, we were going to end up like Grand Funk Railroad or the James Gang—sort of two-dimensional.

JIMMY PAGE   People couldn't get enough of us, so we started touring on the strength of the first album, and it was tour after tour after tour of America. In-between time, we fitted in a small amount of recording at Olympic, where we did "Whole Lotta Love" and a couple of others, and the rest of the second album was recorded and mixed with Eddie Kramer in New York, and that was that. And we were still touring.

JOHN BONHAM   There was an urgency to being in the States. I remember we went out to the airport to meet our wives, got them back to the hotel, and then went straight back to the studio and did "Bring It on Home." We did a lot that year like that.

EDDIE KRAMER (engineer on *Led Zeppelin II*)   I think they'd cut some tracks in England and one in Vancouver. They traveled around with this bloody great steamer trunk full of all the tapes, and they schlepped that thing around from pillar to post.

They called and said, "We're coming to New York, and do you want to do it?" I said, "Absolutely." We had to cut more tracks, which I did at Juggy Sound, a tiny little studio that had opened in the '50s. We booked A&R Studios to do the overdubs and to do the mixing, so I think we spent maybe a day or two there. I don't remember precisely how many days, but

Page and Plant during a session for *Led Zeppelin II*, Los Angeles, spring 1969. (Chuck Boyd)

Jimmy overdubbed some of his guitar parts with his little Ampeg amp. I know I did a tremendous amount of editing, for instance on "Moby Dick," which was cut together from two or three different studios.

We mixed the album in two days over a weekend, and the results speak for themselves. It's a lovely sounding record, and it set the standard for them for many years to come. That's due to the fact that it was mixed at A&R all in one go, and Jimmy had a particular clear-headed vision about what it should sound like. With "Whole Lotta Love," it's all true about the instinctual moment of both reaching for the reverb sound button or knob to put the reverb on to finalize that little mistake that we all laughed about.

JACK WHITE (singer, writer, and guitarist with the White Stripes) When I was very young, there was a girl down the street who had a tape with "Whole Lotta Love" on it. And I rewound it so many times that there was a fuckup on the tape before the guitar solo. I still think that break is probably some of the greatest guitar notes ever played, if not *the* greatest. Just that little section is so powerful, and it was powerful to me when I was *five years old*.

ROBERT PLANT Jimmy's riffs are the things that everybody goes nuts about. His capacity and ability to take teeny-weeny bits and develop them into huge anthemic moments was stunning. He had great diligence and a big, big gift.

BURKE SHELLEY (bass guitarist with Budgie) Page's sound wasn't that big—a quite scratchy sound, a lot of it. It wasn't really thick and huge, but it was all *punched-out*, you know.

BRAD TOLINSKI (editor of *Guitar World*) Everybody thinks Jimmy's guitar sound is big, and it's actually on the *small* side, to allow room for the drums to breathe and the bass to breathe. It's the nerdy, technical detail that makes this stuff great and makes it sound contemporary. Put on *Beck-Ola* or the other Jeff Beck records from that time, and those things sound awful. Then put on the first two Zeppelin albums, and they sound like something that could have been made last week. It's the overwhelming quality and bigness of the production that sucks you in—and the actual beauty of all the different sorts of guitar sounds.

HENRY SMITH (roadie for Led Zeppelin) Bonzo is one of the few drummers, to this day, who plays drums *like an instrument*. He doesn't just play drums to hear the sound. I could listen to him play by himself and be totally enchanted by what he was doing. He took a lot of rhythm 'n' blues drum licks and put them into rock—which at the time was different. Many times, he would turn and look at me with that little smirky smile, as if to say, "I pulled *that* one off!" And I would think, "Where did you hear that in your brain to even *attempt* it?"

SIMON KIRKE (drummer with Free and Swan Song band Bad Company) I've played drums for nearly forty-five years, and to this day I can't figure out some of the stuff he does.

TERRY MANNING (engineer on *Led Zeppelin III*) Bonzo loved Gene Krupa, and in my opinion, Bonzo was playing the hardest jazz ever, as simply as anyone ever did. He really wasn't bashing like a rock drummer. There was finesse to the bashing, if that makes any sense— hitting hard but with incredible time and feel. He's setting his own tempo, and the others had to follow it. He is more of the percentage of the total sound and production and feel of that band than any drummer in any other band. He made the drums important *all the time.*

Jimmy once said to me, "Our time is different, and I don't think the general public or other musicians will ever get what we do or catch up to it." Maybe that sounds egotistical, but I don't think it is. You hear so many other bands that tried to sound like that and had the Robert Plant hair and everything, but none of them had their own sound.

GUY PRATT (bassist with Page's post-Zeppelin band Coverdale/Page) There is stuff that Jimmy does that as a musician you just can't count. Under no circumstances look at his legs. Look at anyone else's legs, and they are tapping time. Jimmy's legs give you no clue.

EDDIE KRAMER   I did "Ramble On" at Juggy's. I'd have to listen to it again, but it was something very silly and spur-of-the-moment. Whether it's Bonzo's knees or beer cans or his head, I can't remember.

ROBERT PLANT   By then, I had developed a wanderlust, and that song was really just a reflection of myself.

PAMELA DES BARRES   Robert was so young and innocent. Singing about all these groovy fairy things with that crazy heavy music—it's an outrageous combination, so it just all fit and worked and touched the girls with his sweet words and that dangerous dark scary shit that Jimmy was doing. The dark and the light.

ROBERT PLANT   During the making of *Led Zeppelin II*, we went to the old Del-Fi and Gold Star studios in L.A. We were always on that trail.

KIM FOWLEY (L.A. producer and scenester)   Del-Fi was at the corner of Selma and Vine. The studio had been bought by a genius engineer called Chris Huston and renamed Mystic Sound. There was a bank next door, and allegedly they would use the empty bank vault or hallways for that tremendous echo.

CHRIS HUSTON (owner of L.A. studio Mystic Sound)   We did the tracks live, with Plant standing in the middle of the room with a hand-held microphone. You can hear that at the end of "The Lemon Song," where Plant sings, "floor floor floor"—that echo was recorded in real time.

Chris Huston and engineer Doug Moody outside Mystic Sound Studios,
Los Angeles, in 1968. (Chris Huston Collection)

MARIE DIXON (wife of Chess blues legend Willie Dixon)   Around
1979, my late daughter Shirley discovered the recording of "Whole
Lotta Love" at a friend's house on the North Side. She was convinced
it was one and the same thing as my husband's song "You Need Love."
Willie had a publishing company, Arc Music out of New York City,
that was supposed to monitor it. You would think they would have
been on top of that, but they didn't care. He was pretty happy that
they'd recorded "Bring It on Home," never knowing they would take
another song that wasn't popularly known and give a new title to it.

DON SNOWDEN (biographer of Willie Dixon)   Willie would never have
heard "Whole Lotta Love" because he wouldn't have been listening to
a rock station, and his management people would never have heard the
Muddy version of "You Need Love" to make the connection. And almost
no one knew of "You Need Love," because it had only been on an early
'60s Chess single in the U.S., before us white kids knew blues existed.
    What I remember finding out is that both "You Shook Me" and
"You Need Love" *did* come out on an EP in England or Europe in
1962, and that's almost certainly where the Zeppelin crew would have

heard it. Giorgio Gomelsky said Willie was leaving taped copies of songs with him in 1963, during the first American Folk Blues Festival gigs in the U.K., and it's hard to believe that Page wasn't part of that circle, given the Yardbirds connection.

The Small Faces' version is credited to Marriott-Lane but is almost identical to the sound of the Muddy track with the organ—not to mention throwing in a verse's worth of "Land of 1000 Dances." Plant really copped Marriott's vocal stylings as his launching pad. Poetic justice, I suppose.

STEVE MARRIOTT (singer with the Small Faces and Humble Pie) "Whole Lotta Love" was nicked off our album. We did a gig with the Yardbirds, which Robert was at, and Jimmy Page asked me what that number was that we did. "'You Need Loving,'" I said. "It's a Muddy Waters thing." Which it really is, so they both knew it. After we broke up, they took it and revamped it. Good luck to them. It was only old Percy who'd had his eyes on it. He sang it the same, phrased it the same; even the stops at the end were the same. They just put a different rhythm to it.

ROBERT PLANT   Page's riff was Page's riff. It was there before anything else. I just thought, "Well, what am I going to sing?" That was it, a nick, now happily paid for. At the time, there was a lot of conversation about what to do. It was decided that it was so far away in time and influence . . . well, you only get caught when you get successful.

JEFF BECK   There was a lot of conniving going on back then: change the rhythm, change the angle, and it's yours. We got paid peanuts for what we were doing, and I couldn't give a shit about anybody else.

ED BICKNELL (former manager of Dire Straits)   Mick Jagger famously said, "We had the best of Chess"—in the sense that they'd pinched everything and not paid for it. The same went for Zeppelin, because both Mick and Jimmy found the idea of money going out to be really quite traumatic.

ROBERT PLANT   Keep your head down and don't say anything, ha ha ha! If you read *Deep Blues* by Robert Palmer, you'll see that we did what everybody else was doing. When Robert Johnson was doing "Preaching Blues," he was really taking Son House's "Preacher's Blues" and remodeling it.

JOHN PAUL JONES   I don't know, the whole question of the appropriation of black music by white musicians is just so . . . the whole thing is that nobody really *owns* any music. There's a lot of white church music in black music. Anybody who can make music is affected by what's going round. They're all materials to be used—to make more music.

CHARLES SHAAR MURRAY (writer for *New Musical Express* in the '70s and '80s)   Nick Kent told me that when he did his first-ever Jimmy Page interview, he raised the point that many alleged Page-Plant songs—notably, "Whole Lotta Love," "Bring It on Home," "The Lemon Song," "Black Mountain Side," and "In My Time of Dying"—are either traditional or else straight lifts from the likes of Willie Dixon. Page got extremely defensive.

NICK KENT (writer for *New Musical Express*)   People like Charlie Murray didn't like Led Zeppelin and were morally offended that they stole songs from his old blues heroes. He didn't get that blues is a very malleable form, and one way of customizing it isn't necessarily irrelevant or sacrilegious.

MARIE DIXON   Willie took Atlantic to court. There was a settlement out of court, but there was no significant money to Willie from record sales. He went to his grave feeling that he was not represented properly. You probably read somewhere where it was seven million dollars, but none of that happened. Not one million, not *close* to one million. It was very disappointing to Willie, but he said he didn't have time to be angry with people. He never carried any bitterness. I believe he passed away as a very happy person.

JIMMY PAGE   I don't know what the outcome was. I haven't made any court appearances, personally. I don't know. I mean, I *might* know. It's probably on file somewhere. I'm just not interested. You should ask Robert these things, because I didn't write the words, did I?

PAMELA DES BARRES   I remember sitting in between Jimmy and Robert. *Led Zeppelin II* was about to come out, and they were working on the order of the songs. I was just sitting there, knowing that history was being made and I was right in the middle of it.

EDDIE KRAMER   One has to think of *Zeppelin II* as a watershed moment. It took the world by storm because, sonically, nothing had been done like that before. It was an amazingly powerful record. Even today, though it doesn't have the sonic depth of what we can do now, it still kicks everybody's ass.

There are a few reasons, I think. One, the band was very united, and all the musicians thought as a unit. Two, the immense power of Bonham's drumming, which drives the whole thing. Three, Page is brilliant in terms of his direction and interpretive qualities, and he's got this amazing ability to absorb all these influences—blues, British folk music, and all that stuff—into one cohesive whole. Four, John Paul is the mastermind behind the scenes, sewing it all together. And five, Robert's voice and his lyrics—you don't get a better combination in rock 'n' roll. It was the dark star of the rock world, in a positive, not a negative, way. Immense power.

It's more than just the sound. The ability to go from extremely quiet low dynamics to an immensely powerful rush of noise carries a tremendous amount of weight. Plus, you've got the huge sexuality of Robert—he's up front doing his thing. It's like a panty-wetter all night.

PHIL CARSON (head of Atlantic Records in the U.K.)   I remember putting on the acetate of the second album and the sound of "Whole Lotta Love" just *erupting* from the speakers. I was scared to death by the middle section, thinking, "What the hell is going *on* here?"

CHRIS WELCH (writer for *Melody Maker*)   Phil Carson had been a supermarket manager before playing bass with the Springfields. I think he was working for MGM-Verve when Ahmet hired him to be head of Atlantic in the U.K. I think he would love to have been Zeppelin's manager. He was always a little bit in the footsteps of Peter.

PHIL CARSON   It was Nesuhi Ertegun who actually hired me. As an ex-musician, I of course knew who Jimmy and John Paul were from the session circuit, but I'd never worked directly with them. When I

"The ears and eyes for Nesuhi and Ahmet": Phil Carson with Zeppelin, backstage at the L.A. Forum, September 4, 1970. (Michael Ochs Archives/Getty Images)

got the job, I think they were relieved that someone they knew had been a musician had got the job as their day-to-day guy.

ROY CARR (writer for *New Musical Express*)   People liked Phil, whether it was the Stones or Zeppelin. He never bullshitted anybody, and he was always ready to muck in. He wasn't sort of, "I'm from the record company"; he *knew* all the musicians.

MARILYN COLE   Phil was really sharp, no messing about. He and Peter had a great respect for each other, and both of them had huge respect for Ahmet. Carson was good with people; he knew how to work relationships. With all the madness that was going on, he kept his ground. He was a character, like Ahmet and Peter were characters. After these guys, the business was just run by accountants.

MIKE APPLETON (producer of BBC's *Old Grey Whistle Test*)   Phil was the eyes and ears for Nesuhi and Ahmet. The thing about him was that he didn't mind being *used* by bands. He didn't see that as demeaning. He accepted that it was part of the job to run around after them. It was one of the cogs that drove the machine.

PHIL CARSON   They used to forget that I was the record company guy. Richard Cole had a stamp made up that said, "Atlantic Records will pay." And he would just stamp any bill at the Speakeasy. So I had my own stamp made that said, "Charge artist."

JERRY GREENBERG (general manager of Atlantic Records, 1969–1980) In America, "Whole Lotta Love" was getting played like crazy on FM stations, but it ran five minutes or something. I called Peter, and I was like, "Can we get Jimmy to do an edit? I think I can get play on some top 40 stations, but they're not going to play a record that's five minutes long." He said, "Greenberg, he's not going to do it." I said, "Well, what if I do an edit and you approve it?"

PHIL CARSON   After we put "Whole Lotta Love" out, I received this irate phone call from Peter: "'Ere, we don't *do* singles." So I was summoned to his office, and I said, "But this is how you promote records." "Not Led Zeppelin records you don't." I was told I had to withdraw them. I think about three thousand got out.

ROY CARR   Everybody had hit singles, and Zeppelin didn't. If you said, "Led Zeppelin," people would say, "Whole Lotta Love." But that was it, unless you were a devoted fan. Whereas with the Stones, the Who, you could rattle off the singles. This whole thing of not releasing singles made them a bit more mysterious.

• • •

PHIL CARSON   The first time I met Steve Weiss was at Madison Square Garden, where he physically threw someone out who was serving him a writ.

CHRIS WELCH   Steve met us at Kennedy airport and got in the limo with us. He said, in a very Bronx-type accent, "I just heard the new album, Jimmy, it's a masterpiece." And Jimmy said, "Don't gimme that New York bullshit." I was in awe that anyone would dare speak to an American lawyer like that.

SAM AIZER (artist relations, Swan Song in the U.S.)   In the Atlantic archives, there's a picture of Page, Beck, Peter, and Steve Weiss standing together. Peter is wearing a suit, he doesn't have a beard yet: he's a businessman from England wearing the only suit he owns. Meanwhile, Steve is dressed up like Jimi Hendrix, with, like, a sash and a vest and long hair. You look at it and think, "This guy must be in the *band*."

SHELLEY KAYE (assistant to Steve Weiss)   I remember Steve going to a meeting at Madison Square Garden in a lime-green paisley suit. It was hilarious. Actually, it was pretty atrocious by today's standards.

JANINE SAFER (artist relations, Swan Song in the U.S.)   Steve didn't look like anybody in New York. He was a short man, skinny as a rail, and he wore tight blue jeans with a big old honkin' Texas cowboy belt, Nudie shirts with sequins, cowboy boots, and this huge mane of silver-flecked hair.

SHELLEY KAYE   He and I used to fight a lot. We would get into it and have some real arguments, because he just drove me crazy sometimes. But he was a very, very smart guy. He got the business side of it.

JOHN PAUL JONES   The main thing I remember is that we worked like dogs. We didn't stop working, right the way through 1969 and 1970. There was *constant* touring.

RICHARD COLE   You could only work New York, Boston, Detroit, Chicago, Cleveland, and maybe pick up a date in Texas. And then you usually had to go out to the West Coast to do L.A. and San Francisco, and that was your whack. Plus, you could only do weekends. So it could take six or seven weeks to do a tour.

JOHN PAUL JONES   People were going to sleep onstage, especially in America. You'd see bands sort of wandering around looking at each other and saying, "What shall we play next?" And we just came onstage and went blam-blam-blam, three or four numbers, and people sat up in shock. You didn't notice that there wasn't a set as such, because the power came from the music.

A lot of people say to me, "You can just see the communication onstage. . . . Why isn't *my* band like that?" Our priority was to make *Led Zeppelin* sound great, and if that meant playing two notes in a bar and shutting up for a bit, then that's what it took. You had the big picture in your mind and in your ears all the time.

JACK CALMES (cofounder of Showco sound and lighting company) We did a one-off using the Showco sound system with Zeppelin sometime in May 1970, and afterward, Robert Plant said, "Fuck, I hate these systems we're using. What about those guys from Texas?" We picked up their tour in the summer of 1970 and were never away from them after that.

JOE JAMMER (Chicago blues guitarist and Zeppelin roadie) In those early days—before Charles and Henry made the scene—the band was just drinking. Bonham was drinking the most. You had to keep up with him. He was the regular guy who'd smack you on the back so hard, it would knock you forward.

BILL HARRY (Zeppelin's first U.K. press officer) I was at the Revolution club one night, and I got a call from Bonzo. He said, "I want to come down and have a drink with you." I said, "Where are you?" He said, "Birmingham." I said, "You must be joking. The club shuts at two o'clock." Ten to two, he arrived. I said, "The bar shuts in ten minutes." So he ordered fifty lagers.

MAC POOLE Bonzo hated the fawners and hangers-on, even in Birmingham. I remember this agent came into a club one night and did the big, "Hey, John!" because he'd heard Zep had made a few quid. John just went, "Fuck off!" and smacked him on the nose. This was a guy who'd always kept hold of the money and never paid anybody. And we all applauded John. The guy got what he deserved.

SHELLEY KAYE Bonzo was very gregarious and very happy. He wanted to sleep with me, and I wasn't interested. I knew they were married, and I was never a groupie. In those days, sexual harassment was not a defined term. Plus, it was just different then. It was a much more innocent time.

ELLEN SANDER (rock writer for the *Saturday Review* and other publications)   There was always a bit of tension. It's not easy having an embedded journo and photographer. And a female journo was not a good fit for them, as it turned out. I got on great with Peter Grant and spent some extremely pleasant social time with him and his wife. I remember them fondly, but Richard Cole was a pain in the ass.

PHIL CARLO (roadie for Bad Company, tour manager on the last Zeppelin tour)   The whole groupie thing was massive. The proper ones—Penny, the Flying Garter girls, Sweet Connie from Little Rock—were the nicest people you could come across. You'd trust them with your life, and they'd look out for you as well. You'd see them year after year, and there was a mutual respect. I remember Penny Lane, who was the head Flying Garter girl, saying to me, "This is bizarre. We have letters of application from girls all over America with a CV." It was like a corporate business.

"SWEET CONNIE" HAMZY (Arkansas groupie of wide renown)   Groupies went back all the way to Sinatra. Power and glamour have always attracted women. When you're a teenager, you're either a cheerleader or in a school band or on the football team, and a lot of people like me didn't fit into any of those molds. So I decided to become a groupie because all those people—the cheerleaders and all of them at my school—thought they were so cool, and I thought I'd show them what cool was really about.

Miss Pamela was, like, the first. She led the way and paved the way for the Butter Queen and then Cynthia Plaster-Caster, and I sort of followed in their footsteps. I decided I wanted to be one, and if I was going to do it, I didn't want to do it half-assed. I wanted to be one of the biggest ones I could be. No matter how many people I had to blow to do it.

PAMELA DES BARRES   Led Zeppelin got to L.A., and it was literally like falling down the rabbit hole. Cynthia Plaster-Caster had a Zeppelin poster on her wall, and they were so gorgeous. She told me how dangerous they all were and how they had this terrible reputation of abusing women and just being wild.

HENRY SMITH   L.A. had a mystique. It's warm, and when you get in the warmth, you kind of let your hair down. Drugs were easy to get, so when we arrived, it was like, "Okay, we've finished the gloomy part of the U.S., which is anything between Cleveland and Denver, where there's nothing to do."

BIG JIM SULLIVAN (London session guitarist and member of Tom Jones' touring band)   When I joined Tom Jones in 1969, every time we got to L.A. we'd always run into either Jimmy or John Paul or one of the lads. The first time I went to the Whisky, Jimmy and John were sitting at the table, and Jimmy was squirming about quite unnaturally. I looked under the table, and there was a girl there.

JACK CALMES   Once, when they were playing Dallas, we put Zeppelin into the Cabana Hotel, and they got thrown out after two or three days. So we thought we'd rent them a house in the country. They were out at this ranch house, and it had a swimming pool, and all these groupies were out there with them. The Butter Queen was kind of like a madam, and they all had their tits out, riding on their shoulders in the pool. Barbara Cope was the Butter Queen's real name. She was a hound herself, but she was the organizer of the girls and would tell them what was needed.

At this point, the Christian owner of the ranch and his two little daughters pull up because they want to meet the band. So we all got thrown out of that place, too.

ROBERT PLANT   I was twenty-one, and I was going, "Fucking hell, I *want* some of that. And then I want some of *that*, and then can you get me some Charley Patton and some Troy Shondell? And who's that girl over there and what's in that packet?" There was no perception of taste, no decorum. It was a sensory outing.

JIMMY PAGE   There was a certain amount of hedonism that was involved, and why not? We were young, and we were growing up. People say, "I grew up to Led Zeppelin." And I say, "So did I."

11

In the Misty Mountains

I live for my dream, and a pocketful of gold.

—Led Zeppelin, "Over the Hills and Far Away"

JOHN PAUL JONES It was much harder to get anywhere in England. We toured England quite a bit and worked very hard, and the press kind of wasn't interested in us at all; 1970 was the first time we felt we got recognized for what we were doing. Up till then, it felt like we were big in America but not in England. Maybe the Albert Hall was the first "Here we are" type of show in England. Here was a band that could fill the Albert Hall, but where did they come from?

ROBERT PLANT It was an absolute shock when I saw the Albert Hall stuff on *DVD*. It's kind of cute and coy, and you see all that naïveté and the absolute wonder of what we were doing and the freshness of it, because the whole sort of stereotypical rock singer thing hadn't kicked in for me. I was just hanging on for dear life, really. I was playing and singing and weaving my way through the three greatest players of that time, and I was coquettish, coy, shy—a bit embarrassed, really.

RICHARD WILLIAMS (writer for *Melody Maker* in the '70s, later the paper's editor) I interviewed Robert in the back of a Rolls-Royce going to Heathrow, and we talked about the Buffalo Springfield and the Flying Burrito Brothers and all the West Coast music he loved. In the piece, I said something like, "Despite being the singer with this heavy group, he actually likes good music." Not long after that, I saw them at the Albert Hall, and Jimmy Page approached me in the interval, with Peter Grant glowering behind him. Jimmy said, "Are you trying to break up my band?"

BILL HARRY (Zeppelin's first U.K. press officer) I only saw Peter appear frightening once, and that was backstage at the Albert Hall. There were some jobsworths who were saying, "You can't do this, you can't do that." He appeared very frightening, and he terrorized them.

JACK CALMES (cofounder and head of Showco sound and lighting company) The first thing anybody would tell you when you went into Frank Barsalona's office in 1970 and you had a Led Zeppelin date was, "Watch out for Peter Grant. You'd better not have anybody selling T-shirts or taking pictures."

ANDY JOHNS (engineer on Led Zeppelin *II*, *III*, and the untitled fourth album) I remember walking down the street with Peter, and he went, "Hang on a second, Andy, we have to go in here . . . got a bit of work to do." And he went in, and they'd been selling bootlegs, and he was trying to stick something up the guy's ass, and it wasn't working because he had jeans on. So he wrapped it round his head instead.

CHRIS WELCH (writer for *Melody Maker*) I witnessed Peter destroying a bootlegger's equipment in Germany. The guy was outraged and fetched a cop, who took one look at Peter and walked away.

MARIO MEDIOUS (Atlantic Records promo man, 1965–1972) On those first tours, we'd be the first off the planes. All the guys who were driving the forklifts and picking up the baggage would call the band "fuckin' faggots" and shit. Robert was a big guy, he'd knock 'em the fuck out. I would go over and jump right in the middle of it, saying,

Grant and Bonham
indulging their shared
passion for vintage
cars, Los Angeles, 1969.
(Chuck Boyd)

"These guys are in first class, and you guys are driving forklifts, so what kind of shit is *that*? They can buy and sell your ass."

JACK CALMES Nobody, other than Elvis, had ever chartered a plane before. Peter and the band wanted to base themselves in cities so they didn't have to get up early in the morning and fly to the gigs, so I found them a charter service that had a field in Dallas. The first one was a fan-jet Falcon that seated six, and there was a stewardess. God knows what they put her through on that little plane.

ROBERT PLANT The brutality of the police in the Southern states in the early '70s was unbelievable. In Memphis, the police brutalized the fans every time they stood up, so I did a Roger Daltrey spin with the mic and hit a cop on the back of the head. That caused a few problems. In those days, we regularly fell foul of paranoid prejudice. I was spat at in the face because I was seen as antiestablishment. We were always potentially in trouble in those areas, just by breathing.

TERRY MANNING (engineer on *Led Zeppelin III*)   The manager of the Mid-South Coliseum in Memphis was a guy called Bubba Bland, who ran it with an iron fist and didn't cotton to those foreigners coming in there. As soon as "Whole Lotta Love" started up, the whole crowd was jumping and screaming—the piece was just throbbing. Bubba pulled a handgun on Peter behind the stage and said, "Make these people sit down, or I will cut the power and everything will be over." So Peter called Robert over, and Robert went back to the mic and tried to calm everybody down. Then the band went into "Communication Breakdown," and everybody was right back up again.

I went backstage at the end, and it was just Peter and Richard and the four guys and me. They were standing there in the dressing room, saying, "Man, America may be cute, but it's just not for us." They had been shot at in Texas the week before, and their limo was actually hit by a bullet between Dallas and Fort Worth. I apologized on behalf of the city of Memphis and on behalf of the South, but they were very upset and never played Memphis again.

JIMMY PAGE   It wasn't until the spring of 1970 that we actually had a real break. That break was only probably a couple of months, but to us it seemed an eternity, because we'd been going nonstop for eighteen months. Robert had this place in Wales that he'd been to with his parents in the past, and he said, "Do you fancy going down there?" I said, "It would do me a lot of good to get out to the countryside." Robert's wife and his daughter were there, and Carmen was only nine months old at the time. It was quite a magical time all around.

JOHN PAUL JONES   A lot of Jimmy and Robert's friendship came out of the fact that they traveled around together during times when we were not on tour. Whereas John and I went home to our families, they went off writing or whatever.

BENJI LeFEVRE (Zeppelin sound technician, 1973–1980)   I think Robert and Jimmy realized they could make even more money than Jones and Bonzo, because they were the main writers. And that drove a bit of a wedge in there that pulled *them* closer together, which was why they used to go off on expeditions and try to expand their musical horizons.

Robert Plant returns to Bron-yr-Aur, September 18, 2003. (Art Sperl)

ROBERT PLANT [Bron-yr-Aur] had no power, no services, and was on the side of a mountain. It was usually pissing down with rain. We had beautiful women with us, one each, an old English army jeep outside, and a blue-eyed Collie. They'd just invented the cassette machine with speakers, so during the sexual act—with the women, not the dog—we could play the tape really loud.

CLIVE COULSON (Zeppelin roadie and tour manager for Bad Company) It was freezing when we arrived. We collected wood for the open-hearth fire, which heated a range with an oven on either side. We had candles, and I think there were gaslights. We fetched water from a stream and heated it on the hot plates for washing—a bath was once a week in Machynlleth at the Owen Glendower pub.

Me and Sandy [McGregor] were the cooks, bottle-washers, and general slaves. Pagey was the tea man. Plant's speciality was posing and telling people how to do things. No, everyone mucked in, really. I wouldn't take any of that superior shit. They were wonderful people to work for, normal blokes, they weren't treated as gods. I'm not sure who got the job of cleaning out the chemical toilet.

JIMMY PAGE It was one of those days after a long walk, and we were setting back to the cottage. We had a guitar with us. It was a tiring walk coming down a ravine, and we stopped and sat down. I played the tune [of "That's the Way"], and Robert sang a verse straight off. We had a tape recorder with us.

ROBERT PLANT In amongst it all, when Jimmy and I set off for the Welsh mountains, was the question, what sort of ambition did we have? And where was it all going? Did we want world domination and all that stuff?

We didn't really have anything to do with the Stones or the Beatles or anybody, but we went to Wales and lived on the side of a hill and wrote those songs and walked and talked and thought and went off to the abbey where they hid the Grail. We were letting ourselves in after dark to places of Celtic historical interest, and no matter how cute and comical and sad it might be now to look back at, it gave us so much energy because we were really close to something. My heart was so light and happy. It was the beginning of a new era altogether. At that time and that age, 1970 was the biggest blue sky I ever saw.

SALLY WILLIAMS (girlfriend of Bonham's drum roadie Mick Hinton) There was one time when they were at Olympic Studios, and there'd been a screw-up with the hotels. So Robert stayed the night in my flat in Holland Park. We sat and talked about Wales—because I was from Wales and he had just got his farm there.

I thought, "This is such a different person. I wonder how many people see that when he's prancing around onstage, when he's that god that everybody's adoring." He was obviously well-read, and he knew more about Welsh mythology than I did. And then he said, "I think I'll turn in. I've got to go back in the studio tomorrow." And that was it. A total gentleman.

ROBERT PLANT I was very content with the environment where I came from, though it never moved that much from the time of my late teens. The people around me that I knew were quite stimulating. They'd been to Afghanistan. They went across that route to India and came back with carpets in vans stuffed with bags full of dope. There was a subterranean condition all around the Welsh borders. There was a whole deal going down then that was really interesting.

HENRY SMITH (Zeppelin roadie)   I remember staying overnight many times at Jennings Farm, which Robert bought in 1970. At that time, only three or four rooms were being used, because the others were being renovated. Robert had a goat called Major and a dog called Strider. Major used to come into the house like a dog or a cat. The only rooms that were really used were their bedroom, the kitchen, and this long, narrow room that had a little fireplace in it. That was where we would sit and listen to Moby Grape and Fairport Convention.

ROBERT PLANT   By that time, we'd really become good friends with the Fairports and the Incredible String Band, and Roy Harper was on the scene. There was quite a lot of moving around, and it was interesting, really. The places the Fairports and the String Band were coming from were places we loved very much. The Zeppelin thing was moving into that area in its own way. It was part bluff and part absolute ecstasy—going from "You Shook Me" to "That's the Way." I actually relaxed enough to start weaving a melody that was acceptable without it having to have that blues-based thing going on.

DAVE PEGG (former bandmate of Bonham's, bassist with Fairport Convention)   When I joined the Fairports, we made an album called *Full House,* and I took the album over to show Bonzo because he'd given me the Zeppelin one, and I thought, "I've made it. I'm in a proper band now." He phoned me up a few weeks later and said, "It's great, mate. I really like it." I took Dave Swarbrick over, and we got there and Bonham said, "Listen to this, Peggy." He'd got his son Jason a miniature drum kit, and he put *Full House* on, and Jason played along with it, and he got it all.

· · ·

Bonzo behind the bar at West Hagley, with Fairport Convention's Dave Swarbrick (left), Swarbrick's girlfriend Vivienne, and Dave Pegg. (Courtesy of Dave Pegg)

ANDY JOHNS   My brother Glyn got me a gig at Morgan Studios, which was this new tiny place in Willesden. There are two songs on *Led Zeppelin II* from Morgan, but they weren't the cool tunes. I must have done okay because next thing I got a call. I think Pagey enjoyed working with me because he figured he could control me.

HENRY SMITH   Andy was a joy to work with. He was such a nice guy; it was like he was your brother.

ANDY JOHNS   I suggested we used the Stones mobile, which was the first mobile in Europe, and I suggested going to Mick Jagger's house. Pagey is a wise fellow, and he doesn't like to expend money when he doesn't have to. "How much would that cost?" "Well, the truck's about £1,000 a week, and Mick's house is about £1,000 a week." "I'm not paying Mick Jagger £1,000 a week! I'll find somewhere better than that." So he found this old mansion in Hampshire, and we went down there, and it was somewhat seedy. There was stuffing coming out of the couch, springs coming out of the bed, but it wasn't a bad place. It had a nice fireplace, and I was bonking the cook.

Headley Grange, Hampshire, in 1973. (Richard Haines/Genesis Pictures)

RICHARD COLE Headley Grange was found by Peter's secretary Carol Browne, who used to read magazines like *The Lady* and saw an advert for it. I was dispatched down there to see if it was suitable and if it had enough rooms and if they'd be able to record there.

It was a bit damp and cold. Jimmy had a room right at the top that was haunted, I'm sure of it. They recorded in the worst fucking places imaginable, and I don't know whether it was because in the back of Jimmy's mind, he thought, "If I can make the outside surroundings as unpleasant as possible, they'll get on with it."

ANDY JOHNS Pagey would come up with ideas that you'd never heard before. He was very much into tunings back then, and it really worked. It wasn't like he was in total control of the situation, because John Paul was just as great a musician as he was and would also come up with super ideas. But Pagey would spend more time in the control room with me.

JOHN PAUL JONES What happened with Zeppelin was very organic. We didn't *feel* a need to chill out, there *was* a need to chill out, and we did—we just didn't think about it first. You find yourself with a bit more time, and you sit down with some acoustic instruments, and you start exploring. Jimmy always had acoustic guitars around, and he often would play things on acoustic. To me, the riffs sound the same on acoustic as they do on electric; it's only the tones that change.

I'd bought a mandolin on tour in America, and I just started playing it. And as soon as I get an instrument, I want to start using it. And we were probably listening to more Joni Mitchell by then, anyway, plus, you know, people like Fairport. I probably learned my first mandolin tunes from *Liege and Lief*. Literally it was sitting around a fire at Headley and picking things up and trying things out. It was never, "Okay, we've done heavy, now we should look at soft."

JONI MITCHELL (high priestess of L.A. singer-songwriters) Led Zeppelin was very courageous and outspoken about liking my music, but others wouldn't admit it. My market was women, and for many years the bulk of my audience was black, but straight white males had a problem with my music. They would come up to me and say, "My girlfriend really likes your music," as if they were the wrong demographic.

ROY HARPER I remember "Immigrant Song," "Celebration Day," and "Since I've Been Loving You" being played at gigs. And they became staples of the Zeppelin set. "That's the Way" was probably Robert finding himself, right at the beginning of his own real writing. If you stand back and look at that album, it really is like their first record.

ROBERT PLANT "Immigrant Song" was supposed to be powerful *and* funny. I was in Iceland, for Christ's sake, and it was light all day, and it was a hoot. People go, "Led Zeppelin had a sense of humor?" But I guess with a riff as relentless as that . . .

KIM FOWLEY (L.A. producer and scenester) Led Zeppelin were both *dangerous* and *spiritual*. They get you with all that maudlin melancholy acoustic music and all the mythical stuff from Wales, but then they have the Willie Dixon–derived blues stuff going on at the same time. The mystery kept people coming to the live shows, and they got to read meanings into the lyrics that weren't there. It was brilliant management. Peter Grant was a genius.

NICK KENT (writer for *New Musical Express*)   Zeppelin had mainly been playing in America, so the Bath festival was very important. They knew they were going to get a big crowd, and they wanted to show that they were now one of the biggest groups in the world.

PETER GRANT   Bath was a turning point in recognition for us. . . . I remember Jonesy arriving by helicopter with Julie Felix and Mo, and we had to get the Hell's Angels to help us get them on site. I'd made contact with the Hell's Angels in Cleveland with the Yardbirds, so we had no bother with them.

ROY CARR (writer for *New Musical Express*)   There were so many big names at Bath—Zappa, Pink Floyd—but Zeppelin came on and it was one of those magic moments where a band just *connects*. They seemed to have all the dynamics you'd expect from an *American* band. They were just on fire.

NICK KENT   When you went to festivals, if the Who or Led Zeppelin were on the bill, the other groups pretty much might as well not have turned up. I mainly went along to see all the West Coast bands, and most of them were very disappointing because they couldn't *project*. They would lock into themselves and just sort of jam. Led Zeppelin were *all about* projecting; they'd worked it out.

AUBREY POWELL (sleeve designer for Zeppelin albums from *Houses of the Holy* to *In Through the Out Door*)   I looked down from the stage at dusk, and everywhere there were little campfires with people wandering through the crowd like ethereal fairies. It was a mystical gathering of tribes, exactly as they describe it in books. Suddenly, Zeppelin come onstage and it's BANG!! Jimmy's there in his long coat and farmer's hat, and I'm going, "Fuck!" It was so cool that this brilliant guitarist was wearing that old overcoat.

ROY HARPER   I was asked to go to Bath by the guys running the festival to help fill out the bill. While I was in the general backstage area, a guy approached me and asked me whether I could play "Blackpool," an instrumental track from my first record. When I'd finished, he thanked me and made complimentary comments. I didn't think that much about it, except I thought the pants he was wearing were too short.

About an hour after I'd played, a band came onto the stage and were tuning up and getting ready to play. I recognized the guitarist as the man who'd asked me to play the instrumental, although he was now wearing a gray tweed overcoat and a hat. The first song was very powerful, but the third song pinned me down. It was "Dazed and Confused" and it was incredibly moving, particularly because I began to realize that most of the young women around me were standing up involuntarily, with tears running down their faces. They couldn't help themselves, and neither could I.

I immediately recognized that I was at a world event. This was going to be planetary. There was no way that young people everywhere were not going to be forever attracted to this.

ROBERT PLANT   Somebody had to have a wry sense of humor and a perspective [that] stripped ego instantly. As we couldn't get Zappa, Harper is a marvelous man and a crucial chum. Despite him being a sage, poet, and muse, that's not to say he didn't occasionally enjoy some of the Led Zeppelin by-products—like the occasional blowjob! No, no, not true! Alongside Richard Cole, they were quite a duo.

JIMMY PAGE   *Stormcock* was a fabulous album [that] didn't sell anything. Also, they wouldn't release [Roy Harper's] albums in America for quite a long time. For that, I just thought, "Well, hats off to you." Hats off to anybody who sticks by what they think is right and has the courage not to sell out. We did a whole set of country blues and traditional blues numbers that Robert suggested. But ["Hats Off to (Roy) Harper"] was the only one we put on the record.

ANDY JOHNS   We finished *Led Zeppelin III* at Island and Olympic. At Olympic, we had this fabulous mixer and the gear really worked. It was somewhat intimidating because they would play so fucking loud.

In a small space like that, the sound pressure builds up and stops other frequencies from happening.

DIGBY SMITH (tape operator on Island sessions for the third and fourth Zeppelin albums) Zeppelin used Island's Studio One at Basing Street extensively for *III* and *IV*. The room was massive, you could get a seventy-piece orchestra in there. The sound was cavernous and reverberant and live; it wasn't a tiny little den. The problem was controlling the live-ness of it, so the sound was heavily compressed by Andy. It seemed like whenever he was at the desk, everything got bigger and louder: the excitement levels rose. The quality of the sound he could create and the speed with which he worked really impressed me. The confidence he exuded fed through to the band. If George Martin was the fifth Beatle, then Andy was the fifth member of Zeppelin at that point.

ANDY JOHNS One night during the third album sessions, Coley was going out to get fish and chips, and Page said, "Can you get us some cocaine as well?" I went, "Excuse me. Cocaine? If you chaps bring cocaine into this, I will just go home." This is 1970, and I'm twenty years old, and I thought cocaine was the drug of the devil.

GLYN JOHNS (engineer on first Zeppelin album) I love my brother to bits, and I think he's fucking brilliant at what he does: if you want to talk about heavy rock, I don't think there's anyone who beats him. But from a very early age he was influenced by those around him, and I was very naïve about it. So naïve, in fact, that I recommended him to the Rolling Stones, which was about the stupidest thing I could have done. Keith Richards got hold of him, and five minutes later he was a junkie.

JIMMY PAGE "Since I've Been Loving You" was already written, because there was a version of it at the Royal Albert Hall. The only unfortunate thing was that the keyboard wasn't recorded; otherwise it would have been really interesting.

DIGBY SMITH My recollection is that the vocal for "Since I've Been Loving You" was pretty much one take, and it was just electrifying. There are occasions as an engineer in the studio when it's your job to

Andy Johns at
home in Los
Angeles, July 2010.
(Art Sperl)

watch the levels for distortion and make sure the reverb's right and the
equalizing is right, but you transcend into this other world where you
actually forget you're recording, where you're actually *present* for a performance. And when I listen to that track, I'm taken right back there
as if it was happening for the first time. I'm right there in the studio
and I'm hearing every breath . . . and it's still magical.

ROBERT PLANT The musical progression at the end of each verse is
not a natural place to go. It makes it a bit more classy than a 12-bar,
and it's that lift up there that's so regal and so emotional. I don't know
who did it or how it was born, but I know that when we reached that
point in each verse, musically and emotively, the projection of it gave
it class and something to be proud of. You got a lump in your throat
just from being in the middle of it.

TERRY MANNING They hadn't quite finished the third album, and
they had an American tour booked. I had taken Jimmy to Ardent, so

he already knew the studio, and he asked if I could help him finish the album there between shows. He and Peter would fly into Memphis, and anyone who was doing a part would fly in for a day or two.

What sticks in my mind is the strength of Jimmy's personality: the ability to discern what ought to be done out of the mélange of just things you *could* do. I would watch him listen to playback, and he had this little dance he would do where he'd shake his shoulders back and forth. And when that happened, I knew we were there.

Jimmy and I had a longer period where we mixed the album, and then I took it to a place called Mastercraft and physically mastered it onto vinyl. Jimmy was there, Robert was there, Peter was there, and a guy called Paul who had to be there because he had the keys. I was about to run "Since I've Been Loving You" down, and I went to the bathroom to give it what we used to call "the hall test," where you hear it somewhat from afar, all mushed together into mono. And that kind of tells you what it's really going to be like. And I stopped in the hallway and thought, "Damn, that one's *really* good." I remember thinking Janis Joplin a little bit in my head.

Right on the spur of the moment, Jimmy said, "I want to write some Crowley things in there." He wanted to write "Do What Thou Wilt Shall Be the Whole of the Law" on one side, but it wouldn't fit, so we just wrote "Do What Thou Wilt." On the other side, we wrote "So Mote Be It." There were two pressings that were different. I said to Jimmy and Robert, "Someday people will have to buy two copies to get both versions!" We all thought that was very funny.

CHRIS WELCH I remember Jimmy showing me a book by Crowley. It wasn't as if it was some great crime. There were a lot of people getting into black magic, so it didn't seem unusual. I think Dennis Wheatley was as much to blame for that as anyone.

TERRY MANNING Jimmy and I talked about Crowley quite a bit. I knew of Crowley before, but Jimmy had really drawn him to the forefront and would talk incessantly about it. We even got into a couple of friendly philosophical arguments about it, because Jimmy was fully buying into the "Do What Thou Wilt" scenario. I said, "Okay, so if I wilt to kill you, shall I do that?" And he said, "No, that's not what it means." I never got the impression from him that he was thinking anything satanic or evil; to me, it was all self-will and the ability to be totally free in the world and decide your own fate.

LORI MATTIX (groupie and Page's main L.A. squeeze circa 1973) Jimmy said it was all about the will—"I *will* have this"—and that's what Crowley believed. He said it was the white light that he liked, and when you want something, you will it. So that was Jimmy's philosophy: "I *will* have success, and I will have everything I want." I think he willed so much success that that's what ate him alive: he got everything he wanted, and it got too decadent. You lose out on love. Every time he tried to find it, he was hurt again and again and disappointed.

MARTIN STONE (English guitarist and dealer in occult books) Black magic paraphernalia became almost obligatory for certain kinds of heavy metal groups, but Zeppelin were the only one where it carried any real weight, apart from a stylistic comic-strip superimposition.

JON WEALLEANS (architect who drew up plans for Page's occult bookshop the Equinox) My take on it at the time, and now, is that Jimmy was a collector anyway of slightly arcane things. Graham Bond had all this stuff of Aleister Crowley's, and Jimmy sort of bought a job lot of clocks and wands. They were props. I don't think Jimmy was seriously into black magic at all. Crowley was an interesting guy and a very bad poet.

PAMELA DES BARRES (groupie and Page's L.A. girlfriend in the late '60s) There was a bookstore that I frequented on Hollywood Boulevard, and Jimmy was always hunting for manuscripts, so I just wandered in there, and the guy had a manuscript by Crowley with all these handwritten notes in it. You can only imagine what it's worth now. I still have it in my diary—a telegraph with the money to buy it and send it to Jimmy, and that was such an honor. Look what I'm doing! He was exploring and trying to be expansive. He was very deeply spiritual. He wanted to be in control and in charge.

RICHARD COLE Right from before I even moved down to Pangbourne, Jimmy would ask me if I could take him somewhere to buy some

Crowley artifacts or books or stuff. But no one ever really delved into what he did. When he bought Boleskine House, which had belonged to Crowley, he never gave any reasons. He didn't speak about it much. It really was a mystery to everyone else.

JIMMY PAGE [Boleskine House] was built on the site of a kirk dating from around the tenth century that had been burned down with all its congregation. Nobody wanted it, it was in such a state of decay . . . [it's] a perfect place to go when one starts getting wound up by the clock. I bought it to go up and write in.

MALCOLM DENT (caretaker at Boleskine House) Jimmy caught me at a time in my life when I wasn't doing a great deal and asked me to come up and run the place. I never did establish why he fixed on me. Initially, I thought I'd be coming for a year or so, but then it got its hooks in me. I met my then wife at Boleskine House. My children were raised there—my son Malcolm was born at Boleskine.

• • •

ROBERT PLANT To go from "Good Times, Bad Times," "How Many More Times," [and] "Communication Breakdown" to "Whole Lotta Love" and "Ramble On" and still only twenty-two, I thought was quite a move for a kid from the Black Country. And then to go from that to the third album—the cottage album—was incredibly important for my dignity. The acoustic stuff like "Friends" made Led Zeppelin much more powerful, not just a hit machine.

TERRY MANNING There's a thing in the music business known as the Third Album Syndrome, because that's where you either make it for a serious full career or you fall by the wayside. Jimmy was aware of that and wanted to be sure they didn't just repeat the role they had played before. He told me in advance, "You may be surprised, because this is different." But in any case, I knew they liked folk music. There was an element that hadn't liked the first two albums. I had friends who said, "Ah, that stuff's just bashing, and the singer sounds like he's falling off a cliff." Jimmy heard some of that, and he thought, "Okay, *I'll* show you."

Zeppelin unplugged: Trentham Gardens, Stoke, March 14, 1971. (Rex Features)

HENRY SMITH   The press wanted Zeppelin to be Zeppelin all the time. All they wanted was for them to come out and howl, and that's not what Zeppelin was about. People had to start realizing that Zeppelin was a continued story, and every chapter was different.

I loved the acoustic part of Zeppelin. I remember Jimmy just sitting around the house playing acoustic, and that was always a great spot to be in. It was a dream of Page's at the time to be like the medicine man in a little horse-drawn cart, going around England, selling potions, but he wanted to do that with a guitar. That was a country side of Jimmy that was almost like a Roy Harper. That was as much Pagey as "Whole Lotta Love" was.

JOHN MENDELSOHN (reviewer of first two Zeppelin albums for *Rolling Stone*)   When *Led Zeppelin III* came out, there was actually a song on it that I really liked. I thought that I might be asked to review it, but Lester Bangs was given it instead, and he praised exactly the song I had liked—"That's the Way." Lyrically, it was extremely bad, but I remember it feeling evocative, and it actually inspired one of my own songs.

JIMMY PAGE   I think [Bonzo] originally had some lyrics about drinking pints of bitter, you know: *"Now I'm feeling better because I'm out on the tiles . . .*" He used to do a lot of sort of rap stuff. He would just get drunk and start singing things like what you hear in the beginning of "The Ocean." He would stomp his feet, and his fingers would get going.

CHRIS WELCH Bonzo would get nervous before shows. I remember walking up a ramp to a stage with him once, and he suddenly shouted, "Christians to the lions!" That's how they felt when they heard the baying of the crowd.

ANDY JOHNS To start with, Bonzo was manageable and seemed kind and all that, but the bigger they got, the worse he became. That had a lot to do with Pagey, because Pagey would wind him and Coley up and let them go. I saw things that I will not mention to you that were abominable. They loved to humiliate females. Jason used to say to me, "Tell me a great story about my dad." I would say, "You don't want to know." "No, tell me a great story." "Your father was a lout and a fuckhead. I told you not to ask."

ANNI IVIL (Atlantic Records press officer in the U.K.) At one Zeppelin gig, I saw Bonham starting to fall off his stool, and I went and held on and shrieked for somebody to come. I was just relieved he didn't fall on *me*.

HENRY SMITH Out of everyone in the band, he was the hardest one to keep under control. And it wasn't because he was disrespectful, it's just because he was out for fun. If there was ever any discord in the band, it was just that Bonzo was getting too drunk sometimes.

We did two shows in Cleveland, Ohio, and it was Bonzo's birthday. In between the shows, Peter said, "Go get some champagne, and we'll celebrate his birthday." He might have given me a hundred-dollar bill, so I went to this liquor store and bought all the good champagne I could get for that money. Well, Bonzo got totally wasted, to where he really couldn't play. And when we got onstage for the second show, I was holding his seat and holding him up by the scruff of his collar, just so he could get through the set.

I think after that show it was like, "Bonzo, if you don't clean up, you're out of the band."

DAVE PEGG Fairport Convention was in L.A. at the Troubadour club. We'd done one night there already, and on the second night Zeppelin were on at the Forum. They were all coming down to the Troubadour to see us. So for our second set, they all turn up after their gig, and it was, "We wanna have a play." So I went, "That's fantastic." So they all got up. Jonesy had my bass. Richard Thompson stayed onstage with them, and Simon Nicol gave Jimmy his Gibson. They did the whole of the second set, pretty much, and it was fantastic. We had to buy Mattacks a set of new heads for his kit because they were heavily indented by Bonzo's playing.

There was a new club opening the following day where Savoy Brown was due to play. Bonzo said, "We're all invited back there. We're going back for a game of pool and for drinks." It was about two a.m. when we got there. It got to four o'clock, and the guy said, "Right, you're gonna have to go now, guys. It's going to be light soon." Bonzo said, "I'll go if you beat me on the pool table." So they had this game of pool, and Bonzo won. He beat the guy, and it got to five o'clock, and the same thing happened, and it's now six in the morning.

We're all very over-refreshed, to say the least, and all of a sudden there's the sound of the police. The room just clears, and Bonzo says, "Come with me!" So I follow him and go onto the stage, and we're hiding behind these 4-by-12 barstools, a big stack. I'm slumped behind one, and he's behind the other. I pass out, and the next thing I know, the sun is streaking through the window. It's nine a.m., the place is deserted, and Bonzo is passed out next to me. I go, "Shit! What happened? Where the fuck *are* we?" He goes, "Oh, it'll be alright. My driver will be outside." There's nobody in the club, so we creep out of the club, and outside there's a big limo. The guy's been waiting all night.

The driver drops me off at the Tropicana motel, and Bonzo says, "I'm off to Hawaii tonight. We're playing in Honolulu tomorrow." I get back to the Tropicana, and at one o'clock the phone goes, and it's Bonzo: "Fancy a drink before I go?" I say, "Oh, alright." So he comes round, and we go to Barney's Beanery just up the road. We have a few beers, and Janis Joplin comes in and sits down next to us. It was unbelievable. At five p.m., I'm going, "You should have gone." Bonzo says, "Ah, fuck it. I can get a later flight, whatever." I say, "You really should go." "Fuck it. Fuck 'em." He really didn't give a shit.

At six-thirty, his flight's gone anyway, and I'm completely blotto. Anthea Joseph, our tour manager, comes to collect us. She's in the middle of us two lumps, and she's walking us three hundred yards back to the Tropicana. We get to the Tropicana, and up the steps there's a swimming pool where Andy Warhol and some other people are sitting round the side of the pool. I've got to go in an hour and a half to do the first set that's being recorded, and Bonzo pushes me into the pool, fully dressed. I think, "I'll get you, you bastard," so I push *him* in the pool, and then he gets out and takes all his clothes off, except for his Y fronts, and he's having a swim, and he's left his clothes by the side of the pool. He comes out, and we're befriended by two Texan girls with a big bag of grass, which we take back to our room and carry on partying for a bit. Then I have to go to the Troubadour to do the first set. I'm drinking black coffee, cold water, in a fucking dreadful state.

Just before the second set starts, there's a phone call from Bonzo, going, "Where am I? Can you help us out?" He was in my room at the Tropicana, and he'd gone out to the pool in his wet Y fronts, and all his clothes had been nicked. So he borrowed some of the clothes out of my suitcase and came down to the club, and we had to loan him the dosh to get the ticket to get to Honolulu. I thought, "Peter Grant's going to fucking murder us." Bonzo made it to Hawaii. Don't ask me how.

BILL HARRY   We used to set up interviews in the Coach and Horses in Soho. I'd be interviewing somebody, and I'd see Bonzo in the bar, and he used to be with people like Stan Webb of Chicken Shack. They'd get a glass and put Cointreau in, put vodka in, put this in. There was one time when they were doing that, and I knew they were up to mischief, and I thought, "Bloody hell, something's going to happen here." So I rushed back into the office because I had Glenn Cornick of Jethro Tull doing an interview there. I locked him in my office, and I heard them coming up the stairs. I rushed into Terry Ellis's and Chris Wright's office, and it was empty, and I shoved the door shut.

Suddenly, I heard a big bang, and they knocked the door off the hinges and grabbed hold of Doug D'Arcy and got all this tape and completely wrapped him up and dumped him in Oxford Street. For some reason, they then came after me and dangled me out of the window. They then went to Morris Berman's and rented out these Arab costumes. They went back to the Maharishi Suite at the Mayfair Hotel. They told me that later that night, when I was in the Speakeasy, there were two blue-rinsed ladies in the lift with them, and they turned around and lifted up their things, and they had nothing on underneath, so the women beat them with their umbrellas.

Bonzo ordered steaks for fifty people, and all the waiters came in with all the trolleys, and after the waiters had gone, they threw the steaks all around the room. That got Bonzo banned from every hotel in London.

GLENN HUGHES (singer and bassist with Trapeze and Deep Purple)   I could give you a hundred stories about Boisterous John that you've probably already heard. The guy I knew was a family man who missed his wife when he was on the road and who loved his fucking music. He didn't know he was an alcoholic, he just wanted to emulate Keith Moon—he definitely wanted to be in the Oliver Reed club. I remember going to the Elbow Room in Birmingham one late night with John, and he probably bought twenty pints of beer and lined them up on the bar. He was a very generous man, let's be clear about that. He would literally give you the shirt off his back. But if you took a sip of his beer, he would go fucking mad.

ROSS HALFIN (photographer and friend of Page's)   John was Tony Iommi's best man, and they were out all night drinking and doing a load of coke—"on the waffle dust," as Tony puts it—and at one in the morning Bonzo orders thirteen bottles of champagne. Eventually, they end up back at Bonham's, and Pat opens the door and says to Iommi, "Fuck off, the pair of you!" Tony goes, "Pat, please, I'm getting *married* in the morning." Pat says, "Alright, but fucking leave him there." And they just leave Bonzo lying on the floor in the front hall.

Eight a.m., there's a knock at Tony's door, and Bonzo's standing there all dressed in his suit, kipper tie and all, waiting to take Tony to the church.

12

Stairwell to Headley

We don't say "heavy," do we? Well, I don't know whether we do. But it's strong stuff and exciting, and the flame is really burning higher and higher.

—Robert Plant, 1971

ROBERT PLANT We had always led a very cloistered existence in Zeppelin. We really didn't know anybody else. We knew each other, and we knew the entourage, but that was about it.

JOHN PAUL JONES Peter never let anybody near us. He wouldn't let them talk to us, and he took care of everything else. Even *he* didn't say, "I think you should do this or you should do that." You'd know when he was really pleased, which was most of the time. I can't ever remember him saying or indicating that we'd done something he didn't like, artistically. And if he'd felt that, he would never have said it, because it wasn't his place.

ANDY JOHNS (engineer on *Led Zeppelin II, III*, and the untitled fourth album) They were very much unto themselves. A clique, as it were. There was a tremendous amount of paranoia, because all they knew

Melody Maker, September 19, 1970.

was one another: "It's us against them because they're going to get us." One time we were taking a break in the middle of the fourth record. I show up at the studio on the day that we'd agreed on, and they say, "Where have you been?" I say, "What do you mean? We said we'd start at noon this Tuesday." "Well, we've been trying to get hold of you, and you haven't been communicating." "That's because I was in Gloucestershire with my family."

I would watch people come in the room, and it was, "Alright, mate!" and then they'd walk out, and it was, "Fucking cunt bastard, he's trying to stab us in the back."

MICK FARREN (singer with the Deviants; writer for the underground press and *NME*) Colonel Parker didn't want Elvis hanging out with Natalie Wood, because he would have met people who'd have said, "That cracker you've got managing you is an idiot." And I think there was an element of that with Grant and Zeppelin. It was like, "Don't let them loose out of the Zeppelin pod."

SAM AIZER (artist relations, Swan Song in the U.S.) The thing that Peter did great was he got them to not talk to anybody for a while. The more you don't talk to the press, the more they want to talk to you. It's a different world now, where people will tell you on Twitter, "Hey, I just moved my left foot, I just moved my right foot." Zeppelin went the other way: *you couldn't talk to them*. Any time they did interviews, they were always sketchy, and half the time they didn't make eye contact.

KEITH ALTHAM (writer for *New Musical Express, Record Mirror,* and other publications)   When you see Jimmy being interviewed, you only get the tip of the iceberg. As soon as his finger goes to his chin, you know he doesn't want to answer the question, and he's going to find his way around it.

NICK KENT (writer for *New Musical Express*)   Page is very contained. He always thinks before he says anything, whereas someone like Keith Richards will just say whatever's on his mind. Page is always editing himself, and inevitably most of what comes out of his mouth is very guarded—like he's got something to hide.

MAT SNOW (former editor of *MOJO*)   If you approach Page with the absolute attitude of being a bit of a fan but also knowing your stuff and loving the stuff he loves, he does warm up. He doesn't exactly get interesting, but he will talk. But my God, the initial prickliness and the beady eye . . .

CHRIS CHARLESWORTH (writer for *Melody Maker*)   Chris Welch told me that even now, if he ever says anything derogatory about Zep, he has nightmares about the phone ringing and a voice saying, "It's Peter here. I'd like a *word* with you." But Peter was also capable of being very kind to journalists. Roy Hollingworth wrote nice things about Stone the Crows and Maggie Bell, and he once went to Holland with them and Peter. The day after the show, they were wandering through a market, and Roy was admiring some jacket. Peter said, "You like that, do you, Roy?"—and just bought it for him. So he was capable of these gestures.

JERRY GREENBERG (general manager of Atlantic Records, 1969–1980)   Peter was a collector of Rolls-Royces, so he takes me out to where he stored a bunch of these cars. Sitting there is a 1957 Rolls-Royce James Young body; there were only sixty of these made. I was like, "Maybe someday I'll own a Rolls." Steve Weiss calls me up, and he says, "Peter is sending you something, but you're going to have to pay shipping charges." I thought it was like a glass case, champagne or something. I get a call from the shipper. . . . He's sent me the car. It was wild, incredible.

Zep press junket: *Melody Maker*'s Roy Hollingworth (center, in sheepskin coat) with Atlantic's Anni Ivil (top) and *NME*'s Roy Carr (right, waving). (Julian Ruthven)

PERRY PRESS (London estate agent to the stars)   I always found Peter a sweetheart. He was very charming to me. He'd call up out of the blue and say, à propos of nothing, "You seen Charlie Watts lately? He looks like Bela Lugosi!" If there was an antique shop, he'd want to rummage through it and perhaps buy you something. That was the sort of generosity of spirit he had.

HELEN GRANT (daughter of Peter Grant)   Perry phoned up when we were still living in Purley and said, "I've found this fantastic house, you've got to come and see it."

PERRY PRESS   There were people who couldn't afford to run big houses anymore, and big houses had, in any case, become unfashionable. It's hard to believe that what we now consider "secluded and beautifully remote" was considered "isolated and undesirable" in the pre-mobile and motorway days. Horselunges Manor was on the market quietly.

I probably looked at dozens of places before shortlisting a few that I thought would suit Peter. He was open-minded about where he'd go, and that bit of east Sussex was where those sorts of houses are. You don't get moated timber-framed houses in Oxfordshire.

HELEN GRANT Of course, Dad went down to see it without Mum. Bought it without telling her, bless him. She was a bit cross about that. I mean, Dad wanted a house, and that was it. And it *is* an amazing house. The woman that Dad bought Horselunges off was very eccentric. She had sort of big boars' heads and stuffed animals everywhere. It was a strange house, definitely haunted.

ALAN CALLAN Peter took his mother to Horselunges, and she looked at it and said, "Oh Peter, what *have* you done?" Because she hadn't come to terms with how successful he was.

GLORIA GRANT (wife of Peter Grant) I'd started teaching dance when Peter was away, and that kept me busy. At Horselunges, Peter turned

Gloria Grant at Horselunges, 1974. (Peter Clifton)

the side part of the building into a dance studio with big mirrors and bars all the way round. I probably had about 150 students during the course of three or four years, and I'd put them in for festivals. Peter was absolutely fantastic about it, because he'd come home and the driveway would be filled with cars.

HELEN GRANT Mum's a very down-to-earth girl. She wasn't interested in the money at all; she didn't like what it brought. Even when we were living at Horselunges, she was still going to charity shops to find things. She would have driven around in an old banger if she could have. Most of the wives spent their whole days in Bond Street. Mum would rather spend her day doing something useful. She kept us very grounded at home. And I'm pleased that she was like that. You've got to remember that she and Dad got together when they had nothing, and I think that's when they were at their happiest.

GLORIA GRANT I remember once when we were on holiday in Miami, and we were all geared up to spend a day by the pool with the children. Somebody called, and Peter had to go somewhere. I was very, very upset. Marion Massey, who was Lulu's manager, said to me, "You've got to let him do it, he's a big noise in the business, and you've got to hold it together."

· · ·

DENNY SOMACH (producer of "Get the Led Out" segment on classic rock radio stations)   I think America fell in love with Led Zeppelin because most people didn't get the opportunity to see the Beatles. Zeppelin was a living, breathing band. They were a legend that people *had* to go and see. It became a religion, and Peter Grant knew it and *made* it a religion. Everything was geared toward America. They just came in and slayed everybody. We never took to the Hawkwinds and the Iron Maidens, but Zeppelin was different. It was blues-rock-based, which, of course, is American music.

BEBE BUELL (Groupie and girlfriend of Page's)   To me, Led Zeppelin was not part of the post–British Invasion thing. I didn't consider them to have anything to do with the Stones or the Beatles. I considered them to be a kind of *rogue fluke* that just came out of nowhere. Much like Jimi Hendrix, they were a band without a color or a country.

MARIO MEDIOUS (Atlantic promo man, 1965–1972)   They were huge in every major market in America: Los Angeles, Chicago, Seattle, Denver, Philadelphia, Dallas, you name it. They didn't really like to do interviews, but because I knew them well, they would talk to the disc jockeys. And so because of that, these guys thought they knew the band. If the band was in town for three days, you wouldn't hear anything on the station except Zeppelin.

CHRIS DREJA (photographer and ex-Yardbirds bassist)   I'm living in New York, and I get a call from Peter saying, "The boys are at Madison Square Garden tonight—why don't you come down with your wife?" I'm thinking, "Madison Square Garden? Doesn't he mean Carnegie Hall?" And he arranges it all and I go down and meet the guys, and they're awfully polite to me, really nice. None of that "I'm a big rock star stuff." They say, "We've got to go onstage now." And Madison Square Garden is a concrete place, and the dressing rooms are subterranean. They start playing, and I walk up the ramp with Peter, and I hear the whole building move. *Shaking.* I come up round the back, and they're playing the "Whole Lotta Love" riff through 15 megawatts of PA, and there's twenty thousand people sitting there. You've got to remember that the Yardbirds never played to those sorts of audiences. The scale of it just blew me away.

JOHN BONHAM   We did three tours last year and finished off feeling, "We've just about had enough." We had done so much in such a short space of time, we were drained. We had offers to go everywhere, France, America, and we could have done them. But what would be the point? We were tired. We had worked hard, and Peter had probably worked harder than any of us. We enjoyed working, but we needed the break before we got stale.

JIMMY PAGE   We were fed up with going to America. We'd been going twice a year, and at that time, America was really a trial, an effort.

HENRY SMITH (Led Zeppelin roadie)   We drove to Bron-yr-Aur in a white paneled truck. It was just four of us this time: Jimmy, Robert, Sandy McGregor, and myself. No wives, no Peter, no Richard, no nobody else. It was like a camping trip. Jimmy was wearing the high wellies and cardigan sweaters and that famous hat he wore at the Bath festival. It was the folksy look.

In some ways, it was grounding for them. Jimmy was a city boy, whereas Robert was more of a country boy. It was interesting to see them work that part of life out to where serenity was. It was a fun place for me, because there were a couple of times Robert and I went out back and sat in the grass by the stream. And he was talking about songs and looking for a little inspiration for some lyrics. I remember talking about little animals in the grass, parting the grass and seeing what was underneath.

JIMMY PAGE   Maybe the spark of being at Bron-yr-Aur came to fruition by saying, "Let's go back to Headley Grange with a mobile truck and get in there and see what comes out of it." What came out of that, with staying in the house, was the fourth album. Although some things were recorded outside of that location, like "Stairway to Heaven," the whole germ of it was Headley.

JOHN PAUL JONES   Headley was horrible. [There was] virtually no furniture, no pool table, no pub nearby. . . . We all ran in when we arrived, in a mad scramble to get the driest rooms.

RICHARD COLE   There weren't any serious drugs around the band at that point. Just dope and a bit of coke. They were playing at being country squires. They found an old shotgun and used to shoot at squirrels in the woods—not that they ever hit any.

JIMMY PAGE   It was really good for discipline and getting on with the job. I suppose that's why a lot of these came at Headley. For instance, "Going to California" and "The Battle of Evermore" came out of there.

ANDY JOHNS   As musicians and performance-wise, they were so fast. You have no idea. You could get three or four tracks done in a night. Jimmy and John Paul were session musicians and the *best* session musicians. I may have only slept two or three hours a night, but I'd wake up in the morning thinking, "Today I have another chance to do something that has never been done before." You had this opportunity, and it was fantastic. You learned from some of the best people that ever walked the planet.

JIMMY PAGE   Whenever we got together from the third, fourth, fifth album, . . . we would always say "What have you got?" to anybody else—to see if Jonesy had anything, to be honest.

JOHN PAUL JONES   I recall Page and I listening to *Electric Mud* at the time by Muddy Waters. One track is a long rambling riff, and I really liked the idea of writing something like that—a riff that would be like a linear journey. The idea came on a train coming back from Pangbourne. From the first run-through at the Grange, we knew it was a good one.

ROBERT PLANT   My daughter's boyfriend, who was in a psychobilly band, started telling me that part of "Black Dog" was a mistake because there's a bar of 5/4 in the middle of some 4/4. Well, my dander was up at *that*, so I pulled the record out and plonked it on and said, "Listen, you little runt, that's no mistake, that's what we were *good* at!"

ANDY JOHNS   We'd done a couple of takes of "When the Levee Breaks," and the sound pressure was building up, as it always did with those buggers. I'd been experimenting with Blind Faith and Blodwyn Pig, and I was always thinking about how to record things with just two microphones.

One night they're going down the pub, and I say, "Alright, but Bonzo has to stay behind." He says, "Why?" I say, "I've got this idea. You're always moaning about your drum sound, and I think this is going to work." So we carted his kit out into this huge lobby, where the ceiling is at least twenty-five feet high. It sounded really good. How can he not like this? "Bonzo, come and listen!" "Fucking hell!" he said. "It's got *thrutch!*"

ROBERT PLANT   "When The Levee Breaks" was a giant step. Nobody other than John Bonham could have created that sex groove, and many have tried.

RICHARD COLE   The first time I heard "Stairway to Heaven," John Paul was playing it on a recorder. Whenever they got together to write or record, he would come down with a carload of instruments, usually acoustic. This particular time he came down with the mandolins, and I remember Robert sitting on a radiator working out the words.

ROBERT PLANT   We just thought rock 'n' roll needed to be taken on again. So we had all these little rock 'n' roll nuances, like in "Boogie with Stu" or ["Rock and Roll"]. And I was finally in a really successful band, and we felt it was time for actually kicking ass. It wasn't an intellectual thing, 'cause we didn't have *time* for that—we just wanted to let it all come flooding out. It was a very animal thing, a hellishly powerful thing, what we were doing.

RICHARD COLE   Ian Stewart, who came down with the truck, had a similar kind of position with the Stones to the one I had with Zeppelin. He was very friendly with Jimmy because he went back to the early Stones days with him. He was a really lovely guy.

DAVE PEGG (bassist with Fairport Convention)   Sandy Denny was big mates with Jimmy from their school days. She knew Jimmy from way back when she was at art school.

ANDY JOHNS   Robert said, "We're going to have Sandy come down and sing on 'The Battle of Evermore.'" I thought it was a brilliant idea. Of course, she fit right in—sang like a nightingale, with Robert singing at the same time. Literally, she was the inspiration for the whole thing. I went, "Wow!"

ROBERT PLANT   For me to sing with Sandy was great. Sandy and I were friends, and it was the most obvious thing to ask her to sing on "The Battle." If it suffered from a naïveté and tweeness—I was only twenty-three—it makes up for it in the cohesion of the voices and the playing.

DIGBY SMITH (Island Studios tape operator)   The band had been in at Island for a couple of nights, and they were due in for one more. I was at home in my little flat in Victoria, looking forward to a well-deserved night off. The phone rang, and it was Penny Hanson, the studio manager: "Bob Potter's not well, can you come in and stand in for him on the Zep session?"

Seventy percent of the drum sound on "Stairway to Heaven" came from a Beyer M500 ribbon microphone hanging four or five feet over Bonham's head. Jonesy was on a keyboard bass. Jimmy was on acoustic guitar, surrounded by four tall beige baffles that almost obscured him. I don't think there was even a guide vocal. It's a complex piece of music, a medley of two or three tunes tied together.

There's a two-inch tape somewhere of the first take that's awesome, no mistakes from beginning to end. Andy called everyone into the control room for the playback, then turned the volume up to hooligan level. Bonham and Jones and Robert all agree that that's the one: "We nailed it." The only person not saying anything is Jimmy. Bonham turns to him and says, "What's wrong?" Page says nothing's wrong. Bonham goes, "No, something's wrong. *What is it?*" "No, there's nothing wrong." "Well, is that the take or isn't it?" "It's alright." "It's alright. So you want us to do it again." "I think we've got a better take inside us."

Bonham is fuming at this point. He grabs his sticks, walks out of the control room and down the stairs. I can still see him sitting at the kit, waiting to come in, seething. When he finally comes in, he's beating the *crap* out of his drums, and all the meters are going into the red. They come back up into the control room, play it through, and it's just that little bit more urgent. Bonham gives Pagey at least a metaphorical hug and says, "You were right."

We overdubbed three tracks of John Paul's recorders. For the guitar solo, instead of headphones we set up some big playback monitors—big orange Lockwood cabinets on wheels, as big as Page was—and he was leaning on one of them with a cigarette in his mouth. We did three takes of lead guitar and comped the solo from those three takes. I was audacious enough, even as a fresh-faced nineteen-year-old, to point out that one of Andy's switches didn't quite work and that there was an alternative solution that might. After the solo, Robert went out and did the vocal—one take, maybe two.

ANDY JOHNS Robert was sitting at the back with me, and I said, "Come on, it's your turn now. You've got to go sing." "Oh, really? I'm not finished. Play it again." He's got this legal pad. So I played it again, and he said, "Okay, I'm ready now." Two takes, one punch-in.

ROSS HALFIN (photographer and friend of Page's)   Jimmy told me years ago, "The reason I always changed engineers is that I'm not having anyone saying they're the sound of Led Zeppelin. *I* am the sound of Led Zeppelin." And you know something? He *is* the sound of Led Zeppelin. You can play any Zeppelin album—apart from *In Through the Out Door*, which is unmitigated crap—and it sounds like they recorded it this morning. And that is 100 percent Jimmy.

ANDY JOHNS   What did piss me off in the end was Jimmy intimating about that he'd virtually invented the electric guitar and could charm the birds down from the trees. He always took responsibility for things I'd done. He said, "Andy was just there. He did nothing, and I did everything." I thought, "Come on, man. You wrote the tunes, you play them, and you won't even give me *that*?"

JIMMY PAGE   [The press] did not really start bothering me until after the third album. After all we had accomplished, the press was still calling us a hype. So that is why the fourth album was untitled.

JACK WHITE (singer-guitarist with White Stripes and other bands)   The genius of Jimmy that people are always missing is the idea of the anti-establishment "punk" things that he was doing. Things like releasing records with no information and no writing on the cover. I mean, that's pretty bold. It's a lot more punk than the Sex Pistols signing a contract in front of Buckingham Palace.

RICHARD COLE   The picture of the old man was Robert's, and none of us could work out why the fuck he wanted that old bit of rubbish he'd found at a garbage dump or somewhere.

PETER GRANT   We had trouble initially, but Ahmet believed in us. Again, it was a case of following our instincts and knowing that the cover would not harm sales one bit. And we were right again.

JIMMY PAGE   I remember being in an Atlantic office for two hours with a lawyer who was saying, "You've got to have this." So I said,

"Alright, run it on the inside bag. Print your Rockefeller Plaza or whatever it is down there." Of course, they didn't want to have to reprint it, so there it is. It was a hard job, but fortunately we were in a position to say, "This is what we want," because we had attained the status whereby that album was going to sell a lot.

RICHARD COLE   I still don't know what Jimmy's *ZoSo* symbol means. For all I know, he could have been having a fucking laugh with everyone. It could just have been some old bollocks he'd thought up to get people at it. Which is not unlikely with him.

• • •

GLENN HUGHES (singer and bassist with Trapeze and Deep Purple)   My band Trapeze was playing as a trio, and we end up playing Mother's. We were coming to the end of the set with the final number, "Medusa." Fifteen or twenty feet in front of me, walking up to the stage as bold as brass, is Bonham with his assistant Matthew.

JOHN OGDEN (pop music writer on the *Birmingham Express and Star*)   They didn't know John was there. All of a sudden, you heard this voice from the back: *"Ey, we gonna 'ave a knock, then?"*

GLENN HUGHES   Bonham gets onto the stage and—without missing a beat—takes the sticks, nicely, from Dave Holland and says, "Right, play that outro section again." And we played the outro section for about fifteen minutes until we'd gone through all the formats of the arrangement the way he wanted it. That was my first real introduction to John.

That night he took me back to West Hagley. He wasn't out-of-his-mind nasty-drunk, he was in a really good frame of mind. He told me in the car that Zeppelin had just finished recording the fourth album, and he wanted to play it to me. We got there, and he proceeded to play an acetate of the album from tip to toe, "Black Dog" to "When the Levee Breaks." We must have played it ten times, the whole album, and he was grinning and crying and smoking and back-slapping and dancing.

What I heard—on an amazing stereo, turned up to eleven—was life-changing. "When the Levee Breaks" just did me in. It became embedded in my soul. I didn't think, "This is going to become one of the biggest-selling albums of all time." I thought, "Here I am with a great guy, we're young, we're fucking rocking, he's becoming my mentor, he's giving me advice, he's dropping the needle back to this moment and telling me how Jonesy did this or that." He's giving me a historical lesson on the making of Led Zeppelin's fourth album, and it was one of the biggest moments of my life.

JOHN OGDEN   I went to sleep in Jason's bedroom, with his little drum kit next to me. Everyone's sitting around hung over the next morning, and in comes Planty, full of beans: "C'mon, then! Time to get going!"

GLENN HUGHES   Robert's standing over me and waking me up, because they're about to leave for the States, and he's come in a car to pick John up.

RICHARD COLE   I think the third album had been more about breaking a pattern than anything else. They didn't want to make it look as though the heavy stuff was all they could do. I don't know that they didn't decide to do the acoustic stuff knowing that they were going to go back to the earlier style. When the fourth one came out, there was no disputing what they were.

JOHN PAUL JONES   There was always a slight resistance to new material. The first time we played "Stairway" live, it was like, "Why aren't they playing 'Whole Lotta Love'?" Because people like what they know. And then "Stairway" became what they knew.

PHIL CARSON   After the first few times they'd played it live, Peter said, "You know what? You've really got to shut up after this song. Jimmy, don't check your tuning. Bonzo, don't hit the snare drum." The idea was that if the band seemed reverent toward the song, then that would impact on the audience.

JERRY GREENBERG   "Stairway" was going nuts on the radio, but it was an eight-minute cut. I called Peter and said, "Listen, we've got the same thing going on as we had with 'Whole Lotta Love.' Will Jimmy

White label advance of the fourth album, Side One. (Courtesy of Rob Mady)

go in and edit the track?" Peter said no. So I did the exact same thing as I did with "Whole Lotta Love": we did our own edit. It had to go to at least five minutes; there was no way you were going to make a three-minute version of "Stairway." But the same thing happened: Peter would not allow it to come out as a single. The only way anybody was going to get "Stairway" was to buy the album. And it was their biggest-selling album ever.

ROY CARR   On the "Back to the Clubs" tour in Britain, not only did the door prices have to be the same, but the *bar* prices had to be the same. And Zeppelin wanted the same money that they'd got at the start, so they were on 125 quid for the night—that's what they got. The only thing that disappointed them was that they couldn't do enough gigs.

RICHARD COLE   They liked the closeness with the audience, but after doing the stadium tours in America, I don't think they were too enamored of the space they had backstage. It was like, "Fuck this, we won't do *this* again in a hurry!"

ROBERT PLANT   It was bollocks: Led Zeppelin go back to the people. Playing Nottingham Boat Club for four cases of Nut Brown or whatever it was. All these great ideas and the great naïveté of the time.

Playing the King's Hall in Aberystwyth was a very well-meant gesture, on behalf of Jimmy and I, to drag John Paul and Bonzo up to Wales to give something back. In fact, we gave it back to some very disinterested bearded pipe-smoking thespians who were not impressed and quite rightly so. They were obviously in the wrong place. They should have been at the lecture room. We came in peace. It was one of those things where Bonzo was playing away, and he looked at me and went, "This was a fucking good idea, wern it?"

13

Heavy Friends

I mean, who wants to know that Led Zeppelin broke an
attendance record at such-and-such a place when Mick
Jagger's hanging around with Truman Capote?

—Jimmy Page, 1973

EDDIE KRAMER (engineer on *Houses of the Holy*)   There was a point
where I stopped working with Zeppelin because I'd said something,
and they pulled out because they were on their high horse. It was silly,
stupid. I was right, and they were wrong, but that's another story.

I didn't hear anything, and then a year later I got a phone call saying, "Do you want to come over and do some work at Stargroves?" It
was a nice mansion, if you like mansions. It was unfurnished, but Jagger's bedroom was done up. I think that was where Pagey was sleeping. What we were there for was to record and sleep and eat, and that
was it. We managed to get six tracks that were split up between *Houses
of the Holy* and *Physical Graffiti*.

LORI MATTIX (groupie and L.A. squeeze of Page's)   *Houses of the Holy*
is very much Jonesy and Jimmy. Jimmy said that was the most

189

composed album that he's ever done, because all the other albums were sort of live. It was way more produced, and it was all about the composition.

EDDIE KRAMER The band was in great shape, and they were fun to work with, and they wound me up something horrible. I'd brought this chick over from the U.S., and Robert bagged her right away. There were all sorts of scenes with Bonzo bursting into the room in the middle of the night. Now it's hilarious, but then it wasn't so funny.

All that stuff is crap, really, because the most important thing was, how did they work in those circumstances? They were focused, they were together, the music was incredible. I think we got some really good sounds. Everybody loves "D'yer Maker," "Dancing Days."

JOHN PAUL JONES When we did "D'yer Maker," [John] wouldn't play anything but the same shuffle beat all the way through it. He hated it, and so did I. It would have been all right if he'd worked at the part: the whole point of reggae is that the drums and bass really have to be very strict about what they play. And he wouldn't, so it sounded dreadful.

ROBERT PLANT There was no place we wouldn't try and joyfully go. Visiting "The Crunge" one minute, because we'd been to see James Brown when he was really on fire. "The Crunge" is not James Brown, it's just Zeppelin going on a crazy moment.

EDDIE KRAMER One of the things that I think is so important in this music is the great joy in the fact that the mistakes were left in. We left them in intentionally, and we rejoiced in the mistakes, if they were good mistakes. Robert Plant says the classic line in "Black Country Woman"—he's recording the thing, and the plane goes overhead, and they say, "What about this airplane?" He says, "Nah, leave it." You can't create that stuff. You can't fabricate it. It has to happen exactly like that.

ROBERT PLANT Someone goes, "I ain't got no bloody lyrics," and a week later I'd come back with "Over the Hills and Far Away" or "The Crunge." That was amazing, because Bonzo and I were just going to go in the studio and talk Black Country through the whole thing.

And it just evolved there and then: at the end of my tether, it came out. "The Rain Song" was just sort of a little infatuation I had. The next morning I'd scribble it out. If I had done it the day after, it would have been no good.

EDDIE KRAMER Jimmy never forgets. I had all my pictures from Stargroves—a great series of pictures of Robert with an acoustic guitar—and I showed them to Jimmy in a hotel in New York twenty years after the event. He goes, "That fucking prat . . ." He just went off like a fucking rocket about Robert: "I told him never to touch my fucking guitar. I went round the corner for a quick gypsy's, and he had the fucking audacity to pick up my fucking guitar, and I told him never to touch it!" I said, "Jimmy, give it up. It was fucking years ago." The paranoia and the suspicion and all that stuff is part and parcel of who he is, and, unfortunately, it manifests itself in some weird ways.

AUBREY POWELL (designer of *Houses of the Holy* sleeve) Storm Thorgesen and I went to the office in Oxford Street, and it was very dark and gloomy. There was a massive Art Deco desk with a statue on it, and behind it was this enormous man with long, lank hair and rhinestone jewelry everywhere. He was very polite but incredibly menacing. Jimmy was standing by the window smoking a cigarette, looking very ethereal and Shelley-like. Robert was superfriendly.

They were very gracious. The dialogue was mainly with Robert, with Jimmy coming in and looking for some deeper interpretation. Robert's enthusiasm drove the thing. Peter sat there going, "Ah, fuckin' great, love that . . ." Or the negative of that. At the end of the meeting, when we'd all agreed on the two best ideas, he said, "We're going off on tour to Japan. You choose which one you like best." Suddenly, the responsibility was completely on Storm and me. And then, as we're walking out the door, thinking, "We've got it," he goes, "And don't fuck it up." Just the way he said that sent shivers down my spine. It was a classic Peter move.

There was a hierarchy when it came to approval. I always showed everything to Peter first, and then if he liked it, he'd say, "Fuckin' great, go and show it to Jimmy." Then it was Robert, and next it was

Jonesy. Bonzo was last because Bonzo often didn't give a shit. The design was presented to them, and it seemed appropriate for the title *Houses of the Holy.* Jimmy didn't give me that title, nor did he give me any other information about the record. We presented many ideas to them, but this was the one that caught their imagination. It had a comic-book, science-fiction atmosphere celebrating some sort of ceremony or holy communion.

STEFAN GATES (the naked boy on the cover of *Houses of the Holy*)　I *am* a bit scared of it. There's this big bad thing out there, and it's got *me* on it. I just feel I'm in the middle of some hellish scene. The one thing [my sister Sam and I] agree on is, we would never let our kids do the same thing.

AUBREY POWELL　You have to place the cover in the context of the time. We live in a world now where every other word is *pedophile*. In the '70s, I never knew that word existed. I was an out-and-out hippie—albeit a materialist hippie because I was interested in becoming well-known—and back then, you could see child nudity with families and with parents on every beach and in every swimming pool. That image on the cover was specifically taken from Arthur C. Clarke's *Childhood's End*, where he describes all the children of the world leaving the Earth in a ball of fire—and they're naked.

• • •

JUNE HARRIS BARSALONA (wife of Premier Talent boss Frank Barsalona)　What was beginning to happen was that promoters like Michael Cole in Canada would go to a manager and say, "I will guarantee you 90 percent, let's cut out the agency." Frank had always been very direct and very honest, and the agency got whatever it was in those days, I think 10 percent. And he was not going to cut his commissions just because one band was greedy.

I'm sure Frank was hurt when Peter decided he was going to do it his way, but he wasn't going to compromise his principles. There is a possibility that the agency contracts were up, and that gave Peter the freedom to do what he wanted. Frank never held a grudge about it. There was no bad blood.

DANNY GOLDBERG (U.S. press officer for Zeppelin and president of Swan Song in New York)   Peter famously left Premier, and I think Steve Weiss was considered complicit in that. By the time I was involved, Zeppelin had already left Premier, and Steve was considered an enemy.

MITCHELL FOX (Swan Song staffer, 1977–1980)   When Peter and the band suggested what they wanted, in my experience Steve got it done.

HENRY SMITH (Led Zeppelin roadie)   Some people looked at it like Peter renegotiating a deal was like the Mafia renegotiating a deal—the take-it-or-leave-it type of deal. Was it English Mafia? Well, maybe it was. Maybe it was *musical* Mafia. Peter had that with Steve Weiss.

MICKIE MOST (producer and owner of RAK Records)   Peter changed the industry . . . he said, "Ninety/ten, take it or leave it." Promote it? You don't have to promote Led Zeppelin. Just take an advert in the *Jewish Chronicle*. . . . You're gonna get 10 percent for just turning up. . . . The Americans had never met anyone like him before.

PETER GRANT   Well, they were greedy fuckers, weren't they? The thing was, there were so many of them that were cheating bands.

MALCOLM McLAREN (manager of the Sex Pistols)   He basically changed it by making—for a *moment*—the band more important than the industry . . . than the record company. He treated everybody else as parasites.

SAM AIZER   You want to know what I honestly believe? *Steve Weiss* was the business brains behind Zeppelin, not Peter. I believe that from my heart. *He* came up with the 90/10, *he* came up with all these remarkable ideas. He always gave the credit to "the Leds," as he called them, but the guy was a genius. Steve could wield somebody else's power better than anybody—he could squeeze every last nickel. And Peter fed off that. He said, "I've got my hired gun, and he's gonna pull the trigger for me."

Steve had everything to do with the business mystique of Led Zeppelin. When you walked into that office in the old *Newsweek*

444 Madison Avenue, New York City: Weingarten, Wedeen & Weiss were on the 27th floor. (Art Sperl)

building, there was a hall from Shelley Kaye's office to Steve's, with a music room in the middle. In this hall, there were pictures of Led Zeppelin from the first album, and then a little farther down you could see Hendrix, Beck, Vanilla Fudge, the Rascals. And you'd think, "This guy's been around the block."

STEVE WEISS (Led Zeppelin's U.S. lawyer)   Before we started to self-promote [Jimi Hendrix's] concerts, there was a lot of difficulty in his obtaining dates in America, because at that time—although it seems ludicrous by today's standards—he was considered to be a very erotic act. Most of the deals available were 60 percent artist, 40 percent promoter. We hired a promoter and paid him a small [10 percent] percentage for promoting the concert. That way, if you did very well, the artist made a lot more of the money. You could only do this with an artist of Jimi's stature, because if you guessed wrong, the artist wouldn't make as much or might even *lose* money.

JANINE SAFER (press officer, Swan Song in the U.S.) Peter Grant had a quite false reputation for being intimidating. He wasn't. *Steve* was intimidating, and Peter let Steve be the asshole. Led Zeppelin had incredible power within the Warner family, and not just because they were a huge band but because Steve was their liaison, their mouthpiece, their roadway into the executives. Steve was respected by those guys, whether it was Ahmet or Mo Ostin or Jerry Greenberg.

I don't know that Jerry liked Steve at all; I suspect he didn't. But he respected him. When Steve spoke, he had the power of a lot of record sales behind him. And he wasn't outrageous in his demands. He had an unerring sense of how much he could get for those guys. And they knew he was the reason they were staying in those huge suites in the Plaza Hotel. They fully recognized that Steve was an essential part of Led Zeppelin. Also, they would get themselves in trouble an awful lot, and he would get them out of it.

TONY MANDICH (artist relations manager at Atlantic's West Coast office, 1972–1997) I was present at the meeting when they introduced the 90/10 split. Certain promoters were making millions from 60/40. They were making a fortune doing fucking nothing but making an announcement.

Peter told us, "Let's go. The band will tour, and we'll call a radio station." The tour would start in L.A., and they would do multiple shows. Ahmet told us to call the radio station to tell them that the first show goes on sale Monday morning at 10:00 a.m. at the box office. In those days, there was only one place, the Forum, where they used to play. The tickets would go on sale at 10:00 a.m., and Peter said, "Call the station and give them that information, and see what happens." By eleven o'clock or noon, we got a phone call from the Forum that they'd sold out. A couple of days later, Peter said, "Call the station and tell them that the second show is on sale." And boom, the second show would go clean in a minute.

Then he said, "Why do we need promoters or anybody else to work our show?" I think we ended up doing seven shows at the Forum. And that's where 90/10 was born. After that, it was a different ball game.

JACK CALMES (cofounder of Showco sound and lighting)   When Concerts West and Jerry Weintraub took over the running of the tours from the agents and the old promoters, Peter and the band were able to tap into the kind of resources that had always been there—having that level of security and having the doctors travel with the tour so that everything that the band wanted could be handled in some way.

JOHN PAUL JONES   We would get people turning up and trying to claim the gig as a free show. It became a bit of a two-way fight. From our standpoint, it was like saying, "Hey, we're up here as well—just listen and enjoy it." Robert was always making gestures for calm. I think we then realized we'd be better off without the police, and we got rid of them and brought in our own security.

MITCHELL FOX (Swan Song U.S. staff, 1977–1980)   Between Phil Carson and Ahmet Ertegun and Joan Hudson, they had a lot of very influential people working for them.

PHIL CARSON (head of Atlantic Records in the U.K.)   Joan was not the original accountant. That was Peter Parker, who worked for the firm that Joan worked for. They decided they wanted Joan to work for them full time, so they took her out of the firm and set her up in her own business. And she's been brilliant for them all of these years.

BENJI LeFEVRE (Zeppelin sound technician, 1973–1980)   As far as I am aware, they all trusted Joan absolutely. She was the legitimate face of Led Zeppelin. She had a very high proper voice, and they just loved her.

EDDIE KRAMER   Ahmet Ertegun was the epitome of a great record man, and he loved the Zep guys. That's what's missing in the music business today, a guy like Ahmet who just knew the music backward, the history of it, and could hang with the Stones all night doing blow or whatever he did. The guy was like fifty men.

TONY MANDICH   Ahmet would go out every night to chat with the bands, see new acts play. You name it, he was there. The dedication was unbelievable.

PHIL CARSON   I used to dread Ahmet coming to London. I would show up at the Dorchester at ten o'clock, and routinely he was still horizontal, though already making phone calls. And he wouldn't come down till eleven, and we would go and do what we did *all day*. There'd be a lunch with somebody, and then later he'd say, "Come and pick me up at eight, we're having dinner with so-and-so." Dinner would turn into going to Tramp or the Speakeasy, and by two o'clock I'm dead, and he's just getting into gear.

BILL CURBISHLEY (manager of the Who and later of Jimmy Page and Robert Plant)   [Ahmet] stood up to Peter and was not at all intimidated by him. Grant knew who Ahmet was, and, in the end, he owed Ahmet. It's okay to come in with a great album and all that, but you cannot minimize what Ahmet put behind that band.

GEOFF GRIMES (plugger for Atlantic Records U.K., 1972–1978)   We had the four biggest British rock bands that worked all over the world, doing what they were doing for Atlantic. So, for anybody who was working here, it was a really big honor to be doing it. If one of the big four was coming out with an album, there was a checklist of things that you had to do. Carson was incredibly good at caretaking. He would be deeply aware of the potential rivalries or competitiveness, and he'd be there to make sure it all worked.

• • •

RICHARD COLE (road manager for Led Zeppelin)   We toured Japan in 1972, and coming back, we stopped off in India.

ROBERT PLANT   We stopped in Bombay, and we ended up playing in an old dive there for a bottle of Scotch. It was superb. I was singing through a Fender cabinet [that] was the size of a 12" telly, and Pagey was playing a guitar that must have had piano strings on it. And the people were so happy because they'd never ever witnessed anybody just passing through, taking the trouble to stop and play. We did some recording in India—yes, they have got studios there, just about.

RICHARD COLE   On the plane back to England, Robert and Jimmy decided that they wanted to be in the limelight. I said, "What sort of publicist do you want?" And I told them about BP Fallon and T. Rex, and they said they wanted that.

BILL HARRY I had Suzi Quatro doing an interview in the Coach and Horses, and Bonzo was in there drinking again. I got up to walk somewhere else, and he grabbed hold of me. I had all my things in my pocket, and he ripped the pocket off me; money went everywhere. I was so pissed off and fed up, I just said, "That's it. I'm fed up with you, and I don't want anything more to do with you. If I see you coming up the street, you better cross to the other side."

I phoned up Peter and said, "Look, I'm sorry, but I'm having nothing more to do with Led Zeppelin." He said, "What did they do?" I said, "They ripped my pocket." He said, "Go out and buy the most expensive stuff you can." I said, "I don't want anything to do with them."

To him, it was a bunch of lads having fun, but for me to be looking after Suzi Quatro and have her witness things like that in front of

"A glamorous Gollum": BP Fallon, New York City, July 2010. (Art Sperl)

everybody, it was humiliating. I can put up with a number of things, but that was the last straw.

BP FALLON (U.K. press officer for Zeppelin, 1972–1976)   Bill Harry was a very nice man but more Pete Best than John Lennon. He wasn't torn and frayed, and I think you probably had to be to work with Zeppelin.

MICHAEL DES BARRES (singer with Silverhead)   BP is like a glamorous Gollum combined with the wisdom of Yoda. He and Marc Bolan were two little imps who gravitated toward each other. He turned me on to everything I know about music—took me under his unbelievable wing and just confirmed to me that three chords and a slide guitar could maybe change the world and certainly get you laid.

ROBBIE BLUNT (guitarist with Silverhead)   Silverhead was in L.A., and we called Robert up. He said, "You a bit 'omesick?" I said, "Well, I *am* a bit." But I was having a bloody *great* time. They let us loose in among all these costumes from some film production, and BP got hold of this outrageous coat made of feathers. You could find where he was in the Hyatt House because there was this trail of feathers every-where. He kept molting.

BP FALLON   Peter and I had a talk. He said, "We're thinking of doing this tour." So I said, "Well, show me the dates, then." And we sat down on the floor and spread them out across the floor. Years later, he said, "I knew we were alright when you sat on the floor." I'm not really one for ceremony. I said, "If we're going to do this properly, and it's a 24/7 situation, you can have me heart and soul." It's very simple, really: if you have something that's good, you just let people know about it. Why hadn't it happened before? Because nobody had applied themselves to it with the correct psychology. All you have to do is let people believe what you're saying, and they can decide whether it's bollocks or not.

ROY CARR (writer for *New Musical Express*)   BP was his own creation. He knew how to handle a lot of artists by tickling their egos. There's a famous quote from Greg Lake: "That man can't do our publicity, he doesn't wear socks!" We were at the Speakeasy one night and a bit the worse for wear, and BP was saying, "People have got to realize that we're the new aristocracy." Everybody started throwing food at him.

GYL CORRIGAN-DEVLIN (Zeppelin friend who traveled on the 1973 tour)   In the beginning, Beep was the court jester. I never remember him even sitting down with a journalist. Whenever everybody else was a bit down, Beep would start throwing popcorn at people. There were many times when we couldn't even find him. We'd be on the plane, and someone would say, "Anybody know where Beep is? Is he under a seat?" "No." "Well, we're not waiting for him this time." I remember flying back to Chicago without him because he'd gone off with some girl to buy rhinestones.

BP FALLON   There's too much darkness been talked about with Led Zeppelin. Things can't happen if it's all darkness. You can say, "Well, look what happened later on," but that's not the point. There was so much fucking joy with that band, so much fun and so much mischief. On one American tour, I said, "I am now the entertainments manager." No one complained.

ROBERT PLANT   Right the way through Led Zeppelin, the majority of the music was built on an extreme energy. It was excessively extreme at times and joyously so, despite people wanting to think it was dark.

MICHAEL DES BARRES   BP validated the magical elements of Led Zeppelin, and that extended their lives. Most people in that position will simply take from you to make themselves feel better. Beep reminded them of what they were meant to be doing.

BP FALLON   The first evening with them in Montreux, I put all my makeup on and all the feathers and furs, and I wore a blue velvet cloak. For Bonzo, who was a good stolid chappie, it was all a bit of a shock: "This guy's gonna get involved with *us*? Fuck, G, what's going on?"

CHRIS CHARLESWORTH (writer for *Melody Maker*)   I always wanted to be in a meeting with BP and the band and Grant, because you'd think they'd have swatted him for being cheeky. He had great lip, did BP. He took me up to Manchester to see Zeppelin at the Hard Rock. Halfway through the show, I decide I need to go to the dressing room for a pee. I open the bathroom door, and BP's in there with *two women.*

BP FALLON   You can do a lot during a twenty-minute drum solo. Especially if you're not the one playing the drums.

CHRIS CHARLESWORTH   Danny Goldberg was the first guy I met in the business who had very long hair in a ponytail, and he was incredibly skinny and laid-back. He was just what Led Zeppelin needed, actually.

DANNY GOLDBERG   Steve Weiss told me that they were interested in me working for them. I'd failed as a journalist, and this was my new career as a PR person. The first time I met them was at the Georges V, and I was very titillated to be flown over to Paris. I think the whole reason for it was to make it clear who the boss was, and that I wouldn't be working for Steve.

It was a short meeting. It was, "Jimmy and I want you to be our ambassador." Peter was very large and scruffy, a mound of a man who wore his shirts outside his pants. It was giant jeans and big shirts over them and a big beard, balding but still with hair on his head. He was very much the gracious, amiable host.

The band had been through some of the demons that people deal with—the disorienting feeling of success where people are extra nice to you and extra mean to you. I think by the time I met them, they had become sort of at peace with it and really knew their place in the world.

Jimmy did very little talking. Later, it became clear to me that he was really the boss. At first, it appeared they were all equals, but they were *not* equals. It was Jimmy's band, and he had to deal with the other guys and keep them happy, but it was like he had two votes. Peter was Jimmy's guy. When he talked about the band, he talked about Jimmy in a very different tone of voice than the other people, and that was their bond and I think their deal from the birth of the band.

I'm not sure that Jimmy was as devoted to Peter as much as Peter was to Jimmy, but on Peter's part, it was like a love affair. When Peter called me to hire me for the label, it was like, "Jimmy says hello," and, obviously, Jimmy hadn't said hello—it was just something Peter said. And to Peter, that was the highest compliment that he could pay somebody.

JAAN UHELSZKI (writer for *Creem*)   When I talked to Danny in the '90s about Zeppelin's relationship with the press, he told me it was a conscious effort to have this conspiracy of silence, because they thought the mystery would add to their sales. But then there was a day in 1972 when they saw the Stones on the cover of *Time* or *Newsweek* and thought, "Okay, we've got to do more in public."

DANNY GOLDBERG   My memory is that Robert felt that his father didn't know how successful the band was, and that was one of the things on his mind. He wanted the people he grew up with to know and thought that the media would help and would recognize what the band had accomplished. So that was part of the agenda. What they really cared about was how the coverage of what they did in America would look in England. They didn't care what it looked like in Philadelphia. At that first meeting, Robert specifically mentioned to me how much press the Stones had got in the last year and how ridiculous it was, given that Zeppelin was bigger in terms of concert attendance.

MARIO MEDIOUS (Atlantic promo man, 1965–1972)   Zeppelin were *very* jealous of the Stones. In '72, I was on tour with them first, and then I had to tell them, "Guys, I gotta leave tomorrow to meet with Ahmet and the Stones for a couple of days." And they said, "Fuck the Stones!" They fell out with me behind it. Plus, the Stones got all these good reviews, and Ahmet was crazy about them. Ahmet loved all that society stuff, because Jagger had that society thing going on. Zeppelin were straight-up hippies; they hated that fucking bullshit. Movie stars would want to say hello, and they wouldn't even let them backstage. Bonzo would say, "Fuck *them!*"

LISA ROBINSON (New York correspondent for *Disc, New Musical Express*, and *Creem*)   Danny called me up and asked if I would go on the road with them. I said, "Don't be ridiculous, they're a cheesy heavy metal band." But I went, because I'd never been to New Orleans before. And then I interviewed Robert and Jimmy and fell in love with Led Zeppelin. I really thought they were great. No one else could be bothered with them—they thought they were over-the-top and a joke—but I started writing this good stuff about them in *Disc and Music Echo.* So they got some good press in England.

DANNY GOLDBERG   Lisa and I were very close, and she went on the tour and wrote a lot of stories about them. She could cover what they were doing in the U.S. for English papers and give them the image they wanted in England. So they always had time for her, and she really got it. She wasn't snobbish about it. She didn't care about what any of the critics thought, and she really developed a relationship with them.

JAAN UHELSZKI   Lisa got a little peek into Zeppelin that most women didn't get, because she was such a kind of society babe. She had complete access to everything, because it kind of gave them more of that appeal to debutantes, and for some reason she's always been that kind of gossip-columnist writer. She was friends with Danny, too, so that kind of opened up that door for her.

LISA ROBINSON   Nick Logan contacted me and asked whether I'd do a New York column for the *NME,* so I jumped from *Disc.* I would file all these glowing reports about them in England, which they were thrilled about because their parents read it, and it was their only good press at the time. I remember Jimmy pissing and moaning about Chris Welch's review of [*Houses of the Holy*] in *Melody Maker,* but I never had a problem with Zeppelin.

MICK FARREN (singer with the Deviants and writer for *New Musical Express*)   They treated Nick Kent like complete shit. Kent, God bless him, is an honest man in his own way, and he went off to somewhere like Cardiff and saw Zeppelin in their early grandeur and thought they were the best thing he'd ever seen. At which point, he got shepherded backstage, where they promptly started to abuse him. It was like "Nick Bent," you know, real low-level homophobic stuff from Bonzo. Nick put up with that shit, and I couldn't understand it. *I* wouldn't have.

Nick Kent with Atlantic's Anni Ivil, circa 1973. (Courtesy of Anni Ivil)

NICK KENT (writer for *New Musical Express*)   I've never claimed I was bullied by Led Zeppelin. What happened backstage was not bullying, it was just getting involved in the old cut-and-thrust of being an interviewer. Any journalist was fair game for them, so you can imagine someone like me walking in, dressed up to the nines. They weren't too keen on this glam-rock thing—though they were using some of it themselves—so I was fair game.

NICKY CHINN (coproducer of RAK acts Sweet and Suzi Quatro)   I remember going to a Zeppelin party at Peter Grant's place, and they kept on playing Sweet's "Ballroom Blitz." So I went up to Robert Plant and said, "Do me a favor, stop taking the piss." He said, "This is one of our favorite records!" Zeppelin were so big that they could afford to appreciate anything. They didn't have that snobbery.

NICK KENT   You really had to learn to tough it out with these guys. You had to be in a room with them and *be memorable*. If it went badly, at least you had something to write about. I remember once being in the Atlantic office in London, and Bonham walks in with Phil Carson. Carson turns to me and says, "Here, John, you know Nick Kent, don't you?" And Bonham just looks at me and says, "Ever since Planty started wearing those silly little frilly tops, we've had benders like this following us around." But then he would say the same thing to Page— they were all calling each other "big girls." You didn't want to get between Jimmy Page or Robert Plant and a full-length mirror in the dressing room—and Bonham was always taking the piss out of both of them.

ROBERT PLANT Nick Kent was with Keith [Richards] or he was with Jimmy. And the psyche of that condition and that platform from where he made his assertions were based on the chemicals and the humor. Nick went where he felt the greatest affinity, comfort, and stimulation, so looking at Bonzo coming in growling, with a suit and a fedora on and carrying a black stick with a silver top, wasn't easy for him.

LISA ROBINSON I went on five tours with them, and they were total gentlemen to me, lit my cigarettes, opened my car door—just stars. But I could see what they were like. Richard Cole, Peter Grant—they reminded me of *Expresso Bongo*. All those guys were heavy, dark, that East End music scene.

MICHAEL DES BARRES I adored Peter, not least because of the incredible gangster power he exuded and that seemed to step straight out of *Performance*. He came from the mean streets of London, which was essentially a "fuck-you" to all of society.

TERRY MANNING (engineer on *Led Zeppelin III*) One time Peter was in New Orleans, and I was in the lobby of the hotel with him. Don Fox, the promoter, was demanding this and demanding that, and they had just delivered coffee to Don and tea to Peter. Peter stood up, pulled down his pants, and put his you-know-what right in the hot teacup. He just stood there looking at Don. It was saying to Don, "There's nothing you can do to me." And Don just sort of went, "Okay, I give up."

JOHN PAUL JONES   Peter didn't heavy *everybody*; he got pissed off at people who tried to stitch him up, but if you played fair with him, he was fine. A lot of stories came from people who tried to pull some number on him and didn't succeed, and then suddenly it's, "Oh, Peter Grant tried to rough me up."

BP FALLON   One is completely against violence, but sometimes people can interpret someone being very forceful as being a threat of violence, just because they're huge. Peter was a big chap, and he knew how to work it. But he didn't become successful by being a horrible, menacing bully. He became successful by being very charming and very bright, and because he loved Jimmy and, by extension, loved the band and would do anything for them.

HELEN GRANT (daughter of Peter Grant)   The temper and all of that, it was all acting. When Dad used to have those moments, he didn't like himself behaving like that. It really used to get to him and make him very anxious and upset. He'd have an angel on one shoulder, going, "Calm down, Peter," and then a devil on the other, egging him and going, "Get in there and show 'em what you're made of!"

When he used to lose his temper in front of me, he would look so ashamed that he'd behaved like that in front of people he was close to. Jimmy felt quite secure and protected by it, but Robert hated it and was embarrassed by it.

AHMET ERTEGUN (cofounder of Atlantic Records)   Peter . . . kept them hidden in a shroud of mystery. They became the most unapproachable band in rock history. My life with them thereafter was a roller-coaster ride. The music and the recordings got better and better, the hits were bigger and bigger, the stories of their exploits on the road kept getting wilder and wilder. They were not only inventing the most important rock 'n' roll music of their time, but they were also inventing the new rock 'n' roll lifestyle, and the mystique about them was turning into legend.

HENRY SMITH   The Beatles kind of opened the door to it, but when the Who and Zeppelin came over, they were the bad boys of rock 'n' roll. Now whether Peter used that as a tool—and in some ways I think he probably did—there's nothing like a bad reputation to take you a long way. The Stones went places because the Beatles were the good boys and the Stones were the bad boys. And Zeppelin were the bad boys, too. I think some of that mystique helped them in that time period.

CHRIS CHARLESWORTH I traveled to Montreux with them and spent the weekend there, and that was absolutely delightful. They used to go over there to do a couple of warm-up shows before a big tour. They were on their best behavior because their wives were there. They'd kept a low profile for the previous six months and had been working on *Houses of the Holy*. Somewhere in my piece, I wrote something along the lines of, "Their popularity may be on the wane as a result of their recent lack of activity." Well, they picked up on this and used this phrase in the adverts for their next tour, which was totally sold out.

BP FALLON Chris wrote something like, "Led Zeppelin may be past their peak" in *Melody Maker*. All the tickets sold out straight away, so the following week, we ran an ad with the dates, all of them "sold out," and with Chris's quote under it. So it was a little message: "Don't fuck us around because otherwise we're going to do things like this to you." Chris and I, we're friends to this day.

NICK KENT The two shows I saw in '72 were truly phenomenal, because there was a sense of focus and natural energy. What really struck me about them then was that no one was on cocaine and no one was drunk. It took three songs for them to lock together. After that, they took flight.

GLORIA GRANT (wife of Peter Grant) I don't think I realized for a long time that they *were* the biggest band in the world. I remember being in Montreux and coming back in a Learjet that Peter had hired. And then I realized it was the big time. We were able to stay in the best places and the best suites, the Dorchester and so on. But I never got embroiled in it. Maybe I *should* have done. I'm not saying I didn't enjoy the rich pickings from it, because I did. I always had a nice car and things like that, but it didn't faze me. I hope I didn't change a lot.

14

Trampled under Foot

It's a bit like amyl nitrate. It's like a rush that you're
not ready for. I didn't know how many people were going
to be there. I had no idea what it would look like. There
was nobody else but Led Zeppelin, four of us, and all those
people as far as the eye could see.

—Robert Plant on Zeppelin's record-breaking show at
Tampa Stadium, May 5, 1973

JACK CALMES (cofounder of Showco sound and lighting company)   At
Showco, we decided that lighting would really end up being the bigger
business of the two. I hired Iggy Knight, who was the designer for a lot
of things. Iggy knew Jimmy from the Zeppelin parties he'd done, and
he was kind of a crazy gnome, a designer with the Royal Shakespeare
Theatre who'd kind of morphed into the psychedelic world and done
the light show at the Roundhouse. I always give Zeppelin the credit for
everything that modernized touring. We did our first big staging and
lighting production with them.

BENJI LeFEVRE (Zeppelin sound technician from 1973 to 1980)   At the end of 1972, Iggy got the job to design Zeppelin's 1973 tour, and Robert asked if he knew anyone who was good with sound effects. I got a call from Robert asking me to come and meet him, so I jumped on the train up to Kidderminster and met him in this pub where they had a stripper.

I liked him a lot because of his humor—Leo, extrovert, outgoing. He had a Jaguar that had been customized into a station wagon, and he drove up what's known locally as Sandy Track at about fifty miles an hour. We got on very well and he said, "Come and work for me." He had all this extraordinary Binson echo equipment that I pretended to know about. I got the nod at the end of '72, and at the beginning of '73, we rehearsed at Shepperton Studios.

I thought to myself, "I'll work for them for six months and make a pile of money, then I'll go back to the jazz and blues I love." Of course, not only did I not make a pile of money—because they were tight as hell—but I carried on working for them.

JACK CALMES   At Tampa Stadium, I brought along this crazy artist from L.A. who was so in awe of Zeppelin that he couldn't talk at all. This guy had turned me on to lasers at the Planetarium in San Francisco. So I said, "Come out, and let's explain this to the band." I took him into the trailer, and he couldn't talk. He was a bit of a drinker and a crazy hippie artist who had shoes that were duct-taped, but they trusted me enough to bring in a character like this. I said, "The bottom line is that lasers would be cool for your show," and Bonzo was always the one who was like, "Fuck it. Let's have it. Right now."

Robert never liked any of this and was always kind of disdainful of any of the production things. It was like, "They're here to see me, and why do we need all this shit?" We got that laser shortly thereafter and carried it all the way through Earl's Court in 1975.

JOHN PAUL JONES   We'd done the stripped-down thing, and it got bigger. There were more lights, so you had to wear things that reflected them a bit more. If you'd wandered onto a well-lit stage in jeans and T-shirts, it wouldn't have looked very good. It was part of Zeppelin tradition never to discuss what you were wearing before you actually got onstage. So sometimes you'd have three blokes in jeans and one in a white suit. Sparkly clothes became available. I got that silly jacket with the pom-poms because the people who'd made Page's dragon suit came by with a van-load of clothes, and we all just went, "Oh, *that* looks fun."

BENJI LeFEVRE   The first gig blew my balls, fifty thousand people going bananas. Very quickly, I realized it was blues-based, and because of the way they approached their music, it was constantly changing. That unit was quite extraordinary. They just had telepathy and could take the music anywhere they wanted to go.

JOHN PAUL JONES   Sometimes you'd walk out on those stages and think, "Bloody hell! Where'd all *this* lot come from?" But usually, once the gig started, you'd forget it, because you had other things to think about. There was nobody in the band who was throwing up in the dressing room, but you got nervous before you went on, and that kick-started the adrenaline. You have to remember that it wasn't suddenly sixty thousand people. It was a thousand, five, ten, twenty et cetera. I can remember going back to Madison Square Garden after playing to sixty thousand and thinking, "Hmm, this is cozy."

BENJI LeFEVRE   My enduring image of the band onstage is of Robert and Jimmy doing their thing, performing together. When there was no singing, it was almost like Jimmy wouldn't let Jonesy *near* Bonzo because it was about *him* and Bonzo—he stood in front of the drums the whole time. He would direct Bonzo and suggest where to go. Jonesy would just be standing there and following along because he was such a fucking brilliant musician, he could handle anything.

The *energy* of the thing was Jimmy and Bonzo. If you watch some of the Zeppelin footage, you'll see Jimmy in front of the bass drum making physical *signs* to Bonzo. And Bonzo's timekeeping was so impeccable that it allowed Jimmy to really go for shit but be reined in, time-wise. I think the telepathy between Jimmy and Bonzo as musicians almost extended to the drug-taking: it was like, "I wonder how fucked up we can get and still play."

Zeppelin limos waiting outside the Riot House, July 1973. (Richard Cole Collection)

EDDIE KRAMER (engineer on *Led Zeppelin II* and *Houses of the Holy*) There was always a tremendous feeling of power—that they could do anything they wanted—and sometimes they took advantage of that. You were in this floating bubble of protection around them because they were so adored.

BP FALLON (Zeppelin's U.K. press officer, 1973–1976) They were the kings of the castle, and one felt untouchable being part of this family. I remember once I went and sat in a park in Boston, and I suddenly realized I was outside the bubble. It was really odd.

BENJI LeFEVRE There was an undisputed loyalty among the four of them because of the amount of money they were making and the amount of fun they were having. There was camaraderie and a sense of invincibility. You get in a gang, and you think you're untouchable. I think we *all* felt like that. Even though we got treated like shit by the band, to anybody else we were *Zeppelin's crew*.

JACK CALMES It was English rock star royalty. You know England—the class system kind of repeats itself at different levels. Based on the money and the fame, they had their slaves and serfs and all that.

MARK LONDON (comanager with Peter Grant of Stone the Crows and Maggie Bell)   For the 1973 tour, they rented a plane called the *Starship*. I was the first one to see the plane with Steve Weiss. We drove over to Newark Airport to check it out. We gave it our blessing.

PAUL RODGERS (lead singer with Free and Bad Company)   The *Starship* was an amazing airplane. It was huge, with bedrooms complete with beds and huge seatbelts. It had video games and all the rock star stuff.

PETER GRANT   The *Starship* was only $14,000 more [than the Falcon nine-seater], because [Boeing] wanted the publicity and that kind of thing—and we thought, "Well, why not? We'll have a 720!" The first day, in Chicago, they'd parked it next to Hugh Hefner's plane, hadn't they? All the press were there, and somebody said to me, "Well, how do you think it compares to Mr. Hefner's plane?" I said, "It makes his look like a Dinky toy." Boomph! Press everywhere!

GYL CORRIGAN-DEVLIN (Zeppelin friend who traveled on 1973 U.S. tour)   At this point, they were what Richard called "Zeppelin'd off." They were stuck in the Hyatt House, and they missed home. American groupies could be great fun and very fascinating, but sometimes Bonzo just wanted to talk about his bulls, and no girl wanted to sit and listen to that. It was never a plan that I would go with them. They just said, "We'll send the plane if you'll come to Chicago . . . just go to the gig!" I think I was a bit of a grounding force. I used to be called "Mum" once in a while. I was the one who sewed the crotch of Robert's jeans when he split them every night.

MORGANA WELCH (L.A. groupie and Zeppelin friend)   There was nobody quite as flamboyant as Page and Plant, though Hendrix came close. While there were a lot of things going on, one of them was the sexual freedom movement. But from a fashion standpoint, it was just *fun* rummaging through thrift stores and your granny's closet and coming out with these things that felt good. And don't the Brits have a history of cross-dressing or something?

GYL CORRIGAN-DEVLIN It's funny how Robert's famous little blue blouse came about. It was just lying around, and this girl showed me how to put rhinestones on it; Beep went off to some factory and bought thousands of them. We'd sit on the plane and put them on everything. And then this girl Corrie came to the Drake in Chicago and brought the suit for Jimmy with all the planets on it and John Paul's jacket with the pom-poms.

MAGGIE BELL (Swan Song artist) Robert used to hate me because there were a couple of lovely antique shops on the King's Road, and I used to wear all the '30s and '40s gear, little silk blouses. He used to say to the guys, "You don't sell that to Maggie Bell if she comes in. Tell her that's for me."

VANESSA GILBERT (L.A. scenester and Zeppelin friend on the 1973 U.S. tour) The Hyatt House used to say, like, "WELCOME, Small Faces" or whoever it was on the marquee. When I learned that Zeppelin was in town, Gyl said, "Call Richard Cole, and tell him I'm going to be back in town tomorrow." Somehow I got through to Richard. The next day, off we went to visit him.

One by one, the guys started walking past, and slowly they came in—like, "Who's Richard got in *his* room?" What I really saw was a bunch of tired dudes. They would tour for a month, go home for a month, and come back and tour for a month. They would just beat the crap out of themselves and then go home and lick their wounds. So this was the tail end of the first pass.

Before you knew it, Gyl and I had keys to our own room on the ninth floor, and we just became part of the family. It was so comfortable, and nobody wanted anything, and there was no hanky-panky. We went to the Forum every night and sat there and came back to the hotel and had some cocktails and a bit of this and that and then went to bed.

GYL CORRIGAN-DEVLIN I first met Vanessa on the *Starship*. She was very un-groupie-looking, where all the other girls were five foot two and wearing next to nothing. Peter Grant fell madly in love with her. She was my right-hand man on these trips. From a distance, people thought she was Robert because she had the same hair. Robert was actually jealous of her.

VANESSA GILBERT I remember tackling Robert's hair one time. It was right after the month that they'd spent at home, and I don't think he'd brushed it once. I was trying to get the tangles out of it. What a scene! We had a very brotherly-sisterly relationship, and our hair looked a lot alike, so people constantly confused us, even though he was five inches taller than me.

LORI MATTIX (groupie and L.A. girlfriend of Page's) Vanessa was a part of the team. Gyl and Vanessa went on the road with them. During that whole phase, I couldn't go because I was underage, but Vanessa and Gyl would fly out with them.

VANESSA GILBERT We get to Seattle, and we're all in our rooms at the Edgewater Inn. The record company was holding a party for them on another floor, and the guys never went; they just sent Gyl and I to get shrimp to use as bait. One of the bodyguards gave John Paul and me a joint, and we sat there looking at the ocean, getting higher and higher and higher. Like, "Do I have *fingers* anymore?"

Next thing we hear this laughter, and it's Bonzo hanging over the balcony: "You guys gotta come and see this!" So we hobble along the hallway and open his door. And he's so proud. He opens the shower curtain, and there are at least eight mud sharks swimming around on top of each other. Peter is lying on the bed like the Jolly Green Giant, with a bottle of ouzo in his hand.

And then the girls started coming in. One of them had fingernails that were probably five inches long, painted green—she scared the shit out of me—and another one was wearing a leotard. And it was like, "Don't let Vanessa see this, don't let Vanessa see this!" Because I was the baby. Which only made me more curious, of course.

They were taking a mud shark and rubbing it on one of these girls. Everything was screwed down—even the ashtrays—and I remember John Paul had a briefcase with all these screwdrivers in it. After that, everything started going out the window. After a couple hours of this, Bonzo realizes it's *his* room, and he turns into a big fucking baby.

He wants to go to sleep, and now he doesn't have a bed to sleep in because it's floating in the ocean.

The next morning as we're checking out, the hotel manager comes out and sort of unscrolls the bill for everything that's been damaged. And he says, "I'm a little disappointed. This band threw out three rooms . . . that band threw out four rooms . . . and when the Mormon Church was here, they threw out *six* rooms."

GYL CORRIGAN-DEVLIN We had a friend in Seattle named Freddie Lightning or something, and we went into his shop one evening, and everyone got dressed up in drag because we were going on to L.A. and giving a party for Ahmet Ertegun at the Hyatt House. Robert wore a Chanel dress with Vanessa's high heels. Jimmy ended up wearing this amazing dress that had belonged to Vanessa's mother. He looked really good because he was a bit more girly than the others. There was nothing feminine about Bonzo. He came as a fishwife.

LORI MATTIX We put the boys in drag, and it was like this big party because George Harrison was down there. Stevie Wonder was visiting, and they wanted to play a joke on him. The guys come down in drag, and Stevie goes, "What's going on, man?" Everybody is cracking up, laughing, and nobody has the heart to tell Stevie what's going on.

CHARLES SHAAR MURRAY (from *NME*, June 16, 1973) It is John Bonham's birthday, and the Forum audience had given him a hero's tribute for his drum marathon on "Moby Dick" earlier in the evening. "Twenty-one today," as Plant had announced from the stage. "This party is probably going to get very silly," he announces. Why else would a man turn up to his birthday party wearing a T-shirt, plimsouls, and a pair of swimming trunks? As things turn out, he was the most appropriately clad person present. . . .

Having flown in from Louisiana that morning, your reporter disgraces himself by falling asleep in his chair at around 4:30 a.m. A little later, he is awakened by the very considerate Phil Carson from Atlantic, and returned, more or less in one piece, to his hotel. The following day he learns that virtually everyone present ended up in the pool after George Harrison clobbered Bonzo with his own birthday cake. Mr. Fallon's exquisite antique velvet costume was totalled by his immersion, as was Rodney Bingenheimer's camera and a mink coat belonging to a lady named Vanessa. Over the rest of the proceedings we will draw a slightly damp veil.

RODNEY BINGENHEIMER (L.A. DJ and club owner) Bonzo wanted me to take a picture of him and George and Patti [Boyd]with my little camera. I'm looking at the camera, trying to take the picture, but it was jammed, and Bonzo got all mad and threw me, Patti, and George in the pool.

VANESSA GILBERT When we got to London, Roy Harper said, "You made it into the paper," and he handed me the *Sun*. It described everybody getting thrown in the pool, "followed by a screaming girl in a mink coat." Which was me. Jimmy didn't go in because he was holding the drugs. Rodney was the first one to go in, because he always got picked on.

ROY HARPER (maverick British folkie and friend of Zeppelin's) There were two people who never ended up in the swimming pool; who you'd never, *ever* think of throwing in the pool—Jimmy and Peter. Oh, and the woman who was carrying for the band and had something or other in her bra.

ROBERT PLANT "I am *the* golden god." I proclaimed this with a smile— and I wasn't standing on the roof of a house; I was at the top of a palm tree on the night of Bonzo's birthday. It was an unfortunate moment, because someone drove across the garden in a Cadillac and wedged it between two palm trees. And I was busy making sure everyone knew exactly who and what I was. I wanted to get it in perspective before the party really started.

BILL HARRY (Zeppelin's first U.K. press officer) I heard that BP was going about in this beautiful green suit he'd bought, and they picked him up and threw him into a swimming pool. And I thought, "That is why I'm not there."

· · ·

ROBERT CHRISTGAU (music editor of the *Village Voice*, 1974–2006) [Led Zeppelin] redefined the '60s in the image of all teenagers for whom hippiedom was a cultural given, rather than a historical inevitability—all the kids forced by economic reality and personal limitation to escape from, rather than into, to settle for the representation of power because the real power their older siblings pretended to was so obviously a hallucination.

ROSS HALFIN (photographer and friend of Page's)   In America, the Rolling Stones were like the Kings of Leon are now: they were cool. Whereas Zeppelin were completely for the working classes. Which is why, when you went to Zeppelin shows, there were people passed out, throwing cherry bombs, all of that. Zeppelin appealed to the masses. And because Zeppelin were so accessible to the working classes, that's why the critics hated them so much.

JAAN UHELSZKI (writer for *Creem* magazine)   At *Creem*, we always loved Zeppelin, but then we were the anti–*Rolling Stone*. We were supposedly the anti-intellectual magazine, we were *of the fans*. Zeppelin really fit into what appealed to Midwesterners; it was big and it was bombastic.

BILL GRAHAM (San Francisco concert promoter)   Led Zeppelin always drew a difficult element. A lot of male aggression came along with their shows. This was during the warp of the '70s, which was a very strange era. It was anarchy without a cause. And there were a lot of rebels without causes out there in the audience whenever Led Zeppelin performed.

MICHAEL DES BARRES (singer with Silverhead and Swan Song band Detective)   The legions of disenfranchised young American warriors had no outlet whatsoever. They're the same kids who grew up worshipping Trent Reznor, they're always there. Their lives became three chords and a stadium parking lot. Zeppelin came along and gave them a hard-on like they'd never had before. There was no TMZ, there was no Internet. There was just this incantation, this wailing to the gods.

TONY MANDICH (artist relations manager in Atlantic's L.A. office, 1972–1997)   When they shut down those house lights, for three or four minutes I thought the roof would blow off from the expectation. It was something you really cannot explain or compare to other bands.

BRAD TOLINSKI (editor, *Guitar World* magazine)   In 1973, I saw Zeppelin at Cobo Hall in Detroit, which was a huge rock city and a big Zeppelin town. I grew up in a suburb that was probably much like a lot of Midwestern suburbs. You'd go down Telegraph Road, and it was just filled with fast food outlets and KMarts, and it was pretty fucking boring. And Zeppelin had this exotic otherworldly appeal. The Stones were ultimately sort of juvenile delinquents, so they didn't take us out of our environment. Zeppelin painted pictures of something otherworldly. But as opposed to prog rock, it had some real balls to it. "Dazed and Confused" turned the sexual act into something very Cecil B. DeMille: orgasm as mystical experience. It sounded super-dangerous. A Led Zeppelin orgasm wasn't pulling a girl's pants down in some alley.

ROBERT PLANT   In the beginning, at the tail end of the Haight-Ashbury phenomenon in the late '60s, playing San Francisco and stuff was a very mellow experience—far out. But then it got [to be] a bit of a rant with cherry bombs and firecrackers and bloodcurdling whoops. I was quite uncomfortable at times. It was just too big, and nobody knew how big it would be. It was too intense. This was a bit weird, we thought; we were playing the YMCA in Kirkcaldy four years ago!

HENRY SMITH   Robert was more of an American type of peacenik than maybe the others were. He was more of a caring soul. I remember times that we would sit down in the '70s and go, "Whatever happened to the peace-and-love generation?"

AUBREY POWELL (designer of Zeppelin album covers)   Robert still believes that we come as one tribe from those heady '60s days. He's much more a peace-and-love man than he is interested in any of the aspects that Jimmy was interested in. But just because Jimmy was interested in the occult and the dark side doesn't mean to say he was a dark *person*. He could be very cutting, and sometimes it could hurt you, but I never experienced him as being a dark force or a messenger of Crowley or anything like that.

I think Jimmy and Robert's relationship was exactly the same as any other creative relationship—Keith and Mick, John and Paul, Waters and Gilmour, Storm and me at Hipgnosis. In rock 'n' roll, you have these fractious relationships where there's a good cop and a bad cop, and somehow they gel to create interesting music.

LORI MATTIX They were such a good combination, Robert and Jimmy, because they were such polar opposites. Jimmy would slither into a room, whereas Robert would strut. You had to have seen the two of them together. It was always like oil and water. Jimmy was the water, and Robert was the oil. It was like rubbing those two egos together.

DANNY GOLDBERG (Zeppelin's U.S. press officer) I talked to Jimmy many, many times, but I always felt that he had a big wall up in front of him. Whereas Robert was very accessible emotionally. He was twenty-five when I met him, but he'd already been famous for five years. And he *loved* being famous. I've never met anyone who enjoyed being famous more than Robert Plant. He wanted to spread it around. He made people feel good. He was the happy warrior.

BP FALLON To me, Jimmy was a lovely man. Once you had his heart, you had it for always. Not everyone would say that, but not everyone has a fucking clue, do they? They prefer to have Jimmy eating virgins at the stroke of midnight. The image of him being this magus of dark uncertainty is wonderful. One day maybe we'll know if it's true.

BRAD TOLINSKI I never really got the evil thing, for all the myths and stories about Page making a deal with the devil. To me, it was always more transcendent and Olympian.

BP FALLON To me, he's the kid in *It Might Get Loud*, playing air guitar along to "Rumble." We had so many moments like that together.

Page onstage with roadie Ray Thomas at Kezar Stadium, San Francisco, June 2, 1973. (James Fortune/Rex Features)

I bought all these Sun singles at Ted Carroll's Rock On stall in Soho and went down to Plumpton Place with them. Jimmy would stand there playing air guitar along to the Roland Janes solos on Billy Lee Riley singles. The guy loves his music.

PERRY PRESS (London estate agent to the stars)   I'd already taken George Harrison to Plumpton. The original owner was a stuck-up Tory who'd sold it to a local solicitor who didn't really have the means to live there. So Jimmy bought it from him. The house was thought to date from the sixteenth/seventeenth century, and then [Edwin] Lutyens had come along and restored it for Edward Hudson, the founder of *Country Life*. The combination of it being a Lutyens house and in that setting meant we all fell in love with it.

Like mine, Jimmy's taste was always Gothic revival and the Arts and Crafts period. He has the most refined architectural taste and interest in houses of any of my clients, without exception.

• • •

Plumpton Place in the mid-'70s.

GYL CORRIGAN-DEVLIN   As soon as the Hollywood scene came around, Bonzo would be like, "I can't be doing with this." He was never one with the girls, except once he was drunk—then he was in party mode, and that was different. He'd always be the one who'd say, "I'm gonna see what's on television." And then the roadies would get him out and get him into trouble, and the next day the headlines would be all about *him*.

VANESSA GILBERT   Bonzo made enough ruckus for *everybody*. So much so that one hardly noticed John Paul, and Jimmy was sort of quiet, too. It seemed to me they would get rooms away from Robert and Bonzo.

ROY CARR   I was up in Bonzo's room in L.A., and we were going out that evening to the Rainbow or the Roxy. He says, "Pagey's in town, I'll get hold of him." So he rings Page up, trying to persuade him to come out. Page doesn't want to, so Bonzo says, "What the fuckin' 'ell do you do—hang upside down in a loft all day?"

BP FALLON   Bonzo was a very warmhearted man. He wasn't necessarily at all times best equipped for being regarded as a deity. But if you freak out every now and then and misbehave, does that mean you're a monster? Not necessarily. It just means you're a bit out of sync with how you should be behaving.

Bonzo was the guy who drove that train, night after night, not for a few minutes but sometimes for four hours. If he'd painted or sculpted, everyone would have said, "How great." But he didn't: he drummed, like nobody in the world. Sometimes I'd be standing at the side of the stage, and during "Whole Lotta Love" he'd give me this almost imperceptible nod that meant I had to go and play the tom-toms beside him. To feel the power of that was fucking incredible. It was like being strapped to a rocket.

TONY IOMMI (guitarist with Black Sabbath)   John was never a snob. We'd go out, and there was never any bragging about anything. He'd have liked to be a farmer, and he even started dressing like one. He really got into going the local pub and dressing like a farmer with the cap and everything. He certainly didn't dress like a rock star.

RICHARD COLE (Zeppelin's road manager)   The band was flying somewhere from England, and Bill Wyman was there with his girlfriend Astrid. She was talking to Bonzo. We were getting off the plane, and she pulled me to one side and said, "Richard, why do they bring a farmer on the road with them?"

JOHN BONHAM (speaking in 1975)   I was never into farming at all. I wasn't even looking for a farm, just a house with some land. But when I saw this place, something clicked, and I bought it. . . . [It] used to be just a three-bedroomed house. My father did all the wood paneling, and I did a lot of the work with my brother and subcontractors.

PAUL RODGERS (lead singer with Free and Bad Company)   There are pictures of him covered in cement and laying bricks. He was a really down-to-earth guy like that, who really got stuck in.

MAGGIE BELL   I loved Bonzo and his wife and kids. Just like a farmer's family, lovely and cuddly. I knew his brother and his little sister. Sweet nice family. Pat was just fab. Kitchen table, everybody sitting round there.

MARILYN COLE (wife of Richard Cole)   Richard and I would go up to the Old Hyde for the weekend, and there was a lot of drinking. I saw

The Bonhams in the south of France, August 1972: John, Jason, and Pat
(Richard Cole Collection)

Bonzo falling over, and I saw him shouting and hollering, but I never saw him nasty or abusive. Pat was one of those salt-of-the-earth women, warm and sweet and nice. She adored John. And he adored her.

BENJI LeFEVRE   On his own, out of the limelight, Bonzo was alright—a loving family man. But it really *was* Jekyll and Hyde: the minute he left the Old Hyde, he resumed his other life.

LULU (Scottish pop singer and friend of the Bonhams')   John and I had a lot in common. It was not about being a star or about doing it to become rich and famous; it was doing it because it's in every fiber of your body, and that's why I think it's kind of sweet that I am able to say I knew him.

   John was very generous and incredibly passionate, which allowed him to play the way he did. John and Pat and Maurice [Gibb] and myself used to hang out a lot together. When John was in London, he was always at our house. Being on the road, it does drive you a bit stir-crazy. You can't go out of your hotel rooms because people want a piece of you. So I think that encourages the excess. It has an effect, this business, of giving you a high adrenaline rush, but at some point you have to come down from that, and it's not easy. And that's why drugs and alcohol numb you out a little bit.

TONY IOMMI   John and I spent many nights doing coke, and it got to a point where he'd tip a pile onto a plate and just throw it at his face. You'd think about saying something, but John was hard to talk to when he was like that. You might say, "You gonna cool it a bit tonight?" And he'd say, "Ah, fuck it, I don't care!" How Pat dealt with it, I don't know. It must have been very hard for her. He and Matthew [Stanislowski] were driving down to London in the Roller once, and John said, "Stop, stop!" So Matthew stopped the car, and John just started beating him up. He was like a wild animal.

LORI MATTIX   If Bonzo got out of control, he was insane. We went to this opening in some theater in L.A., and afterward he was so fucking drunk, he took a picture off the wall and slammed it over Richard Creamer's head.

Lori Mattix on the town with Bonzo and (lurking behind them) Richard Cole, L.A., June 1973. (Michael Ochs Archives/Getty Images)

HOWARD MYLETT (Zeppelin collector and expert) I'd seen them at Wembley in 1971, but I came away thinking a more intimate gig like Brighton would be great. On the 22nd of December, 1972, I went down in the afternoon to the Dome, and there were people around like roadies and riggers, and I bumped into Mick Hinton. I said, "Any chance I could get backstage afterward?" I had these Zeppelin scrapbooks that I'd brought, and they loved looking through them.

Then I heard Bonzo trashing a dressing room—you could literally hear these chairs being thrown around and grunting noises being made, no words being formed. It was like a bear in a cage. I didn't go and pursue it.

JANE AYER (publicist in Atlantic's West Coast office in the '70s) Mick Hinton was devoted to Bonzo and took such great care of him. He did *everything* for him. It was like Bonzo was his *child*.

SALLY WILLIAMS (girlfriend of Mick Hinton) Mick was Bonzo's roadie-cum-dogsbody. His main job was to set up the drum kit. The running-around part, the picking up of John's laundry, was mainly back home in England. They were two of a kind. John was a really nice guy, but he was probably drinking long before Zeppelin came along. There were times when he would floor Mick in some kind of rage—it was the alcohol speaking. If he hadn't been a musician, he would have been very happy on his farm with his toys.

JEFF OCHELTREE (drum tech who assisted Bonham on the 1977 U.S. tour) Mick made £45 a week working for Zeppelin at the beginning. He just kept doing the same things, taking drugs and never really developing as a drum tech. That's why they treated him as a class clown and dressed him up as a butler.

BENJI LeFEVRE Bonzo and Hinton had a love-hate relationship. Being a drum tech is not the most demanding job in the world, and I don't think Mick could really have done anything else. Bonzo regularly used to beat him up. Seeing him getting biffed for no apparent reason put a really bad taste in your mouth.

15

When I Look to the West

Their popularity lay in myriad reasons: their indisputable
talent, their sex appeal, and their sheer power. The
nasty '70s fit them like an iron glove.

> —Peter Clifton, in Chris Welch's *The Man Who Led*
> *Zeppelin* (2002)

TONY MANDICH (artist relations manager at Atlantic's West Coast office, 1972–1997)   They really weren't that demanding. Big parties and hoopla and this and that? No, they were really happy going late at night to the Rainbow, where I would set them up with a section blocked off. Most of the time, they took care of their own tab, and it was no big deal. Bonzo was always the first to come and the last to leave.

LORI MATTIX (groupie and L.A. girlfriend of Page's)   They liked to rule at the Rainbow. It was easy because it was the Strip. That was our domain. They liked to get loud in there and make it loud and crazy. Mario Maglieri let them get away with murder.

Former Atlantic Records general manager Jerry Greenberg (left) at the Rainbow Bar & Grill in L.A. with Mikael Maglieri, the son of Rainbow founder Mario, June 2010. (Art Sperl)

SALLY WILLIAMS (girlfriend of Bonham's roadie Mick Hinton)   Everybody was at the Rainbow one night in the big booth, and people were prowling around trying to get autographs. Robert stood up and shouted, *"Where's the fucking security? Get these people away from us!"* So I shouted over the table, *"Well, if you sat down and shut up, that would be a start!"* Mick told me that Robert later said to him, "Your old lady's got a lot of spunk."

JOHN PAUL JONES   L.A. is so boring most of the time, so as soon as any life arrives, suddenly you rule the town. I'm probably more ashamed of the *reputation* than of anything we actually did. Plus, people seem to have forgotten every other band that stayed at the Hyatt House, because everyone was behaving in a similar way. A lot of people have put this really evil slant on it, and when I read that sort of stuff, I think, "Do they mean *us?*" We seemed to take the heat for everybody.

LORI MATTIX   L.A. was the Mecca of rock 'n' roll in the '70s. New York was way more urban, but in L.A. you could have one scene right here, and it was all within a small radius of the Strip. It will never happen again: the girls, the decadence, the throwing champagne bottles out the window. We used to try and hit the billboards across the street.

MIKE APPLETON (producer of BBC2's *Old Grey Whistle Test*)   There was so much money sloshing around the record business in those days that people referred to Dom Pérignon as "rock 'n' roll mouthwash."

NICK KENT (writer for *New Musical Express*)   People go to Hollywood to attain celebrity. Everyone who goes there has a fame-seeking agenda, which makes it a spiritually bankrupt place. The '70s was the end of Hollywood as a wild frontier town, and Led Zeppelin were the most famous group in the world. When news of them being in Hollywood hit the grapevine, all these nutcases came out of the woodwork.

PAMELA DES BARRES (groupie and L.A. girlfriend of Page's)   Something about Zeppelin's energy really altered the joie de vivre of the L.A. rock scene. They thought they could get away with anything—and they *could*, because everyone wanted to get near them. They were very debauched, and the girls got younger and younger and more willing to do anything. It got to be incredibly sick. I mean, it's weird to see Richard Cole today, because I have images of him kicking people's teeth out.

MORGANA WELCH (L.A. groupie and Zeppelin friend)   Around 1972 is when the Hyatt House became notorious. Prior to that, it was only a small handful of groupies. We knew what was going on. You could walk into the little coffee shop and hang out with a lot of people. And there were always bands staying there.

The word got out that this was a cool place to hang. The coffee shop was open twenty-four hours, so you'd go there after the clubs closed and when all the bands were coming in. And it just turned into a huge party place. It was very intimate, and it was very real in a lot of ways. There weren't bodyguards, and there weren't cops. There was nothing except Richard Cole. And the hotel itself pretty much turned the other cheek.

The Hyatt House, aka the Continental Hyatt, aka "the Riot House," shortly before it became the Andaz West Hollywood in January 2009. (Art Sperl)

RICHARD COLE (Zeppelin's road manager) The second-generation L.A. groupies were younger and more hysterical. Each year there'd be a few of the old ones and a whole slew of new ones. Really, what I think they were doing was trying to live up to what they'd read or heard about.

MORGANA WELCH There was a buzz among all the young girls that these were the guys you needed to go meet. There was something very charismatic about Zeppelin that just drew you. Jimmy was the mysterious dark one, while Robert was just out front center, projecting this love of life. So there was this darkness and light that was also very curious and something to explore. In a way, they were a more sophisticated Beatles. It was more *serious* than the British Invasion groups, going within oneself with music as the catalyst.

NICK KENT The really famous groupies were extremely tough and unpleasant. Jimmy told me that one of his Hollywood girlfriends bit

into a sandwich that had razor blades in it. I mean, seeing these conniving, loveless little girls really affected my whole concept of feminin-
ity for a while. Talk to the bass player from Sweet, and he would
probably say those were the best months of his life, but to someone
with a bit of taste—who wasn't just hopelessly addicted to pussy—it
was pretty sordid. It was a period of time when, if you were skinny and
English and dressed like some horrible Biba girl, you could have anything you wanted.

MICK FARREN (singer with the Deviants and writer for *New Musical
Express*)   I'd be on the road with Hawkwind or whoever, writing for
the *NME*, and we'd check into the Hyatt, and Zeppelin would be
there. And the whole place was full of the stinkiest fucking groupies.
There was something very unclean about the whole deal. Rod and the
Faces sort of kicked it off, but it went to some kind of zenith with Zeppelin. Moon actually blew up hotel rooms, but with Zeppelin it just
seemed to be running in semen and beer and unpleasantness and old
Tampaxes. They were number one on the groupie-target roster, and
Rodney Bingenheimer was pandering to them as they sat in the back
of his cupboard-sized discotheque getting their dicks sucked by thir-
teen-year-olds under the table.

RODNEY BINGENHEIMER (L.A. DJ and club owner)   Nothing could
beat L.A., especially with the music scene and the girls. Led Zeppelin
would land at LAX and load up the limousines with all their luggage,
and before they'd even checked into their hotel, they would swing by
my club, with all the luggage still in the limo. I'd be DJ'ing, playing
Gary Glitter, David Bowie, Suzi Quatro, Mud. I did manage to play
"Trampled under Foot" in the club, but that was the only Zeppelin
track. They wrote a song about the place called "Sick Again."

DANNY GOLDBERG (Zeppelin's U.S. press officer and president of Swan
Song)   I got a very angry call about a picture at Rodney's, and my
response was, "Don't be in the fucking picture!" I mean, what am *I*
supposed to do if someone takes a picture? There was an illusion that
you could control the press. I mean, I *wish*.

Rodney Bingenheimer with vintage wheels and vintage Zep T-shirt, West Hollywood, June 2010. (Art Sperl)

RODNEY BINGENHEIMER The girls would scratch your eyes out if you crossed their path. There were a lot of other girls that were in love with Led Zeppelin, but these girls kept them away. I had a girlfriend at the time who was in love with Jimmy, but she couldn't get near Jimmy because of Lori Mattix.

BP FALLON (Zeppelin's U.K. press officer, 1972–1976) I got to photograph Lori because she was in my room. Why would I *not* photograph her? The thing about groupies that's misunderstood is that it was all consensual. The *girls* were the predators, not the bands. Lori and Sable were very funny, very bright; they wouldn't take any shit from anybody.

CAMERON CROWE (writer for the *L.A. Times*, *Circus*, and *Rolling Stone*) What I was trying to capture [in *Almost Famous*] was the elaborate denial that the girls buy into. They talk about themselves as muses . . . but when you get the rock stars, you realize [the girls] of course are the trinkets themselves. When I ran into rock stars at airports, they would ask me, "Have you seen Lori or . . . ?" and I'd say no . . . and they'd get a wistful look, where you realize later the power of those trinkets. They missed those girls. . . . It's funny how they remembered [them] as a great symbol of their years of popularity. Looking back, those girls had shared many of the most private, reckless, golden moments . . . they had become, over time, as memorable to those musicians as the music itself.

IGGY POP (lead singer of the Stooges)   When I was living in L.A. in very reduced circumstances during that period, I would meet these horrible little girls there who were fifteen and were fearing becoming nineteen. And that's not healthy, that's sick.

SABLE STARR (L.A. groupie, speaking in 1973)   I never want to be anything over fourteen years old. I'm just going to ignore the years from here on.

Plant with Iggy Pop at the Riot House, summer 1973. (James Fortune/Rex Features)

LORI MATTIX Sable and I were best friends, like two peas in a pod. We were the young Paris Hiltons of our decade. She was the one who brought underwear and garter belts and all that to Hollywood, way before the Runaways were around.

Michael Des Barres was staying at the Hyatt House, and Sable and I went to visit him. Michael and Jimmy were best friends, so he went back to England and showed Jimmy these photos, and Jimmy said, "Oh, my God, I have to meet this girl." At the time, we sort of looked alike. I was skinny and had really long curly hair.

Sable and I were up in Iggy Pop's house, which was the Mainman house, and Sable was like, "Zeppelin are coming to town. Let's go down to the Hyatt House. If you go near Jimmy, you're dead." So I was terrified and was not going to go anywhere near him until we got to the Hyatt. And everybody's up at the pool, and Jimmy beelines directly over to me. I'm like, "Oh my God, don't come near me. You're going to get me in trouble." I said, "Sable is going to beat me up. You have to go away."

MORGANA WELCH I didn't like those Rodney's girls. When you're young, it's all about territory, so anybody that came from the Valley was looked down on. I was sixteen when I started out, but these girls were *thirteen* and very immature. I don't think we were troubled, we were just annoyed. We thought they were ridiculous. And look, Roman Polanski got caught, but there were all these forty-year-old men who were seeing young girls on the Strip.

It went both ways: there was a notch in your belt as a girl if you went with a famous guy. And it was going on all the time. There would be parties after the Rainbow closed, just big sex parties. People got loaded, put good music on, and everybody was with everybody. And most of the guys were *much* older.

LORI MATTIX My biggest fear was Richard and Peter, obviously, because Richard said, "If you don't fucking do what I say, I'll 'ave your fucking head."

RODNEY BINGENHEIMER I went to a party at the Hyatt, and they had the whole floor. A friend of mine, Ronny Romano, came with me, and they got all weird about it. Bonzo or Richard ended up picking him up by his heels and holding him over the balcony. Nine floors up. They were all laughing.

LORI MATTIX   When they came down, Richard told me to get in this limousine. It was a bit scary. I was a frail little thing, I didn't know what the fuck was going on. He was like, "Just sit there and don't move." Jimmy had left a long time ago, and I didn't know where he was. They drove me back to the Hyatt House, and all of a sudden I'm being escorted down the hallway by three bodyguards. A door opens, and Jimmy is sitting there in a hat, waiting for me, and he says, "See, I told you I'd have you."

GYL CORRIGAN-DEVLIN (Zeppelin friend, traveled on 1973 U.S. tour)   Jimmy and Lori really were so beautiful together. The longer the relationship went on, the more they looked alike. I don't think I ever thought, "Oh my god, Jimmy could get arrested." The way I saw it then, it was just very Hollywood: like, "You're not in Seaham Harbour anymore." I found those little girls rather annoying, and we'd swat them away.

LORI MATTIX   Jimmy stationed himself in L.A. and would fly in every night just to see me. He would play Chicago and then get a flight out that night so that we could be together. We'd be sitting on the floor, and then we'd be crying because we were so happy to see each other. We really kept to ourselves and were very private. He was my first love, and I didn't know any better. I feel lucky to have had that time with him, because I don't think he'll ever have that innocence again. I didn't love him for his money because I didn't know what that was.

He was always very conventional and conservative. He wanted me to be such a lady. He used to make me wear long dresses and look gypsylike. He caught me smoking a cigarette one night and went crazy and bought three packs, and he made me sit there and smoke all of them so I was gagging and then made me promise I'd never smoke again. If you look at any photos in the early '70s, you'll never see him with a cigarette in his hand. He wasn't even a big drinker. He'd have his gin and orange or vodka or champagne, and he loved the blow, but that was that.

BP FALLON   You never knew what people were capable of. They'd want me to get a message to Jimmy, and you didn't know whether they were going to pull out a knife or what. So instead I introduced Zeppo to people like Les Petits Bon Bons, who were these wonderful raving young queens from California who'd give Bonzo pictures of their cocks with glitter on them. We went to gay clubs because it was more fun, and simply brought the girls with us.

CONNIE HAMZY (Arkansas-based groupie of wide renown)   The first time I met Led Zeppelin was in Dallas. I was about the only real woman around them because they'd brought all these drag queens with them on the plane from New Orleans. Bonham stayed because when he was at the hotel, he looked over the balcony and there was a Corvette on the parking lot that he wanted. I would like to have been with Robert, but seeing as they'd left, I said to Bonham, "I'm very glad that you and I got to know each other." He said, "Well, if you like, I'll put on a blond wig for you." He gave me the impression he didn't fool around very often.

JACK CALMES (cofounder of Showco sound and lighting company)   I always wondered how Connie could do what she did. She was amazingly good-looking for somebody who would just line guys up like that.

MORGANA WELCH   I don't know why Roy Harper was on that tour. Probably just to have a good time. When I think that I was sixteen, and he must have been thirty, it's kind of like, "Wow!" We met at this pool party at the Hyatt House where me, Tyla, and Dewey Martin had gone. The Zep crew comes up, and Richard Cole starts throwing people in the pool. And apparently me, Tyla, and Dewey threw Robert *and* Jimmy in, because we were just so tired of watching them laugh at everyone else.

   That night I was in Roy's room, and about a half hour later, Richard, Bonzo, Plant, and I think Lori and Sable broke down the door. Robert took a picture of me and Roy in bed, which I was really furious about. It was like bored eight-year-old boys, saying, "What we can we do next?"

GYL CORRIGAN-DEVLIN Roy was a complete nutcase on the tour. Somebody lent him a monkey for a while, and he would walk onstage with him. It became huge in the press.

VANESSA GILBERT (L.A. scenester and Zeppelin friend on the 1973 U.S. tour) Roy carried this stuffed monkey around with him, and he would sort of flutter it at Jimmy when the band was onstage. I liked Roy. We stayed at his house in England; he showed us his bird-watching slides, narrating as the slides went by.

ROY HARPER (folk singer and Zeppelin pal, speaking in 1974) By the end of a tour, everybody is getting pretty much blown out. I mean, you have no idea, *you have absolutely no idea*, of what the pressures are like. Peter Grant jestfully referred to me as the social worker on the last trip. There's a limit to what human beings can take, and on a cross-country American tour, you can watch the gradual disintegration. And when you run into the average hotel jobsworth, you don't actually want to play around with him too much.

You're going gray, so life gets into a pattern of activity that's inescapable. You reach the ultimate, which is, "What can we do next to keep ourselves together?" I've seen cars driven into swimming pools and walls blown out of hotels with dynamite. But that only happens when you've reached the point of total stress, when you've gone beyond all endurance.

RICHARD COLE At the Drake Hotel in New York, Jimmy phoned me in the middle of the night because he wanted $600 for a guitar. I went down to the safe, and everything was there. When I went down the next afternoon to get some money to pay off the film crew, everything was gone. The key opened, and there were just the passports in there. They'd even nicked some money that Jimmy had brought over from England for a Yardbirds tour.

VANESSA GILBERT Everybody had their own theory—like, Richard took the money and went to Switzerland and got back before everybody woke up. We were all questioned more than once. It was *very serious*.

UNITY MacLEAN (manager of Swan Song's London office)   The strange thing about the Drake robbery was that Peter wasn't that unhappy about it. And usually if Peter had lost a couple of quid, he'd be miserable. You'd have expected him to turn America upside down to find that money, and he didn't.

LORI MATTIX   Jimmy was like, "Don't worry about it, darlin', it's all under control."

PETER CLIFTON (film director who completed *The Song Remains the Same*)   In *The Song Remains the Same*, I decided to re-create the robbery, and I got away with it.

RICHARD COLE   We were playing Boston, staying at the Sheraton, and I was brought in to meet Joe Massot. That was the first time I knew we were making a film. And it was all rushed together to do the sequences in Pittsburgh and all that business. I remember Joe in England, saying he wanted us to rent him a Range Rover, and I said, "Tell him to rent a fucking Ford Fairlane!"

JOE MASSOT (original director of *The Song Remains the Same*)   Right from the start, Jimmy was against a straight concert movie, though obviously for the band it's the safest way of doing it. Anyway, I don't film that way—a camera here, a camera there. It's just too mathematical. The way I filmed, I eliminated that possibility, and I felt that one concert movie within the medium of film wasn't enough visually. The music is the power that drives the imagery, and just the performance is not enough.

PETER GRANT   We got Massot and Ernie Day over and started filming. It turned out to be traumatic, to say the least. . . . They filmed three dates and never got one complete take of "Whole Lotta Love."

PETER CLIFTON   I saw glimpses of brilliance in what Joe had done— you hold a mirror up to Led Zeppelin, and you're going to get extraordinary things—but again, it was that haphazard thing. There was a scene missing here and a scene missing there, and when you're dealing with rock 'n' roll stars, the only thing they look at is the mistakes. If something's not perfect, they jump all over it. Joe didn't have the savoir faire to deal with people like that, so, of course, they walked all over him.

JOE MASSOT I became a psychiatrist, a doctor. I don't know—it was weird. I'd go to each one's home, he'd show me round, we'd talk about the film, and two days later we'd be making it. If you've made films, you know difficult it is—just bringing down lights, finding costumes. With forty or so people involved, the whole psychiatrist thing came to a head, and the band eventually realized they'd had enough. It was a coup d'état, really, but that's showbiz. What I did find out about Led Zeppelin was that, as individual human beings, they were extremely sensitive and considerate, but as a group they were bloody difficult, if not impossible.

JOHN PAUL JONES When we first had the idea, it was a relatively simple one—to film some shows and then release it as a film. Little did we know how difficult it would all become. I would ask if we were filming tonight but be told that nothing was going to be filmed, so I'd think, "Not to worry, I'll save the shirt I wore the previous night for the next filming." Then I'd get onstage and see the cameras all ready to roll. Nobody seemed to know what was going on.

PETER CLIFTON Joe had been to Boston, he'd been to Pittsburgh, he'd been to various concerts, and they'd had a couple of 16 mm cameras in and out of this place. Even when he wasn't there, there were cameramen roaming around—it was a cameraman who picked up the sequence where Peter Grant is ranting backstage.

When they got to Madison Square Garden, they started shooting in 35 mm film but on four-hundred-foot rolls, which only gave you about three and a half minutes. During the reel changes, the cameramen were missing so much material, so Joe was trying to fill it with documentary footage, but it was out of sync and it didn't match. It was a very difficult thing to film live concerts in those days.

JOE MASSOT They finally came to a preview theater to see the "Stairway to Heaven" segment, and they started to fight and yell when the film began. They thought it was my fault that Robert Plant had such a big cock.

PETER CLIFTON I'd decided to go back to Australia for a while and make a film about reggae. I was just packing up the house when the phone rang and it was Peter, who said, "Come and see me in Oxford Street." I walked into the office, and there were the four of them, just sitting waiting for me. They even had Foster's beer in the fridge.

I pitched a film to them, not knowing at that point that they'd been working with Massot. They eventually told me and said, "It's not working out, it's not what we wanted." When I saw the mess it was in, I said, "There's some great 16 mm documentary material there, but there's nothing that holds together as a film." I thought that if you could make a 35 mm film, then you could re-create the concert experience. I said, "I don't want interviews—I find rock stars have a lot of difficulty articulating themselves—but let's come up with ideas as to how we can reveal your personalities."

The meeting went on and on and on, and the next day I heard from Peter. He said, "Look, Jimmy loves your editing, so we'd like you to make the film." I already had people moving into my house, so I moved to the Churchill Hotel for three weeks and wrote a script—I just winged it.

I took the script down to Horselunges and showed it to Peter. Jimmy was hiding in the back room, apparently. The next thing I know, Peter comes out and says, "Okay, we agree." I said, "Can I have a contract?" and he just signed every page of my script. There wouldn't be any fee, but I was to be made a sixth member of Led Zeppelin and would get an equal share of the whole thing.

I went to see Joe. He was eccentric, long-haired, and ill-disciplined but quite serious. He was a bit of a hippie. I had to play the George Clooney role in *Up in the Air* and sack him.

• • •

DANNY GOLDBERG   They were *all* into cocaine. That was part of the culture then, when a lot of people on Wall Street and all different kinds of people were doing cocaine. The damages of it were not clear to people, and certainly in the rock 'n' roll world it seemed like it was everywhere. So cocaine was not something they wanted distance from, and that was the main drama.

BP FALLON   How do you not sleep for six days and keep going? Pretty easily, actually. Part of the fuel is the lunacy, the being unhinged. A lot of great art isn't made by people who go jogging in the morning. It wasn't all a blur. It was all in high definition. Sensory overload. Driving down the highway with the police escort. Having drugs and sex in the limo. Very vibey.

GYL CORRIGAN-DEVLIN   What started out as a little joint and a few bottles of Dom Pérignon got to be a *case* of champagne, and eventually they got into the *really* bad drugs. At the beginning we would all be together—or the guys would be together—and then it was Peter and Jimmy off in another room by themselves.

Toward the end of '73 is when Jimmy was starting to be a little bit naughty. I think he had already started to mix heroin and coke. I can still remember in Milwaukee, someone had left a line of coke on the dresser, and we thought, "Oh, we can't leave it there." It turned out someone had put heroin in with the coke, and we were all absolutely ill. Jimmy was really the only one who wasn't, and it was obvious to me that that line had been left as a gift for *him*.

SAM AIZER (artist relations, Swan Song U.S. office)   I think it started coming apart in 1973. Before then, you look at all the shows they did from '68 to '71, and this was an animal group. You could never play at that level and be out of it: you had to be hungry and seeing something unfolding and Peter driving a whip. By the time they got to their own jet, the wheels started falling off the cart. Because now they've become what they *wanted* to be.

PART 3

Twitchy Times

I n late 1973, after cruising for a year in a haze of groupies, drugs, and private tour jets, Led Zeppelin took stock of the madness their music had unleashed. John Paul Jones, crying out for quality time with his kids, threatened to quit the group.

Out of this soul-searching came not only *Physical Graffiti* (1975)—a powerful double album that encompassed epic mysticism ("Kashmir") and intense Delta blues dread ("In My Time of Dying")—but the ill-conceived yet initially very successful Swan Song label, home in due course to Maggie Bell, Bad Company, the Pretty Things, and Zeppelin themselves. The band's 1975 tour of America was a behemoth but came at the cost of Page's increasing frailty and the alcoholic antics of Bonzo the Beast. Climaxing with a week-long residency at London's vast Earl's Court, Zeppelin had pushed themselves as far as they could go. Now everything began to unravel.

A car accident in Rhodes almost killed Maureen Plant and left Zeppelin's singer on crutches for months. Punitive tax rates drove the group into exile—specifically to Los Angeles, where a depressed Page kept the curtains closed and sank into a smack habit. When the four men finally regrouped to make the guitar-heavy but strangely cold

Page strums at Oakland
Coliseum, July 23, 1977. (Ed
Perlstein/Redferns)

Presence (1976), the fire seemed to have gone out of their bellies.
With Peter Grant and Richard Cole—not to mention half of the road
crew—in the grip of their own addictions, the overseeing of the Zeppelin empire became dysfunctional in the extreme. Bad Company
aside, Swan Song's other acts were left to dangle, while the label's
London office became a den of thieves and worse.

Add to this punk's belated reaction to bloated '70s superstardom,
and it was clear that Zeppelin were no longer tethered to the real
world: not quite irrelevant but hardly the musical powerhouse it had
been. Page was in trouble, not just with drugs but with his occult dabbling: harboring Satanist filmmaker Kenneth Anger in his London
home was not the wisest thing he'd ever done. On the U.S. tour of
1977, something in the heart of Zeppelin was rotting. Paranoia was
ubiquitous, and Grant's right-hand man was now not Richard Cole
but the psychopathic criminal Johnny Bindon.

All of it came to a head one hideous July weekend. Wired to the gills on cocaine, Grant and Bindon almost beat one of promoter Bill Graham's henchmen to death in Oakland. Two days later, Plant's son Karac died of a viral infection in the Black Country, where the singer's roots were still deep in the soil of Worcestershire.

These events almost spelled the end of Zeppelin, but Bonzo coaxed his old Midlands mucker back into the fold. Exasperated by Page's drug use—and Bonzo's boozing, come to that—Plant nonetheless signed on for the eclectic but misfiring *In Through the Out Door*, as well for two huge shows at Knebworth in August '79 and the scaled-back 1980 *Tour Over Europe*, intended to warm the band up for yet another assault on the American heartland.

The U.S. tour never happened. In September 1980, after reconvening with his bandmates at Page's new home near Windsor, Bonzo drank himself insensible and died from choking on his own vomit. A week later, it was announced that Led Zeppelin was finished.

16

Out of the Maelstrom of Mediocrity

This social phenomenon, in no way was it ever in existence in the past and in no way will it ever exist again. I don't think we'll ever see this again: the adulation, the *massness*.
—Bill Graham to Tony Palmer, in *All You Need Is Love*, 1975

JIMMY PAGE (speaking in 1975)   When I came back from the last tour, I didn't know where I was. I didn't even know where I was going. We ended up in New York, and the only thing that I could relate to was the instrument onstage. I just couldn't . . . I was just totally and completely spaced out.

ROBERT PLANT (speaking in 1975)   I was so relieved to be home again, because I'd missed a season, and I really need each season as it comes. I got back in August after that tour and realized I'd missed spring going into summer that year. I don't want to lose these perspectives in what I consider to be important for the lyrical content of what I write.

I want to take stock of everything, instead of going on the road until I don't know where the fuck I am and end up like a poached egg three days old.

PETER GRANT [John Paul Jones] turned up at my house one afternoon and told me he'd had enough and said he was going to be the choirmaster at Winchester Cathedral.

JOHN PAUL JONES I'd just had enough of touring, and I did go to Peter and tell him I wanted out unless things were changed. There was a lot of pressure on my family.

PETER GRANT He was just generally *peeved*—I think that was his word—with things. I said, "Have you told anyone else?" And he said, "No, I came straight to you." I said, "Well, you're gonna be 'Not Too Well.'"

JOHN PAUL JONES Had I talked it over with the band? Only in the form of general whingeing. It happened a few times that I was the one who was pushed out to the front to ask. I didn't want to harm the group, but I didn't want my family to fall apart, either.

PETER GRANT It was kept low-key. I told Jimmy, of course, who couldn't believe it. But it was the pressure. He was a family man, was Jonesy. Eventually, I think he realized he was doing something he really loved. It was never discussed again.

RICHARD COLE When we went back to Headley Grange to do the next album, I put Robert, Bonzo, and John Paul into a hotel called the Frencham Pond. Jimmy wouldn't stay there. He was quite happy in that fucking horrible cold house.

RON NEVISON (engineer on the *Physical Graffiti* sessions) I drove the Ronnie Lane mobile unit down to Headley. It was state-of-the-art with a Helios console, the same one the Stones had in their truck, sixteen tracks like most of the big studios had.

Jonesy had some personal issues, but I didn't ask and I wasn't told. So we spent a week or so at Headley just running down songs; I don't think we even recorded much. We were just hanging around, doing

Elvis covers and stuff like that. We went home and came back a week later, and that was when the official recording of *Physical Graffiti* started.

I'd made a commitment to Pete Townshend to start the *Tommy* film in late January. Because of Jonesy not appearing for a week, I had to ask at one point to leave the project, and I don't think anybody in the history of Led Zeppelin had ever quit a project before. When I called up and told them I couldn't continue, they were really nasty to me on the phone. They all shouted and screamed at me, and it was very upsetting. Especially Bonham, who called me all sorts of names.

ROBERT PLANT (speaking in 1975)   It's always a case of getting together and feeling out the moods of each of us when we meet with instruments for the first time in six months. We began as always, playing around and fooling about for two days, playing anything we want, like standards, our own material or anything that comes to us, and, slowly but surely, we develop a feel that takes us on to the new material.

Some of the new stuff came directly from this approach, like "Trampled Under Foot," which was just blowing out, and some comes from Jonesy or Pagey or myself—seldom myself—bringing along some structure [that] needs working on. Then the four of us inflict our own venom on it to develop the idea.

RON NEVISON   My biggest fan during the whole recording was Robert, who loved the effect I got on his vocals—probably because I wasn't a guy who looked at meters. I was taught early on, don't listen to the speakers, listen to the music.

The drum kit was set up where it had been set up for the fourth album. I put mics all around it, and Bonham told me to take them down. I said, "Well, just in case . . . ," and he said, "No, not just in case—take them down." So I took them down, and they showed me where to put the microphones where they'd used them before.

There was very little of Ron Nevison in this recording, compared to other recordings I've done. I was not party to any of the rehearsals, which is totally different to how I've worked with other bands.

Even with "Kashmir," when we cut the track, there wasn't even a vocal on it; it was just bass, drums, and guitar.

ROBERT PLANT Bonzo came in with this really nice driving tempo, really laid back, sort of *shoom shoom*. And we thought, "Mandrax? No." And having been traveling a little bit to get the feel of foreign lands, the song developed from that *shoom shoom* . . . and with a touch of the east, a little bit of cholera on the arm . . . what we had left was "Kashmir."

BENJI LeFEVRE (Zeppelin sound technician, 1973–1980) Eventide Clockworks gave me innovative bits of electronics, and I just played with them. Robert's voice would become a chorus of ten voices, because I would feed things back into themselves. And then we had this harmonizer with an actual keyboard so I could make his voice sing chords. It was fantastic fun.

RON NEVISON I'd heard that Eventide phasers sounded great on cymbals, so I brought one in for "Kashmir." I only had two tracks for drums, so what I did was set up the phaser and put one of the tracks through it, just for the hell of it. And they loved it and kept it in, and that's part of the whole sound of "Kashmir."

PETER GRANT They'd go off to recordings . . . and I'd get a call from Bonzo: "Oh, you've got to come down. We ain't half done something today." I remember particularly "Kashmir"—"Come down! Come down! Get in the Porsche and get down here!"

BENJI LeFEVRE Bonzo and Robert arrived in Bonzo's brand-new BMW—"Arrggh, best fucking car I've ever 'ad!"—and Bonzo goes, "'Ere, Benj, look what *I've* got." And he had a bag of about *fifteen hundred* Mandrax [a sedative]. I thought, "Well, this is gonna be a good session, isn't it?" He was handing them out like sweeties, saying, "Don't tell Robert." I said, "Bonzo, you'd better fucking *stash* these somewhere." So a little later he said to me, "Come and look." He'd taped them to the inside of his tom-tom—forgetting, of course, that it was a Perspex kit, so we could all see it.

RON NEVISON I was pretty naïve. They kept saying, "When's Charlie coming?" And I never *met* Charlie. There was a decided change in the vibe after Charlie came. After a few days, I realized what was going on. At some point during the recordings at Headley, I made the decision not to stay nights there but to lock up the truck and drive back to London at the end of each session. The reason was that they kept waking me up at three in the morning wanting to record, and the recordings went nowhere—it was just a waste of time. They realized in the end that I was doing the right thing. They didn't say, "You stay here or we'll get somebody else." They knew they were bad boys and that this would improve the whole flow of the recording.

BENJI LeFEVRE   In the mornings at Headley, us mere mortals used to go 'round the sitting room, picking up rocks of coke to make our own stashes.

GYL CORRIGAN-DEVLIN (Zeppelin friend)   I can remember the night when everything got a little scary for me at Headley. I was worried about Bonzo, I think, because he'd have finished the wine at dinner and then he'd get stuck into the Jack Daniel's. And that was the first time I'd spent time with him at the kitchen table, as it were. This wasn't on the road, he wasn't coming down from anything. And he would get sad at the end of the night and say he wanted to go home.

VANESSA GILBERT (Zeppelin friend)   After the 1973 tour, I was in England for about six months. I was staying near Hampstead Heath with Gyl. One evening the phone rings, and it's Peppy, one of their road guys: "We're here at Headley Grange, and John Paul wants to see you." I said, "Where's Headley Grange?" I hang up the phone, and two seconds later BP Fallon calls, right there and then. Now *he* wants to go to Headley Grange.

The taxi couldn't find the exact location, so we pulled over at a phone box and called Peppy, who came and got us in Bonzo's brand-new BMW. Peppy starts bouncing the car off at least five different obstacles. We're holding on for dear life in the back seat. When we get in the house, John Paul's got his face in, like, a pile of spaghetti—he's on Mandrax or something, and he's talking real slow. Beep, who'd probably also taken a couple of Mandrax, went to sleep in a little bedroom, and the guys went outside into the garden with the sheep and herded them into Beep's room. Like, "How many farm animals can we get into this room?" Poor Beep.

BENJI LeFEVRE   Bonzo came down to breakfast the next morning, and I said, "I think you'd better go and look at your car." Peppy hid in a wardrobe for two days.

RON NEVISON   I was closest with Plant, but Jimmy was a lot of fun. One night we went to Drury Lane to see Monty Python live. At the time I was living in a guesthouse over the garage at Ian McLagan's place in East Sheen. We all went, including the roadies. I had a Bentley at the time, and Jimmy was with me that night. In fact, we spent the night at Ian's guesthouse.

VANESSA GILBERT   Everybody left except John Paul and I, and we went through all the different instruments downstairs. He would often play songs for me, and he taught me about Charles Mingus and oysters. Hey, who needed college when you could go on the road with Led Zeppelin?

GYL CORRIGAN-DEVLIN   John Paul and Vanessa were great friends; they'd sit in the corner and read Henry Miller's *Big Sur and the Oranges of Hieronymus Bosch* together. Robert almost always *did* have a book with him, but he wasn't always reading it: there's a famous picture of all of us on the *Starship*, and he seems to be reading this book, but if you look closely, it's upside down. The idea that he was reading while everyone else was having fun—I don't think he can get away with that anymore.

JOHN PAUL JONES   I just started playing "Trampled Under Foot" on the clavinet, and [John] came in with this glorious stomp that had this great feel. He could play in front of the beat, and he could play behind it, depending on what was needed. "Trampled Under Foot" had this swagger; it was a different type of song for the band.

JOHN BONHAM   John, Paul and Jimmy started off the riff, but then we thought it was a bit souly for us. Then we changed it around a bit. It's great for me. Great rhythm for a drummer. It's just at the right pace, and you can do a lot of frills.

JIMMY PAGE With *Physical Graffiti*, you can see all the different things that we were able to do that people can't do now—constantly working in a positive way, for no other reason than making good music. It wasn't to be on *Top of the Pops* or to be doing an interview.

RON NEVISON Jimmy was so well prepared. He used to come into the truck, and he'd listen to the whole thing. At that time, I thought he just didn't like his guitar. But then I realized that he was doing what I do now, which is to take the guitar down to make sure the drum track is solid.

The essence to me of the whole Zeppelin thing was John Bonham following the guitar. He would take the riff, and he would make that his drum part. If you listen to "Sick Again" or any other song, he listened to the riff, and he made it the drum part. Instead of just doing it 4/4 and getting in with the bass player, he got in with the guitar player.

PHIL CARLO (roadie for Bad Company) I remember Jimmy coming 'round to the flat with Keith Harwood, the engineer at Olympic. They'd just done "Kashmir," and Jimmy was absolutely thrilled to bits with it. He seemed to be more pleased with that than anything they'd ever done.

RON NEVISON I was never party to any discussions about where to take the songs or what they had in mind. Jimmy never talked to me about any orchestrations for "Kashmir" or anything. I had no way of even knowing that *Physical Graffiti* would be a double album. It was only later, when it came out, that I realized they'd gone back to *Houses of the Holy* and before and dragged some other stuff up.

DANNY MARKUS (artist relations manager in Atlantic's Midwest office) Apart from Ahmet and Jerry [Greenberg], nobody at Atlantic heard *Physical Graffiti* till it came out. The mystique was very well orchestrated.

JAAN UHELSZKI (in *Creem*, May 1975) The fans descended on Marty's Records downstairs from *Creem* like dragonflies, clustered around the cash register, furtively clutching the album to their heaving bosoms, slobbering and drooling down the shrinkwrap.

DANNY MARKUS In many respects, the audience was ahead of the company. Everyone knew internally that the next Zeppelin record was going to be really big, but I never saw an album sell as much as *Graffiti*. You'd go to stores, and there were lines, and everybody was waiting to buy the same record.

· · ·

MICKIE MOST (producer and owner of RAK Records)   RAK moved to Charles Street, and Peter decided not to come with us and wanted to do his own thing. He set up Swan Song in Chelsea. I never actually went there.

ALAN CALLAN (president of Swan Song in the U.K., 1977–1980)   I'm told that when the estate agent said, "So, Mr. Grant, what would be your ideal office?", Peter's response was, "Two staircases, so I can get away from all the people I don't want to see."

MAGGIE BELL (Swan Song artist)   Mark London found the premises in the New King's Road facing the World's End pub. It was an incredible set of offices, Georgian: it was next to Granny Takes a Trip, where they used to make all the clothes. It was three floors and then a basement. It belonged to the British Legion, but the only time they used it was for Poppy Day to count up the money or to get the poppies out on the street. These four dear old ladies would come in, and it was all rock 'n' roll upstairs. They loved Peter. He would send a guy round the corner to the Italian restaurant to bring them lunch and champagne and ice cream and chocolates.

UNITY MacLEAN (manager of Swan Song U.K. office)   I've seen better offices for nonprofit agencies. Peter had an office with two rather beat-up old armchairs in it and a telephone on the floor. My office was kind of a long room, and it had a breakfast counter down one wall and that was my desk—they gave me a *stool* to sit at. The two offices next to me had no furniture at all. Richard and Clive Coulson worked downstairs: they had a big old dining table with four chairs around it,

Led Zeppelin storms the Bath festival in Shepton Mallet, England, June 28, 1970. (BRIAN McCREETH/REX FEATURES)

John Paul Jones emerges from the Starship on the 1973 tour.
(RICHARD COLE COLLECTION)

Bonzo in the back garden at West Hagley, September 1972.
(RICHARD COLE COLLECTION)

Robert Plant with Kim Fowley at the Starwood in Los Angeles, September 1976. (MICHAEL OCHS ARCHIVES/GETTY IMAGES)

Plant with *The Song Remains the Same* director, Peter Clifton, Shepperton Studios, 1974. (COURTESY OF PETER CLIFTON)

Roberta Plant in Chanel with Ricardo Cole. (RICHARD COLE COLLECTION)

Peter Grant watching Zeppelin's last show on U.S. soil, in Oakland, California, July 24, 1977, with Janine Safer (left) and Steve Weiss (right). (RICHARD COLE COLLECTION)

Guest pass for Zep's last stand. (COURTESY OF PHIL CARLO)

Reunited at Jason Bonham's wedding, April 30, 1990.
(COURTESY OF PHIL CARLO)

Jimmy Page and Paul Rodgers performing on the ARMS tour in America prior to forming the Firm. (COURTESY OF PHIL CARLO)

Jimmy Page in L.A. in 1983, with (left to right) Richard Cole, Phil Carlo, Michael Des Barres, and Steve Jones. (COURTESY OF PHIL CARLO)

Reunited at Live Aid: Plant, Jones, and Page backstage in Philadelphia, July 13, 1985. (EBET ROBERTS/REDFERNS/GETTY IMAGES)

Jimmy Page cuts the cake at son James' second birthday party; his wife Patricia (née Ecker) is on the left. (COURTESY OF PHIL CARLO)

Page and Plant on the eve of their 1988 tour. (MICK HUTSON/REDFERNS)

Backstage at the O2, December 10, 2007: John Paul Jones,
Robert Plant, Jason Bonham, Jimmy Page. (ROSS HALFIN)

Robert Plant and Alison Krauss at the New Orleans Jazz and Heritage Festival, April 26, 2008. (LEE CELANO/REUTERS/ CORBIS)

Robert Plant with his merry Band of Joy at the Anselmo Valencia Amphitheater in Tucson, Arizona, July 2010. (ART SPERL)

Richard Cole outside the old Swan Song offices, March 2011. (Art Sperl)

and that's where they sat and worked. Many times, I walked in there and saw Jonesy sitting in the corner on the floor because there were no seats left. Being guys, nobody thought, "Oh, give Jonesy a chair."

JULIE CARLO (wife of Phil Carlo)   It was just like a family. These days it's all corporate and laptops, but in those days it was just a load of old hippies together. Nobody was obsessed with money. The girls didn't care about the way they dressed, not like all the WAGs [wives and girlfriends] these days. Peter was like the big daddy. He would always say, "If you ever have any problems, give me a ring." And he was always true to his word. He was such a lovely man. I don't know what he was like to people that he didn't get on with. He must have been quite scary, I suppose.

CHRIS WELCH (writer for *Melody Maker*)   Peter's view of the world was that Led Zeppelin should be an underground band, and they didn't go for flash or bling at all.

BENJI LeFEVRE Part of the whole mystique of Zeppelin was that they wanted to be perceived as answerable only to their fans—not to the promoters, not to the press, not to anybody else. It was for the *people*, man.

CHRIS WELCH The office did shock people. The first thing most successful bands did after starting labels was open a big flash office with potted plants, but Zeppelin never really went in for that. They spent money when they needed to, but if it came to investing in *image*, they weren't interested.

ALAN CALLAN It was *completely* unprepossessing, and they were *always* trying to cut down on expenses. One of them, Richard or Clive, bought a tandem bicycle and said to the roadies, "No more taxis, you're using *that* to get around now."

HELEN GRANT (daughter of Peter Grant) Carol Browne ran the ship, let me tell you. Her desk was called "Mission Control."

MAGGIE BELL Carol had been there from the start. In fact, she'd worked for Don Arden, and Peter took her away from him. She was the mainstay, and she was fabulous.

SAM AIZER (artist relations, Swan Song U.S. office) I reckon it was Carol Browne, Shelley Kaye, and Steve Weiss who really ran the show for five years, '68 to '73. That was all they needed, that and Richard. Everyone else was hired on. Carol did everything for Peter.

SHELLEY KAYE (assistant to Steve Weiss, and manager of Swan Song U.S. office) Swan Song was in the works for six months to a year. When they started the label, there was a quarterly stipend paid to run the New York office. It was a fairly large amount of money, and it paid for the staff. We'd been in that office in the *Newsweek* building for a few years, but it was redesigned. Steve's office was redecorated, and we had this fabulous music room with purple velvet walls and an orange-and-berry carpet that was hideous, and all wood paneling on the walls. Bonzo picked out all the stereo equipment. The office was a good environment and mostly upbeat. When the band was in town, they would hang out there.

JANINE SAFER (press officer, Swan Song U.S. office)   Steve had negotiated the Swan Song deal with Atlantic, so I guess for financial reasons and control reasons, it made sense to have Swan Song and Steve's
firm all together in the same office.

Steve was always drunk. He wasn't *sloppy* drunk or slurring his
words; he was a complete functioning drunk. In the copier room there
was always a bottle of Johnnie Walker Black just sitting there, and
every time you went in to make a copy, you would notice that it had
gone down a little more.

He was incredibly intense, quick to fly off the handle. Partly, it
was the alcoholism, partly the double life that he led with his mistress, Marie. I don't think he was insecure, but he may have been
financially insecure. He had worked hard and fallen into that fantastic net of realizing, "I'm really rich!" And then looking around and
thinking, "What did I do to *get* rich?" and "Oh, my God, perhaps it

Plant with promoter Bill
Graham (left) and Zeppelin
lawyer Steve Weiss (right),
Kezar Stadium, San
Francisco, 1973. (Neal
Preston/Corbis)

will evaporate!" All of this was what led him to be, often, a complete sonofabitch.

DANNY GOLDBERG (president of Swan Song in the U.S.)   They made a deal with Ahmet for this label. It was a label without a name, and the only person signed to it was Maggie Bell. Her record was coming out soon, so I immediately started working on the press for it. A lot of my first work was with Mark London, who comanaged Maggie with Peter. Maggie didn't have a big hit, but we got an amazing amount of press for her. I happened to have an artist that appealed to the press at that moment in time.

MARK LONDON (comanager of Maggie Bell)   Personally, I thought *Queen of the Night* was a weak album. The reviews were incredible, but it just didn't happen. There were no hits on it. To me, Maggie was the greatest female rock singer that ever lived. She made Joplin look like an amateur.

DANNY GOLDBERG   It was all about Maggie, and then Jimmy came up with a name and came up with that piece of art by William Rimmer. By the time the Bad Company record came out, the label was called Swan Song.

ABE HOCH (president of Swan Song in the U.K., 1975–1977)   Swan Song was basically a way to give Jimmy retentive ownership of the catalogue. Swan Song was the primary and principal owner of the masters, and then they basically did a loan-out deal to Atlantic.

PHIL CARSON (head of Atlantic Records in Europe)   I kind of agreed to do Swan Song to start with. In the end, Ahmet said to me, "You shouldn't do it, because you're still going to be working with him here." And at the time I had a pretty big job, I was head of Atlantic Europe. It led to a bit of acrimony between me and the band, and they went through a variety of people who tried to do the job.

UNITY MacLEAN   Phil hardly ever came to the Swan Song office. I don't think he thought the offices were very comfortable.

MARK LONDON   Peter asked me to run Swan Song—I was the second favorite after Carson. I thanked him but said I didn't think I could do the job well enough.

PHIL CARLO   Clive Coulson came round to my flat one day and said, "I'm just putting this band together. They're going to be called Bad Company, and we're looking for a crew. They're going to be fucking huge." Clive knitted the whole thing together with Simon Kirke. They got Boz Burrell in, and Clive went to Peter and said, "I'll do all the day-to-day running of it, and you just turn up at gigs when you can and negotiate record deals."

SAM AIZER   Clive had been Jimmy's roadie. He was a bright guy, very impressive, and he saw an opportunity. They knew they were never going to be as big as Zeppelin, but Clive knew enough to say, "Okay, we're gonna fit ourselves in between the pieces."

UNITY MacLEAN   Clive wouldn't let anybody near Bad Company. They were *his* band and *his* babies. If you tried to do anything, he'd be, "What are you doing? Why are you interfering?" He'd learned from the master.

BENJI LeFEVRE   I did the first tour of America with Bad Company, and it was a completely different level from the time I'd been there with Zeppelin. We were driving ourselves, second on the bill, et cetera. Ironically, I'd done one tiny bit of a tour with Free, so I kind of knew what Paul Rodgers would be like and what Simon Kirke would be like. It was just terrific fun, though Rodgers was a little shit with a huge chip on his shoulder.

DESIREE KIRKE (ex-wife of Bad Company drummer Simon Kirke)   Paul was the prima donna. The rest of the band would be ready to go, but if Paul had had an iffy day, we would all be waiting on him. And he had a terrible temper. I remember one time he knocked out his wife's front teeth. I mean, this is all fueled by whisky.

SAM AIZER   We were at the pool at some hotel, and Paul is standing in the shallow end and says, "Come on, Sam, I know you wanna take a punch at me, so give it a shot." And I tell you, I really felt like clocking him. I think it was either Clive or Boz who said, "If you touch that guy and you break his jaw and they have to cancel the tour, you know they're going to find you in the desert."

JANINE SAFER The first question men always ask me is, "Did you fuck Jimmy Page?" And the answer is no, it never even came up. In fact, they were all perfect gentlemen. Unlike Paul Rodgers, who hit on me at 2:00 a.m. in a Chicago hotel, when I laughed at him. He never forgave me.

BENJI LeFEVRE Bad Company was never going to be as big as Zeppelin, but they desperately wanted to be and thought that here was the chance. I can imagine that Ricardo [Richard] would have tried to make sure they didn't get *too* big. By the same token, Clive wanted to be Peter, but he never stood a chance. I think he was envious of the respect that people had for Peter. Of course, the only way to really get respect in this business is to be a good person and do the right thing. Following in G's footsteps, unfortunately, Clive learned all the *wrong* things.

ELIZABETH IANNACI (artist relations in the Atlantic L.A. office) I called Bad Company "crotch rock." They were so solid. You could have built a fortress on Simon Kirke's playing.

Page makes a guest appearance with Bad Company at the Texas Jam Festival, September 1, 1974. Left to right: Simon Kirke, Page, and Mick Ralphs. (Courtesy of Phil Carlo)

DESIREE KIRKE A lot of people thought Bad Company were American, because their image was quite plain and kind of Western-looking. They were almost like the opposite of glam rock, and people were kind of ready for that.

DANNY GOLDBERG The Bad Company album was number one, and that was the first release on Swan Song. Led Zeppelin signed another band, and it went to number one, and that was an amazing differentiation for Swan Song—what a way to start.

PETER GRANT That whole "Can't Get Enough" era was so fresh. We had Maggie doing quite well and the Pretty Things. I have a framed *Billboard* chart with all our artists listed one week in early 1975.

SIMON KIRKE (drummer with Bad Company) G was an amazing guy. If he was in your corner, then he would do anything for you. Initially, I was afraid of him. I'd heard that he had connections with the East End underworld, and in typical greenhorn fashion, I asked him about it. He said no, of course, and gave me a bunch of charming bullshit. The next meeting we had with him in his office, he started by saying, "Oh, Si, I've got something for you here," and he bent down behind his desk and pulled out a toy Tommy gun—which looked pretty bloody realistic—and loosed off a stream of Ping-Pong balls at me.

BENJI LeFEVRE Zeppelin decided to have their own label so they could make money, but also so they could control their own destiny a bit more. The whole idea of it—with the Icarus logo and everything—*seemed* very appealing. Bad Company got off to a great start because everyone within the Zeppelin camp was focused.

MAGGIE BELL There was a great launch party at the Bel Air Hotel, with pink flamingos and doves—especially for a little girl from Glasgow who'd started out in the Salvation Army playing the tambourine.

ABE HOCH Maggie goes to Groucho Marx, "I'm so honored to meet you." Groucho goes, "Fuck that, show us your tits." Right there in front of everybody.

GEOFF GRIMES (plugger for Atlantic Records in the U.K., 1972–1978) The Swan Song launch in England was on Halloween at Chislehurst Caves, which was like a labyrinth. Everywhere that was accessible, they seemed to find something to put on in it. There were a bunch of naked male wrestlers writhing around in the dust. I just stood in the doorway and looked at this: nuns walking toward you with the complete dress on, and then you looked back and there was nothing on the back except suspenders.

BOB HARRIS (presenter of BBC2's *Old Grey Whistle Test,* 1972–1978)   It was like being at a medieval orgy. Flames from huge torches flickered

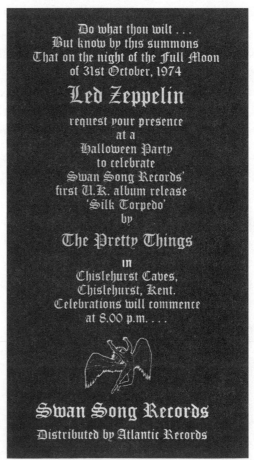

Invitation to the Halloween Pretty Things party at Chislehurst Caves, October 1974. (Getty Images)

Do what thou wilt . . .
But know by this summons
That on the night of the Full Moon
of 31st October, 1974

Led Zeppelin

request your presence
at a
Halloween Party
to celebrate
Swan Song Records'
first U.K. album release
'Silk Torpedo'
by

The Pretty Things

in

Chislehurst Caves,
Chislehurst, Kent.
Celebrations will commence
at 8.00 p.m. . . .

Swan Song Records

Distributed by Atlantic Records

light across the dark, dank recesses of the caves, while a crowd of maybe two hundred people watched George Melly perform jazz tunes and bawdy songs in a nun's habit, naked girls wrestling in jelly in open coffins at his feet. In all, it was a strange and disturbing night.

GEOFF GRIMES Nesuhi Ertegun arrived, and he'd just been to some very posh shop and bought this brand-new burgundy velvet jacket that looked fantastic. There was a naked girl in a coffin covered in jelly, and she leaped out of this thing, and the jelly went all over Nesuhi's coat. He wasn't very impressed.

CHRIS CHARLESWORTH (New York correspondent for *Melody Maker*) After the Swan Song party in L.A., I flew up to San Francisco with Bad Company to see them play at Winterland—they had their own plane, though it wasn't the size of Zeppelin's. On the way back to L.A., I'm sitting, minding my own business, and a roadie wanders up and says, "Peter'd like a word with you." I walk to the back of the plane where there's a private room, and sure enough, Granty's sitting there surrounded by some of Bad Company, with a mound of cocaine in a sugar bowl. He says, "Wanna toot, Chris?" I go, "Oh, well, alright." He goes, "Did you enjoy the band, then?" I said yes, of course. "Well, mind you say so in the paper, won't you." Then he says, "You can go now."

DESIREE KIRKE It was difficult for Peter having two acts on the road at the same time. I remember him saying he would never do that again. There was a lot of that going on between '74 and '77, and it was exhausting for him. And then the commuting into London, an hour and a half on the train, it was too much for him.

SIMON KIRKE Swan Song was initially a great idea. It had that Island Records vibe, in that it was formed by musicians to look after their musical interests and those of other bands. Of course, it was a business and was run as such, but it wasn't a shrine to capitalism, by any stretch of the imagination.

JANINE SAFER Swan Song was for and about Led Zeppelin, primarily. To a lesser extent, it was about Bad Company. To hardly *any* extent, it was about the Pretty Things. Maggie, though, held a very special place in the pantheon, because Peter loved her and Jimmy loved her. Detective had a brief flurry of activity, but it was a case of hurry-up-and-wait, long months of doing absolutely nothing. No one would hear from Peter, and no one would hear from the band.

ALAN CALLAN Why should Michael Des Barres need to speak with Jimmy? This is why I wanted to sign John Lennon, so that people stopped seeing Swan Song in the context of Jimmy or Robert or the others. You might have been introduced to Peter, or Peter might have introduced you to Jimmy, or whatever, but as an artist coming to Swan Song, you shouldn't see your career in terms of another band on that label. The people who complained about not being able to get hold of Led Zeppelin, in a way that was terribly disrespectful—and it's an own-up that they were looking to *them* to make them successful.

SHELLEY KAYE Maggie was really supremely talented, but they just couldn't get it over that hump. They thought she was the next Janis Joplin, but she wasn't.

PAUL FRANCIS (drummer with Maggie Bell in the mid-'70s) We did a six-week tour in the States with Bad Company. It was all under one roof, and Peter was around, trying to look after things. When Bad Company took off, it kind of left Peter in an awkward position because he was trying to split himself evenly. That's really why Maggie got neglected. It's such a shame, because she has an incredible voice.

BENJI LeFEVRE Very rapidly, things descended into chaos at Swan Song. Nobody paid attention to the label, because they were all more interested in getting fucked up. So all these poor people like Danny Goldberg and Abe Hoch—and the artists, of course—were left to flounder. Swan Song turned out to be just another feather in Zeppelin's cap; the artists were really just their playthings.

PHIL CARSON Whoever came in had no real authority. It might have been different if I'd done it—I'd like to think it would—but then I wouldn't have been able to sign AC/DC and all the other things I was fortunate enough to be part of. Robert was particularly passionate about the Pretty Things. And Bad Company obviously were massive.

But no one at Swan Song was really doing that work, it was all the Atlantic people that were working the records. Once the reconciliation took place between Peter and the band and me, business carried on as normal. Goldilocks [Danny Goldberg] was really a PR guy, and he was quite good at it. I really never knew what Abe Hoch was doing, and I'm not sure he did, either.

ABE HOCH   Phil was more their best friend than anything else, and it was all a social circle and kind of a game. He was one of those guys where it was important for him, both business-wise and socially, to be a part of the gang. He felt like he was the inside guy with G and that, because I was American, I was the interloper.

JANINE SAFER   Danny Goldberg was a Krishna person at that time and very serious, so there were always people named Vishnu in the office, and they would be doing the odd jobs.

ABE HOCH   Danny brought a girl into the company called Mirabai. That was pretty much his downfall, as well as his upside. The upside was that Danny would do very funny things, like having shamans over to his house, and was living a very New Agey world and was an interesting guy.

JANINE SAFER   Mirabai wasn't talentless, but Danny was *obsessed*. Clearly, he was looking for some sort of spiritual fulfillment. And, clearly, those who had known Danny before were irritated by this.

SAM AIZER   Danny and Steve Weiss got along at first, and then they *didn't* get along. Steve knew which side *his* bread was buttered, and if Peter and Danny had a falling out, Steve was going to go with what *Peter* said.

The bottom line is that Danny was passionate about Mirabai—much more passionate than he was about anything else on Swan Song—but it didn't work politically, and it got caught in the middle of everything. They put a record out on Atlantic, and I'm sure that was a political move between Weiss and Zeppelin and Ahmet—like, "Just get it out and do what we gotta do"—but do I think Zeppelin was into Mirabai? No. Were they into Danny? Yes. They liked Danny a lot, because he did something for them that no one else did, which was give them a high profile.

DANNY GOLDBERG   Peter was good to me. I was tempestuous and ambitious and had a sense of entitlement, and any problems I had with Peter were, in retrospect, more my fault than Peter's. I mean, the drug thing created a shitty atmosphere, and I was not a druggie at that time, but he gave me a job that no one else had given me, and he gave me a raise. He introduced me to people. This very day I'm talking to you about Zeppelin. So I'm in his debt.

SHELLEY KAYE   Mirabai was terrible. She was like a folksinger who sang all this whiny music. It was so completely different from what Swan Song was about.

ANNI IVIL (press officer at the Atlantic U.K. office, late '60s–early '70s)   I really think it doesn't work when a band forms a record label. I know their intentions are good, but you're either a promoter or you're a record company or you're a musician; you cannot be all of those things.

RICHARD COLE   Jimmy and Robert were in awe of Roy Harper and were trying desperately to get him to sign to Swan Song. But Peter could never make an amicable agreement with his manager. It went on for fucking months.

ABE HOCH   They wanted to sign Roy, and that never came about. They used to call him Harpic, so that was his nickname—Roy Harpic. I didn't know him as anything other than that. He may have been a very talented guy.

ROBERT PLANT   I saw Phil May in a club one night. I told him how great I thought his band's albums were. He was quite amazed that I'd heard of them. So I said, "Listen, one day I'd love to come to you and make you an offer and help you move it along a bit."

DANNY GOLDBERG   The Pretty Things was not a big hit, but it was critically acclaimed and sold some records because it was legitimate and they toured. So I think it had a real vitality to it, and I think that at that moment—if Swan Song had had proper A&R—it would have had a tremendous ability to sign artists.

BOB EMMER (publicity director for Atlantic on the West Coast in the '70s) Danny called me and said Zeppelin had signed the Pretty Things and were going to be playing at the Shrine in L.A. He wanted me to host a party for the release of *Silk Torpedo*, and it should be something special.

JANE AYER (artist relations in Atlantic Records' L.A. office) I first got to meet Zeppelin at the party for the Pretty Things at the Biltmore in downtown LA. It was around March or April 1975, my second day on the job. There were ice sculptures and a lot of lobster and shrimp. And there was an after-party at the Hyatt House, to which I was invited by Tim Hauser of the Manhattan Transfer. The lobby scene alone was like something out of *Almost Famous*. We got up to the penthouse, and all this wildness was going on. John Bonham and John Paul Jones were trying to throw a TV out the window, and Jimmy Page was walking around squirting people with a bottle of ketchup.

BOB EMMER I'd decided I was going to wear a suit and tie to the party, I don't know why. Bonham comes up to me and says, "Bob, could you get me a cup of coffee?" So I get him a cup of coffee, and he says, "Bob, that suit is disgusting." And he takes the coffee and douses me in it. I was a little shocked, obviously. I didn't get the humor in the moment. But everybody else did.

JANE AYER Cameron Crowe and Harold Bronson were there, as was Neal Preston. And I felt like I became friends with all these people instantly in one night. I can remember looking at Betty Iannaci and saying, "You know what? I think this is gonna be a really fun job."

BOB EMMER Jane and Betty had a special place in the band's hearts. If Zeppelin came to town, Betty was no longer the receptionist. She was elevated to a different position. If she didn't come to work the next day, it was understood.

ELIZABETH IANNACI Jimmy called Danny Goldberg and said he wanted me to be the funnel for all their dealings with Atlantic on the West Coast. I was stunned, because I hadn't had five words with Jimmy. Danny said, "You know, Jimmy *watches* . . ."

BOB EMMER One thing that L.A. is great on—or Hollywood, anyway—is that big-screen, bigger-than-life pop culture. A lot of it was created just because of the hype that Hollywood is good at, in and of itself. For someone coming in from outside, it was like, "Wow, I wanna drive down Sunset and see my name on this huge billboard."

Atlantic only had one billboard on Sunset, so there was always the issue of who was coming to town and who got the billboard. When you have acts like the Stones and Zeppelin and Bad Company, you run into issues. I recall times when we literally had a billboard up for two weeks, and then we took it down and put the other group up. Alternatively, when the band was picked up at the airport, the driver was instructed not to take them down Sunset.

JANE AYER In 1975, the Stones were playing the Forum, and I helped Ahmet and Earl McGrath create the guest list for a party at Diana Ross's house. And that was all about the social registry and peppering it with movie business people. It was certainly very different from the Swan Song parties.

MARILYN COLE (wife of Richard Cole) There was a big rivalry with the Stones. Zeppelin really *were* the biggest rock 'n' roll band in the world in those years. Part of Peter's bravado was, "Those fuckin' tossers can't sell out stadiums like *we* can."

BOB EMMER There may have been some competition between them and the Stones for Ahmet's affection. From the outside looking in, it seemed like more of the affection would have been directed toward Mick Jagger. It probably says something that at Ahmet's funeral, there were two keynote speakers: one was Henry Kissinger, and the other was Mick.

DANNY GOLDBERG Ahmet was much closer to Jagger than he ever was to Zeppelin. Ahmet was the symbol of the record company to Zeppelin.

They looked at him as the record company. They didn't look at him as a friend. They looked at him as this colorful guy that they would negotiate with and get money out of, and they liked the general notion of him being the record company, but he didn't spend anywhere as much time socially with Zeppelin as he did with Jagger. Zeppelin didn't want to be part of that world. Even Jimmy. They didn't have aspirations to that.

MICHAEL DES BARRES (singer with Swan Song band Detective)   The difference between Zeppelin and the Stones is that Mick and Keith had a real awareness of glamour and show business. They understood that if you've got princesses trying to get into your dressing room, then America will follow. Jimmy had no concept of that and wasn't interested in it. *None* of them was interested in that. Robert was always more interested in Ry Cooder and Roy Head and Ral Donner. He's always been more interested in Americana than in the glamour of Hollywood.

JAAN UHELSZKI   Someone threw a party for Zeppelin in Dobbs Ferry, New York, and the Stones and all the Jerry Zipkins and friends of Mica were out for that. It was unbearably posh, but it was segmented because Zeppelin kept off to themselves in a little booth, while all the society types floated around. It wasn't that they didn't look like they were at home, but they *weren't* at home. What Zeppelin aspired to was, like, Bebe Buell.

BEBE BUELL (groupie and girlfriend of Page)   I was at the Hyatt House with Todd Rundgren and my pet raccoon Kundalini, and Led Zeppelin were in town for the Swan Song party. There's a scene in *Almost Famous* where the band is walking through the lobby of the hotel, and it's totally accurate. It was more like a *nightclub* than a hotel. You had to step over this legion of girls that would actually *camp* in the hallways.

NICK KENT (writer for *NME*)   I once went to see Page at the Hyatt House, and Squeaky Fromme—the former Manson girl—was in the lobby trying to get to them. When I got to the ninth floor and knocked on his door, three other doors immediately opened. It was like, "You gonna see Jimmy? Tell him Dave's here, and I've brought a guitar for him." These people had booked rooms just to be *near* him.

BEBE BUELL   Todd drops this bomb that he wants to go to San Francisco *without* me—which developed into quite a row. I became hysterical and was comforted by Kim Fowley and Rodney Bingenheimer and Michelle Myer. I get into the elevator, and in walks Jimmy, along with his minders, one of whom was Richard Cole.

About five in the morning, I'm lying in bed and the phone rings. I pick it up and it's Jimmy. He is very, very distressed, because he has returned from doing a session for Joe Walsh, whose daughter has just been killed in a car accident. He was extremely despondent, and he asked if I would come up to his room and have breakfast with him. He said, "I would just like to have a shoulder to talk to." It was a unique Pageism.

When I got to his room, he asked me what I wanted to eat, and he asked what the raccoon would like. He had this amazing fruit basket, so he suggested we put the fruit down for the raccoon in the bathroom. Out came the cocaine, and I started to tell him my plight, and he started to tell me about *his* crazy relationship with Charlotte Martin. We were in the thick of our conversation, and Peter Grant came into the room and said, "Oh, I see you captured your beauty." Peter then asked to use the bathroom, which was when we heard the gasp and the scream. The raccoon had eaten so much of the fruit that she had shat herself. Peter walks out of the bathroom and says, "What've you two been *up* to?"

Jimmy was going to go and see Elvis Presley with the other members of Zeppelin. He said, "Do you want to come and meet the King with us?"

ROBERT PLANT   Jerry Weintraub was operating as our agent at the time, and he was Presley's agent as well. The King demanded to know who these guys were who were selling tickets faster than he was.

BEBE BUELL   There was another knock at the door, and—being naïve—I went and opened it without the chain on it. It was Lori

Mattix with a couple of other girls, and they just sort of *lunged* at me and grabbed me by my hair.

LORI MATTIX (L.A. groupie and girlfriend of Page's)   Peter was trying to distract me, but I pushed my way through and opened the door, and Bebe was laying in bed with Jimmy. I don't think she meant that to happen.

BEBE BUELL   Contrary to the story that's often told, Jimmy did not sit back and laugh as Lori ripped my hair out—that is not the kind of man Jimmy is. He was extremely upset. And it was *because* Lori hit me that he cut her off.

LORI MATTIX   She'd just wormed her way in there, and Jimmy knew I was destroyed. The innocence that we had was gone forever. It would never be the same, and I could never forgive him.

BEBE BUELL   The upshot of all this was that I was left to rest and recover, and I didn't get to see Elvis with the band.

ROBERT PLANT   [Elvis] came over to us, and the four of us and him talked for one and a half, two hours. We all stood in a circle and discussed this whole phenomenon, this lunacy.

BEBE BUELL   I think every girl in L.A.—from Lori to Pamela Des Barres—thought she was going to be Jimmy's date for the Swan Song party. But he told me he had no interest in either one of them. I even lectured him about Lori outside the Rainbow, like, "She's just a little girl, what the heck is *happening* here?"

LORI MATTIX   Jimmy got so depressed after that. I was with him for three and a half years, so I know how happy he was. After Bebe, he got heavily into heroin. He did heroin for seven years straight, and in the seventh year he went to Switzerland and had his blood changed like Keith Richards.

JIMMY PAGE   I only got into heroin because I thought it could make me more creative. That was a big mistake.

BEBE BUELL   Even in the throes of extreme drug intake, Jimmy had class. He would leave the rougher, less savory stuff to the other fellows.

Jimmy always kept himself separate from a lot of the bad behavior. I don't know whether the others protected him or whether he just had the common sense—because of his upbringing—to leave the room. These guys like Jimmy and Mick Jagger were obviously raised a little different from some of the street dogs. The other thing people don't want to acknowledge about Jimmy is that he was very funny.

DANNY GOLDBERG   Jimmy never rode through hallways or threw TVs out the window, but he loved it when other people did. He was more the kind of person who would manipulate someone into doing those kinds of things. And then laugh to himself, watching everyone make fools of themselves.

BEBE BUELL   Todd took me to Europe, and when we arrived at the Savoy, I got this telegram from Peter Grant telling me how excited Jimmy was to see me. I think Jimmy wanted to find his queen, and he was very picky.

I'm sure Jimmy slept with many women just for physical gratification, but when he took that next step of sending you flowers or having Peter send you a telegram, it let you know that potentially he was more serious about you. But I would also compare him to Henry VIII, because it took very little for you to get your head chopped off.

Todd was going to the Speakeasy with Derek Taylor, and I made up some elaborate lie about having to do something else, and I got in a cab and went to the Tower House. And I fell asleep there and didn't wake up till the next morning. I think Kenneth Anger may have been in the basement, because I kept hearing all these crazy noises, and I felt like I was in a horror movie. Jimmy would say, "Don't go down there!"

The next morning I called Derek, who said, "What have you got yourself into *this* time?" Fifteen minutes later, Ronnie Wood came walking into his office to tell me that Jimmy had just stolen his wife and that I was welcome to stay at his house. I guess Woody and Krissy had gone to Plumpton and—in the throes of the evening—Krissy and Pagey disappeared together. I believe Krissy became the mistress of Plumpton for a while.

Page's London home, the Tower House, Holland Park. (Art Sperl)

ELIZABETH IANNACI I was standing in the bathroom at this club once, and here was the epitome of the beautiful English girl—bright blue eyes, long blond hair, wearing a beautiful velvet shawl. It was Krissy Wood, and all of a sudden she's talking to me about Charlotte. She goes, "Well, Charlotte's nice, but she's not *me*." As a woman I was so stunned, because I would never think that or be so full of myself. There was this particular group of guitarists, and this very Machiavellian web of who-wants-to-be-with-whom, and it was just so odd to me. I mean, on certain levels, how much difference is there between Ronnie Wood and Jimmy Page?

BEBE BUELL Todd said to me, "Jimmy is the darkness, and I'm in the light. You go there, you're going to get sucked into something nasty and terrible. Promise me you're going to stay away from him." But I just couldn't do it. I think Todd was probably right. Mick Jagger said pretty much the same thing to me.

BENJI LeFEVRE Jimmy's interest in Crowley was exploding, and the whole "dark side" was emerging. I think Robert had a peripheral interest at first and then went, "Not for me." Jimmy went headlong into it, and nobody followed him. It was irresistible to try and find something that . . . wasn't *there*. I think the whole occult episode was completely meaningless: he *thought* it meant a lot, but I don't think it meant anything.

MICHAEL DES BARRES The norm was never enough, and I caught that virus. What *is* was not enough. Anything to do with magic and the supernatural—with the emphasis on *super*—took you out of the maelstrom of mediocrity and brought you into a higher place. You could be as dumb as a piece of wood and read that "Do What Thou Wilt Shall Be the Whole of the Law" and be exalted into some rarified absurd self-awareness.

MARILYN COLE We were *all* interested in Crowley. I found it terrifyingly taboo and scary but sort of fascinating. I was always asking Richard about the extent of the involvement within the band, with Jimmy, but he would never tell. He was zip-lip, even when he was drunk.

ABE HOCH Jimmy and I had this weird moment with the Crowley world. I came from an Orthodox Jewish background, and I remember he had this book open, and there were these charts, and they were supposed to be black magic writings. I can write Hebrew, and all they did was write transliterations of Hebrew letters.

I started reading it, and Jimmy is watching me read it and going, "You understand this?" I went, "Yeah, it's Hebrew." He went, "I don't want to talk to you about this anymore." It freaked him out that I could literally understand these things that to him were mystical. I just thought it was all a great ploy for him to get chicks.

17

Almost Infamous

The trouble is now, with rock 'n' roll and stuff, it gets so big
that it loses what once upon a time was a magnificent thing,
where it was special and quite elusive and occasionally
a little sinister, and it had its own world and nobody could
get in.

—Robert Plant, May 2008

DAVE NORTHOVER (John Paul Jones's assistant on Zeppelin's 1975 and
1977 U.S. tours)   I used to play rugby in Hellingly, and Peter Grant
would come to the White Hart in Horsebridge with his wife to enjoy
the mayhem we created when we got off the pitch. They seemed very
happy together. Gloria wasn't a typical rock wife at all; I don't think
she even indulged in any chemicals. She was very concerned with her
kids.

HELEN GRANT (daughter of Peter Grant)   I didn't really like a lot of
people *knowing* about Dad. I kept it relatively quiet at school. And
then there was a big article in the *Sunday Times*, and everyone got to
know about it. I used to say, "For God's sake, turn up in something

understated." All the other parents were turning up in Volvos, and Dad used to come screaming round the corner at boarding school in a Bentley and goggles and scarf.

DAVE NORTHOVER Just before Christmas of 1974, Peter invited me round and asked if I'd like to come on tour. I had once been a physicist, and when Peter told the rest of the guys he was taking me on the tour, they thought he said *pharmacist*. Jimmy's ears pricked up, and he said, "Bring him along!"

JACK CALMES (cofounder of Showco sound and lighting company) For the 1975 tour, we went up to a much higher level of production. It went to six or seven trucks and a whole bunch of stuff and a stage. I went over to the New King's Road, and they got me up in the little meeting room above the ground floor. Peter Grant started the meeting and said, "Alright, what have you got for us?" I kind of choked because it was a big number. He said, "Well, let's have a blow first." So he pulled out a big Bowie knife—about a foot long with a three-inch blade on it—and dipped it into this kind of grocery sack of blow. He said, "Here, Calmes, have some." They had to give me five minutes to recover from that.

So they were all sitting there staring at me, which was pretty intense. We unveiled the model and showed it to them. Bonham looked at me and said, "How much fucking money is this going to cost us?" I said, "$15,785 per show." The room went dead silent. Not a word. They started looking at each other sideways. Bonzo got up, walked over to the window on the New Kings Road, and opened it up like he was going to throw me out of it. Then he came over to me, gave me a huge bear hug, and started laughing. He said, "Yeah, go for it. We're in."

DAVE NORTHOVER The first date was in Chicago. It was the 17th of January 1975, it was 17 below, and there were seventeen thousand people at the concert. I had no idea just how huge Zeppelin were until I was standing at the side of the stage with all these kids screaming and jumping up and down.

ROBERT PLANT There was a minute there when I thought we'd lost it after that first show. The whole idea of Zeppelin has always been getting each other off—and that was missing until the second night. Then it suddenly came together—we looked at each other and we all knew it—we were there again. The magic had returned.

DANNY MARKUS (artist relations in Atlantic's Midwest office)   In Chicago, they would stay at the Ambassador, which is two hotels, and there was an underground tunnel between the two. At five o'clock, we would meet in the lobby, climb into the limousines, and go to the airport to fly to Minneapolis or wherever it was. In Minneapolis, the airport was right next to the stadium, and we would go in, play the show, no encore, go off, and on the two-way radios I could still hear the audience calling for an encore as I was being served lobster thermidor on the plane. Hell, you didn't even *need* cocaine.

TONY MANDICH (artist relations in Atlantic's L.A. office)   Everybody always wants to know what it was like being backstage at a Zeppelin concert. The truth is, there was nobody there. It was a ghost town. If they had a great show, the band would meet and greet certain people and all that, but if they had a bad show, they would jump in a limo right after with a police escort. The people were still screaming and yelling for them, and they were already gone.

DANNY MARKUS   The band got along very well. Not like the Who, who were the most impossible thing I've ever seen and where everyone had a submanager. When they did the little acoustical set, Janine Safer and Neal Preston and I would go down in front of the barricade, and Neal would shoot pictures, and they would perform it for *us*. That would be the one point during the show where the three of us would meet, and we would try to make them laugh just to get the vibe going.

JIMMY PAGE   The intention was to cut back in the January–February tour of America. "What are we doing? We're mad, three hours." So we attempted to cut it back to two hours, and I don't know, it just went to three hours again.

DANNY GOLDBERG (president of Swan Song U.S. office)   One night in Cleveland, Jimmy warned Robert that he was tired and to expect short solos. Then he went out and did more than eight minutes in "Over the Hills and Far Away." Afterward, Robert said, "Short solos, huh?" Jimmy just grinned and shrugged.

BENJI LeFEVRE (Zeppelin sound technician, 1973–1980) Zeppelin treated the crew like shit, hardly paid anybody anything. There was this enormous thing between G and Jimmy, which was, "How can we squeeze the last penny out of everybody?"

On the 1973 tour, they gave us an old double-decker Greyhound bus with sleeping bags in the back. In 1975, they wouldn't even give us a *sleeper* coach: we had a Continental Trailways bus and had to do over-nighters just sitting in *seats*. I wrote a letter to G, in which I complained bitterly about the way we were all treated. I said, "This is not right."

Having grown up in the theater environment, I didn't get fazed by speaking my mind. People called me the trade unionist, but it was only because I had the balls to say something. Other people would be just like, "Yes sir, no sir." It wasn't even so much the *money* as just "Cut us some slack and give us some respect."

SALLY WILLIAMS (girlfriend of Bonham roadie Mick Hinton) Peter and Richard gave off this kind of Mafia vibe, this control over the band. I'd say to Mick [Hinton], "Well, surely you've been paid your bonus." And he would say, "Nah, Richard hasn't paid us yet." But then Richard will remind me that Mick would spend his bonus the moment he got it—usually on cocaine.

BENJI LeFEVRE With the *Clockwork Orange* boiler suits, Bonzo *instructed* Mick that this was how he would appear on the tour. Most people were completely shit-scared of both of them. Mick's main role was to set up the drums, but there were many times when Bonzo would just say, "Hinton, you're coming with *me* now!"

GLENN HUGHES (bassist and singer with Deep Purple, 1973–1976) I was in New York and really fucked up. I'd had an ounce of coke flown in from L.A., and I'd been partying pretty strong with Mick Jagger at the Plaza. I was getting a bit too high, and I wanted to get out of there, like, "I'm a little too high for these dudes . . ."

"Mr. Ultraviolence" and his demonic twin: Bonzo and *Clockwork Orange* dogsbody Mick Hinton on the '75 tour. (Neal Preston/Corbis)

Later I call Jagger, and I think I'm speaking to him, but it's *Hinton* I'm on the phone to. They'd put me through to his room by mistake. I invite him to come over, thinking Jagger is coming round. And lo and behold, there's a knock at the door, and it's Hinton. I'm completely off my tree, I'm shaking, I'm twitching, I'm sweating, I'm wearing a kimono, completely paranoid: the last thing I want to see is Bonzo's evil-twin *Clockwork Orange* brother, frothing at the mouth.

Mick goes, "I know what to do with *you*, fucking Hughesy!" And he pulls out a fucking syringe and says, "I'll fuckin' stab you with *this*." Obviously, it was heroin or something, so I was convinced I was going to die. Fortunately, there was a guy in the room who got him out of there. Hinton scared the shit out of me. He was Bonzo's Man Friday. Jason Bonham and I have laughed our asses off with the Bonzo and Hinton stories. Mick would have done anything for John.

JACK CALMES Jimmy got sick in Chicago, and I mean *rockin' pneumonia* sick. I was there, and I came to get paid. Peter says, "You fucking greedy cunt. You're here collecting money when Jimmy's sick!" I said, "Yeah, actually I am. We've got people to pay."

Peter threw a big fit. They'd started the show and gone onstage. They'd thrown a trash can over one of the monitor guys onstage and were just being bastards. So I told Peter, "We're done. We quit. We're not going to be treated like this. We're out of here. I'll give you two days to get somebody else, but we're not doing this. Good-bye."

About four hours later, I get a call from Steve Weiss and Peter, and they say, "You need to come over to the Whitehall Hotel and have a meeting about this." I get to the room, and Steve Weiss is on the phone, putting out a contract on my life. I'm listening to this third-hand thing that Steve is saying: "Bad things will happen to Calmes. We know where he lives." I'm about to shit my pants when I notice Peter looking at me with a twinkle in his eye. I went, "Oh fuck."

CHRIS CHARLESWORTH (New York correspondent for *Melody Maker*)   I was always a bit wary around Led Zeppelin because—Plant aside— there wasn't a very friendly atmosphere coming from them. They were a bit touchy. Every other word with Peter was "fucking" or "cunt."

ROY CARR (writer for *New Musical Express*)   Bad Company were playing Madison Square Garden, and Peter rang me and said, "Do you wanna come over for a few days?" I went over, and he said, "You know, I know people think I'm an evil bastard, but you know and I know that there are so many crooks in the States that just want to latch on. I just want to keep them away from the bands." He said he'd been approached by the Mafia. That was going on, with Zeppelin being so big.

NICK KENT (writer for *New Musical Express*)   Grant was the closest thing to a Tony Soprano that I've ever known, because you wanted to like the guy and because he knew the difference between right and wrong. But what he'd come up with through his life meant that he couldn't trust people.

BENJI LeFEVRE   Peter liked villains because he *was* a fucking villain. He liked getting physical with people. On the New King's Road, we had Krays people hanging round all the time. Poor Carol Browne used to sit there wincing.

BEBE BUELL (groupie and girlfriend of Page's)   Being with Zeppelin was like being Ava Gardner with Frank Sinatra. You had to be part of the entourage in order to do certain things. If you weren't, you were kept at bay. After I went to see a Bad Company show, rumors even started flying around that I was dating Peter. But he never even tried to hold my hand. Most of the time I would sit in his room, crying my eyes out about Jimmy. And I'm sure he'd already had to console many a damsel.

ROBERT PLANT   We had twitchy times at the end, me and Peter, but I owe so much of my confidence and my pigheadedness to him because of the way he calmed and nurtured and pushed and cajoled all of us to make us what we were.

PETER GRANT   By that time, the security thing in the U.S. was getting ridiculous. We started getting death threats; in fact, straight after the '73 tour following the Drake robbery, there was a very serious one. Some crackpot letter from Jamaica stating what was in store for us when we toured again.

It got very worrying. That's how we lost a little of the camaraderie after that when we were in America, because there were armed guards outside the hotel rooms all the time. I think we even talked about wearing bulletproof vests at one time.

PHIL CARLO (roadie for Bad Company)   We actually had CIA and FBI men and a marshal called Bill Charlton, who could move people from state to state and arrest people. All these people were provided by an ex-cop called Steve Rosenberg, who was Steve Weiss's mate. We had this Boston detective on the Bad Company tour who'd go and bust people if the band ran short of dope. He'd take the dope off them and tell them to fuck off and not do it again, and then he'd bring back the dope to the hotel and hand it over to us.

DANNY MARKUS   Ahmet saw Peter as some kind of British version of Colonel Tom Parker. He appreciated the way he operated, even in a primitive sense.

Grant with Ahmet on the
1975 tour. (Neal Preston/
Corbis)

ELIZABETH IANNACI (artist relations in Atlantic's L.A. office)   Ahmet was a lover of the message and not the messenger. This man loved music so much that I don't think he put judgment on what the bands did. He didn't behave badly himself and consequently did not judge those who did. He might have agreed with Dylan Thomas, who said that to create was to always be living on the edge of madness.

DANNY MARKUS Partly because I never did drugs, I wasn't so scared of Peter. I could go in the cage. I'd have Peter doing tricks—not for *me*, but there were channels open. And Ricardo was always very kind to me. His job was to create tension, and mine was to ease it. There was *always* tension backstage, and Richard played it like a piano. You had no fear *inside*, but it created an outside thing that was just incredible. Peter kept a very high intensity of social order, and it was very hard to get inside.

MARILYN COLE (wife of Richard Cole) Peter was warm, funny, powerful, terrifying. He wasn't an *éminence grise*, but there was an aura of ultimate power about him. Zeppelin dealt in intimidation; that's how they got their way. If you knew Richard, really, he was a pussycat. His true nature was far gentler than his aura as part of Zeppelin.

GLENN HUGHES Cole was the scariest man I ever met in my life. I witnessed his behavior in person, saw him in full fucking flight. When he said, "I'll fuckin' 'ave you!" it was like, "I could kill you and nobody would know about it."

JANINE SAFER (press officer, Swan Song in the U.S.) Was Richard raised by really mean wolves? It's like the Eddie Izzard sketch. It didn't matter if he was buying toothpaste at the drugstore, the subtext was always "Fuck you." The glass wasn't even half-empty, it was *totally* empty. But the thought of firing him and hiring someone they didn't know was unthinkable and impossible.

MARILYN COLE We got married at the Playboy Club, and Peter paid for everything. Lionel Bart was at the piano. I remember my mum saying, "Why is there such a long queue for the toilet, and why are they all coming out with white powder on their noses?" Bless her.

After the wedding, I thought, "That was great. *Now* what do I do?" I asked Richard how much he earned. And when he told me, I said, "*What?* That'll do for *me*, Rich. What are *you* gonna live on?" They were the stingiest lot you've ever met. Richard adored Peter. Peter was his father, his god, his mentor. And then along comes *me*.

JACK CALMES I don't think the Zeppelin people thought Richard was ever going to be employed by anyone else, but I got him the job as tour manager on Eric Clapton's 461 Ocean Boulevard tour.

MARILYN COLE Robert Stigwood offers Richard three times what he earned in a *year* with Zeppelin to take Eric out of hibernation for a couple of months. Rich says to me, "Oh, but I couldn't leave the boys." I say to him, "You fucking *what?* You turn this down and it's good-bye." Dear Richard, he had no self-esteem whatsoever. He'd been mollycoddled by Big Daddy G. Of course, they were gobsmacked.

RICHARD COLE   It was a hell of a lot more than Zeppelin were paying me, more than likely ten times as much—something like $16,000 for eight weeks' work. I spoke to Ahmet, and he said, "You should do this." Before I took it on, I called Peter and said, "Are you gonna give me a piece of Swan Song for all the fucking work I've done?" He said no, so I said, "Right then, I'm off in the morning."

JACK CALMES   Richard was still doing a lot of drugs, and Clapton was trying to dry out, so Richard was walking a fine line there. His methodology of dealing with everything was the slash-and-burn mentality of Led Zeppelin, whereas the Clapton tour was kind of frail because he was coming back. But he did a good job and was enough of a pro to pull it off.

RICHARD COLE   Ahmet was a crafty old fucker, believe me. I was out on the piss in New Orleans with him and Eric and Marilyn and Earl McGrath, and he said, "You know Zeppelin are back on the road next year?" I said I had heard. He said, "You'll be doing it." I said, "Nah, fuck 'em." He said, "You've *got* to do it. Who *else* is going to do it?" I don't know if he spoke to Peter, but Jimmy and Robert then came down to see me in Pangbourne.

MARILYN COLE   Jimmy, Robert, and Peter came to our barn—where they'd never been before—and Richard, of course, behaved like the Queen had arrived. I'd cooked this casserole in Guinness or something, which somehow fed everyone. Peter comes out with "I see we're gonna 'ave to deal with Leni." I said, "Who, Riefenstahl? She was *great*, wasn't she?" In the end, they quadrupled his salary, gave him a Jaguar and a much bigger expense account. But he's grossly undervalued by them to this day.

CHRIS CHARLESWORTH   The undercurrent of unpleasantness was so unnecessary. They were the biggest band in the world. They could outdraw the Stones and the Who. They could do as many gigs as they wanted in the biggest arenas, and no one was going to attack them.

The latent violence wasn't there with any other bands of that stature—and certainly not the Who, a band that I spent a lot of time with. There might have been a row in the dressing room after a bad Who gig, but there was nothing like the bad vibes and that hint of menace around Zeppelin. They behaved as if they were a law unto themselves. They could protect themselves with this crew of gangsters, and they could do pretty much what they liked . . . short of murder.

BENJI LeFEVRE If there was something distasteful going on, you tended to have another drink or another joint and go, "Ah, it'll be alright, fuck it. At least, no one's got killed . . . yet." When you're twenty-something and involved in something that enormous, it doesn't *matter*. You just go along for the ride.

DANNY GOLDBERG I didn't see anybody beaten up, but I saw people threatened. I was nervous. I didn't want anybody mad at me. There's no question that you didn't cross Richard Cole, but the person who was the most prone to violence was Bonham when he got drunk. He'd push people around, and then it would be Richard's job to try and restrain him.

NICK KENT Taking cocaine just enabled Bonham to drink more. The combination of cocaine and alcohol is almost as dangerous as heroin, because you end up with two separate addictions. Plus, people were worried about him getting into heroin. It was like, "Whatever you do, don't let him do smack. He'll snort the whole gram and overdose."

JOE JAMMER (blues guitarist and former Zeppelin roadie) Page being a student of Aleister Crowley, they didn't call Bonham "The Beast" lightly. Something made him unhappy as time went on, because he became more and more violent.

JOHN BONHAM (speaking in 1975) I've got worse—terribly bad nerves all the time. Once we start into "Rock and Roll," I'm fine. I just can't stand sitting around, and I worry about playing badly. Everybody in the band is the same, and each has some little thing they do before we go on, just like pacing about or lighting a cigarette. It used to be worse at festivals. You might have to sit around for a whole day, and you daren't drink, because you'll get tired out and blow it. So you sit drinking tea in a caravan with everybody saying, "Far out, man."

DAVE NORTHOVER When we were leaving the gigs in the limos, although everyone was exhausted, Bonzo would be very hyped up. There was no way he would be quietly going to bed. He never wanted to go to bed before it got light.

JOHN PAUL JONES Bonzo drank for *reasons*. He hated being away from home. He really *did*, and between gigs he found it hard to cope. And he was terrified of flying: sometimes he'd drink too much and get the driver to turn around before he got to the airport. So things like that really don't help.

JANINE SAFER Personally, I was never in fear of Bonzo. I thought he was really a doll, one of the sweetest people. Miserably unhappy whenever Pat wasn't with him. Not very bright and not intellectually inclined. Of the four of them, he had the weakest hind legs. He liked playing the drums, and he loved his wife. He would be completely unhinged when she wasn't around.

MARILYN COLE The groupies troubled Bonzo. He called them "those old slags." He couldn't come to terms with it. He'd be angry at them for what they were.

CHRIS CHARLESWORTH I was on the plane with them, and Bonham had passed out drunk. When he came round, he tried to attack the stewardess—literally tried to mount her from the rear. Everyone had been having a really nice time until then. Jones was playing the organ and everybody was singing along and getting pleasantly pissed, and suddenly the whole mood was broken by Bonham's arrival and his futile attempt to seduce the stewardess. The others manhandled him off her and frog-marched him back to the cabin where the bed was.

JANINE SAFER Danny Markus was in Artist Relations, a job that no longer exists in record companies and that basically entailed procuring drugs and women for bands. What a great job! Danny was smart, Danny was funny, and Danny had monogrammed rolling papers.

DANNY MARKUS Bonzo had a way of testing you. He used to squeeze your nipple until it was purple. There was a famous European publisher named Larry who had these amazing goggle glasses, and I found a guy in Chicago who made me a similar pair. So I had just gotten these glasses when I got on the *Starship*, and Bonzo comes up to me, takes the glasses off, throws them on the floor, and stomps on them.

About two nights later, I'm back on the *Starship*, and I'm wearing a new pair that I've had made up because the guy still had the prescription. I see Bonzo coming toward me, so *I* take the glasses off and *I* stomp on them. I never had a problem with Bonzo ever again after that. He just wanted to see that you weren't afraid of him—to see whether you could take a punch. I mean, don't get me wrong, he was an ugly drunk. If you were on the inside, you were okay, but if you were on the outside, it was like he was swinging a ropeful of razorblades and slicing anybody in his path.

NICK KENT   I've never seen anyone behave worse in my life than Bonham and Cole. I once saw them beat a guy senseless for no reason and then drop money on his face. It makes me sick when I hear Plant talking about what a great geezer Bonzo was, because the guy was a schizophrenic animal, like something out of *Straw Dogs*.

DAVE NORTHOVER   I had the suite below John's at the Hyatt House. There's a knock at the door, and here's Keith Moon: "David, I've tried to get into John's room, and he won't let me in." I said, "What do you want me to do about it?" He said, "I've got an idea. I could climb up the outside." Bear in mind, we're on the eighth floor of the hotel. So we go out on the balcony, with the balustrade for John's room about seven or eight feet above us. Keith said, "All you've got to do is just give me a lift up. I'll be fine."

Keith gets up on the balcony, and I've got his ankles. He says, "Right. Lift!" And I'm thinking, "If I let go, it's going to be worldwide news, and I'm going to be dead." But he made it, pulled himself over the balcony, and barged into John's suite. John freaked, rushed into the bathroom and flushed everything down the loo. Next thing I know, I get a phone call asking me to "arrange further supplies."

For some reason, John had a small upright piano in the room, and things got fairly excitable. The music was going, and the piano was going. I was thinking, "I'm going to go out in a minute because they're being noisy bastards." And then I heard a bang, a rumble, another bang, another rumble . . . and then a huge crash. They'd tipped the piano over the edge of the balcony. It missed a limo by about ten feet.

GLENN HUGHES   I remember we were having a bit of a party at the Rainbow with Robert Palmer. John takes an eight ball of coke out of his pocket and throws it into his cupped hands and cups the whole eight ball up into his face . . . and we're catching the crumbs as they fall down. I mean, you've heard of excess, and this is one of those moments where you can't believe what you're seeing.

BENJI LeFEVRE   I have never *seen* so much cocaine. It was fucking insane. Whenever you get into that journey, it's never quite enough, and you always want just a little bit more.

NICK KENT   You had *countless* cocaine dealers in Hollywood, and they would give coke to bands for free because they wanted to be able to say, "Did ya see Zeppelin at the Forum last week? Well, they were high on *my* cocaine."

DESIREE KIRKE (wife of Bad Company's Simon Kirke)   We partied *hard*. Too young to live, too fast to die. But reality always seeps in. It took me *years* to get sober, till the mid-'90s.

GLENN HUGHES   We all know that there was white powder going around other than coke.

BENJI LeFEVRE   Sometimes the "subtle blend"—as Jimmy used to call it—didn't quite work, so he'd try a little bit more of the one and a little bit less of the other. It all just escalated into complete mayhem; 1973 was, without a doubt, the most fantastic fun. On the '75 tour, on the other hand, there were certainly occasions where Jimmy was too fucked up to play.

PETER GRANT   I remember the first time Jerry Weintraub saw Jimmy on a tour. He says to me, "Is that guy gonna *live*?"

PETER CLIFTON (director of *The Song Remains the Same*)   Peter just *loved* Jimmy, and he was incredibly *gentle* with him. And Jimmy was incredibly rude, backed up by Peter. I remember at one early meeting,

Peter just jumped up and ran out of the room—I didn't know he could move so fast! I said to Carol Browne, "What happened?" She said, "Jimmy just caught his finger in a door." It was like a football manager and his favorite player. Jimmy was this fragile genius. He had a sort of incandescent beauty about him and a sense of helplessness.

GLORIA GRANT (wife of Peter Grant)   Peter didn't want the good thing to fall apart. He didn't want to think it was all going to fold up or that he'd messed up. And that's why he helped Jimmy out in lots of ways—with his addiction and things. Peter nannied him. In some ways, Jimmy was like the little brother he'd never had.

I remember walking back from Hellingly School with Warren one afternoon, and Peter drew up in his Porsche and asked if I wanted a lift. I said no, because he'd been out all night. He told me later that Jimmy had OD'd, and he'd been trying to keep it all together.

NICK KENT   At one point, Grant took me under his wing. He'd always say, "You're an ally." So I flew with him to a Zeppelin gig, and after the show he said, "Come up to my room." I'd taken a lot of cocaine, as had everybody, and he gave me a Valium to calm me down. But he also gave me a little talk about heroin, because I was already on that road—and he probably realized Page was on that road, too.

He sat down and really opened up to me, and at one point he pulled out this Karen Dalton album, *In My Own Time*, and said, "This is the greatest record ever made, and I wanted to manage her. So I went out and found her, and she was a junkie."

GLENN HUGHES   At the Hyatt House, you never saw the four of them together. Jonesy was never there, and Robert was sort of in and out. There were all kinds of debauchery going on. People would pop in and out, get a bird, disappear. Smoke-filled fucking rooms of opium and shit happening. It was kind of unsettling to me. I never felt comfortable in that scenario. I was never a big fan of the groupie thing.

BEBE BUELL   I never got to know Robert well, but I always found him really sweet, really peace-and-love. He would shack up with one girl that would be his favorite, and you would never see much of him. He tried to re-create a family everywhere he went.

MIKE APPLETON (producer of the BBC2 show *The Old Grey Whistle Test*)   I always equate Robert to some extent with Jagger, in that they were both in control of themselves. Robert and I could talk about almost anything. I remember being at the Hyatt House with him, and the only thing he was interested in at that particular moment was how Wolves had done that weekend. He had the papers flown out to him so he could read the match reports.

MARILYN COLE   Robert, Bonzo, and Jonesy came into this nucleus of dark energy: the triangle of Jimmy, Peter, and Richard. And those three would always be ribbing "Percy" behind his back. Maybe they were just fucking jealous, but he was the scapegoat, the front man with the golden hair and the little blouses.

Robert didn't seem to give a fuck about the favoritism. Maybe he was more sure of himself, and had enough largesse to deal with it. He wasn't involved in that nucleus of mystery and magick. He wasn't sitting there with mounds of cocaine. He went home, whereas Peter and Jimmy were much more involved with each other.

MICHAEL DES BARRES (singer with Swan Song band Detective)   Robert has white wings that flew him above the fray. He flew above it and smiled and laughed. He didn't need a driver, he didn't need a retinue. The difference between him and Jimmy was that he could step outside the whole thing and observe it. He had a mystical view of things.

MICK FARREN (writer for *NME*)   The normal dynamic of a rock 'n' roll band is like Gene Vincent and the Blue Cats; it's the singer and his backing band. But where you've got a singer who is maybe not actually the top cat in the band, things get decidedly harder and have to be worked out.

DANNY GOLDBERG   I watched [the relationship] change. Earlier, Jimmy really dominated the relationship completely. And he was the founder of the group, the producer of the records, wrote the music, and was just the psychic center of the group. And basically somewhat dominated Robert. Although Robert had his own life and his own thing, Jimmy was the stronger of the two in that relationship. At times when they would disagree, if Jimmy was vehement about something, Robert would go along with that.

But as time went by and Robert got older, he became more and more independent, to the point where, now, Robert is the stronger. He's certainly the more successful. But I would say by the end of Zeppelin, Robert had got the confidence to assert himself as an absolute equal.

NICK KENT   Plant is one of those guys who wants to run his own game. The thing about him is that very, very quickly in America he became a sex symbol, and it was made very obvious to everyone involved in Led Zeppelin that he was as much a powerful image and force as Page was.

When I was with them in 1975, there was one thing that showed me what the Page-Plant dynamic was all about. *Circus* put out a book about Plant, and the guy who'd put it together came to a gig. After the gig, Page said he wanted to talk to this guy and wanted me to come along. So we got in one of the limos together, and Page really went for this guy. Like, "Why have you done a book just about Robert?"

I mean, Page was the leader of Led Zeppelin, you have to realize that. But when Plant became as popular as he did—when he became the Viking prince of rock—all of a sudden Jimmy couldn't tell him what to do anymore. He couldn't pull the whole "I was in the Yardbirds when you were still mending roads in West Bromwich." Plant recognized it, and suddenly people had to treat him differently. Peter Grant could no longer tell Plant what to do: if Plant didn't like something, he was now going to say something about it. And if it got any worse, he might even walk out.

CHRIS CHARLESWORTH   John Paul was a mystery. He showed no interest whatever in having any kind of profile. No one seemed to interview him very much, and he wouldn't be out in bars with the rest of them. He was nice enough, but he just wasn't *there*.

JANINE SAFER   John Paul was incredibly bright, always the most grown-up and detached of them. He taught me how to play backgammon, which we would do for hours on the *Starship*. He was the consummate session musician, and in many ways Led Zeppelin was just another gig to him—albeit one that lasted many years.

Jonesy playing backgammon on the *Starship*, 1975. (Neal Preston/Corbis)

MARILYN COLE Jonesy never really looked like he belonged in Led Zeppelin. He was like a classical musician surrounded by rock stars.

JANINE SAFER Musically, John Paul would butt heads with Jimmy; he was the only one in the band who would do that. He would say, "No, that doesn't sound good," and the two of them would at least discuss it. Jimmy was not imperious with him, which he was with almost everyone else.

DAVE NORTHOVER John Paul wasn't exactly aloof, but he didn't partake in all the silliness that went on. He tended to go off on his own, without any of the minders looking after him. That used to worry Peter a bit.

SAM AIZER (artist relations in the Swan Song U.S. office) John Paul and Brian Gallivan would come up to my little office, and I'd say, "What are you doing today?" Jonesy would say, "We're going to go see a movie." Brian and him, that's what they did. They realized they could get away with it, and they *liked* getting away with it. Jimmy? Never. Everything that guy did had to be a drama.

DAVE NORTHOVER   After one show, this chap invited John Paul out to his house, so we were driven out to see him. Just before we left, the guy said, "I'd really like to ball you both." At which point John Paul said, "Well, David, I think it's probably time we left, don't you?"

• • •

JANE AYER (press officer in Atlantic's L.A. office)   The year 1975 was *huge* for Zeppelin. That was the golden era of rock 'n' roll, and they were the biggest group in the world. For us, this was the Renaissance, and I just happened to be there at that peak time. Maybe I was like Cameron Crowe and an innocent, but on the West Coast—where I was doing press—I really did feel like the Harvey Kuberniks and David Rensins and Todd Everetts were receptive to Zeppelin. Danny Goldberg did an extraordinary job for the band, and I thought the relationship with American journalists at that point was very good.

HARVEY KUBERNIK (West Coast correspondent for *Melody Maker*)   I went up to John Paul Jones at a Swan Song party and said, "I know this is Zeppelin and you're debuting your label, but I just have to tell you how much I love the Lulu and Donovan stuff you arranged." He said, "I haven't been asked about *them* in a while."

JAAN UHELSZKI (writer for *Creem*)   I went to a couple of the gigs with them. I was there as a journalist, but I was also just kind of observing and taking it all in. I really was a little daunted. Richard Cole was more like a big loutish goof, but Peter Grant did scare the shit out of me. You didn't want to look at him the wrong way.

To me, that tour was the apex. Everything that they were and everything they had become and how far out they were taking it . . . those shows to me were mind-altering. People used to say that Pink Floyd took you on some kind of acid trip, whereas Zeppelin was much more physical—hence *Physical Graffiti*, I think. It was the difference between a chemical reaction and a physical reaction. You weren't altered, but you were agitated and tumbled around, and then it was over. Like sex.

DANNY GOLDBERG   In 1973, the band had got a lot of attention for the sheer magnitude of what they were doing, playing these stadium shows. *Rolling Stone* wanted to do something on them, and the band said, "Fuck them. No." So then, in 1975, Jann Wenner called me and said, "Okay, you can pick the writer, and we'll do it in a Q&A, so you don't have to worry about any snarky, sarcastic, or dismissive style. We'll print it verbatim as a Q&A." Jimmy suggested Cameron Crowe because Cameron had interviewed him in 1973 for the *L.A. Times*.

TONY MANDICH   When Cameron showed up at the Atlantic office to interview Led Zeppelin, I thought, "This kid must have come to pick up a poster or something." But he really smoothed out the relationship between *Rolling Stone* and Zeppelin.

DANNY GOLDBERG   Cameron was never one of the snobbish critics. He was like a champion, a cheerleader for music he loved. There's not a mean bone in his body, either as a writer or as a person. So he was not similar in temperament to the *Rolling Stone* or New York writers. Jimmy thought of the next generation, and he thought of Cameron and suggested him, and I was freaked when I was told that this kid in high school was going to interview them. But I went with what they wanted, and it turned out to be a very good thing for the band.

Zeppelin just wore everyone out with their success and the sheer fact of what they were doing. One way or another, it was going to wear down the resistance. There were too many people who love rock 'n' roll who loved Led Zeppelin for it to be ignored.

●   ●   ●

JAKE RIVIERA (manager of Dr. Feelgood)   Ahmet and Earl McGrath and all the strippers were at Earl's Court. The band were pleasant to us because they were courting Dr. Feelgood. Robert was very nice, talking about "Riot in Cell Block No. 9" and Big Joe Turner. Jimmy loved Wilko's lead-and-rhythm playing, and they had a good old chat about Mick Green. But Lee Brilleaux didn't like the hierarchy of it all. Even at that point they were strutting around, and Bonzo was being boorish.

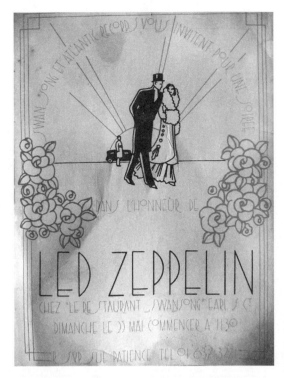

Invitation to the Earl's
Court after-show party,
May 25, 1975. (Courtesy
of Phil Carlo)

ROSS HALFIN (photographer and friend of Page's) Earl's Court was
more of an event than a week of great concerts. "No Quarter" went on
and on and on, and the sound was very boomy. And all the songs from
Graffiti were epically long.

DAVE LEWIS (editor of Zeppelin fanzine *Tight But Loose*) On the last
night, they played for three hours and forty minutes. They did "Heartbreaker" and "Communication Breakdown" as extra encores, and
played a reggae improvisation in the middle of them. They seemed to
be in their own little world, oblivious to the 17,000 watching them. It
was astonishing. Tell me that's not the greatest band that ever lived.
When they walked off the stage, it was the end of the glory days.
Nothing was ever easy again.

18

Invocation of My Demon Brother

Peter Grant: "Hello, Bob, I'm Peter Grant, I manage Led Zeppelin."

Bob Dylan: "Do I come to you with *my* problems?"

—As overheard by Ian McLagan and others,
Los Angeles, 1974

ROBERT PLANT   On the Monday morning after the last gig at Earl's Court, I was on my way to Agadir with Maureen. And three weeks later, Jimmy flew out to meet me in Marrakesh, where we spent several nights at the folk festival. . . . We wanted to get down to a place called Tafia, which is not very far from the border of the Spanish Sahara. We got as far as we could, but eventually the road got so bad, we had to turn back.

It was devastating leaving Morocco behind and suddenly finding ourselves in Europe. For two months, I'd lived at a Moroccan speed, which is no speed at all, and then suddenly I was in Spain, being frisked. We saw the jazz festival in Montreux, living on top of a mountain in a total extreme of climate from what we'd had for the past two months. After a while, I started pining for the sun again, not just the sun but the happy, haphazard way of life that goes with it, and Rhodes seemed a good idea.

BENJI LeFEVRE (Zeppelin sound technician from 1973 to 1980) Everything in Robert's world began to change at the time of his car accident in Rhodes. When you have a physical experience like that, you really have to think about who you are and what you're doing. At twenty-seven, you still think you can recover from anything, but he never has. He can't move his arm completely to this day.

ROBERT PLANT   I had the normal instant reaction of anybody, and that was for my family who were in the car with me. I didn't know what the implications and the final outcome of the wounds or whatever would turn out to be, but they were of minimal importance at the time. I had to . . . not so much grow up very quickly as be prepared to face odds that I never thought I would come up against.

JIMMY PAGE   It was just strange that it happened within a week of rehearsals. It was just like something saying, "No, you're not gonna do it." It's personal.

RICHARD COLE   I went down to Rhodes with the doctors because Maureen was dying, and her sister Shirley couldn't give any more blood. I remember looking at the X-rays and the doctor saying, "We've got to get her out of here, the bones are setting in the wrong way." So I got them back to England, where Willie Robertson, our insurance guy, got them to Jersey to save their money.

BENJI LeFEVRE   When they got Maureen to Guy's Hospital, she technically died for a few minutes.

JACK CALMES (cofounder of Showco sound and lighting)   Benji and his wife and I visited Maureen in the hospital when she was there, and she was wacked out on the pain pills. She was lying there with pins in her body and slings in the air, with casts and everything, so that was a pretty tough time for her.

WILLIE ROBERTSON (Zeppelin's insurance broker)   Richard asked if I knew anybody who lived in Jersey. I said, "As a matter of fact, I know the king of Jersey." Because Dick Christian was a heavyweight there. So Richard asked me to call Dick to see if Robert could go over and spend some time there while he recuperated.

Dick was more of an overture-and-symphony man, but Richard, Robert, myself, and Marilyn flew over to Jersey, where a great big Roller picked us up. We got to Dick's huge house, and he came out and told us that Robert, Richard, and Marilyn would be in the lodge at the end of the garden. I left after a couple of days, and, eventually, Marilyn and Richard went back to London. Then Dick invited Robert up to the main house. They became huge friends. He was a fanatical snooker player, so all they did all day was play snooker and enjoy a beaker.

UNITY MacLEAN (manager of Swan Song office in the U.K.)   Like Robert, Bonzo had another life, apart from coming up to town and doing speedballs. He'd go back down to his pub in the country and sit around entertaining his crowd there. They were mainly farmers and people interested in cars and things like that—very normal and ordinary people.

Bonzo loved his prize bulls, so he fit into that lifestyle very well. He'd built up a tolerance to drink, and of course if you're taking coke, it helps you to stay awake so you can drink even more. But I think when he was at home, he'd go down to the pub and have a few beers and a couple of chasers and then go home.

CHRIS WELCH (writer for *Melody Maker*)   I went up to the farm to interview John in the summer. Pat was in the hospital, expecting Zoe. John confessed to me that he found it harder and harder to do the long solos. He was hale and hearty. There were no sides to him. I remember going to a disco with him in Birmingham, and there were all these transvestites swanning around. He said, "You can't find a bloke to have a pint of beer with these days." It was the sort of thing his dad might have said.

SALLY WILLIAMS (girlfriend of Bonham's drum roadie Mick Hinton)   The time I really got to know Bonzo was when they were tax exiles in the South of France. Mick and I drove down there with a drum kit John wanted. Pat and Jason were there, and I think Zoe was a few months old. I ended up staying because I could speak French, and the cook couldn't speak English. John really didn't want any of this fancy French food, he wanted steak and chips, and he was very reluctant to try different things. I had to convince the cook it was nothing personal.

RICHARD COLE Bonham was very meat-and-potatoes. He'd say, "Fuck all this foreign food." When you went to his house in the South of France, his pantry was like the corner shop. Bird's Custard, you name it, it was in there, right down to the curries he'd send his chauffeur back to London to pick up in his mobile caravan.

SALLY WILLIAMS Away from the limelight, John was a very ordinary guy. There was none of that greater-than-thou attitude, which I think was just kept for the crowds and the hangers-on. All the Zep guys, when they were on their own, were very nice guys. Put them in a room together and they became totally obnoxious.

DEBBIE BONHAM (sister of John Bonham) *The Song Remains the Same* shows John as a real down-to-earth guy, really. It's just everything John was about. He's got his wife, he's got Jason playing the drums, the home, the farm, his passion for driving his cars. He couldn't envisage doing a fantasy scene like the others did—it wasn't really John—so he kept it very real.

PETER CLIFTON (director of *The Song Remains the Same*) I knew the only chance I had with *The Song Remains the Same* was to put them in the studio. But it took a long time to convince Jimmy, because there was a certain integrity in people knowing that this was filmed live.

We booked Shepperton Studios, and I spent a couple of months editing the three nights from Madison Square Garden, which had been recorded on 24-track. I created a whole template for the whole concert and then put that all in order so that we had a complete soundtrack. Then I filmed that with pictures from the Madison Square Garden footage that worked and then put the rest of it in white spacing. Then we put up a huge screen directly in front of them and rebuilt the stage at Shepperton.

BENJI LeFEVRE   If you watch the film carefully, you can see how much fatter Bonzo is in certain shots. And then we had to do everybody's dream sequences. It was fucking mental. You have to be a Zeppelin fan to watch that film.

PETER CLIFTON   They hadn't played for a while, so they came to the studio and wound themselves up on the usual substances. There was just me there at that stage, and they played this version of "Black Dog" that was just dynamic.

JIMMY PAGE   *The Song Remains the Same* was an incredible uphill struggle. We'd done a bit of work on it and stopped, did more, then stopped again. Three times in all. At that point, we'd decided to redo the thing.

PETER CLIFTON   Jimmy had an enormous ego. I remember at Shepperton he'd put on a little bit of weight, so sometimes he'd have a look at a shot, and there would be this little roll of tummy over the top of his trousers, and he was *very* conscious of that. When we had to reshoot him climbing the mountain, and I used a wide-angle lens, he didn't speak to me for months afterward because he thought his bum looked too big. His roadie finally told me, so I just dissolved the shot into the full moon.

BENJI LeFEVRE   When I went to Raglan Castle with Robert, it was a case of, "Can you bring some shit down just in case?" A few flares, a couple of paraffin cans. Nobody had any *plans*. It was like, "I think I want to pick a magic mushroom. Can you make a magic mushroom?" Amateursville all the way round.

PETER CLIFTON   The fantasy sequences really became the bits where I just couldn't re-create the energy or the mood of Madison Square Garden strongly enough. Plus, I wanted to give the audience relief from just looking at a concert.

JIMMY PAGE   When we did all our fantasy sequences, nobody was allowed to be around the others while we did them, because they'd all take the piss.

PETER CLIFTON I interviewed them all at great length, and one of the questions I asked them was what their great ambition in life was. Jonesy, who was two different people, said his ambition was to play the biggest organ in the world. In his sequence, we had him with a mask on, and what that meant was that when he was with Led Zeppelin, he put his mask on and raped and pillaged his way through society, whereas when he came home he took his mask off and became himself again.

Robert's fantasy was about finding the perfect woman. He decided that, as a warrior, he would fight all these adversaries until he reached the castle where the princess was. And when he finally found this perfect woman, he knew she didn't exist, so she disappeared before his eyes.

With Jimmy's thing it was all about finding himself, and so he climbed the mountain of life, and when he reached the top he found himself as an old man. I got scrapbooks from his family and went back through the whole period of his life to a fetus.

Bonzo's sequence was just about teaching his son the drums and riding fast cars and motorbikes.

A lot of the reviewers found the sequences self-indulgent and narcissistic, but it was really just an attempt to explain what they were like as people.

JIMMY PAGE The whole point of the bit in *The Song Remains the Same* where Peter plays a gangster was just to send up all that and show how it was just a joke anyway.

PETER CLIFTON The idea of playing an Al Capone–type of mobster was just metaphorical, but it appealed to Peter's ego—and, of course, he loved those old cars. What people never noticed was that the guys he shot were the faceless businessmen counting the money—the people he most hated. And the little guy that ran into his own reflection had a Nazi ring on.

ABE HOCH I think Peter liked the illusion he'd created for himself as being this gangster. He loved the sense that people were scared, but we had some very sensitive moments together. We did a lot of talking on a personal level and became friends. I liked him very much, and I trusted him. Then he would do weird bad things.

PETER CLIFTON   When I had to take Jimmy to the studio and put plaster makeup all over his face and everything, he did it without complaining.

JIMMY PAGE   It's a horrible medium to work in. It's so boring! So slow! Just shooting the fantasy sequence—"Can you do it again so we can get a different angle? Can you do it again?" I'm not used to that.

PETER CLIFTON   One night I had three of them—all except Jonesy— down at my studio in Warwick Gardens, and I told them we had to finish by midnight because I needed to get to a screening of *The Rocky Horror Picture Show*. As usual, I had to pay for the coke out of my own petty cash.

I turned the light out in the editing room, and the boys were waiting for me in my office. They didn't want to go, and they were abusing me. Bonzo took my picture of Australia and turned it upside down. They'd left one long line of coke for me, but as I looked at it, I noticed it was brown. Still, I snorted it—as you do—and jumped into the car. As I was going through Hyde Park, the feeling just hit me, like I'd sunk into a warm bath. By the end of the film, I realized what had happened. It was to pay me back for kicking them out.

AUBREY POWELL (designer of *The Song Remains the Same* album sleeve)   I lived in the Plaza Hotel for three months, with a limo outside for my personal use. I did all the artwork for the film and the album in that hotel suite. Peter wouldn't let me leave. I spent a lot of time with Robert and Benji in New York. We went to see Mott the Hoople play, and Bonzo stumbled onstage, trying to play drums with Buffin.

ROSS HALFIN (photographer and friend of Page)   Buffin refused, and there was a fistfight. Years later, I was in the dressing room at the Freddie Mercury tribute show with Ian Hunter, and Plant walks in and says to Ian, "I really must apologize for that night."

AUBREY POWELL   Robert and I really cemented our friendship when he was in a wheelchair and then on crutches. You could tell there was a separation going on, that the days of dressing up in drag were gone. I think Robert was delicately stepping back, and I think he was a little frightened about what had gone down in his life.

PETER CLIFTON Because the film took so long—the editing took two and a half years altogether—I did get to know them extremely well. When it was over and it was time to sign my contract, that was very difficult. Because they never signed *anything.*

I basically had to deliver the film myself to Warner Brothers. David Geffen was the vice president, and Frank Wells was the president. At the big meeting where we all had to sit down and do the deal, Peter didn't even turn up. There must have been twenty people in this huge, huge office, and I had to explain that Peter Grant was still in London. They were all incredulous.

It seemed like the band was just killing time in Los Angeles. I was at the Beverly Hilton until they threw all my stuff into the swimming pool. I then moved to the Beverly Wilshire. That was when they searched my hotel room because I'd used a Zeppelin limo to pick up my Chuck Berry film from MGM. They asked me if I was using the car for other purposes, and apparently my eyes flickered—I was never a very good liar. Richard picked up on it, and by the time I got back to the hotel, they were waiting for me. They searched the room and found the can of Chuck Berry.

I was really deeply hurt by that. It was absolute drug paranoia. In the end, they really turned on me. They thought I was bootlegging the film. What I'd done was make up a reel of each of their best moments to give them as a present. I knew Robert was madly in love with his son Karac, so I put together a sequence on that. In the Peter Grant reel, I had lovely stuff that I'd filmed with Gloria in the ballet school. And then Richard Cole and Joan Hudson came to my cutting room with a court order when I wasn't there. The nanny let them in, and they took anything that had the words "Led Zeppelin" on it.

SAM AIZER (artist relations, Swan Song in the U.S.) I realized how powerful Led Zeppelin was to people when they had the premiere for

The Song Remains the Same in New York. It was like a riot, it was Beatlemania. People were jumping on their cars. Mick Ralphs said to me, "Bad Company is a big band. We'll play Madison Square Garden, we'll play the Forum. But Led Zeppelin is *show business*." They portrayed themselves that way. They followed in the footsteps of Sinatra and Elvis, the way they carried their own touring, the way they had their own jet.

CHRIS CHARLESWORTH (journalist)   I was living in New York as *Melody Maker*'s U.S. correspondent when *The Song Remains the Same* premiered there, and they came over for it. They promptly headed down to this club called Ashley's on Fifth Avenue at 13th Street. I was in there, quietly minding my own business, having dinner with a girl, when Cole and Robert wandered in.

It was obvious that Richard was out of his tree, and he comes over and starts chatting up the girl I'm with: "'Allo, darlin', whatchoo doin' with this cunt? Wanna come back to my hotel?" So I'm like, "Richard, please," and the girl is embarrassed. He tries to hit me. The staff in the restaurant see this, march him to the door, and kick him out on to the street. Robert then comes over to me and is profusely apologetic. He says Richard has been terrible all day and that he'd thrown cutlery at Telly Savalas on the plane.

The coda was that I wrote something about the film and was, I think, unduly kind about it. One night I was sitting at home reading the paper, and my phone rings, and it's Robert saying, "I just want to thank you, Chris, for not taking it out on the band after what happened with Richard. At least you didn't slag off the movie because you were angry."

UNITY MACLEAN   *The Song Remains the Same* came out, and we had a big party at a huge old warehouse in Covent Garden. We climbed up these creaky iron staircases, and at the top were these private rooms where Paul McCartney and some of the Pink Floyd guys were.

RAT SCABIES (drummer with the Damned)   I blagged my way into the party after the premiere. All the Zeppelin lot were upstairs in the posh bit, and we were all down in the riffraff area. I just remember looking up and seeing Robert Plant's silhouette against the window and thinking, "Fucking hell, there must be a thousand people here, and they don't even bother to come down."

MIKE APPLETON (producer of the BBC2 show *The Old Grey Whistle Test*) *The Song Remains the Same* came out at least two years too late. It should have hit when they were at their peak to elevate them even further, and it would have done that.

MICK FARREN (writer for *NME*)   I went to see the film, and it was like all the nonsense coming to a head: the gangsters and Crowley and the spirit of Albion. It was not entertaining, and it was out of control. That's when I lost any remaining sympathy I had for them. I don't get guys who need to have double-necked guitars hanging round their necks. Mick Jagger said, "I could go eat *dinner* while Bonham's playing his drum solo." And the histrionics and the bare chest and the Greek-statue shapes. I really think they created punk rock, because it was a case of *"Stop this shit!"*

Things really started tightening up. Everything from the Pistols to Rockpile, things were being pulled back into focus. Rock 'n' roll suddenly became human-sized again. We were getting back into Dingwalls, back into the Nashville [club], back to reality. The punk bands had to give respect to the Who because they were stealing furiously from them, and Patti Smith had Keith Richards on her T-shirt. But punk never stole from Zep, because they didn't have "My Generation" or "I'm Waiting for the Man" or those sort of seminal tunes that punk rock bands played. And they were all real flash cunts as instrumentalists.

RAT SCABIES The Who were the working-class band you went to see, and the Faces and the Kinks and those sort of bands were okay. But the whole hobgoblin thing was a bit beyond the pale. Zeppelin hadn't been to university, but they'd read *The Lord of the Rings*. I really didn't like any of the songs they did that were long. "Dazed and Confused" just made me hate the blues. But they had those really cool short-riff rock songs that motored along with a pretty good energy. In 1975, we might even have admitted that "Communication Breakdown" had punk energy—a bit like Hendrix doing that really fast version of "Johnny B. Goode" on *Hendrix in the West.*

By 1976, you couldn't admit you'd ever liked a band like Zeppelin. And quite rightly so. When you're coming up with a new thing and you're the next generation, the last thing you want to be saying is, "Oh, we like the hippie guys." Once I'd got hold of *Kick Out the Jams* and *Back in the USA* and *High Time*, it was quite easy to dump all the English past and say the MC5 were doing what I wanted the Damned to be doing.

PAUL SIMONON (bassist with the Clash, speaking in 1977)   Led Zeppelin? I don't need to hear the music—all I have to do is look at one of their album covers and I feel like throwing up.

ALAN CALLAN (president of Swan Song in the U.K., 1977–1980)   Most of the people one spoke to in the industry had the attitude of "Fuck Led Zeppelin," just because they were unassailable. Yet from the *inside*, the band would often come in and say, "That new Sex Pistols single is really great."

DAN TREACY (singer and guitarist with the Television Personalities) We recorded our first single with money I'd saved from [a job at] Swan Song, and we printed up 867 copies, which was all we could afford. Jimmy came into the office one day as I was reading about our single in *Sounds.* He said, "Got a band, have you? Are you punks?" I explained we were doing it all ourselves: the recording, the mastering, printing the labels. He was fascinated.

JANINE SAFER (press officer, Swan Song in the U.S.)   Robert was aware of punk and interested in it, but as far as their sense of their own music was concerned, it was like a T-Rex flicking a gnat away from its hide: "Call me a dinosaur? I step on you with my big brontosaurus foot!" I don't know that I even *talked* to them about the Pistols or the Ramones.

JOHN PAUL JONES   I didn't really like punk when I first heard it. You heard guitarists struggling with blues solos of the kind you remembered the guitarist in your first band having a go at. Punk did clear the air, though, and it made us feel we ought to look at the way we were doing things—to look at what we'd perhaps become.

RAT SCABIES We used to get phone calls from bands' managers, asking if they could come on the guest list. Robin Trower's manager called Jake and said, "If you put Robin on the guest list, I'll put the Damned on the guest list for *him.*" And Jake just said, "When the fuck are the Damned ever going to go and see *Robin Trower?*" and just hung up. We had a very closed-door policy to the Old Wave, unless it was mates like Dr. Feelgood. BP Fallon was a big help, because he was working at Stiff, so he was the link between us and Zeppelin.

BP FALLON (U.K. press officer for Zeppelin, 1973–1976) I took Robert and Jimmy and Bonzo down to see the Damned at the Roxy. They all loved it because it was the essence of what they'd all listened to, which was wild savage rockabilly from Arkansas. It was the same concept: you get up there and twang like fuck, and you shout and scream. That's what primal music is.

JAKE RIVIERA (manager of the Damned and founder of Stiff Records) Jimmy and Robert came to see the Damned. I was at the door when they arrived. I remember it because Jimmy was wearing his fucking Luftwaffe outfit.

RAT SCABIES We were about to go onstage, and Jake comes in and says, "Led Zeppelin have just walked in." So you're looking out from the stage as you're playing, and there's all these hairy shapes at the back of the room.

JOHN LYDON (lead singer with the Sex Pistols, speaking in 1977) When Robert Plant went down to the Roxy, he had about five heavies with him—half the band and others. There were about twenty of them. They, like, took a corner, posing and hurling abuse at people that walked by as if they were something special. . . . People shouldn't worship stars like Robert Plant. . . . These superstars are totally detached from reality.

RAT SCABIES I remember talking to Robert and then getting this really hideous hard time off Mark Perry for talking to an old hippie: *"What you talkin' to that cunt for, we should be giving him a good kicking."*

• • •

JON WEALLEANS (architect employed by Page and Peter Grant)   Paul Reeves was an Arts and Crafts antiques dealer who'd previously been in fashion with a shop called Universal Witness. Jimmy had bought lots of clothes there, and they were more or less school friends going back to adolescence. Paul said to me, "Jimmy wants a black magic bookshop. Would you design it?"

It was quite a pretty little shop on Holland Street. Jimmy was very worried about the budget, but he got an incredibly good deal because I was doing another building and used the workforce from that on a part-time pirate business. The Equinox was not a very happy thing, because Jimmy was off his head a lot of the time and delegated responsibility to this ghastly guy who was clearly on smack and would try to interpret what he thought Jimmy wanted.

4 Holland Street, London W8: the former site of Page's occult bookshop Equinox. (Art Sperl)

NICK KENT (writer for *NME*)   Eric was a friend of Jimmy's from New Orleans who worked at Equinox and found old books for him. I wasn't into the occult—it was always very Dennis Wheatley to me—but Eric and I had heroin in common.

JON WEALLEANS   Jimmy said, "We've got to get a sound system for the shop." So we got a taxi to the Tottenham Court Road, which he thought a bit of an extravagance. A couple of people half-recognized him, and we ended up with these two big boxes of Wharfedale speakers and were standing on the pavement with them. It started to rain, and he suggested we take a bus. He was wearing this old brown overcoat he seemed very fond of, and he was looking at buses rather yearningly. He's a strange man—a *nice* man, basically, but very, very weird about money.

The Equinox didn't last very long, probably because Jimmy didn't pay anybody or pay the rent. It had a sort of fetid musky smell when you went in there, as if somebody was actually squatting there.

MARILYN COLE (wife of Richard Cole)   Peter Simister ran the bookshop, and everybody, of course, referred to him as "Peter Sinister." He was one of those short-sighted bookish types who had to peer very hard at you before he recognized you.

JON WEALLEANS   It was difficult to get paid. Joan Hudson was marvelously evasive and elusive, and clearly for years had protected Jimmy from anybody. She just said, "I've had no instructions to pay you." I said, "Well, can I speak to Jimmy or can you get a message to Jimmy?" She said, "No." I thought that was a bit shitty. She is an absolutely ghastly woman, much hated by myself and Paul Reeves.

PETER CLIFTON   Joan Hudson was like a villainess out of a James Bond film. Boy, they were tough.

DAVE NORTHOVER   Peter was often on the phone to Joan, checking up on things. She once said to me, "David, please don't submit expenses under the names Charlie and Henry." She wouldn't castigate us, but she would rather it was kept under the counter.

UNITY MacLEAN   Joan was so odd because she was the classic accountant, with twin set and pearls and a tight skirt and high heels. Very, very straight. Pretty clever. You couldn't get anything past her.

PHIL CARLO (roadie for Bad Company)   Joan wouldn't question bits of paper that came in with £500 spent on "supplies" or £2,000 used for "pocket money" during a recording session. I would go, "Well, it's bits and bobs, Joan, you know what they're like." She'd go, "Right, okay, jolly good." The band thought they were getting it for nothing because someone would just go off to London and come back with a huge slab of dope and a bag of Charlie that they didn't have to pay for. They all loved that.

PETER CLIFTON   Jimmy asked me to help him with *Lucifer Rising*, the Kenneth Anger film he was doing the music for. We projected the film onto a wall, and I didn't like it at all. Marianne Faithfull was in it, and it was all devil worship and candles, and I didn't want to be around that. I said, "Jimmy, don't do it, mate." Jimmy wanted me to meet Anger, but I made a point of not doing that.

KENNETH ANGER (director of *Lucifer Rising* and other films)   I met [Jimmy] at Sotheby's when he was bidding on some of Crowley's books. The problem with people like Jimmy is that he has enough money to buy the books, but he doesn't *read* the books. He doesn't use them. He doesn't understand them. He just keeps them locked up.

MARTIN STONE (guitarist and dealer in occult books)   Every now and then, Jimmy and I would meet or just recognize each other. The book thing became part of that. He was a real brother—gentle, alert, aware that the world is full of interest, with a great aesthetic sense—and a very sophisticated book collector.

I lived out in a cottage in the country, and I decided I wanted to sell some of my occult books. Jimmy by now had the bookshop, so I called them up and said I had some Crowley and other books, and did they want to buy them? This delicious pre-Raphaelite beauty came out to my place and bought my books, and that started a relationship with the bookshop. I would hang out in the flat above the shop, taking drugs and talking about occult subjects.

One day I went there, and this girl told me Jimmy was incredibly upset. A couple of weeks before, Nick Kent had interviewed him in the *NME*, and in the photo he was holding a mug of tea. He'd been asked about the nonappearance of the *Lucifer Rising* soundtrack and had said something quite innocuous about it. Now Kenneth Anger is an incredibly spiky and nasty piece of work—barking mad but definitely sinister—and Jimmy, under the full-blown kosh of Crowley, believes in the power of magick and curses. And Anger has sent him a letter care of the Equinox, and Jimmy opens it up, and there is the picture from the *NME* with a skull and crossbones drawn on the mug of tea he's about to drink. And Jimmy is absolutely freaked.

NICK KENT   Kenneth Anger told me he was going to put a spell on me. I said, "I've already *got* a spell on me. I'm a homeless junkie. How much lower do you think I can get?"

MARTIN STONE   I remember thinking, "Well, Anger is just this old Hollywood queer, he doesn't have any power." But on the other hand, he *was* deeply involved in the Ordo Templi Orientis, so who's to say? I felt really sorry for Jim, and I thought, "Well, maybe one shouldn't mess about with all this stuff." Because if you're susceptible to suggestion—which under the influence of lots of drugs, one always is—it can be terrifying.

KENNETH ANGER (speaking in 1977)   I haven't laid eyes on Jimmy Page since early June. I've been trying to get in contact with him since then; I've fixed meetings through his office and been stood up half a dozen times. I've left messages on his Kafka-esque answering machine. All I've had is promises that the soundtrack is on its way, but nothing's materialized. I've got a fucking film to finish.

The way he's been behaving is totally contradictory to the teachings of Aleister Crowley and totally contradictory to the ethos of the film. Lucifer is the angel of light and beauty. But the vibes that come off Jimmy are totally alien to that—and to human contact. It's like a bleak lunar landscape. I'm sure he doesn't have another "Stairway to Heaven," which is his most Luciferian song.

I'm certainly jaded with the rock superstar syndrome. They're like renaissance bandits. Who needs those people?

JON WEALLEANS I used to go round and see Jimmy, and he'd be in bed, and Charlotte would be off her head. Several times I took Scarlet to school because Charlotte couldn't cope. She was a nightmare when she was drinking. I talked to Jimmy about that once, and he said, "I never spotted it. But now I see that anytime we went out anywhere to a party, we would get in the car and Charlotte would say, 'Oh, shit, I've left something behind.'" Jimmy would be sitting in the limo, and she'd shoot back into the house, and he said, "I now know that she was shooting in to drink a quarter bottle of vodka." But he didn't seem to know, and I just thought she was a druggy rock chick.

MARILYN COLE Charlotte was frosty, very French and very aloof. They were together for a long, long time, but they never married.

PAMELA DES BARRES (groupie and L.A. girlfriend of Page's in the late '60s) Charlotte looked down on the groupies. Of course she did. Even though she *was* one.

* * *

AUBREY POWELL When I first met him, Peter was a softer presence. At Horselunges, he was very much a family man. He'd say, "Come and watch Helen dance."

ELIZABETH IANNACI (artist relations in Atlantic's L.A. office) In 1976, when I visited England, I was invited down to Sussex, and it was absolutely lovely. It was a manor with a moat and black swans. I could stand up in the fireplace. It was like a movie set. I was very pleasantly surprised. And Peter was so gracious, so different to how he was on the road.

HELEN GRANT (daughter of Peter Grant) Dad didn't have homes all over the place, he just had the one base. Lots of people you see will have a home here and a home abroad, but Horselunges was his sort of haven. I think it depressed him quite a lot being away. To be honest,

I think he was sick to death of the business. From a manager's point of view, it's a hell of a lot to take on. It's like being at home with four kids by yourself. I don't think Dad should ever have *been* in the music business. He was quite an old-fashioned kind of person. My mum and dad's marriage would have stayed stable if all the other crap hadn't been going on.

ED BICKNELL (former manager of Dire Straits)   When you're a manager of a successful act, you become an obnoxious twat because you have people pulling at you all the time, wanting stuff. You move from being a fan of the music into controlling this enormous economic asset, and people want a part of that—either for economic reasons or because they want some reflected glamour.

It's like the covered wagons: you're trying to exist inside this circle with all these people trying to get into it *with* you. And it can drive you completely potty. Very, very few people taste the top of the pile, and Peter and I both tasted that and both felt a slight . . . *guilt* about having done so well. It's a very British thing. There's a certain element of "pinch me" every day.

RICHARD COLE   For as long as I'd known Peter, he would always call home and speak to Warren and Helen: "How was school today? Did you have a good day?" And then it stopped. He got involved with coke, and he stopped calling. And when you've got mountains of coke, you can get anyone you want. It went to his head.

ELIZABETH IANNACI   I have very vivid recollections of Peter Grant with a *bag* of cocaine. It was like, "This is my coke spoon," . . . and it was a *ladle*.

UNITY MacLEAN   He never even chopped it, he'd just stick a key in it and shove it up his nose—or *your* nose. He was very generous with his coke, actually. There was a lot of sitting up till three or four in the morning, and then he'd start getting angry and start getting mean . . . and that's when he'd start making his phone calls.

He fired me on many occasions. The first time, he phoned me at three in the morning and said, "What have you done about such-and-such?" I'm half-asleep, and he goes, "You're fucking fired." I called

Richard and said, "I can't believe it, Peter fired me!" Richard said, "Go back to sleep, he'll have forgotten about it in the morning." So from then on, I just took no notice.

NICK KENT   When I was on the road with Zeppelin in 1975, there was a woman with Peter. I don't remember her name, but she was a professional woman in the music industry in her late thirties—American, short-haired, ample-shaped. And that was the woman who broke up his marriage. She was very nice, she wasn't a druggie, she wasn't neurotic, and they seemed to be in love.

RICHARD COLE   I was going through [a] divorce from Marilyn myself when I got a call from Peter, and he was devastated: "Gloria has run off with Jim." It was obvious that he hadn't been calling her, and she'd smelled a rat. I don't think Gloria had ever been on tour with us, but she'd been in the entertainment business, so she knew what people on the road get up to. If you do something out of the ordinary with women, they're going to fucking pounce on you.

MARILYN COLE   Gloria didn't take any shit, she was no fool. Already by the time I was on the scene, there was a *lot* of cocaine, and I don't think Gloria wanted it. She wasn't fly-by-night. From what little I knew, she was a real, strong, bright woman. Peter was never home, and I think she was lonely. It was *horrendous* to be a female within that orbit. When she said good-bye to Peter, I reckon she was saying good fucking riddance to Led Zeppelin. I think she wanted an ordinary life.

DAVE NORTHOVER   Gloria ran off with the farm manager and disappeared to Hastings. I think he must have been a very brave guy! There was talk about . . . stuff that might happen to him.

RICHARD COLE   I remember driving over and thinking I was being very clever by taking the distributor out of Gloria's engine so she couldn't go anywhere. And Peter sent me to put it back again. He didn't want to upset her anymore.

MARILYN COLE   It was a *huge* humiliation. He'd never imagined a life without her, and when she left, there was no anchor—the boat went adrift. He fought her tooth and nail for everything. And he got nastier and nastier. He held all the cards, so the Atlantic executives would be kept waiting outside Horselunges for days. He wouldn't see them. I'd say, "What's that car outside?" He'd say, "Oh, it's just some cunt from the record company."

UNITY MacLEAN Peter was a shithead to Gloria. He went off to America because they were doing those nine months out of the country, and Gloria would try to reach him to say Helen wasn't well or Warren was doing this or that, and they wouldn't put her through to him. And then she'd speak to him, and he'd say, "Don't gimme all this fucking grief . . . all these transatlantic phone calls with you yelling at me!" And she'd say, "Peter, I'm trying to keep a family together here, and you're avoiding me and ignoring me!"

And so she went off with the farm manager. Why? Because the farm manager was kind to her. He saw an opening, and he moved in pretty quick. And they lived in a caravan, and Peter never gave her a cent.

JON WEALLEANS We designed a mews house in London for Peter that was supposed to be a surprise present for Gloria, but in the interim she ran off with that chap, and she never saw it. We always thought he must be the stupidest man in the world.

AUBREY POWELL Without the stability of Gloria, Peter became sort of immersed in a delusional part that he was playing. I was at Horselunges many times when there were guns and characters from the London heavy side and things like that.

NICK KENT Cocaine really did something to Grant. He became a kind of wounded animal.

HELEN GRANT I was at boarding school, and it was a really horrible time for me. I don't think it's ever *stopped* affecting me, actually. It really did hurt Dad. I think he would have gladly had Mum back, but she didn't come back when he asked, and a year later when she wanted to come back, he said, "Nah, I only asked you once, and that's it."

PERRY PRESS (London estate agent to the stars) I remember going to see Gloria in a house just outside Hastings. It was all a bit uncomfortable, because I just couldn't get it out of my mind just how distraught Peter was when she left.

HELEN GRANT We weren't allowed to see Mum. I breached that, true to form. I think Dad was quite determined. Mum said, "He had better lawyers than me." But I didn't stop going to see her. At thirteen, I was still pretty much determined not to do as I was told. I said, "I love you, Dad, but she's my mum and I need to see her."

DENNIS SHEEHAN (assistant to Robert Plant on the 1977 U.S. tour) You knew Peter was unhappy. You knew what was going on, though not from the horse's mouth. He suffered internally—psychologically— from Gloria leaving him. It was quite amazing that she should leave a man who had succeeded so well and was worth an enormous amount of money.

BENJI LeFEVRE I think the band were probably . . . *touched* by it, but in the steamroller that was Zeppelin and Swan Song, it was insignificant. Because to the outside world, the only thing that was important to them was *them*. I'm sure Robert would have had a much more sensitive reaction to it than Jimmy and Bonzo—who probably didn't have *any* reaction to it because they were so fucked up.

ALAN CALLAN Peter, to me, was a person who was so committed to friendship that he could not fail in it. And the ultimate friendship was with his wife, and I don't think he ever understood how that had failed. And there were a lot of times where he was incommunicado because he was trying to deal with it.

PHIL CARSON (head of Atlantic Records in Europe) Peter referred to that time as his "dark period," and the phrase covered a massive amount of sins. He became really very badly affected, to the point of being totally reclusive. I would make an appointment to go and see him, and I'd always be very precise when I did it. I'd say, "I'll be down Wednesday at two o'clock," knowing that if I was *lucky*, I'd see him on Thursday evening. He just wouldn't come down.

AUBREY POWELL A typical day would involve being summoned to Horselunges for twelve o'clock, and you would sit in the kitchen for several hours. The house had descended into something out of *The Fall of the House of Usher*, with all these red drapes covered in cobwebs.

Finally, you'd go up to the first floor, where Peter's bedroom was, with this massive four-poster bed. He would be there in his tracksuit and looked as if he hadn't washed for weeks. The meeting would start at six in the evening and go on till four in the morning. There was a lot of rambling about things that were going on around Led Zeppelin and many threatening phone calls. There were other evenings when I'd be there with Jimmy or with Clive Coulson, and we'd sit around drinking absinthe that had just arrived from New Orleans. There was always this overhanging fear that if you put a foot wrong or said the wrong thing, you'd get clouted.

Finally, toward the end of the night, Peter would say, "So what about the artwork, then?" and he'd suddenly come alive because it was something to do with Zeppelin.

MARILYN COLE   After Gloria left, the guys who looked after the kids at Horselunges were the minders who'd worked on the tours, guys like Ray Washburn.

HELEN GRANT   Ray was fantastic, but Ray couldn't be there *all* the time. There were so many idiots around. I'd come back from boarding school at the weekend and find people sleeping in my room—hangers-on, liggers, ponces. Thieves walking out the house with stuff. Dad didn't even know these people were in the house. And I was the one turning around and saying, "This is enough, all of you get the fuck out!" I was the big baddie. It was like the pit bull had come home.

DAVE NORTHOVER   There was a time at Horselunges when I was asleep, and Warren was playing up somewhere at two in the morning and he wanted something to eat. I was expected to get up and do it, and I didn't. When I came down the next morning, Peter lost it and smacked me on my shoulder with a hammer. I was very upset by the whole thing.

You really didn't want to mess with him. You could almost certainly have run away from him, but you wouldn't have been able to run away from the people he sent after you.

19

Turning into the Storm

They're like a lot of those groups. Not only aren't they doing
anything new, they don't do the old stuff so good, either.

　　　　　　　　　　　—Bruce Springsteen to Dave Marsh, *Creem*,
　　　　　　　　　　　　　　　　　　　　　　　　　October 1975

RON NEVISON (engineer on *Physical Graffiti*) It was the time of coal
strikes and power cuts and oil embargos, and the Labour government
closed all the tax loopholes, so everyone was leaving. I fled, too.

PETER GRANT Joan Hudson told us of the massive problems we would
have if we didn't go. It was an 87 percent tax rate then on high earners.
Disgusting, really.

SHELLEY KAYE (manager of Swan Song office in the U.S.) They were
vagabonds for more than six months of the year, but they also couldn't
live anywhere *else* for more than six months. So we were very, very
careful to count the number of days. If they went over 181 days in the
United States, they would have been subject to U.S. tax.

BOB EMMER (publicity director in Atlantic's L.A. office) Bob Greenberg called me and said, "We've got to find some houses for Zeppelin."

I spent a day with a real estate agent taking me 'round rental houses in the Malibu Colony.

BENJI LeFEVRE (Zeppelin sound technician and assistant to Robert Plant) Robert went along with the whole tax-exile thing because it seemed like a good idea, and they'd all signed up to it. It was like, "We'll make it work. We'll find a way to write some music, and we'll make a new album." We had five houses that we rented in the Colony, one for each member of the band and one for G. The house Robert and I stayed in was right in the middle of the Colony, and when El Niño raged for days and days, it took all the sand away from the beach, and a couple of houses collapsed.

Every single day I would drive Robert into L.A. for physiotherapy for his arm and his ankle. There was lots of smoke and lots of Charlie, and I said to him, "You've got to slow down, man, because otherwise you're not going to get better." So we had an agreement that if he did his physio, I would dispense a certain amount of drugs.

He and I became very close because I was with him 24/7. I mean, I had to lift him into the *bath*. So there was nothing we didn't talk about or know about each other. At the same time, in Jimmy's house up the road it was closed doors and closed curtains. We used to refer to it as "Henry Hall." Robert started to get very disillusioned about the whole thing. It was a time of real reflection for him.

NICK KENT (writer for *NME*)   By 1975, half the group was getting fed up with the debauchery. Page was sequestered with Krissy Wood, so there wasn't even much serial infidelity anymore.

UNITY MacLEAN (manager of Swan Song office in the U.K.)   Robert had been so good to Jimmy. They were in a greasy spoon in London once, and Jimmy was so out of it that he couldn't get the sugar into his tea. Robert would pick up the sugar and put it in his tea and stir it for him. He was very soft and very kind to Jimmy.

ABE HOCH (president of Swan Song in the U.K., 1975–1977)   Jimmy liked Mandrax, heroin, and Dilaudid. I went to see him once in Malibu, and he was lying on the bed naked, sprawled out unconscious.

I came back, and Peter said, "Did you see Jimmy?" I said, "I did." He said, "How is he?" I said, "I've seen more movement in a Timex." Peter wrote that down. He said it was the funniest thing he'd ever heard.

MICHAEL DES BARRES (singer with Swan Song band Detective)   Jimmy and Robert really weren't communicating with each other that much. It was very much along the lines of "Tell him yes." Everybody had their own little posse—Rodney and Richard Creamer and Lori. Meanwhile, Jimmy was isolated with Freddy Sessler, the Dr. Nick of heavy metal.

NICK KENT   Jimmy told me a lot about Sessler. Freddy was Keith Richards's best friend. Fuck, if someone gave you an ounce of pure cocaine every month, he'd be *your* best friend. When the Rolling Stones weren't around, Freddy would be with Led Zeppelin. And if Zeppelin weren't around, he'd be with the Who. And if the Who weren't around, he'd be with the New York Dolls. He was an ugly old guy who wanted young girls.

ELIZABETH IANNACI (artist relations, Atlantic's L.A. office)   In one of my few real conversations with Jimmy, we were at the Rainbow, and he asked me why I'd split up with my husband. It was a complicated answer, but I finally said, "The truth is, I loved him more than he loved me." And he said to me, "Oh my, aren't *we* the martyr." I almost stopped and said, "Who made you dislike women so much?"

All the women these men came into contact with *wanted* something from them, other than conversation and companionship. It was all about fucking the star, rubbing up against this bright light to get some of that shine on you. I really, really, really got it in that moment, and I would have liked to take Jimmy by the hand and have him meet some real women. But that wasn't going to happen—because he didn't know they existed.

RICHARD COLE   Ray Thomas was looking after Jimmy—he was *Jimmy's* accomplice. And Bonzo was really out of control in Malibu. Mick Hinton was there with him.

PHIL CARLO (roadie for Bad Company)   We had a couple of FBI men and a couple of Pacific Coast Highway department cops who'd park in front of each house every night and get paid for sleeping there. One night we all went into Hollywood, and we got this phone call from Bill Dautrich, the FBI guy who'd been doing the rounds. He'd spotted the light on in Robert's house, so he went in, and it was two of the Manson girls sitting on the bed, with all of Robert's clothes on.

ROBERT PLANT The L.A. musicians who lived in Laurel Canyon avoided us. They kept clear because we were in the tackiest part of town with the tackiest people, Rodney Binghenheimer and Kim Fowley. I wanted to know about the history of the Hollywood Argyles or who the fuck the Phantom was on Dot Records singing "Love Me," and I would never have found that out at a candlelit dinner in the Canyon. Those people didn't come out from Laurel Canyon to see us at the Forum, because it was mayhem. For me, it was much more relevant to go out to the beach and spend time in the Colony than to be in the canyon.

KIM FOWLEY (L.A. producer and scenester) I had two wild girls in the car, and we were going over to Robert's house in the Colony. So we walked in, and Robert had over twenty women in the house. It looked like a cattle call for Paris fashion week. He had surf goddesses; he had Euro, Asian, black; he had tiny, tall, tattooed; otherwise, it was just Robert and some roadies. And Robert just wanted to talk about obscure records.

The girls *I* was with were rock 'n' roll beasts, and they got tired of sitting there with these other bitches while Robert discussed vinyl. They were also bisexual, so they decided to put on a lesbian floor show. It was like wrestling or something—everybody started yelling and screaming. And Robert said, "I don't need to see this, let's go outside and talk about Jill and the Boulevards." So we went outside, and Robert told me he was willing to pay $25,000 for one of their singles: "Please say you know about it." I said no. He said, "By the way, are you in love with either of those girls?" I said no.

The next day, one of the security guys called me. Robert wanted to invite the blonde girl to come back to Malibu. I turned to her, holding the phone, and said, "You got lucky—Robert Plant sent for you." She was a surf goddess from Huntington Beach and quite beautiful. The next day I got a call from the security guy, saying that she'd insulted two female friends of his who'd shown up. Apparently, she'd said, "Why are these bitches here? *I'm* supposed to be with you tonight." And apparently Robert said, "These girls are *friends* of mine. I don't make love to every woman I meet—and that includes *you*."

I think Robert was a connoisseur of women. Wouldn't it be interesting if he'd studied all those women and then put their physical movements together with his old vinyl blues records—and if *that* was the whole Zeppelin stage show right there? Could that have been the secret of Robert Plant?

ELIZABETH IANNACI Robert called the Atlantic office, and I answered the phone. I said, "Oh! How are you feeling?" I think he was quite nonplussed by that.

JANE AYER (press officer in Atlantic's L.A. office) He was in a wheelchair with a cast, but Benji would wheel him into the office, and it was like royalty coming in. I never saw the problems with Jimmy, but I was aware that something was going on.

ELIZABETH IANNACI Occasionally, Jimmy would need some money. He would need $2,000, and I was making £200 a week. They were looking at houses that cost $5,000 a month to rent, which was half my yearly income. Plus, I had a little boy who was Karac's age, and sometimes Robert would come and pick me and David up in the limo, and David would fall asleep in his hotel room. Robert was always lovely around children.

Robert was very protective of me. There was never anything romantic between us, but there could easily have been. We spent many long nights where we would talk—or I would listen—all night. We talked about everything, his experiences coming up in the music business. It was never gossip, it was just about experiences. Everyone *thought* I was sleeping with him, because I spent a lot of time in his room. But it was unbeknownst to me, which is how naïve I was. Even my *boss* thought I was sleeping with Robert, which was absolutely fine with him as long as the boys were happy.

On one occasion, I told Robert I was going over to the hotel to drop something off for Jimmy, and he just stopped me for a moment and said, "You know, Jimmy has a dark side." It was all he said, but the point was taken.

MORGANA WELCH (L.A. groupie and Zeppelin friend) I spent a bit of time with John Bonham and got a whole other sense of a very nice man, rather than somebody you just wanted to avoid. They were at the Beverly Wilshire, and he must have had a kitchen, because we went to Safeway in Beverly Hills and got pulled over by the police for speeding. I fixed him breakfast. It was nice sometimes just to give something back to the musicians, and a home-cooked meal meant something. It was almost like a maternal instinct.

JANE AYER We'd go to the Rainbow; we'd go to Trader Vic's, where Robert had to wear a borrowed jacket that didn't fit him. I saw Little Feat with them in Venice. I saw Bob Marley at the Roxy with Bonzo, Ringo, and Keith Moon, and I had to pinch myself, thinking, "I'm sitting here with the three greatest rock drummers in the world." I used to watch Marx Brothers movies with Bonzo, and all of them were heavily into Derek & Clive and Monty Python.

ELIZABETH IANNACI Robert coped by actually surrounding himself with a few people who were grounded. I was certainly a spark of . . . if not sanity, at least hope.

ROBERT PLANT Everybody was aware there was a crisis in the band, so we got together and went forward as if nothing had happened—like turning into a storm instead of running from it. In L.A., we just rehearsed and rehearsed. It was so strange for me the first time because . . . I was sitting in an armchair singing, and I found myself wiggling inside my cast.

PETER GRANT There was a lot of tension about that period, [with all of us] all holed up in houses we didn't really want to be in. In fact, John moved out to the Hyatt House. . . . "Tea for One" sums that period up for me, really. That was Maureen's song. She used to come out at weekends, and Robert was pretty depressed.

JIMMY PAGE   It's true that there are no acoustic songs [on *Presence*], no mellowness or contrasts or changes to other instruments. Yet the blues we did, like "Tea for One," was the only time I think we've ever gotten close to repeating the mood of "Since I've Been Loving You."

JOHN PAUL JONES   It became apparent that Robert and I seemed to keep a different time sequence [from] Jimmy. We just couldn't find him. I wanted to put up this huge banner across the street saying, "Today is the first day of rehearsals."

Myself and my then roadie Brian Condliffe drove into Studio Instrument Rehearsals every night and waited and waited until finally we were all in attendance, by which time it was around two in the morning. I learned all about baseball during that period, as the World Series was on, and there wasn't much else to do but watch it.

ELIZABETH IANNACI   When they decided to go to Munich to record the album, I got each of them a present. I made Jimmy an amazing wizard's hat—the front of it was a satin appliqué that I had gotten off a blouse the Fool had made. I'd cut the blouse apart and put it on the front of the hat.

I got Bonzo a wind-up racing car called the John Player Special, and I got Robert an amazing book of fantastic stories at the Bodhi Tree. Jonesy's present was this beautiful leather-bound book. I walked over to him and said, "This book is representative of our relationship." He opened it up, and it was blank. It wasn't that John Paul was shy, nor was there a disdain. It was that he didn't waste his energy. And his ego was as right-sized as it was possible to be in that situation.

MITCHELL FOX (staffer at Swan Song in the U.S.)   There were times when John Paul flew commercial with his family. He felt comfortable with that. There was a spotlight on Led Zeppelin at all times; it was just whether you *stood* in the spotlight or not. Onstage, John Paul was as much a star as anyone else. Offstage, he took the low road.

ELIZABETH IANNACI   Just before they went to Munich, we had been hanging out at the Record Plant, because a lot of people were recording there. One particular night, Robert and most of Bad Company were there, and everybody just kind of picked up instruments and started to play. We were all singing along to "Stay" by Maurice Williams and the Zodiacs. It was so much fun. We dubbed it "The Night the English Left Town." The next day, Peter Grant demanded the recording. He didn't want it to fall into someone else's hands.

●   ●   ●

RICHARD COLE John wouldn't do his tax-exile trip abroad because Pat was having a child. He and I flew to Munich from London, and the others flew in from L.A. When we got there, they'd been [in Germany] two days before us, and it was very cold. But one of the crew was laughing and giggling. I said, "You don't seem very worried by the cold." And he said, "No. We've found the solution." And he pulled out a bindle of heroin. "That'll warm us up," I said.

JIMMY PAGE [*Presence*] was recorded while the group was on the move, technological gypsies. No base, no home. All you could relate to was a new horizon and a suitcase. So there's a lot of movement and aggression—a lot of bad feeling toward being put in that situation.

JOHN PAUL JONES There were good times and . . . frustrating times. The band was splitting between people who could turn up on time for recording sessions and people who couldn't. I mean, we all got together and made the album in the end, but it wasn't quite as open as it was in the early days: what band *could* be, after all that time and the amount we'd been through?

These days, everybody knows so much about helping people and what goes on, but in those days, you kind of didn't, really. And while you'd say, "For Christ's sake, don't do this or . . . be here then," you didn't really know enough to start telling people how to live their lives. You didn't know whether what you were doing *yourself* was totally the right thing. But we were *beginning*, I suppose, to think, "Well, wait a minute, it *may* be coming apart more than it should."

ABE HOCH We go to make *Presence*, and they ask me to come to Munich. We get to this hotel called the Arabella, and we're in the basement of the hotel. Keith Harwood, the engineer, is there. Robert is hobbling about on a cane, and he's lying in bed a lot. He's writing lyrics for this record that we were supposed to do that seems to never happen because Jimmy is not awake. They set Bonzo's drums up in the dining room, and he drives out all the diners, but nothing is happening. Robert is saying things to me like, "What rhymes with Achilles?"

ROBERT PLANT "Achilles Last Stand" was prog rock gone mad, and it was brilliant. I remember when we wrote it, it was such a beautiful bird to release. It was about going back to Morocco and getting it back again. The music was stunning, and when we did it live some nights, it would be unbelievable, and other nights it was dreadful. But at least it wasn't "Great Balls of Fire."

ABE HOCH One day Jimmy wakes up, ruffles his hair, goes into the studio, and starts to fiddle around on the guitar, and it reverberates information around the building, which is that *he is in the studio*. Jonesy and Bonzo run like demons to the basement. They play together and bring food in, and seventeen days later we have this record.

I don't care what illusion anyone has about the process, it was so remarkable to watch as a casual observer, because it looked like a jam, and it wasn't. It was well-crafted, beautifully articulated songs that didn't have the whole verse-bridge-verse concept, and yet you could walk away humming and singing lyrics to them. It was the most bizarre thing you ever saw.

JIMMY PAGE There are certain times where people would say, "Oh, Jimmy wasn't in very good shape." Or whatever. But what I do know is that *Presence* was recorded, finished, and mixed in three weeks, which was done on purpose not to mess about.

ROSS HALFIN (photographer and friend of Page's) *Presence* is Page's favorite Zeppelin album. I personally can't bear "Achilles Last Stand," I think it's so pompous. To me, it's everything that's *wrong* with Led Zeppelin. But it's a very *metallic* album, and that's what Jimmy likes about it.

GLENN HUGHES (bassist and singer with Deep Purple and Black Country Communion) When people abuse drugs and alcohol that much, they lose their muse. You can hear the blow and the horse on the later Zep stuff, just as you can hear it on the Deep Purple albums and the Stones albums. There are moments on *Presence* that I really like, but for me, the peak was *Graffiti*.

JAAN UHELSZKI (writer for *Creem*)   Lester Bangs used to say he could always tell when someone was on a particular drug when they'd written an article. And *Presence* feels like an album made on painkillers, which, of course, Robert was.

RICHARD COLE   After we made *Presence*, Peter and I flew to Paris to bugger around with Abe Hoch. Then we met up with Jimmy in Los Angeles. I flew home with Jimmy because Scarlet was in a pantomime at school. Then they all met up in Jersey again. I think they got the plane home on Christmas Eve. And then Bonzo became a tax exile in the south of France.

ABE HOCH   Po from Hipgnosis came up with the plinth. We didn't know what it was called, everybody just said "the object."

Led Zeppelin make their *Presence* felt on the Sunset Strip. (Courtesy of Phil Carlo)

AUBREY POWELL (designer of *Presence* sleeve)   When we did *Presence*, Steve Weiss sat me down and said, "Po, you've designed this black object, and we've got to think about how this is gonna be perceived by people." I'd sit there for hours with Steve, pontificating about what the design was going to do.

The best thing about Steve was that he held the power of Peter Grant and Led Zeppelin in America. When I was trying to get Atlantic to approve album covers and other things, I'd call Steve and say, "They're fucking me around." And he'd get on the phone and say, "Po has the authority from Peter and the band to do whatever is necessary to get this artwork right, and you fucking do what he asks." He was a very powerful spokesman.

He was also the guy who got everybody out of trouble, whether it was Led Zeppelin or Bad Company. Some bad stuff went down with Bad Company—I was there when it happened—and Steve was the first guy on the plane down there to sort it out. He certainly knew where the bodies were buried.

SIMON KIRKE (drummer for Bad Company)   A bouncer in a bar in New Orleans threatened Boz Burrell with a blackjack, and they all set on this guy and beat him badly. I believe he lost an eye. They were all arrested and spent the night in jail. Strings were pulled and money was paid, but Bad Company never played New Orleans again.

ABE HOCH   *Captain Fantastic and the Brown Dirt Cowboy* had come in at No. 1, and that was a big achievement. It was one of the first times an album had come straight onto the American music charts at No. 1, and they really didn't want to not have that happen with *Presence*. Danny Goldberg and I devised this idea for the record to be released worldwide simultaneously, at the exact same hour, minute, and second. It was a massive feat of coordination, but it worked. So the record came in at No. 1 on one chart and No. 2 on other charts.

DAVE NORTHOVER (John Paul Jones's assistant on Zeppelin's 1975 and 1977 U.S. tours)   Benji and I were looking after Robert in New York, and we received a phone call around three in the morning from Jimmy. Could I come up straight away? It was really important.

BENJI LeFEVRE Jimmy said, "Where's Northover? I need Northover right now!" I said, "Actually, he's in my room here with me."

DAVE NORTHOVER So we got up to his room, and there was Jimmy at a desk, and Ray Thomas passed out in the corner. Jimmy was quite agitated. When he wrote, he always wrote with a fountain pen. And he had a bottle of ink on this desk, along with a little bottle of cocaine. By mistake, he'd emptied the pen into the bottle of cocaine, rather than into the bottle of ink.

He said to me, "Dave, can you separate the ink from the cocaine?" I could probably have done it, but it would have meant buying ether and various other things. So he gave me this foggy blue mess, and I dried it out on a hot water cylinder. For the next few days, we kept seeing these people coming out of Jimmy's room with blue snot.

BENJI LeFEVRE After the Blue Charlie episode, we flew to L.A., and Bonzo got really, really drunk before we took off—so drunk that he pissed the seat. Hinton was sitting in the row behind, and Bonzo said, "Hinton! When I stand up, you've got to stand up and follow me to the toilet so no one can see I've pissed myself." When they came back from the bathroom, Bonzo made him sit in the wet seat for the rest of the flight.

GLENN HUGHES I knew Pat Bonham as a friend. When John was touring, Pat's sister Beryl worked behind the bar at the Club Lafayette in Birmingham, and we'd hang out. There were never any shenanigans. We were just mates, and we liked to have a couple of cocktails.

What happened was that John heard something other than that, and he was very upset about it. It was just a vicious rumor. Truly, nothing happened. Pat *adored* John and thought the sun shone out of his bum. All she wanted to talk about was John, John, John, John. But he heard different, and he was very upset by it, because we were really good mates.

John and I went out and had a few cocktails, and we cried and we laughed and we hugged, and we ironed it all out. Then Trapeze were playing at Radio City Music Hall, and Zeppelin were in town. Bonzo had the bowler hat on, he was in full *Clockwork Orange* mode. My friend was unhinged, and he had that look in his eye that something was about to kick off.

I was fucking frightened, but I loved this man, and I wasn't about to lose a friendship with him over something as serious as having a relationship with his wife. I've never been a cocksman, that's not part of my story. He kept saying, "What 'appened? What 'appened?" *Nothing* happened. I've been there myself: I know cocaine paranoia, and I know what it's like.

That morning I did a runner after he passed out. He was getting pretty mad again.

• • •

ABE HOCH   Peter said to me, sitting by the fire one night, "We'd like you to come and run our record company." I said, "What does the job entail?" He said, "Oh, you'll know." I said, "What do you mean, 'I'll know'?" He wasn't very descriptive. But I thought, "Wow, this is an opportunity to run a record company for the biggest band in the world."

I go to New York—leaving my wife and kid in California because we haven't figured out yet how to make the transition—and check into the Plaza Hotel, an enormous suite where all types of bacchanalia take place. But there's no band in sight. Zeppelin has gone, and I'm there waiting for them to tell me when I'm going to go to London. Word never comes. Peter is paying for everything. I had a huge suite with a pool table and a grand piano in it, and I was living the life of Riley on somebody else's dime. It was bizarre.

At the end of September, I get a call saying, "Okay, come to London." I said, "Great." I get on a plane and go to London, and I say to Peter, "Where will I stay?" He said, "You'll stay in my mews flat in Gloucester Place." I said, "What's a mews flat?"

Carol Browne ran the show. It was Carol's company. So I got in and introduced myself. "Hello, how are you?" She said, "We've been expecting you." I called Peter a day and a half later and said to him, "There *is* no record company." He said, "See, I knew you'd know." And he hung up on me.

ELIZABETH IANNACI   Everyone thought that the Pretty Things, with the strength of Zeppelin behind them, would explode. And nobody cared. As innovative as they had been years earlier, the music was ho-hum at that time.

ALAN CALLAN (president of Swan Song in the U.K., 1977–1980)   The Pretty Things were signed purely as a musical adventure, to give them the opportunity to be creative. The trouble is, they would come along and think, "I'm on Led Zeppelin's label, so I can party." I had to say to John Povey, "I'm not sure you have a future in this band. You should either leave or consider how this band is going to organize itself." Mostly, it was just human insecurity multiplied.

SHELLEY KAYE   By the time of Detective, Peter's involvement was definitely tapering off. The band wanted another hit act for the label, and they never got it. They didn't get it with the Pretty Things, and they didn't get it with Maggie or Detective.

MICHAEL DES BARRES   Miss P and I were together, and they all adored Pamela. We got a band together, and it was super-loud and super-powerful. Every label wanted it, but we chose to go with the Zeppelin mystique—the greatest force in rock 'n' roll at that time. Jimmy's gonna produce? Oh my God, where do we sign?

For a year, we sat around getting more and more fucked up, with unlimited sums of money, waiting for Jimmy to produce. Eventually, he said, "Let's get Steve Marriott to do it." And then it was another six months' waiting for little Steve. So much of rock 'n' roll is waiting on junkies to make up their fucking minds.

SAM AIZER (artist relations at Swan Song in the U.S.)   Peter showed up on Bad Company dates less and less often. Clive Coulson would pull his hair out because he couldn't get Peter on the phone for days. When something like drugs own you, they own you. Peter had another master, and it wasn't Led Zeppelin, it was his own hell.

I once went to Elliot Roberts's office in California when he was managing Detective. He was looking for support from the label, he wanted answers: who was going to give him an *answer*? He said to me, "I'll bet you ten thousand dollars against your life you can't get hold of Peter right now. Would you call him and say, 'Put Peter on the phone, or Sam Aizer's gonna be killed'?" I looked at him and thought, "He's got a point."

DANNY GOLDBERG (president of Swan Song in the U.S.)   When it came time to take a Swan Song signing photo, I got a limo to pick up Jimmy at the Malibu Colony [and] brought him to my room at the Beverly Hills Hotel, where the members of Detective were to meet us. Jimmy was nodding out the whole time we were in the car, and when we got to my room, he lay down on the couch and immediately fell asleep.

When the band got there, Michael and I tried repeatedly to wake him, even going to the extreme of throwing cold water on his face, but it was to no avail. Although he was breathing, Jimmy was out cold. After around a half hour, I had Andy Kent photograph Detective sitting next to the sleeping Page and then sent him and the band members home. A few hours later, Jimmy roused himself.

There had been rumors that he was doing heroin, and this behavior made me believe them. Not surprisingly, Page had a different explanation. He said he had taken a Valium and must have overreacted to it. He was furious with Michael and me, disbelieving that we had really tried to wake him. He let me circulate the photo but later complained that, in doing so, I had "made me out to be a twit."

In retrospect, he was absolutely right. The photo should never have seen the light of day. Detective was lucky to be on Swan Song, and it would have been no big deal to schedule another photo session. I had forgotten who I was working for.

ELIZABETH IANNACI   I don't think Michael was under any illusions about Led Zeppelin, and Detective wasn't a *great* band—we referred to them as Defective. My speculation is that he knew the music wasn't going to be enough to carry the band, so there was a level of feeling that they were on Zeppelin's coattails.

MICHAEL DES BARRES   Talking about Swan Song is almost like talking about the Luftwaffe. It wasn't a record company, as far as *I* could see. I didn't see any ads or promotion for the Detective record. So I think it *was* an indulgence on the band's part. Rodgers and his crew had hits, but we didn't. Danny Goldberg became my brother-in-arms, but you couldn't get anybody on the phone.

You certainly couldn't get hold of Steve Weiss, who seemed to be some gangster lawyer on Long Island, while I was in West Hollywood with a bunch of decadent ne'er-do-wells. We were promised a support tour with Zeppelin, which was a huge thing. Never happened.

And then suddenly, guess what, the Sex Pistols show up, and I wanted to go out and be part of *that*. By the time the record came out, I was totally disengaged from the thing we were supposed to do.

MITCHELL FOX   Frankly, as much as Swan Song was a record label, in retrospect it was really a management company. By the mere fact that Led Zeppelin were so big, they were given their own imprint, but it was a by-product of the fact that Peter and Steve looked after everything—publishing, merch, touring. It was really the quintessential 360-degree management deal

SAM AIZER   It was the American office that ran the Zeppelin operation. The office in London was just a great place for people to come hang out at.

UNITY MacLEAN   I soon learned, after being there for a few months, that not much was going on. Led Zeppelin were paramount, the rest went down the pecking order. Swan Song had money that should have been used on the acts, and Phil Carson should have steered the label in that direction.

ED BICKNELL (former manager of Dire Straits)   Peter told me Swan Song was the worst thing he ever did. He basically ended up managing all the acts on the label. As hard as you try, you can never train your acts to speak to the other people in the office—they only want to speak to *you*. If they've just gotten a parking ticket, they don't want to speak to the accountant, they want to speak to *you*. You can build a brick wall round yourself, but the artists will still find a way through.

Zeppelin could be on top of the pile, but they could still be professionally jealous of *somebody*. So you end up with the acts becoming competitive with one another within your own stable. And even if you get one act away—which they did, obviously, with Bad Company—you still have three others that are dragging the whole thing down.

RICHARD COLE   Abe Hoch wanted to sign Iron Maiden, and I think Danny Goldberg at one point wanted to sign Waylon Jennings. But they couldn't sign anything because you had to get the five guys in the room together to sign off on it. So what did you do? You went to the pub and got fucking drunk.

DANNY GOLDBERG   In May of 1976, Peter gave me the choice of giving up Mirabai's management or leaving. I don't think he expected me to choose an unknown act. But I was filled with the irrational confidence and self-righteousness of youth. As fierce as he was to outsiders, Peter romanticized his team and didn't like confrontation. "I never thought it would come to this," he said, large tears dripping down his massive face.

"You know, all those friends of yours wouldn't talk to you if you didn't work for Zeppelin," he'd ominously said to me not long before [this]. Peter, I felt, was also talking about himself. Jimmy Page virtually controlled his self-esteem.

JOE JAMMER (guitarist and Zeppelin roadie)   I left the organization because Zeppelin got way too big and way too busy, and they were having trouble just staying sober and staying awake and staying alive. There had been a lot of love and a lot of care there, but the wrath of Satan was unleashed on others right around me. I knew I was going to end up like Maggie Bell, who was so loyal to Peter that she ended up as the receptionist at Swan Song. It was the only way she could see them as they rolled into the office.

ALAN CALLAN   It wasn't as if you could say to her, "Look, Peter's not around, just go off and do it yourself." Her attitude was always, "No, I need to talk to Peter about it." I think it would have been really interesting with Steve Smith, who was at his hottest at that moment. He had a great relationship with Little Feat, and he had a great relationship with the guys in Muscle Shoals, and it would have been great to throw Maggie into that mix.

STEVE SMITH (producer of Robert Palmer and other artists)   Jimmy's favorite band in the world was Little Feat—with whom I'd worked on Robert Palmer's *Pressure Drop*—so Alan approached me to produce

Bonham, Page, and Maggie Bell celebrate wins at the *Melody Maker* awards, September 17, 1975. (Central Press/Getty Images)

Maggie. I thought she was an absolutely fabulous singer, so I said, "Let's do it." He said I needed to fly to New York to meet Jimmy to get the royal seal of approval. The next day a ticket on the Concorde arrived, so I went over to meet Jimmy and Peter Grant to sign off on the deal. They put me in a suite at the Plaza, and I went to see Zeppelin at Madison Square Garden. I never even got around to *meeting* Jimmy. So it never happened with Maggie.

UNITY MacLEAN   Maggie was in the office virtually every day, and we had a lot of fun and silliness together. At one point, Peter was supposed to book her some dates and get her an agent, but he never did a damn thing.

MAGGIE BELL (Swan Song artist)   He never knew what to do, Peter. Nothing was ever good enough. It was always, "Let's wait, let's wait." But he didn't want anybody else to run my career, either, so I was in a Catch-22.

ABE HOCH We had one Telex machine, and I would try to get to the Telex to move the product out there or try and get the promotion guys involved. One time, Robert had lost a robe somewhere in a spin dryer, and he wouldn't let me near the Telex, because the priority wasn't really to get this record placed but to get his robe back.

UNITY MacLEAN There was one nice piece of furniture in the office, which was an etched mirror of Wolverhampton Wanderers [Football Club]. Robert would stand in front of it and comb his hair. Cynthia Sach once said, "Oh, do look at Robert enjoying his two favorite things in the world."

CYNTHIA SACH (secretary in Swan Song's U.K. office, 1977–1981) Robert was a bit of a whinger. He'd studied accountancy, so he was well into the figures. A bit preening, because he had that beautiful hair like the golden fleece. He loved Wolves. For his son's birthday, he wanted me to get him a black and gold Wolverhampton Wanderers cake.

MARILYN COLE (wife of Richard Cole) Abe Hoch was a nice Jewish boy from the States, and they cut his bollocks off from the word go. His hands were totally tied, so he couldn't do anything. There was abuse everywhere, and it escalated like a mushroom cloud.

SIMON KIRKE Drink and drugs took their toll not only on Bonzo but on Jimmy, Peter Grant, myself, Boz Burrell, and—to a lesser degree— Mick Ralphs. Coke does terrible things to people over a long period of time. Lack of sleep adds to the paranoia that coke induces, drinking escalates, and the brain turns mushy with the downers that a lot of users take to get some form of sleep.

MARILYN COLE There was a dealer down the end of the King's Road named Byron. He was very near the office in that golden triangle of pubs: the Roebuck, the Water Rat, the Man in the Moon. He had a shop there, and you scored in the back office. Richard and him were tight, tight, tight.

BENJI LeFEVRE It was always, "Let's go back to the office and do some more drugs. Or let's go up the Water Rat. Oh, look who I've met,

Johnny Bindon. He's a *real* laugh. Someone's on the phone? I'll talk to 'em tomorrow . . . they'll always come back because of *who we are*."

UNITY MacLEAN   There was some girl calling up to Swan Song from the street: "Richard! Richard!" And he shouted down, "Clear off, you old skank!" "Please, Richard, open the door!" "I told you to fuck off!" And he opened the window and peed on her head.

PHIL CARLO   It wasn't an office where anybody went in at 10:00 a.m. It was waifs and strays and heroin dealers and odd people, a bit like the American tours but a scaled-down version. The Colonel with his mustache and blazer, like the Major in *Fawlty Towers* sorting out the poppy tins. Dealers in dark glasses, girls in flowery dresses, people with pit bulls who came along with John Bindon. Terry DeHavilland, the shoemaker. Vicki Hodge, who—when she got pissed in the Water Rat or the Man in the Moon—would lift her skirt up and moon anyone who was walking up the King's Road, while Bindon roared his head off. They were very strange days.

MAGGIE BELL   Carol Browne had an argument with Peter. It should never have happened, because Peter loved Carol, and Carol loved Peter very much, but it was going a bit crazy and Peter was under a lot of pressure. A call came through from his son Warren, and Carol failed to give the message to Peter straight away.

UNITY MacLEAN   Peter was being more and more offensive to Carol. And if she made a decision on his behalf, Peter would phone her up and chew her out left, right, and center. She got to the point where she didn't want to take any more of it.

MAGGIE BELL   She walked out. She never got a penny. She held her head high, walked three streets up to Lots Road, and started a secretarial service.

UNITY MacLEAN   I was absolutely shocked. I was like, "Carol, *come on*." And she said, "If you'd been through all the stuff that I've been through, you'd have some self-respect, and you'd leave, too." I sat back and thought, "She's right." People say, "What an incredible manager

Peter was, he really wrung the last buck out of everybody for his group." But why put people through the misery he did?

MAGGIE BELL Unity took over from Carol. Cynthia was wonderful as well, but she was as soft as butter and not for that office.

CYNTHIA SACH Jimmy only wanted to talk to *me* at the office. He knew I was straight-talking and not in awe of rock stars. He appreciated the fact that I wasn't a sniveling, groveling fan. I wasn't terribly impressed by Swan Song. With all their money, the offices were so scruffy.

PHIL CARLO Dolly the cleaner was over eighty and about four foot eight and always wore a black dress and didn't have any teeth. She'd known G for a long time, and she used to tell him off. If it was a really cold day, she would say, "That boy's been in here again with no coat on. He'll catch his death of cold." G used to love it.

One day we were all in the office talking, and Dolly said, "We've 'ad trouble with people lurking about in the flats." She lived in the council flats across the road, and there'd been some yobs hanging about, causing trouble. So G said to Richard, who was there with Terry DeHavilland, "You'd better go home with Dolly and make sure she gets in alright." Dolly turned round and said, "Don't worry about me, son." She put her hand in the carrier bag and pulled out the handle to a mangle [a clothes wringer]. Terry went, "Fuck me! Dolly's tooled up 'n' all!"

CYNTHIA SACH Warren Grant and Jason Bonham used to sit outside the office, writing notes and throwing them out the window at the postman. The notes said, "Postman, we think you're a bastard." Unity told them off. I would take Helen to the ballet at Covent Garden for Peter, and he bought me a dress to thank me for it. Helen was a lovely kid, but Warren was a little monster.

UNITY MacLEAN Peter would ask me to take Helen out to lunch, because he wanted Helen to know which knife and fork to use. I did take her out a few times, and she was actually a happy little girl. Peter gave her everything she wanted.

DAN TREACY Peter was like Shrek meets *The Long Good Friday*. Unity sent me to cash a check for £350 at Swan Song's bank in Mayfair, and I accidentally went to the wrong branch. The cashier refused to give me the money. When I got back to the office, Grant came stomping up the stairs, lifted me up, and pinned me to a wall. He goes, "You've really fucked it up for me and Jimmy, you little bastard." Then he let go, and I slid down the wall. I later found out that half the money was for a dress for Grant's daughter, and the other half was for a bike for Page.

ABE HOCH Jimmy would stay over and sleep on my floor and be maudlin about what to do with his relationship with Peter—and whether he wanted that to continue or not. He would open up to me, and then I was stuck with the information. Because what could I say? I'm a loser either way.

He would sit me down and say, "I think the band will need to make a move against Peter." Now that I look back on it from a rational perspective, it was more a test of me and how I would play it. It was manipulative, because either way, I get the boot.

I said to him, "Leaving him is not the way to help him. That will drive him further into the toilet. You need to be a friend and an ally, rather than an adversary here." I think that cemented something for Jimmy, because at least I didn't look at it as an opportunity for myself but as a loyal and caring friend. Jimmy may have been serious and I'll never know, but in advising him, it may have just stemmed the flow of what he was feeling at that time. It was a test. It was *always* a test.

Everything about Swan Song was a game. Just being *involved* in it was a game.

20

A Powerhouse
of Madness

Everyone's a bloody roadie or something, and they're all
terrified of Grant. It's sickening just to observe those people
crawling around. Just seeing all that—just having to be
around it all—was enough to make me want to leave.

—Nick Lowe to Nick Kent, *New Musical
Express*, July 1977

BP FALLON (Zeppelin's U.K. press officer, 1973–1976) They all
thought it would be cool to have Dave Edmunds on the label, so I went
down to Rockfield and talked him into coming to Swan Song.

UNITY MacLEAN (manager of Swan Song office in the U.K.) It was
perfect because Dave wanted to rekindle his career. And I remember
saying, "That's a good idea, because he's going to bring fresh breath to
Swan Song—he's going to lighten us up from the Pretty Things and
Maggie Bell and Led Zeppelin."

DAVE EDMUNDS (Swan Song artist, 1977–1982)   It was heaven, from an artistic point of view. Besides the figures involved, which were generous, it freed me from the usual hang-ups that artists have with labels. The boys were interested in what I was doing but wouldn't interfere.

ABE HOCH (president of Swan Song in the U.K., 1975–1977)   When they signed Dave, they sequestered him in the Gloucester Place mews house. I remember standing outside, knocking on the door and saying, "Can I come in?" They went, "No, go away." I went, "That's it, I'm done." I called Peter in Paris and said, "I want to quit." He said, "Well, we refuse to accept your resignation."

UNITY MacLEAN   Peter did nothing for the Pretty Things, and nothing for Dave. One night my husband, Bruce, came over and told Peter that all he had to do was pick up the phone to Asgard and just get Edmunds a support slot. A couple of days later, I called Peter at Horselunges, only to be told that he was not available and would call me back. He never did.

This was the heartbreak that Dave would come to know. The realization that this was the end of the road, not the beginning, must have been awful. One night Dave, Bruce, and I were shooting the breeze, and Dave said, "Perhaps I could get out of my contract." "Perhaps," I agreed, knowing that you don't leave Swan Song. You're not going anywhere. You wait till the contract is up.

ABE HOCH   I'm in the third-floor office, and I'm informed that Peter wants to see me. I go in, and everybody is going home because it's the end of the day. Peter gets up and locks the door behind us. He goes, "You wanna quit?" He opens his briefcase and takes out a pound of cocaine and puts it down and says, "Let's talk about it."

We never leave the room. I'm white, and I can't see anymore. After three days, I'm like, "Oh, I'll give it some time, you know." I just want him to let me out of the room.

I stayed and allowed myself to deteriorate as a person, both financially and creatively. I was really in a bad place. I find it sad to this day that all of the guys, like Mick Hinton and Brian Gallivan, they all died in poverty. Richard Cole ended up in a council flat. There's a better way to take care of your own.

MARILYN COLE   Richard was married to the band. If he'd met me halfway, maybe we could have got somewhere. But I realized he was just always going to be working for Peter Grant on salary. And I was very unhappy. I had already done quite a lot; I'd traveled, I'd lived in Positano in the '60s. I hadn't aspired to being with someone who was going to stay in the same job like a bank manager for the rest of his life. Having said that, I loved him in my mad way.

RICHARD COLE   It was a very difficult position. You weren't always getting the cash in hand, but I'd get exactly the same hotel suites and treatment as they got. It was a lot better than erecting scaffolding. If you end up with nothing, you end up with nothing. I could have left any time, and maybe I should have done. The sensible ones got out.

Page on the top floor of Swan Song, New King's Road, October 1977. (Ray Stevenson/Rex Features)

ALAN CALLAN (president of Swan Song in the U.K., 1977–1980)   One day Jimmy just called up and said, "What are you doing? Would you like to come and run Swan Song?" I said, "Sounds great, Jim. What are you talking about?"

RICHARD COLE   Out of the blue, Jimmy and Peter turned up one day with Alan, and we were told he was going to be running Swan Song.

UNITY MacLEAN   The first thing Alan did was paint the office upstairs red. I said, "My God, whatever did you paint it that color for? It's so dark." He said, "So it won't show the blood."

ALAN CALLAN   The one thing we *should* have been famous for is a sense of humor. I can't tell you the countless number of times people came up to Peter and said, "G, I hear you've got a grudge against me." And Peter would go, "Don't worry, it's all forgotten now." The guy would leave, and Peter would say, "Any idea who that was?"

MAGGIE BELL (Swan Song artist)   It was a strange situation with Alan. He started ordering everybody about. I said, "Excuse me. Who are you?" He says, "I'm in charge of you. Anything you lot want to do, you ask me first." I thought, "He can fuck off as well."

ALAN CALLAN   Peter's assumption was that I'd already started just by having the phone call. So I said, "What's my job?" He said, "Go and see Ahmet, come back, find artists, and sell records." Ahmet said, "To tell you the truth, Alan, if you call me and tell me you want to sign a kid who shakes matches, I'll pay for it. This band is that important to us." He said, "I've built Atlantic's international offices on the back of Led Zeppelin's cash flow."

He said to me, "What do you want to do?" I said, "Well, before I go too far, I want to sign a great artist, so we can make our mark as a label." I thought John Lennon was the greatest unsigned artist of the moment. He was sitting in New York, doing nothing. And for nine months, maybe longer, I kept phoning and asking, "Can we meet? Can we talk?" It went from "Fuck off" to "Okay, I appreciate that you keep calling," to David Geffen just walking in and offering him an enormous amount of money. That was the one moment when I would have liked Peter and Jimmy to have phoned another artist and said, "Come on our label."

PETER GRANT What I regretted about Swan Song was not getting someone in to run it properly. We kept getting it wrong, or I did. It didn't work with Abe Hoch, and in America, Danny Goldberg became another pain in the ass. I think if we'd had Alan in from the start, it might have been okay. . . . In the end, he fell foul of Steve Weiss's ego problems.

ALAN CALLAN Steve was the only Italian-mobster Jewish cowboy in New York. He was also the only one in that organization that I thought was *not* a straight shooter. He was the Salieri in the mix. He was obstructive, mostly because he wanted something out of the deals for *himself* that was outside of Swan Song. Weiss's ego was the thing that distracted Peter and Jimmy—the way he fucked Zeppelin around with Atlantic. That was why I couldn't get anything happening with Maggie. It was like, "Alan, we just can't go there right now."

UNITY MacLEAN Steve was a very smart man. Very suave and very cool. A shadowy figure and probably the brains behind the whole operation. I would only hear whispers and rumors about him and his circle of cronies: he was connected, and he knew how to get 'round the unions and all that that entailed. I met this DEA guy once, and when I told him I'd worked for Led Zeppelin, he said, "Oh, yeah, we helped those guys out a lot. It was the only way I could get my daughters tickets for the concerts."

SAM AIZER (artist relations, Swan Song in the U.S.) Steve was a prick. This was not the kind of guy you would invite over for a meal. He was an egotistical, insecure man who was a bully. And he was able to be a bully because of the clients he had.

ALAN CALLAN I had one incident in London when Steve came over. I went to meet him at the Montcalm Hotel, and he started off on one of those "Do you know who you're talking to?" numbers. So I walked downstairs, paid his bill, and told him he was leaving. And I went back to the offices and told Peter, who gave me a round of applause. Because whenever anybody got too close to thinking they could live off the band without laying the table, Peter was very anti that.

NICK KENT (writer for *NME*) Page couldn't stand Weiss. It was always, "What's that fucking Steve Weiss doing here?" They didn't like him basking in being a power broker in Led Zeppelin's world.

BP FALLON Swan Song wasn't a failure; it's just that there's a difference between running a record label and getting on an airplane to go to some gig with eighty thousand punters going crazy. Peter liked all that. Anyone would like it.

MAGGIE BELL It all got too much. Two years after Swan Song moved into 484 New King's Road, Mark London said to Peter, "I'm going." He just left with Stone the Crows and some publishing he had. That was it, but the funny thing is, a lot of Mark's beautiful furniture was left in there.

UNITY MacLEAN I used to go and see Dave Edmunds's manager, Jake Riviera, who was the most sarcastic and difficult man. He *hated* Peter because of the way Dave was being treated, just *loathed* him. But he would take it out on *me*. I'd suggest a few things we could do, and he'd say, "Oh, where are you from, Unity? Are you from the *sixties*?" He reduced me to tears once. I think the hostility that many of the punk bands showed to Zeppelin sort of trickled down from Jake.

PETER GRANT Dave Edmunds and people like that, I just didn't have time to oversee them. Dave had Jake Riviera anyway, which brought its own set of problems.

ALAN CALLAN The unfortunate thing about Jake was that he really felt he had to compete with Peter. It was like, "I'm as important as Peter Grant." In a way, Peter was quite chilled out, and then Jake comes in, and there's a lot of attitude.

SAM AIZER Jake was the angriest man of all time. It was him against Swan Song, him against the world. And sometimes you need that. Dave Edmunds needed it, because he was basically dicked around.

JAKE RIVIERA (manager of Dave Edmunds and the Damned)   Unity and all that lot were very nice, but they couldn't do anything. They were hogtied, waiting on Peter and Jimmy. Alan Callan was nice but ineffectual. I'm coming from Stiff Records, where—if I like somebody—they go up to Pathway Studios, we record them, and we put the record out the next day. And here we have Swan Song, where Dave's album has gone back a month because Jimmy's trying to airbrush the devil into his hair on the cover.

UNITY MacLEAN   Peter really dropped the ball with Dave, and it was a tragedy. So I understood why Jake was so angry.

JAKE RIVIERA   It came to a head when we did Nick's *Labour of Lust* and Dave's album back-to-back in the studio. We were all burning out on a vodka-and-cocaine diet. So I say, "Let's do the Beatles in reverse and make a Rockpile album." Edmunds's contract is coming up, and suddenly he's very amenable to me. He says, "You've got to tell Peter we want to do a Rockpile record."

I'm busy, I'm shaking, I'm twenty-eight and on top of the world—the male ego holding court—and the phone rings. My assistant says, "It's Peter Grant on the phone," and everything goes quiet. Immediately, I'm like, "Oh, hello, Mr. Grant," very polite and subservient." 'Allo, Jake, I fink we need to talk."

So I'm summoned to Horselunges to have a meeting about Rockpile, the problem being that Nick Lowe is already under contract to Columbia, whose executives are shit-scared of Peter. Ahmet and Jerry Wexler were good people, but Steve Weiss was a fucking slippery creature. On my way down there, I think, "What would Michael Caine do?" I'm going to do whatever I have to do to get Edmunds out of his contract.

Richard Cole rings and says, "D'you need a ride down there? I'll send a car." Ten in the morning, he comes round in a Rolls-Royce with a chauffeur in a gray hat. I think, "This is intimidation, but if you wanna ride the roller coaster, you gotta pay the fare." Richard says, "We gotta stop off at Jimmy's to drop some speakers off." I'm not sure what sort of speakers you can get inside a big brown envelope, but we pull up outside Plumpton Place, and Richard says, "Stay in the car, don't get clever."

We drive in to Horselunges, and I'm thinking, "Why am I doing this for fucking Dave Edmunds?" I'm introduced to this twenty-stone gardener named Ron or something and told that he'll be looking after me. "Peter'll be down in a minute," he says. "Don't go snoopin' around." I sit there for an hour, and Ron comes back in: "He's not ready yet." *Another* hour and a half goes by, and I'm trying to stay cool.

Finally, Peter comes down in this Japanese toga, three hundred pounds of hungry and clearly a very unhappy man. He sits down and pulls out this big brown bottle of cocaine. He says, "'Ello, Mr. Punk Rock. You fink you're a bit of a clever boy, doncha?" I say, "I think I'm pretty smart, but only like *you're* smart, Peter."

He says, "I 'ear from Phil Carson that you're a bit of a ducker and a diver." I try to make him laugh, but it's very hard to make someone laugh who's coked out of his brains.

He says, "We wanna sign Rockpile." I say, "That's good, but, unfortunately, Columbia is never going to let Nick Lowe out of his contract." The pitch to Peter goes on for two hours and is basically this: "I'm young and I'm shaking—I'm *you* twenty years ago." I say, "You're my hero. I want to build up a label as cool as Swan Song. Dave Edmunds is a wanker, and you don't need the grief, so why don't you leave him to me and get on with running your empire?"

He says, "You fink we're all dinosaurs." I say, "Not at all. Jimmy and Robert came down to see the Damned twice, and that's nothing but respect. I'm just a Mod from Eastcote, and I've got a little record label, and this is my big chance." I say, "If we don't do this, there won't be a Rockpile, and you'll get stuck with Dave." I lay it on with a trowel, and much to my surprise, he says, "Alright. I like you. I'll let you do it."

We shook hands, and I walked out. I could have leaped over that fucking moat.

UNITY MacLEAN It all starts at the top. You had all these minions down below who loved being aggressive and were being told, "Yes, go ahead, I'm paying you. Do your worst."

ED BICKNELL (former manager of Dire Straits)   If, as the driver of the thing, you are a complete shitbrain, it's likely that everyone *else* is going to be a complete shitbrain. And when you lose the plot, there's an awful lot of people who want to lose the plot *with* you. Because it's fun and glamorous and all that.

AUBREY POWELL (designer of Zeppelin album covers)   I'd go 'round to Swan Song, and Richard would greet me by saying, "What the fuck do you want, you cunt?" I'd say, "I've just come to have a meeting with Robert." And he'd say, "What d'you wanna fuckin' talk to that long-haired git for?" It was just this powerhouse of madness.

JAKE RIVIERA   I don't know where they dug these people up. They were like rock apes. There was a guy called Magnet, and every other syllable he had to swear: it would be "Los-fuckin'-Angeles," in a Brummie accent. I once asked him if I could put some guests on Nick Lowe's list. He said, "I'll 'ave to check with the fuckin' office." I got a bit shirty, and he said, "Don't fuckin' get smart with me, ya fucker." I'm figuring, "I really don't need this shit." Dave knew he was trapped in that thing, but he loved Robert Plant telling him how fantastic he was.

DENNIS SHEEHAN (assistant to Robert Plant on 1977 U.S. tour)   Johnny Bindon used to hang out with Cole at the World's End, opposite Swan Song. Maybe Richard felt Peter needed somebody like Bindon, but to me, it was like the blind leading the blind.

UNITY MacLEAN   Bindon was born to a big Irish family in Fulham and I think was pretty badly treated as a child. Then he got these bit parts in movies and did all right for himself. Richard was friendly with Lionel Bart, who knew Bindon. A load of wide boys [hustlers].

Peter would have said, "We need tough guys like you." And Bindon could be very sociable. He was a great raconteur and moved in some pretty smooth circles. He could chat with Peter about Princess Margaret, and Peter would probably hang on his every word. I don't think they realized they were unleashing the creature from hell. He was sitting in the office one day with that slagette Vicky Hodge, and she had a dress on that was all poppers, and he ripped it off her in

Peter with John "Biffo" Bindon, Edgowater Inn, Seattle, July 1977. (Richard Cole Collection)

front of everybody. Everybody else seemed to see the fun side of Johnny Bindon, but I never did.

BENJI LeFEVRE (Zeppelin sound technician, 1973–1980)   It was truly frightening whenever Biffo came into the office or when we went to the Water Rat with him. But up to a point, it was also extraordinarily *funny*.

ALAN CALLAN   I believe there was a huge turning point with Zeppelin when they got their first death threat. I think that changes the entire environment around you. The justification for having someone like Bindon around was that if things got bad, he would take a bullet for you. Richard was tough, but John could look you in the eye and intimidate you. You knew you would really have to hurt him badly to stop him coming after you.

MARILYN COLE   Peter was desperately lonely—he had all the money in the world, but no woman in his life—and along comes Biffo. Personally, I *loved* Biffo. He was hugely bright and very entertaining, quite apart from the fact that he'd whip out his old John Thomas. He would recite

Shakespeare in the middle of a pub and do it beautifully. But he was also very unpleasant and dangerous, if not actually psychopathic. You didn't really want him in your home.

Biffo sort of moved in and elbowed Richard out of the way, and Richard allowed it to happen. If Richard was ever sober enough to think about it, he was probably quite put out.

CYNTHIA SACH (secretary at Swan Song in the U.K., 1977–1981)   Bindon was always trying to intimidate people. He'd go into the Water Rat and get his willy out. It was the most hideous willy I'd ever seen, thin and pale and vile. And he'd wave it around and hang beer mugs off it.

PAMELA DES BARRES (L.A. groupie and girlfriend of Page's in the late '60s)   They just hired the wrong people, like the Stones hiring the Hell's Angels at Altamont. It wasn't so much the band. It had a lot to do with Jimmy not wanting anyone to know anything about the band, so it was doubly insulated in that way.

BP FALLON   Bindon was bad news. That's not what this is meant to be about: people going around beating people up. Everyone knew about him. Very charming and very funny and all of that, but at what price? You might as well have a tarantula in your handbag.

21

Roundheads and Cavaliers

1. Never talk to anyone in the band unless they first talk to you.
1a. Do not make any sort of eye contact with John Bonham. This is for your own safety.
2. Do not talk to Peter Grant or Richard Cole—for any reason.
3. Keep your cassette player turned off at all times, unless conducting an interview.
4. Never ask questions about anything other than music.
5. Most importantly, understand this—the band will read what is written about them. The band does not like the press nor do they trust them.

> —Rules of Engagement on Led Zeppelin's 1977 tour of America, as outlined to journalist Steve Rosen by Swan Song press officer Janine Safer

BENJI LeFEVRE (Zeppelin sound technician, 1973–1980) We rented ELP's studio in Fulham Broadway, Manticore, for a month. And I think Zeppelin rehearsed there twice. Robert and Jonesy would turn up at midday, and we'd go to the Golden Lion. Jimmy and Bonzo would show up later, and we'd all get fucked up. Someone would say, "Shall we go and rehearse, then?" And they'd say, "Ah, not today."

BP FALLON (Zeppelin's U.K. press officer, 1972–1976) I took Rat Scabies down to Manticore. They loved him because he was a Keith Moon type.

RAT SCABIES (drummer with the Damned) We got down there, and Bonham was off his face, banging the timpani and gongs in all the wrong places. So that was quite entertaining. I think the *Sounds* poll had been published that day, and he'd been voted the No. 1 drummer, and I was No. 2 or something. So he pinned me against the wall and said, "Listen, you little fucker, *I* used to be that fast!"

Janine Safer gives Bonzo a neck rub on the 1977 U.S. tour. (Neal Preston/Corbis)

ALAN CALLAN (president of Swan Song in the U.K., 1977–1980)   Immediately after I started at Swan Song, Zep were going on tour. So for the next eighteen months, it was just Zeppelin.

JANINE SAFER (press officer at Swan Song in the U.S., late '70s)   We opened in Dallas, and everyone was very excited because the Butter Queen was there. The initial vibe on the tour was good. There was no tension between any of the members. Jimmy was clean. They were always punctual and professional and never kept the crowd waiting very long.

RICHARD COLE (Zeppelin road manager)   We got into Dallas a day before, and the next day we were getting ready to go to sound check when Peter arrived on a private jet. There was a knock on the door, and there was Peter with Steve Weiss and Bindon. None of us had any idea that Peter was bringing Biffo with him.

DAVE NORTHOVER (assistant to John Paul Jones on the 1977 U.S. tour)   I couldn't really figure out what Bindon was doing on the tour. Robert was one of the most vocal when it came to not wanting him around. Bindon was a very funny guy, as well as being in possession of one of the biggest penises you've ever seen.

AUBREY POWELL (designer of Zeppelin album covers)   I remember sitting with Bindon on the Zeppelin plane, and we were talking about Steve O'Rourke, the manager of Pink Floyd. I said I was pissed off with O'Rourke because he hadn't been paying us, so Bindon turned to me and said—in all seriousness—"Shall I fucking 'ave 'im away? I mean, he's a cunt, right?"

I sat there thinking, "I don't really want to be having this conversation about killing Steve O'Rourke." And meanwhile Vicki Hodge was doing cartwheels down the center aisle without any knickers on. Eventually, Peter came up to me and dragged me to the back of the plane. In a funny sort of way, I think he was being fatherly.

JACK CALMES (cofounder of Showco sound and lighting company)   I showed up on the third date at the start of the tour. The mood was ugly, and there had been a buzz in the P.A., and Jimmy had come over and thrown a trash can over one of the main techs, one of our guys who had been with us for a long time.

GARY CARNES (Showco lighting director on the 1977 U.S. tour)   During the acoustic set one night, Jimmy put his guitar down, walked over, and spat in Donnie Kretzschmar's face. Donnie jumped up and was about to have a go at him in front of fifty thousand people. The security guys said, "Donnie, technically you are well within your rights to beat the shit out of him. But if you touch him, we are going to have to kill you."

JACK CALMES   Jimmy was prancing around in his storm trooper uniform backstage, goose-stepping and stuff, and it didn't go down too well with Steve Weiss. He would say it in a way like, "What's the purpose of this?" Jimmy would just look at him like he was crazy.

JANINE SAFER   Jimmy Page? Not a very nice person. He was a looming presence in my life for several years, and my theory was—is—that he was a horrible four-year-old, a horrible eight-year-old, a horrible sixteen-year-old . . . and so on. If a child is born a bad seed, I don't think you can love him out of it. I think he's a profoundly lonely man. He has no friends, and the minute anybody tries to approach him in friendship, he spits on them. The only time I ever saw Jimmy exhibit affection was toward Peter. There was real warmth there. Why, I have no idea.

SAM AIZER   Jimmy made Janine's life miserable. He was out of control, insane. I saw him in the storm trooper outfit after a Bad Company show in Fort Worth, and I said to myself, "What the fuck is *that*?"

UNITY MacLEAN (manager of Swan Song office in the U.K.)   Jimmy had a problem eating, so they often had to put him into rehab just to fatten him up. Charlotte did her best to cook big meals, but by the time the food was ready, he wasn't interested.

JANINE SAFER   I don't think I ever saw Jimmy eat. We would go out to dinner, and it was, "Fine, Mexican sounds good." He would nibble at hors d'oeuvres, but that was about it.

JAAN UHELSZKI (writer for *Creem*)   I remember him saying he had a blender in his room with vitamins and bananas. He didn't mention the alcohol content.

Grant and Page, O'Hare Airport, Chicago, April 17, 1977. (Neal Preston/ Corbis)

JANINE SAFER   When we went out, it would be the band, Peter, Richard, Rex King, Benji LeFevre, Brian Gallivan, Danny Markus, sometimes Tom Hulett of Concerts West, the doctor—a slick, smarmy Californian guy—and the security man Don Murfet.

ABE HOCH   Peter could be a little scary when he was surrounded by guys like Murfet. Don owned a security company, and he supplied the band with guys who had names like Paddy the Plank.

DAVE NORTHOVER   Murfet had some very serious connections. They were owed some money in New Orleans, and they took Don down there to recover it . . . with a few well-chosen words.

RICHARD COLE   The 1973 tour was still harmonious and friendly, as was 1975, to some degree. The last American tour was fucking horrible. There was no camaraderie between *anyone*.

JAAN UHELSZKI   There were bodyguards *everywhere*, and that was a real big sea change from '75 to '77. There was just a cloud that seemed to hang over everybody. There had been much more of an *ease* in 1975. They'd joked around together, and they'd laughed and had much more of a back-and-forth between one another. In '77, it just seemed much more solemn.

JACK CALMES   Part of it started out, in my mind, as the creation of a mythology that starts to consume. A lot of the mayhem was tongue-in-cheek and staged in the early days, but then it became real mayhem and turned into violence and worse.

SAM AIZER   When you went to a Zeppelin show, it was like an FBI outing, the most paranoid thing. Everybody was nervous: "Should I stand *here*?" "Did you see *that*?" "What's *he* looking at?" It was just a constant look-over-your-shoulder. When the band would stroll in an hour late, nobody had the balls to say, "By the way, those people out there, they made you rich."

MITCHELL FOX (staffer at Swan Song U.S. office)   Beyond the mystique, from a dollars-and-cents point of view Zeppelin was a big moneymaker for *everybody*. So the preservation and safety of the band members was the utmost priority to anybody who worked with them. The band was surrounded to the point where, under most circumstances, you couldn't get near them.

GARY CARNES   We were told, as the crew, never to speak to the band or the manager unless they spoke to us first. Peter Grant said one thing to me at a show one night. It was the 25th of April at the Freedom Hall in Louisville, Kentucky. I was sitting stage left, house right, and I got a tap on my shoulder. It was Peter. He said, "I don't *like* this gig, do you?" And I had to think real fast, because I could have gotten thrown off the tour for saying the wrong thing. So I said, "Well, I've seen better venues, and I've seen worse venues." He said, "Alright, mate," and walked away.

MITCHELL FOX   On the plane, there was a front section and a middle section. And then there was the back section, to which I was never quite invited. They established boundaries and guidelines pretty early on. If you were smart, you took a couple of steps back even from the boundaries.

SAM AIZER   There were times when they shouldn't have been onstage. If Jimmy Page has fallen asleep in the bathroom, hey, you've got all kinds of problems.

BENJI LeFEVRE   They would come onstage God knows how many hours late because they'd been trying to pump caffeine into Jimmy to get him to function. Then Jimmy would make a sign, and a follow-spot would pick him up from behind, and he'd start "The Song Remains the Same" on his double-neck. But sometimes he'd have the chord shape on the twelve-string, and he'd be strumming the *six*-string. You could just see Robert *cringing*.

One night Jimmy was doing his fucking half-hour egotistical over-indulgent bullshit—which is what it *and* Bonzo's drum solo became—and Robert said, "Ladies and gentlemen, Mr. Jimmy Page," and just stood there onstage, *watching* him. Whereas normally he went off-stage and had a blow job.

ROBERT PLANT   Whatever was going on, to me it did go on a little bit. It's not that it wasn't that good, it's just that I had to start thinking about things to do, because after a while you can start to look a little bit of a jerk, wobbling your head around like some sort of Indian tradesman.

ROSS HALFIN (photographer and friend of Page's)   Once, during "Dazed and Confused," Plant went to the side of the stage and said, "Look at it, it's all just one big guitar solo, and what am *I* meant to do?" And, apparently, Peter prodded him and said, "Just remember whose fucking band it is, and it's not fucking *yours*."

DENNIS SHEEHAN (assistant to Robert Plant on the 1977 U.S. tour)   By 1977, Peter had tried to lose weight a few times. He was very top-heavy, with little pins as legs. On the tour, at times he was unable to go to shows. He'd call me, and I'd go up to his room, and all he wanted to do was sit and chat. The instructions were basically that no one should come into the room unless I'd been in to clean up and make sure none of the glass-top tables had white powder on them.

HELEN GRANT (daughter of Peter Grant)   Warren and I went on the 1977 tour with Dad. We were kept away from all the hubbub. We were never allowed to stay for the encores, which really used to piss me off. "Stairway to Heaven" came on, and I was always sort of trundled off by this person I didn't really know. You could see my grumpy face as Dad shoved me into this horrible black funeral car.

JANINE SAFER We were in Phoenix, which was one of our bases on the tour, and *Star Wars* came out. Peter, me, Warren, and Helen went to see it. At that point, I had no perspective on parent-child relationships, but even I was touched. It was very sweet, and it was very sad.

SALLY WILLIAMS (girlfriend of Bonham's drum roadie Mick Hinton) The band always seemed to end up in Los Angeles, and I would sometimes join them there. Seeing the shows, I was really proud of them as this kind of Brit phenomenon. I was just sad about everything else that went with it.

ELIZABETH IANNACI (artist relations, Atlantic's L.A. office) When I think about Led Zeppelin, I feel . . . *blue*. I ask myself why, and I think it has to do with the amorality of the time. The Eastern mystics say that if you go into a salt mine, you come out tasting like salt. It is impossible to be in a society of amorality and not be affected by it, because what becomes normal—what becomes the standard—is different.

SALLY WILLIAMS Everyone was falling apart by then, anyway. Mick Hinton was just drunk the whole time. Probably he was an alcoholic, but in those days you didn't get labeled as such. The last time he came home, I said to myself, "That's it, I've got to separate from all of this. It's time for Mick to go." Benji was still holding it together, but Benji started off with . . . not quite a silver spoon in his mouth, but he wasn't short of money, and he had his head screwed on differently. He was one step removed from the madness that was around the other roadies.

GARY CARNES Benji could be the most outrageous, out-of-control person that ever lived and then, on a dime, turn and be Mr. Businessman better than anybody else. We all looked to Benji to keep things as calm as they could be. If he hadn't been there, we'd all have been in trouble.

Benji LeFevre (right) with Brian Condliffe, 1977 U.S. tour. (Courtesy of Gary Carnes)

ROBERT PLANT (speaking in 1977)   I see a lot of craziness around us. Somehow we generate it and we revile it. . . . What we are trying to put across is positive and wholesome; the essence of a survival band and almost a symbol of the phoenix, if you will. I don't know why the fans toss firecrackers. I think it's horrible. That's the element that makes you wonder whether it's better to be halfway up a tree in Wales.

SHELLEY KAYE (manager of Swan Song office in the U.S.)   It was all over the top. The plane, the hotels, it was all top of the line. I remember flying out to Seattle with Steve and Marie, and Peter telling the manager at the Edgewater Inn, "Have a TV on me . . . kick it in!"

JAAN UHELSZKI   The limos were unbelievable. It really was like a cavalcade for the president. They would even have *fake* limos to thwart the fans. To this day, I have never been on a tour that was so beyond the norm. They suspended all the normal rules of behavior.

SHELLEY KAYE   I actually don't think they made a lot of money on any of the tours, because were spending a fortune. It wasn't like it is today, where you have a T-shirt deal, and you get a million dollars up front for it. Merchandise was a minimal part of the deal. Curtis Lentz, who did the T-shirts, would show up with a bag full of cash, and that was about it.

BENJI LeFEVRE   Raymondo [Thomas] completely fucked up one night. He wouldn't put the guitar in this room where we had everything locked up. Next day we come in, and it's gone. Three hours before the show, a truck driver shows up at the back door with the guitar. He claims he picked up a hitchhiker who's completely out of it and says, "You'll never guess who this guitar belongs to . . ." The driver chins the bloke and brings the guitar back. Richard Cole is summoned to the door, takes the guitar off the bloke, and chins *him*.

DENNIS SHEEHAN   Richard was in a fairly sorry state then. One of my jobs was to stop him from jumping off balconies. But he was still a great tour manager.

MITCHELL FOX   What Steve Weiss did for the band relative to the business and legal aspects, Richard did as far as roadside logistics went: protecting the band and making sure they were where they were supposed to be when they were supposed to be there. He was ruthless to that extent. He would not be swayed otherwise by anything.

DENNIS SHEEHAN   Robert had respect for Richard in the beginning, but by the end Richard was treading a very unsavory path, and Robert was very aware of that. He was quite vocal in pointing out that Richard was lucky to be there.

GARY CARNES   Everybody was scared to death of Richard. He was just so mean to all of us. We would be up for days, so if you could catch a thirty-minute nap, you would. And Richard would walk around kicking anybody who was asleep.

SHELLEY KAYE We'd flown in on the plane to Scottsdale to do a show in Tempe. Richard was busy getting everyone into the cars. I wound up in a car with him and Janine, and in the front seat were two people who were unknown; how they came to be there, I have no idea. It's July, and it's a hundred degrees. The young lady says, "I need to go to the bathroom," and Richard tells her to piss off; the rule is that nobody ever stops on a short journey like this one.

A little while later, the young lady turns around and says, "I'm going to pee in the car if you don't pull over." So we pull over, and all the other cars pull over. The couple gets out of the car, and she's running into the bushes with her boyfriend. And all the cars take off again. We just left them there, because nobody cared who they were. It was typical Richard Cole stuff.

ELIZABETH IANNACI The difference between the way I was treated and the way I saw them treat *other* women was very difficult to reconcile. Bonzo was the only one who treated me like I was one of *the girls*. I was on the plane going to San Diego, and Bonzo came over and grabbed me by the wrists and lifted me up—I was very tiny, five feet tall and maybe a hundred pounds. He carried me over to his seat and put me on his lap and tried to kiss me.

Now, I wasn't going to knee him in the groin—which is what I would do today—and at that time there was no such phrase as "sexual harassment." This was what came with the territory, and you learned how to fend off advances from men. So I was putting his hands where they belonged, and he was very drunk and kept going, "Why not? Why not?" And I finally just said, "Because I'd never be able to have tea with your wife." He just looked at me, dead serious, and said, "Well, why the fuck would you *want* to?" I said, "Honey, it's a metaphor." But it was beyond him. Finally, he said, "Ach, you're *Robert's* girl," and kind of tossed me off his lap. But it was perfectly in keeping with "Why are you *here* if you're not here to *fuck*?"

I do feel I was complicit in many ways. In *looking the other way*, you were almost being "a good German." One time, Jimmy sent me to go get Lori in a limo, and she and her mother were staying in some motel on Sunset near the 405 freeway. I knocked on the door, and they were having an argument about a little beaded dress that Lori had borrowed from her mom: "You're not going out in that dress!" It was clear to me that Lori was *groomed* for this, which is why I have mixed feelings about Roman Polanski. There is a culture of older women who groom younger women to do their bidding, so to speak: "You're gonna land someone, and *I'm* going to benefit from it."

JANINE SAFER The thing I enjoyed most about the tour was, in fact, the music. It was a wonderful life lesson in perspective, to see the same band perform the same show seventy-eight times. You learn a lot about crowd dynamics. Of course, they could have stood onstage with kazoos playing "Oh! Susanna," and everyone would have been apoplectic with joy.

BENJI LeFEVRE Some nights "Since I've Been Loving You" made me cry, it was so mesmerizing. Other nights, it made me cry because it was so *pointless.* The word *roller coaster* doesn't come close to addressing the way the thing was so *turbulently disturbed.* Mainly, it was down to what state Jimmy was in, because when you play a wrong note on the guitar, everyone can clearly hear it.

GARY CARNES When all four of them were straight onstage, nobody could touch them. But all four of them straight was pretty rare. Sometimes Plant would announce a song, and Page would go into the wrong number. I was seven or eight feet away at the Chicago show when Page sat down after the first few songs and passed out . . . and that was the end of the show.

JAAN UHELSZKI They had to stop the Chicago show because Jimmy had a stomach ache, and there were all these little blips. You could really see the cracks, and you could also see that the whole tension between Robert and Jimmy was getting bad.

BENJI LeFEVRE When they did the acoustic set at the front of the stage, Bonzo would sometimes nod out while he was playing the tambourine. I think there must have been an enormous amount of personal frustration for him and for Jimmy, because they couldn't understand why they couldn't play properly anymore.

JOHN PAUL JONES   Some nights the tempos would be really slow, and you'd just try and push them up, and sometimes Jimmy would start things off strangely.

JIMMY PAGE   I don't regret [the drugs] at all, because when we needed to be really focused, I was really focused.

DANNY MARKUS   I remember we were in New Orleans, and it was the first time Jimmy had gotten up while the sun was still up. He came to the window when everyone was down at the pool, and he got a standing ovation.

BENJI LeFEVRE   It categorically divided into two camps: Bonzo and Jimmy, Jonesy and Robert. It was astonishing, the labored friendship that had to be portrayed onstage because of the famous Robert-sidling-up-to-Jimmy. They still had to do that, but I think Robert *hated* having to do it.

DAVID BATES (A&R man for Robert Plant and for Page and Plant in the '90s)   Robert always said there were two camps in Zeppelin: the Cavaliers and the Roundheads. The Cavaliers were Page and Bonham and a number of the road crew—the ones that just partied, that went for the chaos and madness. The others were the ones who said, "Look, we're in Rome. Shall we go and have a look at the Colosseum?" Robert was never fully committed to one or the other. It all depended on his mood: "Today I feel like a bit of culture. Tomorrow? Hmmm . . . let me see what's on offer." He can pull the "I'm Robert Plant" if he needs to, but he's also quite happy with people not knowing who he is. He is really quite secure, but he can also be very *in*secure. He is *not* the Viking that you see.

BENJI LeFEVRE   When I went to work for the Stones, I had an interview with Jagger and immediately realized, "Wait a minute, I've been here before—here's the together extrovert Leo singer with his mate, the fucked-up guitar player."

JAAN UHELSZKI Jimmy asked me how I'd liked one of the shows, and I told him I'd seen better. He said to me that the daily papers had said how good *he* was, and that was why Robert had hated the show so much. It was like he was taking great pride in the fact that he'd been able to outshine Robert.

JACK CALMES Robert had his own massive ego, but he did make an effort to keep that from bringing him down, and he was more an observer of everybody else crumbling. I never saw him with his face in the mud, fucked up and crawling around clubs.

ROBERT PLANT I think I could probably remember how to roll a spliff, but I know I haven't touched anything at all since 1977. . . . I make sure that, socially, I keep away from anybody who's unclean like that, because it is that eight-minute cycle of enthusiasm.

DENNIS SHEEHAN Robert was dead easy. He would go out to a club, order one drink, and that drink would be with him the rest of the night. When he got back, he'd slip a little note under my door, telling me what he wanted for the next day: "Can you wake me up at 12 and have a cup of tea ready?"

TONY MANDICH (artist relations, Atlantic's L.A. office) I took Robert to see the New York Cosmos, and he was driving a convertible Cadillac because he loves driving around the country. Anything shorter than five hundred miles, he would drive from city to city, so the two of us went to the Cosmos game in L.A. There were ninety thousand people there. I said, "We need security." He said, "No, there's only two of us." We talked about Wolves. We would talk about *everything*. I saw every moment of him, driving around the country and absorbing all those sounds and melodies and harmonies and guitar playing. When I heard *Raising Sand*, I remembered how he used to soak it all up.

JAAN UHELSZKI Robert was already becoming this kind of cross-pollinator . . . and he was so much more *sociable* than Page. You wouldn't see Page hanging out at the bar, but you would see Plant there, holding court. Jimmy was the dark to Robert's light, which was the thing that made it work musically. But whatever made it work was also what pulled it apart.

• • •

JANINE SAFER   Why did they surround themselves with people like John Bindon? I think there's a one-word answer: cocaine. Or another, related word: paranoia. Peter and Jimmy were the most paranoid people I have ever met in my life, bar none.

Bindon was Richard Cole cubed. He was presented as a long-known quantity. I don't know that I have ever met anyone in my life who so thoroughly embodied all that is negative and all that is violent. I don't think anybody found him charming on the Led Zeppelin tour. Maybe Peter was charmed. He did seem to find Bindon amusing, and he was certainly the only person to whom Bindon was deferential. He was thoroughly bad news, and it infected the entire atmosphere and society around him.

DANNY MARKUS   I met Bindon, but don't forget that I'd had to deal with Freddy Sessler when I worked with the Stones. There's always *somebody* like that. There's always a carousel of people passing through, so many people that get swept along.

ELIZABETH IANNACI   Bindon seemed to be the unofficial jester, and all the crew were quite taken with his antics. It was most likely he who, at the Rainbow one night, slapped a slice of hot pizza onto Phil Carson's crotch. He was not unattractive, just unbelievably crude. His little joke was that he would make a gesture that looked like fellatio. I once turned to him and said, "You know, John, you would be okay if you just didn't do that so much." He never looked me in the eye again. It was as if I'd crippled him.

DANNY MARKUS   I decided to leave Atlantic in the middle of the last Zeppelin tour. I said farewell to Zeppelin at the Forum, and Robert dedicated a song to me during one of the shows: "We will miss your credit card, and we will miss *you*."

ELIZABETH IANNACI   Things seemed to spiral downward after I left Atlantic. The tone changed. There was a velocity of being on the road that carried with it all this detritus. The people that were on the road were different from the people who were there in 1975. It was so much more isolated and insular—like being on a movie set. And because it's a synthetic world that only exists at that moment, the rules of real life don't seem to apply.

DENNIS SHEEHAN With Zeppelin, there was nothing else around like them at the time, so therefore their life *was that*—and it was *only that*. With U2, their lives are about so many other things.

JANINE SAFER In Detroit, for the Silverdome show, we stayed one night in a really crappy motel to be as near as possible to the venue. I had to get Jimmy up for a phone interview, so I knocked on his door, and he was out cold. He woke and said he wanted a cup of tea. I prevailed on someone to bring him a cup of tea, but the water in the pot was so tepid that the water wouldn't even diffuse. He sort of looked at it, half-asleep, half-comatose, took a sip and just spat it out. And we both started laughing so hard. It's one of the few amusing memories I have of him on the tour.

Later that night I actually found him unconscious, because he had started using heroin again by this point. I believe it changed in New York, because Keith Richards had turned up. And that wasn't good for Jimmy.

ALAN CALLAN I was at the Silverdome show, and the collective energy of seventy-six thousand people having a good time was intoxicating and fascinating. To sit and watch the audience from a privileged position was just joyful. It was like having the best seat at the World Cup Final.

DAVE NORTHOVER Everybody was worried about how frail Jimmy was: how could he possibly do a three-hour set after two or three hours' sleep? But he did. Once in Los Angeles I had to wake him up and get him mobile for the concert that night. I walked around the suite and couldn't find him anywhere. Eventually, I realized there was a little bolster thing right at the end of the bed, and he was *hiding* in there.

JAAN UHELSZKI I'd been on the tour for about a week and had interviewed Robert, but I couldn't get Jimmy to commit to an interview time. And this was going to be a cover story for *Creem*. Finally, the day before I was supposed to go home, he agreed—but only on the condition that he had Janine there.

When I got to the room, he looked at me and said, "You have to put the questions to Janine." So I had to ask *her* the question, and then she would turn toward Jimmy and say exactly what I had said to him, and he would answer to her, and she would tell me his answer. And we thought Michael Jackson was weird. It was not a particularly long interview, maybe forty minutes for a cover story, and at the end of it, Jimmy said, "I'm sorry, but this interview has come to an end." It was like a line out of some drawing-room comedy.

JANINE SAFER I was the press wrangler, and there was no question that they were going to talk to John Rockwell at the *New York Times* and Robert Hilburn at the *L.A. Times*. But my agenda was more, "I'd like you to talk to my friend Dave Schulps from *Trouser Press*."

DAVE SCHULPS (writer for *Trouser Press* magazine) At first sight, I was struck by how extremely frail he appeared, escorted by a bodyguard who seemed almost to be propping him up. [He was] remarkably thin and pale, his sideburns showing a slight touch of gray, his skin exhibiting a wraithlike pallor. I found it hard to believe this was the same person I'd seen bouncing around the stage at Madison Square Garden earlier that week. [He] spoke slowly and softly in a sort of half-mumble/half-whisper that matched his frail physical appearance.

ELIZABETH IANNACI When the Jaan Uhelszki article came out, Robert called me and said, "Oh, things at home aren't good . . . my wife read the article." I was stunned. My reaction was, "She didn't *know*?" How would I know that the farm in Kidderminster was out of touch with all of that?

NICK KENT (writer for *NME*) I think they expected that people would be afraid enough of their reputation to delete any references to groupies.

JAAN UHELSZKI When I put in the *Creem* piece the thing about "I hope this doesn't get back to England," they were so mad at me that Janine said they would never talk to me again.

GARY CARNES   At the Tampa show, people had sat in the boiling sun all day, consuming whatever they were consuming. That was the first time I ever saw anyone killed before my very eyes. A guy got pushed off the upper level of the stadium and died instantly. That was not a good omen.

The band came on, and they were just going into "Nobody's Fault but Mine" when the sky exploded. Within minutes, everything was under water. And when it was announced that there would be no show that night, war broke out. The cops called out to us through megaphones, "Everyone lay down behind the speaker cabinets and cover your heads. Do not get up." And this huge riot squad came in through the back of stadium. There were bodies lying everywhere, bleeding. It was pretty scary.

ELIZABETH IANNACI   They were at the fabulous Forum on that '77 tour, and I was standing at the edge of the stage, watching. During "Going to California," someone threw a bouquet of flowers onto the stage, and Robert picked it up. As he sang the line about the girl with flowers in her hair, he walked over and presented the bouquet to me. Twenty thousand fans went fucking wild, and I thought to myself, "*This* is why they do cocaine." Until you have that kind of energy directed toward you, there really isn't any way to get it or to understand it.

GARY CARNES   I used to get so sick of hearing "Stairway to Heaven." Every night Plant would say that line "Does anybody remember laughter?" and sometimes he'd look over at me and say, "Gary, do *you* remember laughter?!" It was like he was saying, "Gary, are you still awake?"

ALAN CALLAN   You put your album together, you record it and release it, you have all these preproduction thoughts about the stage show and the arrangements for the tour, you execute the tour . . . and at some point the thought must strike you, "We've got to figure out how to do this all over again." To sustain that for twelve years takes an enormous amount of courage. Where's the inspiration? You've got to find something. And it's that search, that internal quest.

JANINE SAFER The band was very unhappy when I left Swan Song. When I said I was leaving, it was *incomprehensible* to them. It was like the Mafia.

I wanted to go work for Rockpile and Elvis Costello and Stiff Records, because that was *cool*. It was through Dave Edmunds that I met Jake Riviera and then Nick Lowe. Jake was one of the most brilliant people I've ever met in my life. A marketing genius with a tremendous visual flair. But so quickly, you could see the wide-eyed naïveté of Jake turning into something awful and assholey. He was always incredibly aggressive—like Cole and Bindon, ironically. I'm assuming Elvis fired him, and I'm assuming it was because he became unbearable.

JAAN UHELSZKI I always say to Brad Tolinski, "I just need one more crack at Page, now that I'm older and wiser and a better interviewer." Jimmy likes me, apparently. He said to Brad, after I wrote a big *Q* piece, "Tell Jaan I really *did* steal the Quaaludes from Dr. Badgeley." Then again, Lester Bangs and I used to say to each other—and it's a line that made it into *Almost Famous*—"Rock stars are not our friends." And that's something we always have to remember.

. . .

PHIL CARLO (roadie for Bad Company) There was a girl who used to work at the Rainbow, who was affectionately known as Linda Rainbow. She and Bonzo were really close, but there was never anything physical with them. She said to me, "All Bonzo talks about is his family and how much he misses being at home. He's such a lovely bloke, and everybody thinks something is going on between us. But there isn't."

PAMELA DES BARRES Bonzo was a sweet, cuddly, goofy fella until he got drunk, and then you wanted to avoid him. I saw him slug my friend Michelle Myer right in the jaw just for being in the doorway with him at the Rainbow.

KIM FOWLEY (L.A. producer and scenester)   Michelle was a fighter. A sensitive girl, but she could battle, and she and Bonzo had a bout of Greco-Roman wrestling on the floor of the Rainbow.

ABE HOCH   I think Bonzo was a brute. I'm sorry to say that, but deep down inside the guy just did things sociopathically. He was terrifying at times. My dad was an alcoholic, and when you're around alcoholics, it is scary.

STEVEN ROSEN (writer for *Guitar Player* in the '70s; traveled on the 1977 tour)   Just about everything written about Bonham these days is pretty positive. But he was one mean bastard. I was afraid to even look in his direction when I was with Zep. People don't really talk about that.

SIMON KIRKE (drummer with Bad Company)   Amazingly enough, he still played well. Such was the pride between all of them that being impaired during the show was a big no-no. That's not to say that a drink or a line of coke before a show wasn't taken every now and then, but nothing to seriously affect the performance.

After the gigs, however, John was pretty much a loose cannon. He was not a womanizer, he didn't seek solace in the arms of ladies. He just liked to raise hell. He was the proverbial duck out of water. I remember going to the Whisky to join him for a tipple, and after asking which table he was seated at, I was told by Bear—the enormous four-hundred-pound bouncer—that John had been restrained after drinking fifteen Brandy Alexanders and taken to jail. Bear was quite apologetic because he'd had to apply a choke hold on a very drunk and combative Bonzo and had actually rendered him unconscious.

BENJI LeFEVRE   Rex King was a carpet-fitter who used to drink in the Beehive in Marylebone. Bonzo was not particularly responsible for himself now and needed someone to pack his bags and get him out of bed and into the limo. Rex was considered a good candidate because they thought he would be neat and tidy. One day a carpet-fitter, the next day on tour in America on Zeppelin's private plane . . .

PHIL CARLO   Rex was basically like a playmate for Bonzo on the road. I think he was a mate of Bindon's. They all looked the same: him, Bonzo, and Cole. Facially, they all had black hair and the same beard.

AUBREY POWELL   On the last American tour, I knocked on the door of Bonzo's room at the Plaza to talk to him about some piece of artwork. Mick Hinton answered the door and said, "Er, he's not great today, so watch out." And Bonzo was leery and incoherent, totally out of control. He'd obviously been doing smack, and he was nodding out and then fading back in. This was the middle of the afternoon, and I just could not have the conversation. Basically, he was bored, so heroin and alcohol passed the time of day.

DENNIS SHEEHAN   The days between shows really got to Bonzo. If he could have got a jet to go home, he would have.

DANNY MARKUS   At Swingo's in Cleveland, I had this room that was like something out of Indiana Jones, with bamboo furniture and a fan and a four-poster bed. The four guys came to the room one night, and each grabbed one of the posts and pulled it away so that the bed collapsed. Then Bonzo took one of the posts and battered the fan. I came back a month later, and they still hadn't finished repairing the room. Everyone has a story like that about Zeppelin.

GLENN HUGHES (bassist and singer with Deep Purple)   It all ended up badly with me and John. When *The Song Remains the Same* premiered in L.A., he called me and said he wanted to meet me at the Rainbow.

The incident with Pat never comes up, we're having a drink and a couple of lines. We're having a good time, *kinda*, and we go back to the Beverly Hilton and have a couple of lines with Jimmy. The next night I go to the premiere, and there's no problem.

Then Robert invites me to go to the premiere in Birmingham. I get to the party, and I see little Jason playing drums. I go to the bar, and out of the corner of my eye, I see—fifteen or twenty feet away—the unmistakable figure of Bonzo in full Bonzo mode. Lo and behold, he springs up like a bear and clocks me right on the chin. Hurts me

Invitation to the premiere of *The Song Remains the Same*, Birmingham, November 1976. (Courtesy of John Crutchley)

pretty bad, chips a big tooth out of the bottom of my mouth. And the same security team that did Deep Purple with me, only months before, now escorts me out of that venue.

The story was that outside the venue, there were six Rolls-Royces lined up, and John threw a house brick through the front window of one of them, thinking it was mine. That was the last time I saw him, and it still saddens me. I had so much love for him that it broke my fucking heart.

22

Does Anyone Remember Laughter?

Egos and territories and domains and kingdoms and pecking orders and all the kind of crap that is rock 'n' roll came into being. It had nothing to do with money. It just had to do with that kind of intangible thing that hovers somewhere between your feet and the top of your hair. It's that *power*, you know?

—Robert Plant (1992)

AHMET ERTEGUN (cofounder of Atlantic Records)   I hated some of the tactics they used. They had a very, very embarrassing encounter with Bill Graham in San Francisco that was totally uncalled for. But they got carried away with their own success and power.

BENJI LeFEVRE (Zeppelin sound technician)   Oakland was a horrible and regrettable incident. I was not in any way present in the backstage area where the mobile dressing rooms were, so I was not aware that it was going down at the time. From what I've been told, Warren

371

was being a pain in the ass . . . and, unfortunately, John Bindon was an animal.

DAVE NORTHOVER (assistant to John Paul Jones on the 1977 tour)   Warren was spoiled and everything else—turned out all right, but he was a little toad back then. I can imagine that when he wanted the sign on the front of the trailer, he would have made a huge fuss about it.

JIM MATZORKIS (security guard for Bill Graham)   He was just a young kid, seven or something like that, so I took the signs from him. It wasn't a violent act of any kind.

DENNIS SHEEHAN (assistant to Robert Plant on the 1977 tour)   When Warren protested that he was the manager's son, the security guy sort of pushed him to one side, and he fell. Bonzo saw this and thought this was the wrong thing to do to any child.

DAVE NORTHOVER   I didn't know that the security guy had smacked him, and I'm not even sure that he did. I remember Benji coming to get me, and we all ran round to see the trailer where it was all going on.

JIM MATZORKIS   Bonham came up the little stair where I was standing, and he kicked me right in the crotch—a good unobstructed shot. I keeled over and fell back into the trailer. He wasn't alone, he had a couple of the bodyguards right behind him. All of this was happening fast.

DAVE NORTHOVER   Within seconds it got to Peter, who unfortunately had Bindon with him—he was at Peter's right-hand side most of the time.

JIM MATZORKIS   Peter Grant kept saying, "You don't talk to *my* kid that way." Bonham was kind of backing him up. [Grant said], "Nobody does it. I'll have your job." I remember saying to him, "No, you can't have my job."

BILL GRAHAM (San Francisco concert promoter)   I opened the trailer and went in first. Jim was sitting in the cubbyhole. Peter went in. I said, "Peter, after you." Jim got up to say hello. I said, "Jim, Peter is the father of the young man." In one move—I was behind Grant—[Grant] just grabbed Jim's hand, pulled [Jim] toward him, took his fist with the fingers all covered with rings, and smashed [Jim] in the face. I lunged at Grant. He picked me up like I was a fly and handed me to the guy by the steps, who just shoved me out, threw me down the steps, and shut the door. I was now outside the camper. Grant and one of his guys was inside, and the other guy was stopping me. I couldn't open the door, there was no way to get in.

JIM MATZORKIS Grant just started working me all over, punching me in the face with his fists and kicking me in the balls. He knocked a tooth out. . . . Grant sort of half-pounced on me, and Bindon reached down and was trying to rip my eyeballs out of their sockets. . . . I don't know how I did it, but I squeezed the hell out of there and ran.

DAVE NORTHOVER Matzorkis comes out, and his nose is a little bit bloody, but he's walking. Since then, I've heard stories that he couldn't walk, which isn't true.

JACK CALMES (cofounder of Showco lighting and sound company) I was outside the door, literally five feet away from this poor guy getting the living shit beaten out of him. It just shows you how disconnected from reality all of it had become at that point. It was totally unjustified. There was no incident that required any type of retaliation, nothing. Warren was just running around a little bit out of control backstage, as a kid will—nothing that caught my eye—but all of a sudden they come rushing out of the trailer and drag this guy in there, and he starts wailing.

MITCHELL FOX (staffer at the Swan Song U.S. office) What actually happened behind closed doors, I really don't know. It was a clash of the titans between Bill Graham and a band that had sold out two dates in front of fifty, sixty thousand people. It's all about whose playground you're playing in at that moment.

SIMON KIRKE (drummer with Bad Company) It was all drug-fueled, of course. G would normally have talked everyone down, but he was doing as much blow as everyone else, and tempers were constantly frayed.

JANINE SAFER (press officer at Swan Song U.S. office)   Would Oakland have happened without Bindon? Absolutely not. Bill Graham and his pals were not exactly saints, but I lay the episode entirely at the feet of Bindon, with the flames stoked by Richard Cole and then bellowed by the paranoia of Peter Grant.

It was like a cross between *The Sopranos* and the final episode of *Blackadder*. *The Sopranos* is heart-wrenchingly real, but this had the added element of absurdist theater. Bindon was spoiling for a fight, as was Richard. They were looking for drama, and all hell broke loose so quickly. They were winding Peter up, saying, "Are you gonna take it?" and in their delusional, drug-fueled madness, within a minute and a half it was, "Go get 'em, boys!"

DENNIS SHEEHAN   As far as the group themselves were concerned, I don't think they knew a lot about what was going on.

PETER BARSOTTI (Bill Graham staff)   Plant seemed like the only decent human being there, although there were no innocents. *There were no innocents.*

ROBERT PLANT   I had to sing ["Stairway"] in the shadow of the fact that the artillery we carried was prowling around with a hell of an attitude. It was this coming together of two dark forces that had nothing to do with the songs Page and I were trying to churn out.

JIMMY PAGE   I don't know what happened because I wasn't there. I mean, I only heard about it afterward when we were all being whisked away from it, so I don't know. I don't really want to talk about it. . . . I don't know that either of them beat up anybody, so I'm not sure what they did. All these horrific stories about what's supposed to have happened there—I don't think it was as bad as it was built up to be, to be truthful with you.

JOHN PAUL JONES   In Oakland, there was some fracas there, but . . . look, there's no way I like all that sort of thing. . . . I don't like the reputation . . . but there's two sides to every story.

BENJI LeFEVRE   We were now taking villains on the road to maintain the position of physical power. Robert and Jonesy absolutely hated it.

Bonzo found it amusing. Distasteful doesn't even cover it. I certainly didn't think when I went to work for Zeppelin at the end of 1972 that it could ever possibly degenerate into meaningless violence.

ELIZABETH IANNACI (artist relations in Atlantic L.A. office) There was a part of me that wasn't surprised, but more than anything else I was really disappointed, in the same way that Altamont felt like a death knell. There was the high that had been created by Woodstock, and then a very short time later came this dreadful dark energy.

UNITY MacLEAN (manager of Swan Song office in the U.K.) It was so damn petty. I don't think even the Sopranos would have reacted like that. They'd have said, "Don't ever do that again, Warren. You leave that till the end of the show." But Peter didn't say that to Warren. And Bindon and Cole wanted to please Peter, instead of pleasing Robert and Jimmy. So the band got tarred with the brush of being out-of-control, hotel-smashing loonies, and it just wasn't true: that's not what they were like. On one hand, it was wonderful what Peter had done for them; on the other hand, it was terrible.

HELEN GRANT (daughter of Peter Grant) I think the Oakland thing caused a lot of bad feeling between Dad and the band. Specifically, Robert.

JANINE SAFER I remember being back at the hotel, and there was a warrant out for the arrests of Bindon, Cole, Grant, and Bonham. We split in the middle of the night, and I don't believe they were ever charged with anything. Steve Weiss did *something*, and it was contained. But Bill Graham never forgave them.

CYNTHIA SACH (secretary at Swan Song office in the U.K.) We weren't allowed to be told what had happened in Oakland—especially not by Peter, because he had this Secret Squirrel type of behavior. Nothing must taint his boys.

DENNIS SHEEHAN After Oakland, we flew to New Orleans and arrived about six-thirty in the morning. I went to Robert's room and asked if there was anything he needed. He had Maureen on the phone, and he said his son wasn't well. After about half an hour, I came back to the room, and Robert was sitting on the side of the bed. He'd just had the call to say Karac had died.

RICHARD COLE   Robert asked Peter if I could take him back to England. We were on a plane out of there in the afternoon. It was me and him and Bonzo and Dennis. It was one of those things where it's best to say nothing than to say the wrong thing.

MITCHELL FOX   Richard looked at me and said, "Keep it together. This is a horrific situation." All of a sudden, they've canceled a show in a really large venue, and everything is thrown into complete disarray. It was a reality check of cosmic size, on everyone in and around the band.

ROBERT PLANT   If ever you want a quick reminder of what's going on in the real world, one minute you're in New Orleans and the toast of the new world, and you get a phone call without any warning. He'd gone. I was lucky that I didn't lose my will to sing altogether, because I could have blamed everything on singing.

JANINE SAFER   I was on the plane with Robert from New Orleans to New York, and he was just mute with grief. I didn't even know what to say to this man. Only now that I have children do I realize how *huge* it was. But I also cannot believe that Jimmy and John Paul and Peter didn't go to the funeral.

RICHARD COLE   John Paul was out of contact; he only knew to be back in New Orleans for the show at the Superdome. And no one knew where Jimmy was: he was either in New Orleans or he'd stayed in San Francisco with a Moroccan belly dancer. Peter and his kids and Biffo were in New York, and we didn't know when they were coming back.

NICK KENT (writer for *NME*)   I'm told that Plant was very upset about Page and Jones and Grant not being at the funeral. It meant that Led Zeppelin was no longer a family situation.

BENJI LeFEVRE   I don't think Robert would have *wanted* Jimmy and G at the funeral. I think he felt cheated by life—not that he held them responsible in any way, but he was angry with himself for going on tour when they were all fucked up anyway.

MICHAEL DES BARRES (singer with Detective)   To even conjecture as to why Jimmy and Peter weren't at Karac's funeral is to misread a situation that is so dominated by narcotics. It had nothing to do with lack of love or respect.

RICHARD COLE   After the funeral, we went back to Jennings Farm and just sat there drinking whisky straight out of the bottle.

ALAN CALLAN (president of Swan Song in the U.K.)   I can't imagine how deep the hurt must be to lose your son. There must be moments even now when Robert sees someone and thinks, "Karac might look like that." I don't think it was a question of walking away from the band; I think you just have to walk into your own emotional walled garden and try to deal with it. And everybody around you must respect that and let it roll.

Against losing Karac, the Bill Graham incident was trivia. One was vanity, and the other was humanity. In that moment, Robert's invincibility was rendered as nothing: that was the emotional bullet that got him. It doesn't matter whether you're the singer in the biggest band on earth or you're a bartender, what you're now reduced to is your basic humanity.

ABE HOCH (president of Swan Song in the U.K., 1975–1977)   Robert and Maureen used to come over to my place on the Old Brompton Road. When Karac died, it was the first time we'd had to tell my son Jamison about somebody dying. Rob and Karac would come over, and Rob would let him run around naked like he was the embodiment of Thor.

BENJI LeFEVRE   When Karac died, it was like, "What's the fucking point of *any* of this? I've been here with my fucked-up mate, who can't even play, when I should have been home looking after my *son*." And that had been brewing for a while. If it had been the most fantastically creative time of his life, the guilt wouldn't have been anywhere near as intense.

SIMON KIRKE   When Karac died, I heard a strange thing from Bonzo: "Fucking Jimmy and his magic shit." As if Jimmy's dabbling in the occult had anything to do with this child's death. A knee-jerk reaction maybe from Bonzo, but the dark clouds of bad karma seemed to be rolling in for them. The ultimate tragedy for any parent is to bury a child, and I believe Robert never really recovered from it.

CYNTHIA SACH   Elvis sent a wreath for the funeral. Colonel Parker rang and wanted to know where to send it.

GYL CORRIGAN-DEVLIN (friend of Robert Plant)   Robert will be the first to tell you he sat on a barstool with a bottle of Jack Daniel's. As tough as his exterior is, he's quite a softie underneath it all. And I think that's when everything started to fall apart with Maureen.

CHRIS WELCH (writer for *Melody Maker*)   You tended to skate around subjects like Oakland and Karac's death. You were frightened to ask. I did once ask Jimmy about the issue of "bad karma," and he got really uptight about it. He said, "We're just musicians making music."

RICHARD COLE   After Karac died, I thought, "What the fuck am I gonna do with myself?" I hadn't been doing heroin on the '77 tour. My problem became a real problem when the tour finished.

DENNIS SHEEHAN   I didn't see Richard for many years after Led Zeppelin. When I did see him, he was walking up from the Sunset Marquis to Sunset Boulevard, and I was walking down. I was quite surprised because he looked very healthy, and I said, "Richard, I'm glad you're alive." He probably didn't know all the instances where he'd been almost at death's door and where I'd stopped him from going overboard.

When I said good-bye to him, he said, "Dennis, did you learn anything from me?" And I said, "Richard, I learned how *not* to do it."

23

Polar Opposites

> Powerless the fabled sat, too smug to lift a hand/Towards
> the foe that threatened from the deep . . .
>
> Robert Plant, lyric from "Carouselambra"
> (*In Through the Out Door*)

JOHN PAUL JONES   Robert was wondering whether it was worth it after the grief. I suppose we were questioning things.

ROBERT PLANT   Led Zeppelin had gone through two or three really big changes. The whole beauty and lightness of 1970 had turned into neurosis. It was like a very big tackle from Vinnie Jones—bang! And then you had to pick yourself up.

My own condition and my family had suffered quite a bit. I'd lost my son, and at that time I found that the excesses surrounding the group were such that nobody knew where anyone was. The 1977 tour ended because I lost my boy, but it had also ended before it ended, really. It was just a mess. Where was the actual axis of all this stuff? Who do I go to if it's really bad for me? There was nobody. Everybody was insular, developing their own worlds.

DENNIS SHEEHAN (assitant to Robert Plant on 1977 U.S. tour)   I think I saw Robert about five or six times in the months after Karac died. I went up to Jennings Farm and also to Wales. At that point, he had no inclination to ever want to do anything again.

ROBERT PLANT   When I came back to my family, I received a lot of support from Bonzo, but I went through the mill because the media turned on the whole thing and made it even worse. I had to look after my family, and at that time—as we regrouped—I applied to take a job at a teacher training college in Forest Row in Sussex, the Rudolf Steiner Centre. I wanted to get out of it.

I was heading off up this path where I couldn't hack it anymore because I didn't know where anybody was. And then Bonzo came over and worked on me a few times with a bottle of gin and was very funny. Because he and I had a history that went so far back, it was wonderful. He said, "Come on, we're all going to go down to Clearwell Castle to try and do some writing."

PETER GRANT   Robert kept saying he'd do it, and then he'd back down. But Bonzo was a tower of strength. We had a meeting in the Royal Garden Hotel, and they started talking about Bad Company and Maggie and all that, with their Swan Song hats on, and I said, "What the fuck are you talking about? You should worry about your *own* careers!"

JOHN PAUL JONES   Getting back together at Clearwell was a bit odd. I didn't really feel comfortable. I remember asking, "Why are we doing this?" We were not in good shape, mentally or health-wise. Perhaps nobody was strong enough to stop it—including our manager, who wasn't that well himself.

JIMMY PAGE   Someone approached me saying that Abba had this studio called Polar and were desperate to get an international band to play in there. Plus, they'd give us three weeks' studio time for free. We went over there, and it was bitterly cold and snowing, and we were commuting from the hotel to the studio. We did have quite a few numbers that had been routined, and we rehearsed those in north London, but things still came up in the studio.

JOHN PAUL JONES   Robert and I were getting a bit closer—and probably splitting from the other two, in a way. We were always to be found over a pint somewhere, thinking, "What are we *doing*?" And that went into *In Through the Out Door*. Basically, we wrote the album, just the two of us. I'd got a brand-new instrument as well, the Yamaha GX1—"the Dream Machine"—which was inspiring me. And suddenly, there was no one else to play with. Bonzo turned up next, and we had it all worked out by the time Jim turned up.

JIMMY PAGE   Jonesy hadn't really come up with anything on *Presence*, and he was to be encouraged. The Dream Machine really inspired him to come up with some things.

BENJI LeFEVRE (Zeppelin sound technician)   On the fourth floor of the Sheraton we had four suites, one in each corner for each member of the group. Then there was me, Rex King, and Andy Leadbetter, who looked after the Dream Machine. The band decided they were going to work Tuesday, Wednesday, and Thursday and go home at weekends. They kept the suites on over the weekend, so me and Rex had the run of the hotel, with birds in every suite.

We'd waltz over to Atlantic's office in Stockholm and say, "Oh, we need another five grand for expenses." It was never a problem, but at the end we had to try and account for *tens of thousands of pounds*! I went to Robert and said, "Look, we've been scoring for Jimmy and Bonzo and this and that. Joan's going to be saying, 'Where's all the money gone?'" He said, "Oh, don't worry, just write up something for fish and chips." So I got a piece of paper and wrote, "Giggle and Spend Ltd: Fish and Chips, $25,000." And Robert signed it.

ROBERT PLANT   Jonesy and I, who had never really gravitated toward each other at all, started to get on well. It was kind of odd, but it gave the whole thing a different feel: things like "All My Love" and "I'm Gonna Crawl." We weren't going to make another "Communication Breakdown," but I thought "In the Evening" was really good. Parts of "Carouselambra" were really good, especially the darker minor dirges that Pagey developed. I rue it now because the lyrics on "Carouselambra" were *about* that environment and that situation. The whole story of

Led Zeppelin in its later years is in that song, and I can't even hear the words.

BENJI LeFEVRE　The engineer, Leif Mases, was a great guy. Initially, I felt he was a bit out of his depth, because he was so used to being part of the Abba machine. Polar was a fantastic facility, but the fire alarm was a bit dodgy. One time Bonzo was laying down a groove, and the alarm went off, and all these firemen burst in. He looked up at them and just carried on playing.

Jonesy had this fantastic new toy, and because this machine made fantastic noises, Robert suddenly became interested again and thought it might be a new departure. It was like, "Is this where we can turn things around a bit and move forward in a different direction?" Which is something he's always looked at, right through his solo career. So, creatively, there was a shift in the balance of power, and I think that gave Jonesy the confidence to do what he's done since.

Whether it was *better* or not, who knows; it was certainly different. I'm guessing Jimmy tried to re-exert his influence over it and sucked Leif in, because Leif ended up working for him at Sol Studios.

SAM AIZER (artist relations at Swan Song in the U.S.)　They could have had a number one with "All My Love" if they had released it as a single, because it was the most-played record on the radio.

ROSS HALFIN (photographer and friend of Page's)　I would say that Jimmy is embarrassed by *In Through the Out Door*. He hated "All My Love," but because it was about Karac, he couldn't criticize it.

JIMMY PAGE　It's a bit scary because it looks like I'm moving into the '80s, and we all know what happened in the '80s—absolutely horrendous. Maybe we would have come to our senses, sooner or later.

ROBERT PLANT　I love "Wearing and Tearing," which Page and I wrote together. We were so pissed off with the whole punk thing saying, "What do those rich bastards know?" First of all, we knew that we didn't have *that* much dough. Secondly, we knew more about psychobilly and the psychotic side of Hasil Adkins than they did.

RICHARD COLE We'd leave Stockholm, and something completely different would have turned up in the studio on a Monday. Jimmy may have had the same Neve desk at home, but all I know is when the stuff came back after the weekend, you wouldn't even recognize it.

AUBREY POWELL (designer of *In Through the Out Door* cover) Peter said to me, "We could put the album in a brown paper bag, and it would fucking sell." I said, "Peter, what a great idea." Atlantic didn't want the aggravation, but Peter said, "We're fucking *doin'* it." *In Through the Out Door* ended up having six different covers.

MITCHELL FOX (Swan Song, U.S.) Steve [Weiss], Shelley [Kaye], and I went over to Atlantic and played the record to Ahmet and Jerry Greenberg. I was certainly aware that delivering a new Zeppelin record to Atlantic and WEA was a very big thing. And when I pushed play and "In the Evening" came off that tape machine, you just saw everybody light up. It went on to debut at No. 1, with eight other catalogue albums entering the Top 100. That meant that Zeppelin owned 10 percent of the chart.

ROBERT PLANT Nineteen seventy-nine dawned with the album done. There was something going on, and it was lifting again. We decided that we could work, and we should start all over again. It was agreed that we should play in England.

SAM AIZER I was in England when Logan Plant was born, and that was a very joyous day. Benji came down, and Peter was there telling jokes.

DAVE LEWIS (editor of Zeppelin fanzine *Tight but Loose*) Peter told me, "Look, if we're coming back, we need to do the biggest fucking thing there is. If it's Knebworth, then we do Knebworth." That year I think the Who did the Hammersmith Odeon and the Rainbow, and Zeppelin could have easily done that. Instead of doing two Knebworths, they'd have been better off doing one Knebworth and then a week at the Rainbow. They'd have got their audience back.

JACK CALMES (Showco lighting and sound) After Peter and I did the Knebworth deal, he invited me out to Horselunges. I think he really wanted to have a friendly relationship. We'd sit there and talk for a while, and then he'd drift off and disappear. Then he finally just drifted off, and I took the car back the next morning.

RICHARD COLE I'd flown over to Copenhagen for the Knebworth warm-ups. I had their money for drugs, because Jimmy and Bonzo and I needed the fucking gear. My dealer was in the next room in the hotel, and when I was pulled about it in this big meeting that Robert called, Jimmy said he knew nothing about it. Bonzo said, "Don't be so fucking stupid. If there's no gear, there's no show!" And Peter knew what was going on: he sort of winked at me as if to say, "Don't worry about it."

PHIL CARLO (roadie for Bad Company) If you didn't know that Bonzo was dabbling, you'd never have noticed. With Jimmy, it was quite obvious. Bonzo was a big, robust, rambunctious person, whereas Jimmy was always nodding off.

ROBERT PLANT When you love somebody, you're prepared to take any amount of excuses. So long as it doesn't really do that much damage, you tend to put up with it.

SAM AIZER Robert is watching it right in front of him and praying to God nothing crazy will happen. He's already taken a hit-and-a-half losing his boy, and he's coming back from that, and now he sees Bonzo out of control. He must have thought, "What the hell is going *on* here?"

JOHN PAUL JONES Robert didn't want to do Knebworth, and I could understand why. But we really *did* want to do it, and we thought he'd enjoy it if he did it . . . if we could just get him back out there.

GARY CARNES (lighting technician at Knebworth shows) It was on the 1979 shows that I actually got close to the band, because we rehearsed for Knebworth for a whole month. Page used to walk into rehearsals with this big box of Popsicles and give us each one. We would say to each other, "Wow, he used to spit on us, and now he's handing out Popsicles."

They booked themselves into these shows in Denmark under a different name, some off-the-wall name like Jimmy and the Blackheads.

There we were, loading all this gear into the venue for a band nobody had heard of. People were coming up to me and saying, "Who *is* this band?" And everybody kept their mouth shut because they didn't want the wrath of Peter Grant on their heads.

The band members were nervous and scared because they hadn't played in front of anyone for a long, long time. On the first show, there were only about sixty to eighty people there, and they all went *nuts*. Of course, the next night, in Copenhagen, was out of control.

ROBERT PLANT During the preparations for Knebworth we were really very nervous, but the great thing that happened was that it did bring us back together.

TOM FRY (assistant to promoter Freddy Bannister on Zeppelin's Knebworth shows) Freddy advertised in the newspapers for somebody to help him with the Knebworth Festival. A flatmate of mine got the job, and they needed somebody else as well. So we went along, and our initial job in those predigital times was to send tickets in the stamp-addressed envelopes.

Peter Grant was this big ogre at the end of the phone somewhere. I remember one day picking up the phone and saying, "Hold on a minute," and flinging this phone down and coming back to it three minutes later, saying, "Sorry, I forgot you." "It's Peter Grant." "Oh, I'm sorry." He said, "Doesn't matter at all." I do think that with many of these monsters, it's actually the people who surround them who create a lot of the fear.

AUBREY POWELL For the program photos, I arranged for a stripper to try and lighten the mood a little. Bonzo turned up and looked dreadful: he was bloated and fat and sweating and belching, with a bottle of Pepto-Bismol in his pocket.

GARY CARNES The night before Knebworth, Mick Hinton had bought an ounce of blow and was chopping some of it up on the end of a wooden bench. Bonham came in without Mick seeing him and went "Shhh" to us. He jumped on one end of the bench, so all the coke went flying up all over the room.

BENJI LeFEVRE   For the sound check, Bonzo asked Jason to get behind the drums and came to the mix tower to hear what it sounded like. He said to me, "Fucking hell, man, I've never heard it like this. It sounds amazing." That's the problem for most musicians: they never really get to hear themselves.

ROBERT PLANT   As we got to Knebworth, it was dumbfounding to see that people had bought 220,000 tickets for the first night. Freddy, who'd booked me in the Town Hall in Stourbridge for eight quid, was going, "I say, Robert, I think you've made a bit of a killing here." In some ways, it was a shambles, and in other ways I think I was a bit embarrassed about how big it was.

JIMMY PAGE   I didn't feel very happy at all, and I wasn't well on the second weekend. For me, it was that thing of getting families in position. My parents had split up, and they both had different families, so one was coming one weekend and the other the next. It was fantastic,

Grant with Plant and Jones in the VIP enclosure at Knebworth, August 4, 1979. (Ian Cook/Time & Life Pictures/Getty Images)

though, the reality of it: coming in by helicopter, you could see this huge sea of people. It was astonishing.

HELEN GRANT (daughter of Peter Grant)   Dad had a VIP enclosure and a liggers' enclosure. Anybody that looked a bit suspect, it was like, "Oh, get 'er in the liggers' tent."

TONY MANDICH (artist relations manager in Atlantic's L.A. office) They said, "Don't compare this to L.A. backstage." There was nobody there. It was family members and a few kids running around, and that was it.

ROSS HALFIN   I went with [photographer] Chalkie Davies, and I remember we climbed the scaffolding by the stage and found ourselves on the video ramp. And this big security guy threatened us, so we said, "Oh, Peter Grant said we could come up here," so we were able to stay.

There was a real malevolence about things backstage, whereas previously you'd been able to wander around and take pictures of anyone. That was the first time I'd encountered that kind of *heaviness*. We eventually ran into BP Fallon, who was out of his brains on speed, and he marched us through the security into the dressing room.

Zeppelin were totally personable. They posed for us and everything. I was shocked, because I expected them to be a bunch of cunts. But all the people *around* them were cunts, absolutely fucking horrible. You couldn't work out whether it came from the band or from Grant. My experience with bands is that it always comes from the artist, no matter how much they dress it up. They *want* that, even if they don't admit it.

DEBBIE BONHAM (sister of John Bonham)   John had come 'round to the house and said they were going to do this big show. I said, "Oh fantastic, I can't wait to see it." He said, "You know what, I don't think you should come to this one, because it's outdoors, and I don't really want family there. We've got some indoor shows coming up, and you can come to *them*." I just looked at him and said, "No, I'm *coming*." I remember thinking, funnily enough, that if I didn't see him then, I wouldn't see him play again.

I got there, and I tried to get in backstage. I told the guy I was John Bonham's sister and he said, "Oh yeah? Where's your pass?" And then it got quite frantic because I didn't let it go, and he threw me against the fence. At that point, Richard Cole came out and said, "It's Bonzo's sister! Let her in!" John came round the corner and he just saw me, and he ran and picked me up in the air, and I burst into tears. And he hugged me and held me for ages, and then he put me down and said, "What did I say to you about not coming?"

TOM FRY The interesting thing to a young punk rocker was that Led Zeppelin were on the banned list. I seem to remember they were all in white, with white light hitting the stage, and we were a long way back because we'd been in the enclosure, but then they came on, and they were terribly impressive, even to someone who was programmed to loathe them. It was an extraordinarily powerful, professional, compelling, can't-take-your-eyes-off-it show. My feeling was that they played too long, and the show got sort of diluted a bit. But the first half hour was just sensationally good.

JOHN PAUL JONES The biggest lie ever told about Zeppelin is the whole dinosaur thing—that we were musically bloated or pretentious. We were *never* pretentious.

ROSS HALFIN I didn't see Led Zeppelin as dinosaurs at that point. It was *Plant* onstage who was always making snide remarks, like, "Are we gonna do the dinosaur rock?" He kept making all these sorts of digs at the punk thing, which is what he always does when it's something he's jealous of. I don't think they were even disliked, particularly, 'cause I've got pictures of Mick Jones, Chrissie Hynde, and Paul Cook backstage at Knebworth—they were all there.

But Zeppelin had, in a sense, *become* elitist and lost touch with their audience, whereas Pink Floyd never *were* in touch with their audience but were accepted nonetheless. That was one of the sad things about Zeppelin, that they'd become this sort of steamrolling giant. I don't know if they would even have survived the '80s.

PETER GRANT Do you remember at Knebworth, [Robert] sang the wrong words in "Stairway"? Unforgivable, really. He was in a difficult frame of mind. And then there was all that speech onstage: "We're never going to Texas anymore . . . but we will go to Manchester," and all that, and as he's saying it he's eyeing me out at the side of the stage.

ROBERT PLANT I watched Knebworth on *DVD* and thought, "That was a shit gig, and I know how good we had been and how good we could be, and we were so nervous." And yet within it all, my old pal Bonzo was right down in a pocket. I'd thought he was speeding up, but I must have been so nervous myself that every single blemish or twist that was a little bit away from what I expected was making me hyper.

If you listen to "Achilles Last Stand"—from all that had gone on and all that had gone wrong—it was absolutely spectacular. At the end, I don't know whether I was breathing a sigh of relief because we'd got to the end of the show in one piece without anything going wrong, or because we'd actually bought some more time to keep going.

UNITY MacLEAN (manager of Swan Song office in the U.K.)   On the day of the second gig, Peter decided he wanted more money. So Freddy's running around having kittens, shouting, "Where's Peter? Where's Peter?" Well, Peter had gone to ground. He'd presented his fait accompli: "I want more money, or the boys aren't going onstage."

TOM FRY The problems happened between the two gigs that were on consecutive Saturdays. Zeppelin were on a cut of the take and were asking to be paid in cash.

Freddy wasn't thrilled about this arrangement. It took place in his house at night with the curtains closed, because I remember coming in the following morning and him being very shaken up. Zeppelin's management had arrived, and Freddy was up there, and they had £300,000 in cash. It was 1979, so it was a hell of a lot of money.

Doubt was expressed by Zeppelin's management company about whether this did legitimately fulfill the percentage arrangement or whatever it was of the total box office. Freddy always gave the impression that he was scrupulously honest and said, "How dare he doubt it!" They said, "Well, we've flown a helicopter over the site on the first week, and we've counted 120,000 people, and you're saying it's only 95,000 or whatever the figures were." Freddy said, "Well, I'm not 100 percent sure."

They then began to make threats and said they wanted to take control of the box office for the rest of the second show. The impression I got was that Freddy was initially quite resistant to this, and they then pointed out gently that several people had died on their American tour in suspicious circumstances, and they wished to remind him that they did have friends on the East Coast of America. Freddy said, "My lawyer is in the room, and you're saying this! What on earth are you suggesting?" He was clearly was very shaken and deeply offended.

On the Tuesday, I think, we came in, and Freddy was in this fretful state about this meeting. He said, "They're basically going to take control of the box office, and we've got to start to counsel some grievances because this is going to cost us a fortune."

By the Wednesday or Thursday of that week, Freddy had given up the ghost—like, "If they want the tickets, they can have the fucking tickets." He asked me to take them up to the site for him. He said, "This is John." John was about six foot six and an SAS [Special Air Service] sort of bloke, who said, "I'll be driving you up, and I'll be accompanying you for this mission." I was nineteen or twenty years old and said, "Great"—me and my kind of Rug Rat impersonation of Mick Jones's haircut, with light green trousers and winkle pickers.

We put what must have been about £30,000 to £40,000 worth of tickets into the back of this car and drove up to the site, where I'd been told to go up to the Zeppelin management tent. This guy came out who'd walked straight off the set of *Mean Streets*. It was as cartoony as that. The crowds parted, and this small guy in tinted shades—about five foot three, with nicely parted hair and beige slacks—said, "Tom, is it? Nice to be doin' bidness with you. I believe you have a consignment for us." I said, "This is John." He said, "Yeah, this is Billy." So he had one, too.

The guy said, "Shall we go somewhere?" So we brought these tickets out of the car. We went to a café and sat down in a trailer, and I lifted out the tickets and put them on the table. Billy was assigned to count them, and he picked up a book of tickets—"One, two, three, four . . ." I said, "Can we accept that there are five hundred in each book?" He said, "Tom, you're a man of honor. Of course we will accept that.

The interesting thing is that the mob had always tended to be involved with mediocre artists like Tommy James or Lloyd Price and Larry Williams, but somehow they'd got their claws into Led Zeppelin. You're really gearing up when you're dealing with these guys. I think Peter was getting out of his depth. It was a bit of a date with the devil.

UNITY MacLEAN My husband reckons Commander Cody and Todd Rundgren never got paid. As for the New Barbarians, they couldn't get Keith Richards out of the limo because he was so out of it. And then when they got him onstage, they couldn't get him *off* it.

TOM FRY The Barbarians wouldn't come on and sat in their dressing room. Word got out that they'd been told by Peter not to go on until they were paid. I think in the end it must have been Peter who paid them, because Freddy said, "I'm not paying."

BENJI LeFEVRE There was a huge political thing going down with the New Barbarians. It was like, "We are Led Zeppelin, and you *may* play on our bill." Jimmy never even came out to say hello to Keith and Ronnie.

TOM FRY I went back the following week to tie up loose ends, and Freddy had had enough and said, "God, I thought it was difficult working with the Stones until I came up against this lot." Freddy rarely promoted stuff after that. It was a thoroughly unpleasant experience for him.

CAROLINE BOUCHER (writer for *Disc and Music Echo*) Freddy's house was a huge former embassy. He bought it for not much and spent a fortune on it. He was going to make a shed load of money on this building, and the decorator was in there putting the last gold leaf touches to something when a team of people burst through the door, ran to the top of the house, and spray-painted it black from top to bottom and ran out again. Everybody went, "Oh, Peter Grant."

• • •

ALAN CALLAN (president of Swan Song in the U.K., 1977–1980)   I remember thinking, "I'm working too hard and taking too many drugs, and so is everybody else. I'm not finding the fulfillment in the nature of the artists that I'd like to achieve." There were too many fights going on, and there were too many drugs around, and what they really needed to do was figure out whether they could rebuild themselves as a band. Until they did that, it was always going to be, "Well, call me tomorrow."

I said to Peter, "I don't think this is going to work anymore." I don't think he even *heard* me. Some months later, I bumped into Storm Thorgesen, and he said, "Where've you been?" And I said, "Oh, just around. Why?" He said, "Well, I was at Swan Song last week, and Peter wants to know why you haven't been in the office."

RICHARD COLE   Ray Washburn sent me 'round to the office to get Alan Callan's company car. That was how we found out Alan had gone.

SAM AIZER   Boy, did Alan get eaten up alive. *Abe Hoch* got eaten up alive. There was no chance. Would Bad Company have been as huge if they'd been on Columbia? Yes. They had great songs, a great band, they had Rodgers, who was the best singer going. But none of the other bands happened.

Look, Led Zeppelin was a huge band: this was a full-time operation *all the time*. They would sign bands, but it was just a vanity thing. And yet it was the most powerful label at Atlantic. If we blinked, they said, "What do you need?" We want a full page, they give you a full page. But the other bands really didn't have a chance.

I'm sure if they'd signed Roy Harper that Robert would have been involved. But it was hard enough just to keep them physically together as people in England. Think about trying to schedule tours and merchandising and this and that. Who's going to do that? Not Peter. Peter got iller and iller and iller.

I left in the middle of 1980. I wrote them all letters, saying, "I've been offered a job on Wall Street by my brother." I said, "If you guys are going to work, I'll stay. If you're going to sign bands, I'll stay." I don't think anyone even read the letter.

DON MURFET (head of security for Zeppelin in the late '70s) Paul McCartney's company, MPL Communications, hired us to provide men to handle the overall security at a very prestigious award ceremony that the Guinness Book of Records was holding at Les Ambassadeurs off Park Lane. I was just checking out the members of Pink Floyd when one of my men said there was a call for me upstairs. At the reception desk, I found out the call was from Ray Washburn—and it wasn't the best of news. They'd just found one of Jimmy's guests dead at Plumpton Place.

I arrived at the same time as the police. Obviously, that was because they'd been called out by the ambulance crew—which is standard procedure. Their presence meant that I couldn't "clear up" the way I'd have liked to. All I could do was confine their investigations to the guest room where the guy—whose name I later found out was Richard Churchill-Hale—had popped his clogs.

KEITH ALTHAM (writer for *NME* and other publications) Phil Carson and Ahmet Ertegun drove down to Horselunges for Warren's fourteenth birthday party. Ahmet asked Phil what he should buy for Warren, and Phil said he thought he was into archery. So Ahmet bought Warren a crossbow. Eventually they get to the house, and it transpires that Peter has been winched out of his bedroom for the first time in two years. Ahmet tells Peter he's bought Warren a crossbow, and Peter goes, "That's really nice of you, Ahmet, but you won't spoil my surprise, will you?" Ahmet asks what the surprise is. "I've got 'im an 'arley Davidson."

AUBREY POWELL Peter asked me to film this helicopter that was bringing in the bike, which Barry Sheene had given him. But then the helicopter came over the house with a chain hanging from it and no bike on the end.

You could feel the shudder that went 'round everybody. Richard and Ray were there and, I think, Bindon. The helicopter landed on the front lawn at Horselunges, and you could see Peter's face was dark. He sent Warren away.

The pilot got out and came into the house: "I'm terribly sorry, Mr. Grant, but the chain broke, and the bike is in a field about three miles away." The guy said he would have to sort it out with the insurance company. Peter said, "Forget that, you're not leaving here. I want you to call your boss and have him bring me £5000 in cash right now for the bike." The guy said he couldn't leave the helicopter, so Peter told Richard to go and dismantle it.

The pilot was freaking out. He called his boss and then came back in and said it was all settled. Peter sat there and looked at him and said, "What does it feel like to be called a fucking liar?" You could see the pilot was sweating and very nervous. Peter said, "Here's the recording of your conversation with your boss"—because by this time he was so paranoid, he would record every phone conversation he had, even conversations with Ahmet. The guy had told the pilot to get the fuck out of there.

Peter said, "You go to your boss and say if I don't get five thousand pounds this afternoon, the helicopter doesn't leave." He then turned around to me and said, "Call Barry Sheene and get another bike." I was like, "I don't *know* Barry Sheene." Suddenly, I was part of the whole equation, phoning Australia, trying to get hold of Barry Sheene! I didn't leave till four in the morning, and Peter was *still* raving and groaning.

BENJI LeFEVRE Steve Weiss came over for some apparently unbelievably important meeting, and G just wouldn't come up to London to talk to him. Limos were sent. *Helicopters* were sent. Eventually *I* was asked to go and talk to him, and I got there, and I asked Ray Washburn where he was. He said, "He's out by the moat." I found G sitting on a wooden bench with a shotgun, going, "I know that fuckin' pike's in there, Benj . . . I'm gonna 'ave him."

I said, "What about Steve Weiss?" He said, "Fuck Weiss, I've gotta get this pike." Ray said he'd been there for three days.

24

Dinosaurs Rule!

I tell you, if this band ever drops from favor with the public,
a load of people are going to come down on our asses so
fucking hard. They're just waiting for us to drop.

—John Paul Jones, 1977

BENJI LEFEVRE (Zeppelin sound technician)   The idea that everyone
was in a good place before the Tour Over Europe is not quite how I
remember it. The issue of the drug use certainly hadn't gone away.
Promises had been made, but people thought they could get away with
certain things.

UNITY MACLEAN (manager of Swan Song office in the U.K.)   Richard
had got himself into an awful lot of scrapes, so it probably was best
that he was on time out: "Go and sit in the corner for a bit and chill."

PETER GRANT   I'd paid for the doctor's visits and all that, and it just wasn't
getting better. [Richard] had a massive problem, so I thought the only way
to shake him up was to blow him out. I told him I wouldn't want him in
Europe, and he says, "You can't do it without me." I said, "Well, we've got
to." He was shattered and spoke to Jimmy, but I made the decision.

PHIL CARSON (head of Atlantic Records in Europe) Richard was really a good-hearted individual, and he got completely screwed over by Peter at a certain moment.

RICHARD COLE Robert was the one who finally drove Peter to get rid of me. Whether he thought I was the bad influence on the others I don't know, but I was easier to get rid of than Pagey or Bonzo. Him *and* Jonesy were getting pissed off. They'd had their fill of the fucking chaos when they were making *In Through the Out Door.*

ROBERT PLANT Richard Cole, over the years, had shown deep frustration at not being in a position to have any authority at all. He was tour manager, and he had a problem [that] could have been easily solved if he'd been given something intelligent to do, rather than check the hotels, and I think it embittered him greatly. He became progressively unreliable and, sadly, became a millstone around the neck of the group.

MARILYN COLE (ex-wife of Richard Cole) Richard was in jail, and there was always a question mark about whether he'd been set up. He was a liability, because he knew everything. Nobody went to rehab or 12-step programs. There was so much madness going on, plus all those crooked maniacal lawyers in the States making millions. Peter had pretty much lost the plot at that point.

PETER GRANT We did the Europe tour, but before it, we had this big meet down at [Horselunges] that went on all night. But all the others said it was down to me to get Robert to agree to go back to the States.

BENJI LeFEVRE Robert was coerced back into it, and he almost laid down the conditions under which he agreed to do it. It was, "Let's just play our songs. Do we *really* have to have a half-an-hour guitar solo?" It was an attempt to acknowledge the passing of time and the fact that they needed to get out of the starting blocks in a slightly different way. The whole European outing was a tester to see if it would work in America—to see if they could stand each other.

PHIL CARSON On that last tour, Harvey Goldsmith—who was promoting it—just could not get Peter on the phone. Jimmy and

Robert said, "You've got to help, Phil." So I drove down to Horselunges, and eventually I got summoned up to the bedroom, and I said, "Look, you've got to talk to Harvey so he can book the halls," because the juggernaut was starting to roll, and Harvey was getting very nervous.

Peter goes, "'Ere, I understand you do an impersonation of me." I said, "Wherever would you have heard that?" He goes, "Don't gimme that. You fucking call Harvey and say you're me." I ended up negotiating the whole deal with Peter sitting three feet away from me. It wasn't till years later that we told Harvey.

PHIL CARLO (road manager for Zeppelin's 1980 Tour over Europe)   Richard had got locked up in Italy, and Peter phoned me one day and said, "Get a train to Eastbourne, and I'll pick you up at the station." I thought, "Fucking hell! What have I done?" So I got there, and he picked me up in his black Porsche, registration BAD 1—which Bad Company had bought him—and whizzed me off to Horselunges.

He said, "How do you fancy being Zeppelin's tour manager? Richard's not around, and the lads want to do things in a completely different way to previous tours." I remember my exact reply was, "I'll do my best." He said, "That's not fucking good enough. Can you do the job?" He said I would have plenty of help: "You won't just be dumped. You'll have Harvey, who'll be the coordinator. I'll be there. Carson will be around." So we did a stripped-down, bare-bones European tour, and people absolutely loved it.

SAM AIZER (artist relations, Swan Song in the U.S.)   The last tour they did was a turnaround for them. They were really going to put together a great, great show. They cut the guitar solos, they took the drum solo out. It was two hours, and it was fantastic. Shelley told me that Peter thought it was great.

SHELLEY KAYE (manager of Swan Song office in the U.S.)   In 1980, I hadn't seen them in three years, and I flew over to Brussels. I wound up being with them for a week. We went to Amsterdam and Bremen, and then I flew back to London from Frankfurt. In Amsterdam, I went out on one of the canal boats with Robert and Jonesy. That was a magical day. Everybody was very excited that they were going to come back to the U.S.

HARVEY GOLDSMITH (promoter of Tour over Europe) At that point, Bonzo seemed to be tired. There were no signs that he was giving up the ghost or anything like that, it was just that it was a grueling tour.

DENNIS SHEEHAN (assistant on Tour over Europe) Bonzo sometimes got a little aggressive, and you had to try and calm him down. I knew the soft talk would eventually work. One night in Hamburg he was hungry, and they'd stopped room service at the hotel. So I went out in my station wagon and found him some burgers and fries. When I handed them over, he just bit straight through the greaseproof wrapper. I said, "Bonzo, the wrapper's still on there!" He sort of grunted and said, "Tastes just as good!"

DAVE LEWIS (editor of Zeppelin fanzine *Tight but Loose*) Nineteen eighty was the tour that time forgot. They went on fourteen dates and got *one* review in the U.K. press. Think of that now! That was off the back of Knebworth, which two hundred thousand people had seen. Jimmy didn't really know what to do, and I don't think Peter knew what to do, but they had to keep going. They had to hope that their audience was there.

I know there were a lot of drugs going on, but they'd made some very bad decisions. The Europe tour was done to avoid England, because they were so worried about the press. But they could have done five nights at Hammersmith Odeon and got their audience back.

It was a funny tour that started well and dipped a bit. Bonham collapsed in Nuremberg, but then it went up a bit, and the music was good, and I think they could have gone to America.

RUSTY BRUTSCHE (cofounder of Showco sound and lighting) As I recall, they played well but not fantastic. To me, they never got back to match their peak years of 1971–1975. It was a really short tour, and its purpose was just to get the band playing together again.

DAVE LEWIS Before the show in Cologne, Jimmy came into the foyer of the hotel, and he had this sort of baggy suit on, and the pocket of it was hanging down. I'm talking to him, thinking that someone is going to have to say, "Jimmy, mate, your pocket is hanging out." But no one dared. He was a bit of a mess, and it was a

Plant, Phil Carson, Bonham, and Grant in the lobby of the InterContinental Hotel, Cologne, June 18, 1980. (Tom Locke)

shame. But then when they gelled in Europe, there were great nights. Frankfurt was a great night. It was a good set, a bit leaner and scaled down. They were trying to be a working band. They wanted it to be 1973 again.

JIMMY PAGE   Bonham and I discussed what the next album was going to be—hard-hitting. On the 1980 tour, things were getting quite interesting and hard. Maybe the band would have broken up, I don't know. But what I do know is what was discussed between Bonham and myself was that we really wanted to do that.

JOHN PAUL JONES   It was just coming around again. There was a kind of rebirth. Everybody was trying hard to get it back on course. It had hit a low and was just on its way up again.

SIMON KIRKE (drummer with Bad Company)   I last saw Bonzo onstage in Munich. One of the best nights of my life was being included in Zep's lineup on a second drum kit next to him, playing "Whole Lotta Love" . . . all fifteen minutes of it. It was John's idea and, amazingly, the others in the band agreed. Bonzo's idea of a rehearsal was for me to come to his hotel room. I sat on one bed across from him on the other, and, banging on our knees, he guided me through the complex arrangement. It went like a dream, and the hug he gave me after the gig was something I carried around for a long time.

DAVE LEWIS   When the tour was over, I went to the Swan Song office to take something in. Jimmy was upstairs with Rick Hobbs, his driver. I was there until six o'clock, and Jimmy wasn't going anywhere, by the looks of things. After Unity went home, Rick said, "Do you want to go and see Jimmy?" I said, "Yeah, okay."

So I went up. They had a model of the stage that they were going to use in America. It wasn't going to be massive, because in Europe they hadn't taken a lot, but it was definitely innovative. They were working with Iggy Knight again.

Jimmy was great. No matter how bad he looked, he was very proud that they were going back to America. They were going to do seventeen dates and then go home, then come back and then go home again. And that would have probably worked. So it was all on.

DAVE PEGG (bassist with Fairport Convention)   I heard lots of things through the grapevine, and they worried me to death. You heard stories of monstrous things Bonzo had done, just abusing people and stuff like that. Personally, when I knew John, I never saw that side of him. He was always a real gentleman and would go out of his way to help people, but he did have that dark side. It worried me, and I lost touch with him for a while. I did write him a letter saying, "Please stop drinking." I thought something would happen to him, and he'd have an accident, or somebody would upset him.

TONY IOMMI (guitarist with Black Sabbath)   There was always an accident waiting to happen. I saw John a few times when he'd throw up and then do a line and have another drink.

BENJI LeFEVRE   I just remember Bonzo being very drunk, *most* of the time. Robert would say, "Oh, he's just waffling on and on." He wasn't saying, "I'm really worried about him." It's quite possible that Pat had given John a hard time about going off on tour and getting fucked up again, and maybe subconsciously that was coming through in him.

GLENN HUGHES (ex-member of Deep Purple)   Toward the end, he drank so viciously. There was something eating him so badly. Alcoholism took him out. It isolated him, took him to one side, and fucked him up. The guy was miserable, and it doesn't matter how much fucking money you've got or how many fucking cars you've got, alcoholism will take you out. It was horrible.

PHIL CARLO   I think Zeppelin had hit the crossroads. I don't think it would have lasted much longer. Jimmy and Bonzo were doing heroin. The music was nowhere near as good as it had been. People had to clean their acts up and start writing good songs again. Robert had become Mr. Straight and was pissed off at the others that weren't. He'd get up at nine in the morning and wander around Bewdley and Kidderminster. At ten, he'd want to phone to speak to someone about something and get fobbed off for the second day running because they'd locked themselves away.

ROBERT PLANT   As we drove to the rehearsal, [John] was not quite as happy as he could be. He said, "I've had it with playing drums. Everybody plays better than me." We were driving in the car, and he pulled off the sun visor and threw it out the window as he was talking. He said, "I tell you what, when we get to the rehearsal, *you* play the drums and I'll sing."

MICK HINTON (Bonham's roadie-cum-dogsbody)   We set up in Bray. Come the first rehearsal, Bonzo arrived looking, well, worse for wear. It was the first day, and nobody was too worried, though. He got on the drum stool, fell off it two or three times, and I think Robert said, "Let's call it a day and sort it out tomorrow." In fact, I don't think any rehearsing was done.

BENJI LeFEVRE   Robert, Jonesy, and I were staying at Blake's in London, and we drove to Bray the next morning. I said, "Shall we stop off at Jimmy's and make sure they're up?" We swung round, and Jimmy was sort of wandering about. "Is Bonzo up?" "No." "Where's he sleeping?" "Top of the spiral staircase." I went, "Alright, I'll go tip him out of bed." Jonesy was about five or six steps behind me. We went up the stairs. And there was Bonzo, dead.

JOHN PAUL JONES   I remember after we found him, I came out, and Jimmy and Robert were in the front room, laughing about something. I had to go in and say, "Hold it," and tell them what happened. It was such a shock.

BENJI LeFEVRE   When I came down, Jonesy had gone out to the garden, and Robert was standing there. He made as if to go upstairs, and I said, "Please don't." I got hold of Ray Washburn and said I had to speak to G.

PETER GRANT   Ray said, "Come downstairs." He sat me down, handed me some Valium, and said, "Take these." I said, "Why do I want to take them?" And he said, "Take them." I said, "Tell me what it is." He said, "There's somebody on the phone for you." I said, "What is it?" He said, "John Bonham's died."

DON MURFET (head of security for Zeppelin)   I had to get down to Jimmy's place sharpish. It was down to me to contain the situation, limit the damage—and that probably meant keeping the police and the press at bay. Professionals to the end, Benji and Rex King and Rick Hobbs had already cleaned up, by which they meant that they'd got rid of anything potentially incriminating or embarrassing to the band or John's family.

By the time Peter and Ray arrived and John Bonham had left the building for the last time in the ambulance, the road had filled with reporters, and the mob was growing by the minute, as the circling vultures homed in on the smell of death. The three of us discussed all the angles, analyzed the kinds of problems that might ensue, made contingency plans, and decided how we would box for the next few days. That resolved, Peter and Ray went off to console the boys in the band.

JAAN UHELSZKI (writer for *Creem*)   The fact that they even admitted that Bonham's body had been found at Jimmy's place was amazing to me. You'd think they would have hushed that up.

BENJI LeFEVRE   We then decided that Robert and I should drive as fast as humanly possible to go and tell Pat, because he didn't want it to get out to the media and for her to hear it secondhand. He wanted to be there to hold her hand.

UNITY MacLEAN   I got a call at the office: "Close the office right now."
Why? "Close the office right now and get everybody out. Just do as we
say, and don't ask any questions." I went back to my house, and I got a
call from David Wigg at the *Daily Express*. "Is it true that John Bonham's dead?" Even now as I say it, I go cold. He said, "Unity, I'm so
sorry to break it to you like this. Did they not tell you?" I thought, "You
assholes. Why didn't somebody tell us, so we could grieve in our own
way and not to have to find out from the *Daily Express*?"

MITCHELL FOX (Swan Song, U.S.)   I was sitting at my desk, and we'd
just sold out the first leg of the 1980 tour. I was listening to WNEW,
and that was how we found out. We all congregated in Steve's office,
and there were ten lines on the phone console, all flashing at once. We
just stood there, absolutely stunned, looking at the lights flashing.
Thirty years later, the shock still tears me up.

PHIL CARSON   I got the call from one of the East End plonkers who
worked at Horselunges: "G says you've gotta drop everything and come
down. He's sending an 'elicopter." I spent about thirty-six hours with
him fielding the phone calls and writing the press release.

RICHARD COLE   My lawyer came to visit me in prison. He said, "One
of your band members has died." I said, "Fuck me, not Jimmy." He
said, "No, Bonham." Unity was the only one who wrote to me about it.

UNITY MacLEAN   Peter found out about it and sent one of his heavies
round to the office. The guy said, "You're not to contact Richard Cole
again." I said, "I'm going to contact him, and there's nothing you can
do about it." And the guy said, "If I go back and tell Peter that, there's
gonna be trouble." I said, "You can go back and tell him what you like."
I knew it was something Bonzo would have wanted, because Bonzo
was a big teddy bear and would never have hurt Richard.

BEV BEVAN (drummer with the Electric Light Orchestra)   It was the
most horrible funeral I've been to. The church was absolutely packed
with people. . . . I went with Jeff Lynne and Roy Wood. . . . There was
a lot of absolute weeping and wailing going on. People were just hysterical. Just out of control, sobbing and weeping.

Rushock Parish Church, where Bonham's funeral was held on October 10, 1980. (Art Sperl)

ANDREW HEWKIN (painter and friend of Plant's)　It affected the whole village. It wasn't just the music. It affected Stourbridge and Hagley very much, because he'd died so young.

HARVEY LISBERG (manager of Herman's Hermits and other groups) Peter was terribly cut up about Bonham's death. I'm not even sure whether, by that point, he wasn't closer to him than to any of the others. He was so desperately unhappy that I think he'd built a relationship with Bonham that he didn't have with the others.

PETER GRANT　[Bonzo was] probably the best mate I've ever had in my life . . . yeah, I've seen him wreck hotels—I helped him! But he was always there for the band, he was always there for his family.

ALAN CALLAN (president of Swan Song in the U.K.)　Peter loved those guys like his own children. He tried to anticipate their every need, and I don't think he ever got over the fact that he hadn't anticipated that Bonzo would go crazy that night. I don't think he wanted to do anything but distract himself from the grief he was feeling.

Bonzo's grave in the Rushock church graveyard, March 2010. (Art Sperl)

BENJI LeFEVRE   It was a terrible, terrible, terrible time. Robert asked me to stay at his house because we were able to talk about anything and everything. We used to drink about twelve pints each every night. I became eighteen stone.

ROBERT PLANT   I knew how much Bonzo loved what he did, and I thought it would be terrible to just fob the whole thing off and say, "Well, that's it. We'd better get someone else now so that we can carry on this incredible sort of amoebic carnage game," you know.

PETER GRANT   There was no question of it. Never any thought. The group went off to Jersey and made their mind up. We met in the Savoy, and I said, "It can't be." It wasn't a case of sitting down and, "What do you think we should do?" It was "Bang!" That was it.

ROBERT PLANT   Standing there on the street corner, clutching twelve or sixteen years of your life of knowing Bonzo, holding it close to your chest with a lump in your throat and a tear in your eye, and not knowing which way to go, was a most peculiar experience. Apart from anything else, I knew that all of the dream was over, just like that.

PART 4

Wearing and Tearing

For Jimmy Page, the '80s were all but a lost decade. Addicted to heroin and then to alcohol, he stumbled through a succession of unwise career choices, from Michael Winner's deadening *Death Wish II* to the sub-Bad-Company stadium sludge of the Firm. Meanwhile, John Paul Jones kept busy with arrangements and productions of no great distinction.

Plant, grieving both his son and his best friend, pulled himself together to commence a career whose initial mission was to distance himself as far as possible from Led Zeppelin. A series of interesting, if overproduced, albums, from 1982's *Pictures at Eleven* to 1988's *Now and Zen*, proved his willingness to experiment with both new influences (including those from the world music he loved) and new technologies. When the three Zeppelin survivors did reunite—at Live Aid in 1985 and at Atlantic's fortieth anniversary in 1988—the results were shambolic and, for Plant, regrettable.

Revisiting Zeppelin's legacy with Page in 1995–1996 was a happier experience for all concerned. The "unledded" North African reworkings of some of the band's best songs were in the main invigorating, however much ill will it provoked from the unforgivably uninvited John Paul Jones. Zeppelin's multi-instrumentalist linchpin, who'd found a new lease on life in arranging for R.E.M. and performing with the terrifying Diamanda Galas, swallowed his bitterness for long enough to rejoin Page and Plant for 2007's triumphant O2 tribute to Atlantic honcho Ahmet Ertegun.

As massively hyped and oversubscribed as the event was, Plant had by this point proved he needed a Zeppelin crutch less than ever. He scored six Grammys and three million sales with *Raising Sand*, a superb Americana collaboration with the divine Alison Krauss that remains by some distance the most successful solo work by a former member of Led Zeppelin.

The more time goes by, the less likely a full-fledged Zeppelin reunion seems. Page and Plant's love-hate relationship aside, the group's former front man appears to feel ever less interest in resting on his laurels. Yet it would take a fool to bet against it happening.

25

Staggering from the Blast

> I think I will go to Kashmir one day, when some great
> change hits me and I have to really go away and think about
> my future as a man, rather than a prancing boy.
>
> —Robert Plant, July 1977

ROBERT PLANT   When Bonzo went, I was thirty-two. Washed up and finished. That's what I thought.

BENJI LeFEVRE (Zeppelin sound technician)   I think all three of the guys realized that it could not be perpetuated. We all went to Jersey, the three of them and Peter and the crew. It was pretty clear that we were there because John wasn't—and that we were all going to go our separate ways.

JIMMY PAGE   After having had all those years of having this total free spirit to everything, to have to sort of clamp it down and compromise at that time of the passing of John didn't seem at all palatable.

PHIL CARLO (road manager on Tour over Europe)   G said to me in the months after Bonzo's death, "Phil, you would not believe how many messages were left on the answer machine within days, asking if they were looking for another drummer." A lot of people went down in my estimation. G said, "I can't fucking believe any of them. When are they going to get the message? This is not about money or anything. That's it. That's the end of it."

DEBBIE BONHAM (sister of John Bonham)   The realization was that they weren't going to do Led Zeppelin anymore. Which I think we all felt great relief about.

DESIREE KIRKE (ex-wife of Simon Kirke)   After Bonzo went, the relationship between Robert and Peter got really strained. *Everything* got really strained.

DAVE LEWIS (editor of *Tight But Loose*)   Jimmy was in a dreadful state. Peter was in a dreadful state. Robert was a changed man, without a doubt, and you couldn't mention Led Zeppelin to him. Led Zeppelin stock fell dramatically. It was gone. In that early 1980–1982 period, it wasn't a very cool thing to be a Zeppelin fan anymore.

JOHN PAUL JONES   I was supposed to be managed by Peter still, but during those first couple of years, it was hard to get hold of him. He wasn't coping very well at all. It was a frustrating time. [*Coda*] seemed to close the book on that chapter. We had a bit of a job finding enough tracks.

PHIL CARSON (head of Atlantic in Europe)   There was a complete void when Zeppelin stopped. Jimmy still wanted to make music, and so did Robert. But neither of them wanted to play *Zeppelin* music. It took three records, I think, before Robert would approach Zeppelin tunes again.

ROBERT PLANT   I cut my hair off, and I never played or listened to a Zeppelin record for two years.

AUBREY POWELL (designer of Zeppelin albums and friend of Plant's)   When Robert went out for the first time after Zeppelin, I think he felt the first taste of freedom in a very long time. He was able to express himself without his old partner. And Jimmy was hurt by it because Robert wouldn't go back and re-form Led Zeppelin.

BENJI LeFEVRE   I was living in the barn across from the house above Robert's snooker room. With the Queen's Head football team, we would go away annually on these fucking bonkers trips. We would arrange a match on a Sunday morning with a local football club in Penrith or wherever.

The deal was that they should provide us with somewhere to pitch Robert's Moroccan tent—which slept twenty-eight people feet to the pole—and we would do an impromptu gig at the local social club on the Saturday night. It happened about three or four years on the trot. There were these local musicians that had already been kicking about: Andy Sylvester, Robbie Blunt, Wayne the Gasman. We were talking about music, and I said, "Maybe I could put a little studio together for you, and we can have some fun." Andy and Robbie came up and pratted around. We actually pressed up a version of "Little Sister."

That became the original Honeydrippers. We did maybe fifteen or twenty gigs over two or three months, nearly always at weekends because a couple of the guys had regular jobs. Robert's stipulation was that everything had to be north of Watford. I contacted all the promoters and said that if they used Robert's name in the advertising, we wouldn't show up for the gig.

ROY WILLIAMS (live engineer for Plant)   Robert and I used to get together in the Bull and Bladder in Brierley Hill, and that sort of developed into the Honeydrippers thing. I ended up booking all the Honeydrippers' club dates, on the basis that nobody could mention his name, other than inside the club itself.

Robbie Blunt was in the band. Peter Grant was sitting in the background, though he wasn't hands-on managing him, so we had that Zeppelin machinery of sourcing anything in the press. I think the clubs were more than pleased that they got what they got.

ROBBIE BLUNT (Plant's guitarist post-Zeppelin)   Benji put together a little studio at Robert's farm, with a little four-track TEAC, and we just started playing. Andy Sylvester and I did a couple of recordings, and then it went from there. This thing had already started without me, so I just did what I was told. Robert had got all his old tunes that he'd loved and had never had a chance to do. I suppose it was just to play for the pleasure of it and not forget why we'd all started doing this.

ROY WILLIAMS I even booked them into the Keele University ball. The social secretary said, "Who the hell are the *Honeydrippers*?" And I said, "I can't tell you, just trust me on this one." I don't think there was anybody in the room for the first four numbers.

ROBBIE BLUNT Obviously, Robert couldn't just keep doing that. He'd put his toe back in the water, but he said to me, "I'm getting a bit fed up with this." At the last gig in Birmingham, he said he was going to tell the chaps he wanted to jack it in. So I said, "Well, I'm not going to stay with it, either."

ROBERT PLANT The idea that if all else fails, you can go back—that was never in the equation. Led Zeppelin had been incredibly successful, we'd had a lot of fun, spent a lot of money, been in a lot of limousines, half of Peru had already been inhaled, but there was no way to go back to where I'd been before. Best to just do whatever I feel like doing.

ROBBIE BLUNT I said, "Look, just give me a chance to write some stuff with you. That's all I ask." I guess I bullshitted myself up. I don't think I realized the consequences of my actions till later. It wasn't like we had a board meeting to specify what we were going to do; it was just, "Let's play and see what happens organically."

ROBERT PLANT It was so uncomfortable to begin with that I wasn't sure I could handle it. I started getting so many flashbacks of the night Page and I wrote bits of "Stairway to Heaven" or of doing the lyrics of "Trampled Under Foot" or whatever. I found myself getting all these great swirls out of the mist, and at first I couldn't cope. But I got used to it. And once I'd done it once, I realized I could do it a million times.

ROSS HALFIN (photographer and friend of Page's) I remember photographing Robert at Shepperton, and Robbie Blunt was there. I said, "Can we get you with a guitar, Robbie?" And Plant goes, "Why can't he have a *fishing rod*?" There were all these jibes at Page that I didn't realize at the time *were* jibes.

BENJI LeFEVRE It evolved organically through the Honeydrippers thing. It wasn't forced or pushed, it just started to happen. Robert asked me to be his manager, and I said I really couldn't do that.

It got to the point where we decided to do some real rehearsing. Robbie knew this really good bass player, Paul Martinez, and we found a keyboard player called Jezz Woodroffe, whose dad had owned a music shop in Birmingham. Andy Sylvester was very wary of the whole thing.

We ended up at Rockfield studios, in the second house by the river, trying to write some songs. Cozy Powell came down. It was all pretty mad. Robert was starting to put Robert-type pressure on things, but Robbie was okay with it. It all was going very nicely—we're a brotherhood and all that—until it came to the publishing. It had been a complete cooperative, and then Phil Carson and Peter and Joan came in on it. I'm sure Robert was advised this, that, and the other.

PETER GRANT In the early '80s, I was disappointed and hurt by [Benji's] plan to become Robert's manager, which all went wrong in the end. I used to phone up, and I'd never get a return call or any communication. . . . Robert and I did have a bit of a falling-out, and I said the best thing would be for him to manage himself. But you've got to realize Robert always wanted to be the boss of the band anyway. He finally got his own way.

HELEN GRANT (daughter of Peter Grant) Dad got Robert a very, very good deal after the demise of Zeppelin, and, actually, he never made any money out of that. That was a little bit of a fly in the ointment. Robert always said he'd had enough of the whole drug thing with Jimmy and that he didn't want to be around it anymore. But then, Robert's not the angel fucking Gabriel.

PHIL CARLO I never ever heard G say a bad word about Jim, but there were times when he'd go, "That cunt Plant." Robert was the only one who could really piss him off—and did hurt him a couple of times.

ED BICKNELL (former manager of Dire Straits)   I was sitting in my office one morning, trying to become a tycoon, and my secretary buzzes me and says, "There's a bloke in reception who says he's Robert Plant." So Robert comes in, plonks himself down, and says he's looking for a manager.

I go, "Does Peter Grant know you're here?" And he says, "Well, I've written to him." I say, "When?" "About a year ago." I said I didn't want to end up being hung out of a window. We went for lunch in Walton Street, and Robert was extremely personable, very funny, and very, very committed.

We went through this romance, as you do, and I was fully aware he was romancing other people. He decided to go with Tony Smith, which was fine, though eventually he ended up with Bill Curbishley—who was *exactly* the right person for him.

DENNIS SHEEHAN (road manager for U2)   My first tour with U2, I got a call from Benji to say he was at Rockfield with Robert, and would we like to pop in? I didn't tell the lads, in case it didn't happen. I told them instead that we were just going to have a cup of tea at this nice place I knew.

We pulled up to Rockfield, and Benji was standing there. He told me Robert was over at the house up the lane. So just as Bono was waking up next to me in the van, I drove up the lane to the top of the hill, and Robert was standing on the edge of the hill, looking out across the valleys. He turned around toward us, and Bono goes, "Is that Robert Plant?" I said it was. He goes, "Does he come and have his tea here as well?"

ROBBIE BLUNT   A lot of what we achieved would not have happened without Benji. He would take on the responsibilities of three people on the road. When we were doing our pretour rehearsals in Dallas with the Showco personal assistant, Benji put the lights up and just said, "This is not acceptable." He made the entire crew stay there the whole night, take the desk apart, and clean *everything*. That was the type of guy he was. In the studio, he helped me get a lot of my sounds. Indispensable.

ROBERT PLANT   Phil Collins and I were both on the same label, and he'd had some dealings with Carson and mentioned that if I was doing anything, he would love to join as a contributor. He was really very concerned that it should be right. Considering it was a project that he was just visiting, he was a real contributor, and I was very moved by him.

ROBBIE BLUNT Phil didn't have a lot of time, recording-wise. We probably only had him for about five or six days. But we were pretty well rehearsed without him. And then he came out to Las Colinas in Texas. I think he thought it was going to be easier than it actually was.

BENJI LeFEVRE I think Robert controlled his own destiny, but Carson advised him on certain things. It was Carson who put the Es Peranza label together. But the first time any real management figure came in was Tony Smith on the first tour, on the back of Phil Collins saying he'd love to be the drummer. Robert said it's time for a playback, so there was a big playback, and I don't think G was there.

ROBBIE BLUNT *Pictures at Eleven* had four very good components that you could strip down and it would still sound really good.

Plant snogs Phil Collins, New York City, September 12, 1983. (Ron Galella)

There weren't a lot of overdubs, not a lot of padding. Pat Moran was a fabulous engineer and would get me great sounds. We got there in the end, after we'd emerged from our own orifices.

The album was like a melting pot of all these things we'd been involved with in the past. "Fat Lip" was the first thing Jezz and I really put down at Palomino, Robert's place. When we came back the next day, Robert had put this vocal on. It was like, "Where did *that* come from?" I do remember Robert playing us some Arabic or other world music, and for "Slow Dancer" we did try and push it in that direction. But most of the others just came out of the ether.

· · ·

ED BICKNELL   Robert picked up the ball and said, "I've got lots of music in me, and I'm going to go forth." Jimmy, on the other hand, sat with his thumb up his bum and his mind in neutral and waited for Michael Winner to stick his head over the garden wall and say, "I'm filming *Death Wish 90*, and would you like to do the music for it?"

MICHAEL WINNER (director of *Death Wish II*)   I'd lived next door to Jimmy for many years; I'd never seen him, never spoken to him. So I rang up the number, got on to Peter Grant, and actually Peter was very clever because although Jimmy wasn't paid anything . . . what he wanted to do was restore Jimmy back to creativity.

[Jimmy] rang the doorbell, and I thought, "If the wind blows, he'll fall over." He said to me, "I'm going to my studio"—at the time he owned a studio in Cookham, later bought by Chris Rea. He said, "I don't want you anywhere near me, I'm going to do it all on my own."

DAVE NORTHOVER (assistant to Peter Grant post-Zeppelin)   Getting Peter to attend to business was very difficult. When Jimmy did the music for *Death Wish II*, I constantly had to make excuses to Michael, who would say, "What do you *mean*, 'He's not available'?" The excuses got stranger and stranger. One time he rang and said, "Is Peter there, David?" I said, "No, he's gone to . . . the Isle of Wight." "What's he doing in the *Isle of Wight*?" I said, "Well, he goes there and then . . . he flies back in a hang glider." He said, "A *hang* glider? Good God, the man's thirty stone if he's a pound!"

PETER GRANT   We stalled it a bit, but eventually Jimmy came up with the goods. But Michael wasn't happy. He sent some heavy down to my house to get the contract signed, but he was wasting his fucking time doing that. I just left him outside all night.

AHMET ERTEGUN (head of Atlantic Records)   The members of the band and also the members of Bad Company were having trouble getting hold of Peter, and he was beginning to lose control of the musicians he was representing. Every time you called, there was always an excuse. One of the members of Bad Company said to me, "He must the cleanest man in the world, because every time I call he's in the bathtub."

DONOVAN (Scots-born folk-pop singer)   I got to know Jimmy . . . when he lived near Windsor, in the house he bought, twice, from Michael Caine. He was mourning because Bonham had died. I said, "Is that it?" He said, "That's it. No more Zep." He took me down to a cottage. He said, "This is the Guitar Cottage. These are my guitars." And they were all in little cases, maybe three hundred of them. I said, "Can I open one?" He said, "Yeah." I said, "It's in tune, Jimmy!" He said, "They're all in tune." It was Spinal Tap.

DESIREE KIRKE   Jimmy had always had the shroud of mystery around him. It wasn't until later when I became good friends with Charlotte that I started spending more time with them as a family.

   Charlotte and Jimmy really looked after me when I was going through my divorce from Simon, which was very unexpected. I didn't see too much of anyone else during that period, because usually what happens is once the star walks out the door, people forget you. But they were incredibly supportive. Charlotte would say, "Come down and spend the weekend in Windsor," and it became almost like a family thing.

PHIL CARLO   Charlotte used to say to my wife, "I love it when Jimmy's out of it. He's no trouble at all. It's when he's straight that he's a fucking nightmare." We spent one Christmas with them. It was the weirdest Christmas ever. Jimmy is the only man I know that can look sinister in a Christmas hat. We all sat round the table for a haunted Christmas lunch.

JULIE CARLO Charlotte used to ring me at two in the morning, and I'd say, "Jesus Christ, I'm in bed!" She'd say, "Why do you go to bed so early?"

PHIL CARLO Poor old Rick Hobbs—who was camp, to say the least—had the plumbers round at Windsor. And the plumber had an assistant with one of those big pink Mohawks with safety pins and his legs tied up in those funny trousers they used to wear. Charlotte spotted him and screeched from a window on the other side, "Rick, I told you before, I don't want your fucking gay boys round here!" Rick went, "Charlotte, it's the plumber."

When you worked for Jim, if you came out of it alive, you did well. Ray Thomas is dead. There's the guy from Plumpton who died. The doctor took me into his office at Harley Street and said, "I'm going to put my cards on the table: Jimmy'll be dead by Christmas unless you can get hold of him. There's nothing I can do anymore."

26

The Swan Song

Phil Carlo used to send me postcards of old broken-down shacks, with comments on the back saying, "This is where you end up when you work for Led Zeppelin."

—Sally Williams

AHMET ERTEGUN (head of Atlantic Records) [Peter] was a person with a lot of personal problems. As a result, we had a lot of ups and downs, especially in the later years after the group broke up.

PETER GRANT Ahmet was the only one who ever said to me that I mourned too long over John. Maybe he was right.

ED BICKNELL (former manager of Dire Straits) After Bonham died, Peter went into what he called his "black period." He literally pulled up the drawbridge at Horselunges and took cocaine. The house was sort of falling down around him. He had these two brothers who looked after him, and they'd go into the Marks & Spencer in Eastbourne and stock up on sandwiches and jellies for him.

We know you're in there, Peter: piping at the gates of Horselunges. (Art Sperl)

JOHN "JB" BETTIE (dogsbody for Peter Grant at Horselunges) I used to go down to M&S every day and spend fifty or sixty quid on sandwiches and trifles. [The manager] said to me one day, "What do you work at?" And I just didn't have the heart to tell him I was buying it all for one guy, so I told him I worked for a children's home.

HELEN GRANT (daughter of Peter Grant) Dad was alone. A lot of people turned their backs on him. I gave up everything, really, to look after him. I had a very promising dancing career, but I had to get him through it all. He did have people around him, but they weren't his friends. And I used to tell him that. I would drive people out of the house. But then, I wasn't on drugs. When you've got a parent that's like that, it really does turn you the other way. It doesn't make you want to go *near* anything like that.

MARILYN COLE (ex-wife of Richard Cole) We'd sit there with an ounce of coke; it never ran out. He blew *huge* amounts of his fortune on it. I'd be up for a week or more with him there. He used to send a

Roller for me in London; I think he did the same thing with Krissy Wood. He'd always call around 11:00 p.m., knowing that I'd be high by then and be malleable. *"Wot you doin', Marilyn? Fancy comin' dahn? I'll get the champagne in."* And he'd wake up this poor fucking chauffeur at midnight and have him drive me down to Horselunges.

DESIREE KIRKE (ex-wife of Simon Kirke) Jimmy and Peter used to watch *The Night Porter* over and over. The two of them were *obsessed* with Charlotte Rampling in that movie. Then I would watch it with him, and then *Marilyn* would watch it with him.

MARILYN COLE He knew every line. He'd say, "I'm just gonna freeze-frame *this* one!"

DESIREE KIRKE You didn't want to get in his bad books. He could become very vicious if you crossed him. I once upset him with something, and it was like, "The car will be waiting to take you back to London."

MARILYN COLE There was one night there when we'd been up for days; I really felt as if the dark forces had come for me. It was probably cocaine madness, but it felt like one of those archetypal confrontations with the darkness. I tell you what, I wouldn't have wanted to be off my tits up at Boleskine.

DESIREE KIRKE I remember Joan Hudson sitting downstairs, getting cobwebs. She was there for at least twelve hours, and she must have been pretty pissed off. Most people had to wait to see Peter for at least a day and a half. It depended on whether he was sleeping or whether he was just cocooning. He did a lot of business on the phone in his bedroom. But if he didn't want to see anybody, he wouldn't *see* anybody.

BILL CURBISHLEY (manager of the Who) When Grant was really in a bad state, Ahmet did a lot to shore him up and cover his ass. He went to see Grant in his house in England and sat down for twelve hours, but Grant wouldn't come out of the bedroom. Toward the end, it was quite insane, and Ahmet never got that far with him because it all spiraled into madness.

JOHN "JB" BETTIE The house, which was quite fun and bright and breezy, was a bit like a morgue, really, for a while. People were frightened to make any noises. People were whispering, rather than talking. You were, like, walking on eggshells. You didn't know what to say, in case you said the wrong thing and he would take it badly.

ALAN CALLAN (president of Swan Song in the U.K.) The sad thing is that Peter and I had just started talking again about what we could do with Swan Song when John died. And then it really *was* all over.

DAVE LEWIS (editor, *Tight But Loose*) I went into Swan Song a few times after that, and they were dark days. It wasn't a nice place to be. It all fell apart and went grim, and I think we all went grim with it.

SALLY WILLIAMS (ex-girlfriend of Mick Hinton) When it was all over, I was glad I had a day job and people to talk to, other than a bunch of drunken stoned roadies. I left all the madness behind for good when I moved to Canada in 1981.

PHIL CARLO (roadie and assistant to Jimmy Page) When Swan Song went into liquidation, I said, "What happens to *me*?" They said, "You'll get two weeks' wages from the government redundancy fund." I said, "Come on, you're all multimillionaires!" "Yes, but that's nothing to do with us."

SALLY WILLIAMS Phil was very loyal: a good, good person who was treated really badly. None of those guys had any clue about the real world or the sort of salaries they might have been paid.

UNITY MacLEAN (Swan Song in the U.K.) I was pregnant with my son, and I thought, "I'm all done with death. I've got to think of my own future and my own family. If you guys are all hell-bent on death, that's fine." When my son was three months old, Jimmy and Charlotte invited us down to a party at the Old Mill House. It was just a phenomenal party, and we had a wonderful time. Then after that, I said good-bye and good luck and thanks for the memories, I'm off to do something else.

I'd had enough. It was just Cynthia and Sian Meredith left in the office. And in New York it was Shelley, Mitchell, and Steve Weiss.

After that, it was just Joan Hudson, who more or less took over. I think she was led by Steve, but she was a very smart cookie, and she made sure that every penny the band earned, they kept.

SHELLEY KAYE (Swan Song in the U.S.) Things became very problematic at Swan Song. It was literally all the people I had worked with just drowning in a sea of drugs and alcohol. We did other stuff, but really there was nothing going on. And then Atlantic pulled out its backing from Swan Song, and it was done. We moved the office out to a wing of Steve's house on Long Island and worked there. After a while, I couldn't watch it anymore. In 1985, I left Steve. I was done. And once I was gone, it was over. I never talked to Steve again. I decided it was time to get on with my life and grow up.

SAM AIZER (Swan Song in the U.S.) Steve just sat around, waiting for the other shoe to fall. He had plenty of money, though I got the feeling it was never enough. I mean, working out of Steve's house? Who would do *that*? But he turned a personal page in his life. He married Marie, who helped him put his life back together as regards his health, and they moved down to Florida.

I think Steve was always hopeful that Led Zeppelin would get back together. He got very prosperous, because he was able to keep his financial situation with Zeppelin and Bad Company and Swan Song without selling the rights, when they sold *their* rights. When CDs came into play, you're talking about a brand-new revenue stream. If CDs had come out in 1980, before Zeppelin had finished, the band would have made *untold* amounts of money. Unfortunately, they sold a lot of their rights when Steve Weiss didn't. But he went underground. When he died in 2008, I looked for an obituary, and I couldn't see one anywhere.

ALAN CALLAN There was a moment after John's death when the band made an agreement with Atlantic that Steve negotiated. What he never declared was that he was a beneficiary of that deal. He remained a shareholder in the deal but never declared it, so while he appeared to be negotiating on behalf of Peter and the band, he just wanted the deal to go through so he could take his piece out of it.

MAGGIE BELL (Swan Song artist)   I'll never forget the day I walked up to the World's End to the offices, and the door was wide open onto the street. I went up to the first floor and shouted, "Is anybody there?" I went up to the next floor, and there was Mark London's velvet couch and a beautiful big desk. So I went up to the third floor, where Mark had kept all his files and stuff, and there was nothing in there except a leather chair and a little toilet and a kitchen where Dolly used to clean for us.

I heard rustling downstairs, and I went into the toilet and shut the door. I sat on the toilet seat, looking through the keyhole, and people were coming in and taking stuff out. In the toilet, there were four mirrors of all the albums that Zeppelin had ever made. I've still got them. I sat there for fifteen minutes; I was too frightened to go out. They tried to get in the door, but I'd locked it and put my foot against it. They even took the kettle and the toaster.

It was a strange feeling to come into a place that, years before, was so happy. I was the last person to leave that place. They'd taken everything. The carpets, the curtains, everything.

PHIL CARLO   I worked for Peter for a couple of years, just being at Horselunges for a few days a week, talking to G and listening to him. Ray Washburn would be there Monday and Tuesday, and then me and a poor woman called Betty would do the rest of the week between us. I usually ended up doing the weekends, and then Ray would reappear Monday.

The food bill and the heating bill weren't cheap, and the swimming pool would have steam coming off it fifty-two weeks a year. You've got the gardeners, shopping, days locked up in a room with other people—it came to a lot of money. When you've got more staff than Robert and Jim put together, and you're doing a couple of grand's worth of coke a week, that's £100,000 a year. And if you don't bother paying the tax man, and you've got cars lying about the place, I can quite believe that at the end of it, the main part of G's fortune had gone.

• • •

BENJI LeFEVRE (producer for Plant) When we finished Robert's first album, the temptation was to go and play some live dates. But it was decided instead to do a second album, so that when we did perform, there would be no question of using any cover versions or any old Zeppelin stuff.

ROBBIE BLUNT (Plant's guitarist) It was a conscious "No-Zeppelin-Will-Be-Played" agreement, and Robert stuck by that deal. I remember Phil Carson trying to shoehorn it in through the back door. I took Robert to one side and said, "This is not what we were going to do, is it?" And he said no. I don't think Phil liked me very much after that.

BENJI LeFEVRE We spent some time at Roy Harper's house and some time in Ibiza. We got enough material together and went back to Rockfield. I really wanted Robert to do more blues-rock singing, and "Sixes and Sevens" was about as close as it got. He had this bee in his bonnet about wanting to be modern and up-to-date, but I could never get my head round what he meant by that at all. He put pressures on Jezz and pressures on Robbie.

ROBBIE BLUNT At one point, Robert disappeared and came back, and he'd made this video. I think it was Phil Carson's idea. Having the guitarist's face swathed in bandages was to try and stoke up this bloody thing where people thought Robbie Blunt might be Jimmy. When the girls from the New York office came over to England, one of them said to me, "Oh, you really *exist*."

ROBERT PLANT I had the strangest feeling that at the back of everyone's mind was the conviction that—after a few months—Led Zeppelin would re-form, and we could go back to how it was before. They didn't realize how serious I was about it, for better or for worse. Atlantic soon came to realize I was serious, particularly when "Big Log" was a hit. The song they chose, "Other Arms," was a top-requested record for four weeks, but I flatly refused to put it out as a single. I said, "No, I'm not a hard rock artist, I can sing from anywhere."

JOHN OGDEN (pop writer on the *Birmingham Express and Star*) Maureen's sister Shirley had married Johnny Bryant, who was one of the singers in my band Little Acre. Robert came to see us quite a few times, and then he later nicked Shirley off JB. They were a nice couple, Johnny and Shirley, and seemed well matched, and then I suddenly heard she was living with Robert.

DENNIS SHEEHAN (assistant to Plant, subsequently road manager for U2)   When Robert and Maureen were breaking up, he asked if I had a month or so I could give him. Carmen, I think, was fifteen or sixteen and had a friend; Logan was three or four. They were going on holiday to Madeira, and he couldn't go, so I went with Maureen and looked after the kids. When we got back, Robert thanked me. It was only later that I realized he and Maureen had been breaking up. She would have been suffering inwardly.

BENJI LeFEVRE   In Worcestershire, there's Jennings Farm, there's the house he bought for Shirley, and there's *his* house. I call it the Plant Triangle: things go in there and just disappear.

ROBERT PLANT   I was actually having to relearn and expand my gift just to see what I could do alone, because everything had been a four-way decision before, with Jimmy working in close collusion with the engineers or whatever, and everybody having their say. So to be left in that control room, suddenly controlling everything and bluffing a bit, was fantastic. I was flying by the seat of my pants.

BENJI LeFEVRE   We put the tour together, and it was almost like going out with Bad Company again: brand-new territory, and would people come? And they did, and they fucking loved it.

ROBBIE BLUNT   That first tour was the culmination of everything I'd ever hoped and wished for. The first show in Peoria, I suddenly realized what Robert meant to the American public. That was powerful, walking out on that stage. I still get chills thinking about it.

ROBERT PLANT   I walked onstage, and the place just went nuts . . . and I wept. I looked at the microphone, and I looked to my left and my right, and I was the only one there who'd carried this thing, this myth state, to the center of the stage in a new time. There was a huge feeling of loss.

27

Jimmy'll Fix It

I'm past middle age. But what do you do when you get to middle age? There was no one for me to look up to who said, "This is what you do next."

—Jimmy Page, May 1985

ROBERT PLANT I was so attracted to the technological developments that came along in the studio that I became just like any other nerd. Sampling this and fiddling about with that. Countless hours of my life. If I could put them in a row now and subtract them from my current age, I'd probably be around thirty. But we all went through that. Even Neil Young had his electronic moments.

ROBBIE BLUNT (Plant's guitarist) Robert had this guitar synth delivered to my house. When I moaned about having to use it, he said, "Well, Jimmy's getting on fine with *his*." So Benji called Jimmy's guitar tech and came back and said, "He says Jimmy's thrown his one out the fucking window." Trying to overdub with the thing was a bloody nightmare. To add insult to injury, I was invoiced for it.

BENJI LeFEVRE (Plant's producer)   I kept saying to Robert, "I don't understand why you don't do more of the stuff that you're really good at. Why do you insist on trying to be different, at the risk of putting your own nose out of joint?"

ROBBIE BLUNT   Robert said, "We've got to get a drummer." Years before, I'd gone to see Little Feat, and Richie Hayward just blew me away.

BENJI LeFEVRE   Having seen Little Feat all those years before with Robert and loving them to death, I managed to get in touch with Richie and invited him to come and stay at my house. I rented a disused carpet factory in Kidderminster and put the boys to work with Richie. After they'd learned each other's chops a bit, I said to Robert, "I've got a surprise for you, man." It was a cathartic moment, because at last there was someone who *could* fill that role, without it having to be Phil Collins or Cozy Powell or Barriemore Barlow.

ROBBIE BLUNT   The next thing I know, Richie's at John Henry's rehearsal rooms in London. Wayward Hayward—God rest his soul.

BENJI LeFEVRE   We were at Roy Harper's house, rehearsing for *Shaken 'n' Stirred*, and Robert just disappeared to do the Honeydrippers with Ahmet Ertegun. It was like, "Oh. Alright. Thought we were a unit here." Anyway, it happened, and it was a fantastic success, and the time was right for that to happen for him. He'd simply jumped at the chance to have Ahmet produce him, and that was probably very cathartic for him, too.

ROBERT PLANT   It probably took thirteen years of my life before I even had time to listen to Roy Brown or even Big Joe Turner. Especially Joe Turner, because I'd always thought the productions were a bit smooth and the brass parts, the Kansas City hangover, just a little bit hackneyed. But then I started hearing people playing it and adding a little bit of a rock thing to it. When Jeff Beck played guitar over it, it started to have a bit more of a life.

ROBBIE BLUNT   Robert came back, and he was a little bit coy. Me and Benj said, "Where you been, mate?" Sort of taking the piss a bit. I think he was a little bit embarrassed. I just thought, "Couldn't you have given me *one thing* to play on?" We all felt a bit sidelined, I guess.

BENJI LeFEVRE   I came up with this insane-looking set for the *Shaken 'n' Stirred* tour—which required six or seven trucks—and I budgeted it and costed it. And then Phil Carson and Atlantic, in their infinite wisdom, decided to put the album release back two months in America. I said, "So are we going to put the tour back, too?" They said, "No, it's all booked." I said, "Are you fucking insane?"

I never got to the bottom of it. I suspect that Robert was convinced by the powers-that-be that the success of the Honeydrippers record would carry the tour, but the people who'd bought that record were not the same demographic as the people who were going to be buying *Shaken 'n' Stirred*. As a result, we played to 75 percent audiences and sometimes even *less* than that. It was like the first time in Robert's life that he'd seen empty seats. It then became economically unsound, and a little bit of hump and needle crept into the whole thing.

At the end of all that, there was a bit of disillusionment, and Robbie started playing up a bit around money and publishing. This time I *didn't* become the trade unionist, but I could see his point of view. I like to be able to go to bed at night knowing I've told the truth. And Robert went, "Right, well, you're not supporting me 100 percent." Eventually, he said he wanted to have a change of blood right the way across the camp.

That was the end of my involvement with him on a professional level, but we've stayed friends, and we remember each other's birthdays, and we give each other a big hug and a kiss whenever we see each other.

ROSS HALFIN (photographer)   I once told Robert that *Shaken 'n' Stirred* was horrible, and he said, "How dare you! It's the spirit of Julian Cope!"

ROBBIE BLUNT   Things were starting to get a bit fragmented. I had a major falling out with Robert in Barcelona, but I'd already made up my mind to leave. I'd got a load of guitars at his place, and I went to get them. He stood on his rather large doorstep, glaring at me: "So you're going to throw away six years of work." And I said, "Yep." I think it had run its course. We get on fine now; we've done a few charity things together. When we do "Big Log," I think we both get a bit of moisture in the eyeballs.

*   *   *

CHRIS DREJA (former bassist with the Yardbirds)   Jimmy played with us on the Box of Frogs project. He went off into the toilet and came back, and I don't know what happened to him in the toilet but... he did something on the wah-wah that Paul Samwell-Smith beautifully stitched together, so he made the track. But physically, something was not quite right.

MARILYN COLE (ex-wife of Richard Cole)   When I first cleaned up my act in the '80s, I went to the ARMS [Action into Research for Multiple Sclerosis] gig at the Albert Hall, and Jimmy looked horrendous. He didn't have any magic *then*, I can tell you. Well, that is until he picked up his guitar and played "Stairway to Heaven."

JIMMY PAGE   That Ronnie Lane thing did me a world of good. You can't imagine. It gave me so much confidence—I realized people did want to see me again.

KEITH ALTHAM (former *NME* writer and PR for several major '80s stars)   With all the superstars that were playing, I have *never* seen a reception like the one Jimmy got when he stepped on the stage of Madison Square Garden for the ARMS show. It was almost like John Lennon had come back from the dead.

JIMMY PAGE   I just felt really insecure. I was terrified. I guess that's why I played with Roy [Harper] whenever I could, because I knew his stuff, and I knew him well. After the split, I just didn't know what to do. I lived in a total vacuum.

TONY FRANKLIN (bass guitarist in Page's post-Zeppelin band the Firm)   Roy was a free spirit—rebellious, highly intelligent, with an outrageous sense of humor. He was a gifted poet, lyricist, vocalist, and

Page backstage with Ahmet Ertequn on the ARMS tour, Los Angles, 1983.
(Courtesy of Phil Carlo)

musician, and he wasn't afraid to take chances. He was deeply serious and deeply silly. There was an unspoken understanding and respect between him and Jimmy.

The *Whatever Happened to Jugula?* sessions were very relaxed, a little loose. It felt like a bunch of mates coming together to play and record music. The clock wasn't running; there was no deadline for completion. Jimmy and I started to get to know each other personally and musically during this time.

ROY HARPER (folk singer and friend of Page's)   The '80s were just about the worst time in my whole life. It was a period in time that was just absolutely horrible. And neither Jimmy nor I seemed to be able to dedicate enough time to it. I always take a long time to prepare before I write new stuff, but I think Jimmy was distracted as well. He'd just come out of the biggest band in the world and was kind of looking for something to do. But at the same time, he wasn't. He didn't have to do anything.

I've no idea how Jimmy feels about that time now, but I'd think he probably regrets not making more of it, too. He'd had so many opportunities to do so many different things, but the big problem was: What do you do after Led Zeppelin?

CHRIS WELCH (writer for *Melody Maker*)   When I went to see Jimmy playing with Roy at Cambridge, he seemed appreciative of someone coming to support him. But he was still very shy about appearing onstage. I think he admired Roy as an artist who stood by his beliefs, but it was a disappointment to Jimmy that the magic didn't work musically.

MARK ELLEN (copresenter of BBC2's *Old Grey Whistle Test*, 1982–1987)   Trevor Dann, who was the producer of the *Whistle Test*, said, "We've been offered Roy Harper, but we don't really want him." But Roy had been touring with Page, so that was the additional bait. Sure enough, the phone call came back that Page was prepared to be part of the joint interview and possibly to play as well.

In 1984, Led Zeppelin's critical standing was at its lowest ebb, so I was under pressure from Trevor to give them a bit of needle. We were dispatched to stay in this little pub in Ambleside in the Lake District, and when I went to the bar, there was a girl who turned out to be nineteen years old and asked if I'd come to see Roy and Jimmy. I said yes, so she said, "Did you know he wrote 'Stairway to Heaven'?"

It transpired that her friend, who was only *eighteen*, had met Roy backstage at a concert and become pally with him. And Roy had said something like, "Listen, I'm going to the Lake District with my mate Jimmy, d'you wanna come and maybe bring a friend?" So for the nineteen-year-old, it was a *blind date* with Jimmy Page, who was then forty. I'm thinking, "Wow, this really *is* very rock 'n' roll."

Later on, we shuffled into this baronial upstairs room in the pub, and it was like walking into the cover of *Beggars' Banquet*, with a roaring log fire and pewter mugs of ale on the table. The whole evening was then devoted to massive amounts of drinking and *huge* consumption of cocaine—though not by the BBC gang. The two particular tipples were "Red Tackle," which was flagons of fine claret, and "White

Tackle," which was mounds of chizzle. Roy would go "White Tackle!" and a roadie figure—in rather medieval fashion—would produce this kind of clasp-purse, then pour the holy powder onto the table for snorting.

At one point, the BBC became terribly alarmed, saying, "How are these guys going to be ready for nine o'clock in the morning?" Roy said something like, "Nine in the *morning*? You are fucking joking, aren't you?" I said, "Well, that's when we've booked the crew for." Jimmy then had a brilliant idea. He said, "I'll tell you what, we'll stay up *all night*." As if they weren't going to do that anyway.

The next morning, this caravanserai of old jeeps comes lumbering up the drive, and out of them gets the straightest-looking bunch of BBC people you've *ever* seen, carrying clipboards and such like—I think they'd just done *Jim'll Fix It*. At that point, I look up at one of the bedroom windows and see one of the girls dressed only in her underwear. I say to the crew, "I think this'll be a bit different from *Jim'll Fix It*."

Eventually, Roy and Jimmy come down looking absolutely shocking, and they're mumbling about red and white tackle. We finally end up at a place called Scafell Pike, and they are by now *completely* out of their heads, wearing very rakish scarves and Jimmy wearing knee-high motorcycle boots. They did a version of "Same Old Rock" and then "Hangman," and then I did the interview, which we had to keep stopping so they could go and have a wee. At one point, one of the girls had to manually assist one of the boys in directing his stream of urine into the bushes.

It was difficult for me, because I adored Harper and I adored Led Zeppelin, and I was under pressure to be a little bit snarky and treat them as relics from the dark ages—as opposed to the delights of the Wedding Present or the Wonder Stuff. I said something like, "Led Zeppelin—a little overblown, perhaps?" And Jimmy just didn't know how to react; he thought this was going to be a nice easy little ride, so he went very defensively into this whole thing about light and shade—he may even have used the term *chiaroscuro*. He really clammed up, and then they both started to be very, very aggressive.

Just to compound my misery, a flock of sheep wandered into the shot and were now audible—at which point Roy and Jimmy started to *impersonate* the sheep, who sounded as if they were calling my name: *"Maaaaark! Maaaaaark!"* Trevor and I drove back to London in almost complete silence.

JIMMY PAGE   I thought, "If I stop now, I'm just a bloody fool." I had to carry on—but the only vehicle I had was playing with Roy and also with Ian Stewart. Those were the only things I'd done.

ROBERT PLANT   I'd go back and see Jimmy now and again, and I'd try and say, "Now, come on. It's quite *nice* out there, you know." And so he started stepping out as well, leaving his great shell at home. It was like the metamorphosis; he'd step out a bit and then go home and climb back into his shell, and the shell would grow. It's like Kafka. Kafka could have been writing about Page.

BILL CURBISHLEY (manager of the Who and subsequently of Page and Plant)   Page was drinking a lot throughout that whole period, and he used to close down. He was very insular. The bonding Plant was trying to achieve with him never really happened, and it hasn't happened as of today.

PHIL CARLO (assistant to Page in the '80s)   Peter called me and said, "Jimmy wants to get some stuff together, and he really needs somebody to help him out." So I went to see Jim, and he wasn't at all well at the time. He was doing heroin or trying to get off it. He said, "I want to get back to playing music. G's out of the picture. I've got nobody, and I've got nothing. I just need some help." So I said, "Of course."

He said, "You know a lot of people. I want to form a band, and I want Paul Rodgers to sing in it." I said, "Fucking hell, Jim. You sure this is going to work? 'Cos you're like chalk and cheese." He said, "He's a brilliant singer." I said, "There's no disputing that, but personality-wise, we know what he's like. I've had eleven years of it." Jim says, "No, it'll be fine. I want the band sorted out—all the songs rehearsed, so when I phone him up, all he's got to do is come in and sing."

TONY FRANKLIN   Shortly after the Cambridge Folk Festival show that I played with Jimmy and Roy, Jimmy asked me if I'd like to sit in on the rehearsals with a new band he was forming with Paul. I was not formally asked if I'd like to be in the band until about eight weeks into the rehearsals. After that, we pretty much went straight into the studio.

JIMMY PAGE   At the back of my mind, I wanted to engineer it so that Paul would want to come in. For a while, I did a lot of jams. Everyone was invited.

RAT SCABIES (drummer with the Damned)   Phil Carlo called me up, asking if I'd like to come down. I probably put in two or three days, just messing about. At this point, I'd learned a bit more about guitarists and how they work, so just to sit next to Page and watch him play was quite special.

He was very reserved and didn't ever offer an opinion or dominate. He had this crappy old Telecaster and an AC-30 and an echo box that kept getting stuck so that he'd have to go over and bash it every time he did a solo. He just tore his nails off constantly when he was playing and had to keep super-gluing them back together. When you see that, you realize that this bloke is a guitar player, and that is his life, and that's all he'll ever be.

I played him the Dickies' version of "Communication Breakdown," and he took it off me and said, "I'll swap it for this rare tape of Jerry Lee Lewis arguing about God and the devil with Sam Phillips."

PHIL CARLO   Rat said, "Why d'you keep calling me Chris?" I said, "'Cos I respect you, mate. You ain't Rat to me. That's just some daft punk name." He went, "Oh, cheers for that."

RAT SCABIES   The problem was that Jimmy always wanted Bonham, and any other drummer he worked with had to replace him. And I wasn't too keen on that, because there was only one of him. If you were going to do something, it should be because it's *you*.

I told him he should go the Ozzy Osbourne route and have a few dead chickens onstage. At that time, everyone's preconception of him was Aleister Crowley's house and his interest in magic, so I said he should just throw it back in everyone's face. He wasn't at all impressed with that idea. That's when the audition stopped.

PHIL CARLO   When it was all done and dusted, Rodgers came down. I said, "Jimmy, who's going to manage it?" He said, "Carson." I said, "Oh, right." He said, "But don't worry. You're the tour manager. Fuck me, we wouldn't have a band if it wasn't for you."

TONY FRANKLIN   Jimmy was focused, energized, and wanted to play. He was partying a bit, but then again we all were.

CHRIS WELCH   In a weird kind of way, the Firm was almost like going back to Zeppelin in 1968, when we were all saying, "Whatever happened to the Yardbirds?" It was like, "Whatever happened to Led Zeppelin?" There were millions of fans out there wanting to hear them, and yet their music was being ignored and they'd almost been written off. Jimmy seemed to be in bad health, and Jonesy had almost gone into hiding.

JOHN PAUL JONES   I'd moved to Devon—moved out of town—thinking it would be nice to spend between-tour times out in the country, well away from London. And my family was growing up, so I hardly saw [Jimmy] at all.

CHRIS WELCH   I was pleased that Jimmy had managed to pull himself back from the brink. The Firm was like therapy, though I'm not sure I'd have chosen Paul Rodgers as part of *my* therapy. The real problem was ticket sales. Phil Carson was getting quite cross that they weren't selling more.

TONY FRANKLIN   There were ups and downs, as there are with any band, but overall they were both focused. The respect and chemistry were good between them, and they felt like they both had something to accomplish musically.

PHIL CARLO   The first time we went to L.A., there were loads of paparazzi outside the Rainbow. As we pulled up in the car, Lori Mattix spotted Jim and flew across the car park and leaped on him with her legs around his waist and her skirt up to here. The cameras were going nineteen to the dozen, and Jimmy said to me, "Fucking hell, this can't come out. I'll get slaughtered by Charlotte."

CONNIE HAMZY (Arkansas-based groupie)   Jimmy called me up late at night and said, "Connie, this is Jimmy Page." I said, "I don't believe you." I mean, I love English accents, but there were a lot of English roadies who played little jokes on me. Anyway, he said, "This really is Jimmy, and we're coming to Dallas. Let me get Phil Carlo." He put Phil on, and Phil said, "Connie, it's Phil." And I recognized Phil's voice. He said, "Jimmy wants you to come to Dallas."

Jimmy was drinking, and we were doing a little blow, and he was saying that he and Robert didn't get along. I asked why, and he said, "Because he blames me for John Bonham's death." I said, "Why?" He said, "Because he died at my house." Jimmy was not doing any heroin. He told me he would not do that again. He'd had hell with heroin, and I asked him quite frankly, lying on his bed in the suite, "How did you get involved with that drug?" His exact words were that Keith Richards had turned him on to it.

PHIL CARLO   Halfway through the first tour, Jimmy came off heroin, but he had a hundred and one pills to take. He turned to other things. Of course, being with him twenty-four hours a day, your head spins off. It got to where I couldn't tour-manage *and* be with him all day.

Carson, to his credit, did the right thing. He said to me in the break in the tour, "He needs you to be with him twenty-four hours a day, and you can't tour-manage properly when you've got to spend over half the night with him. He's happy as shit when you're around, and that's all that matters."

DAVE LEWIS (editor, *Tight But Loose*)   The Firm was hard work. It was difficult at the time, realizing that Jimmy wasn't living up to his potential.

GUY PRATT (bassist with Coverdale/Page)   The only story I ever heard Jimmy telling me about the Firm—and I think it was meant to be a warning—was that they were playing Madison Square Garden, and Tony Franklin was being such a showoff that Jimmy went up and pulled his guitar cord out halfway through a bass solo.

SAM AIZER (ex-Swan Song in the U.S.)   I took my wife to see the Firm at Madison Square Garden. Backstage, it was just like Zeppelin, all the guys with the earpieces in their ears and seven limousines. I'm saying to myself, "I'm sure this isn't the way the Rolling Stones tour." It was so uncomfortable.

TONY FRANKLIN   Jimmy was disappointed that the second Firm album didn't do better—we all were. But the shows were still selling out, and the tour was going well, so it didn't affect us too much.

JIMMY PAGE   It just wasn't the way I wanted to continue. Paul Rodgers is a difficult guy to get close to. It wasn't the most comfortable band to be in, particularly toward the end.

PHIL CARLO   When you weren't on tour or rehearsing, if a goat needed to be taken to the market, you had to do it. Or you had to take the kids down the playground and keep them amused for the afternoon.

One of Jim's guitar techs laid down a set of rules to him. He said, "I don't take children for walks, I don't pick up dog shit, I don't fetch drugs, I don't do building work, and I don't mow the fucking lawn. I'm a guitar technician, and that's all I do." Jimmy was surprised. No one had ever spoken to him like that before.

EDWARD ST. AUBYN (author of *Mother's Milk* and other novels)   My friend Adam Shand Kydd knew Jimmy and told me about a three-day coke session that the two of them had, with the music from *The Killing Fields* playing day and night for seventy-two hours. The entire house was wired, so there was no escape from the music. You couldn't even have a pee without hearing the *Killing Fields* music, again and again. He said the coke was on the billiard table—it was the only thing that was big enough.

Toward the end of the binge, the firearms came out. Jimmy came in with a pistol, and Adam said, "Is that loaded?" Jimmy said, "Of course it is." So Adam said he took the pistol and went into the garden and fired it into the flower bed. The Windsor suburbs were echoing with the sound of gunfire.

It sounded like just the sort of place I wanted to go, so we drove down in my car. To my disappointment, Jimmy was not there, but Charlotte was. She took me on the house tour because Adam knew the house well—as you would if you'd been locked in for seventy-two hours with *The Killing Fields* and the killing flower beds.

The house had two generations of bad taste, because Michael Caine had owned it before Jimmy and put in a fabulous gray armchair with a console above—very James Bond villain, with all these buttons to open all his Venetian blinds. The idea was, if you didn't want to get up and do anything for yourself, there were these little buttons that could. I also vividly remember the tarot-card dining set. There was an oval table surrounded by chairs whose backs had been painted as tarot cards.

Charlotte was very apologetic about Jimmy's absence and clearly felt that we should see him in some form. So we were taken up to the bedroom to watch a film of him on this enormous screen. There was this curtain of black hair, and he was swaying to this music, and you couldn't see his face at all—just occasionally the tip of the nose breaking through.

Charlotte said, "Ah, Jeeemy, he's so good looking." We had to politely agree. He had a nose—that's all I can tell you.

28

Dark Days for a Cocksman

Last night while I was crouching and leaping up in the
air and doing a spiral, as I came down again I thought, "I
wonder if David Coverdale does that yet."

—Robert Plant, March 1988

JOHN PAUL JONES At first, I didn't realize that I'd be pigeonholed,
because before Zeppelin I did television, radio, films, all of that. So I
never worried that I'd have to go get a real job, but it was kind of hard
in the '80s.

When I first decided to try and get some work, nobody took me
seriously at first. I was like, "Now wait a minute, I'm a professional
musician and an arranger and a producer. I've worked with more
people than you can possibly imagine." Once I did the production
for the Mission, it got better, but even then it was tough. I remember wanting to produce a John Hiatt album, and these record
company people would say, "We really can't see your relevance to
John Hiatt."

I like to do arrangements, because they're usually very quick projects, and they're really a lot of fun. The most I usually get in terms of instruction from the artist is something like what happened when I did the arrangements on *Automatic for the People*. Michael Stipe wrote me this little handwritten message, saying, "We like what you're doing and if you could have the strings come in about halfway through 'Everybody Hurts,' that would be great."

DAVE LEWIS (editor, *Tight But Loose*)   It's incredible when you tell people what it was like in the early '80s, because until Live Aid it was not happening for Zeppelin, and their catalogue was shoved under the carpet. The likes of Def Leppard and the Cult were all to follow. Live Aid changed it a bit, and Robert started doing Zeppelin numbers again. Suddenly, you're in the '80s, and you have the Beastie Boys sampling them, and it all took off again. Then came the 1990 remasters. It was evident that I should bring *Tight But Loose* back, which I did in 1992. And we had a big convention that year in London.

JACK WHITE (singer-guitarist with the White Stripes)   American rock radio just played the shit out of Zeppelin, to the point where it was almost embarrassing to like them. Because it was *too obvious*. They kind of represented so much in that realm, because of punk rock destroying prog rock and all the big regular rock. It was almost like you were more likely to have a *statue* of Led Zeppelin in your house than to actually mention them in conversation.

DOMENIC PRIORE (L.A. music historian)   One day, my two super-garage gal-friends Audrey and Neala and I were all sitting around, and quietly—after years of knowing each other—we slowly began admitting that we'd all found out about the Yardbirds because we'd been fans of Led Zeppelin first. We never could have admitted that to each other on the Mod/Rockabilly/Garage scenes we were all basically living inside of during the '80s and '90s.

JOHN PAUL JONES   At Live Aid, it was great when we got there. I forced myself onto it, really. I guess that was the beginning of not being asked to do these things.

BENJI LeFEVRE (producer for Plant)   We were in the middle of Robert's tour, and it was all a bit bonkers. Jimmy's brain was scrambled: brain cannot tell fingers what to do. He was incredibly nervous, but he wanted to prove himself.

PHIL CARLO (assistant to Page)   We rehearsed at a place called the Warehouse in Philadelphia. We had a break in rehearsing, and Robert announced that he didn't want to do "Stairway." Jimmy said to me, "I fucking knew this would happen. We've just got to play this game all fucking afternoon until we get up tomorrow morning, when he'll announce that he'll do it. It's just a fucking game, and he's a fucking old tart." So at Live Aid, I'm sitting with Robert watching Queen on a TV, and he goes, "Fucking hell! We've got to try and top that."

PHIL COLLINS (drummer with Genesis)   I got together with them in the dressing room, and I had the funny feeling of being the new boy. Tony [Thompson] is a great drummer, but when you're playing with two drummers, you have to have a certain attitude—you have to back off and not have so many egos. . . . Tony didn't seem to want to do that, and within five minutes of me being onstage, I felt, "Get me out of here."

PHIL CARLO   It was a shambles. Phil came on, but when it came to "Stairway" we had to turn all his mics off because he couldn't play it. He'd been given tapes to listen to and told what we were going to do, and he said, "I apologize, I didn't realize how complicated your stuff was."

ROBERT PLANT   We virtually ruined the whole thing because we sounded so awful. I was hoarse and couldn't sing, and Page was out of tune and couldn't hear his guitar. But on the other hand, it was a wondrous thing, because it was a wing and a prayer gone wrong again—it was so much like a lot of Led Zeppelin gigs. Jonesy stood there, serene as hell, and the two drummers proved that . . . well, you know, that's why Led Zeppelin didn't carry on. The rush I got from that size of audience, I'd forgotten what it was like.

PHIL CARSON (head of Atlantic and Plant's Es Peranza label)   After Live Aid, we did a sold-out Robert Plant show at Meadowlands, and I invited Jimmy and Paul Shaffer and Brian Setzer to come along. And when Jimmy stepped onto the stage, the roof came off the place. On the way back to the hotel, Robert was kind of unhappy. He said, "Is it always like this when Jimmy steps onstage?" And I said, "No, only when he steps onstage with *you*."

GLYN JOHNS (engineer on first Zeppelin album)   I was asked to put together the English contingent for the Atlantic 40th Anniversary show in 1988. We get a truck behind the stage, and Zeppelin go on— and then a monitor amp blows up in the truck. I can't hear anything, and I'm screaming for someone to give me a pair of headphones, anything. Eddie Kramer, who's crept into the truck, sneaks off and tells Jimmy I'd fucked it up and run screaming from the truck.

JIMMY PAGE   There were a lot of nerves involved in the Atlantic bash. Jonesy and I had rehearsed with Jason [Bonham], and it had gone particularly well. We'd agreed on what we wanted to play. Then at the eleventh hour . . . Robert decides he doesn't want to do "Stairway." So there's this running confusion and harsh words between us, right up to literally the last minute, and that shook me quite a bit, I can tell you.

PETER GRANT   [Live Aid was] fairly dreadful, really, in my view, because they were obviously underrehearsed. But it was nowhere near as bad as the Atlantic anniversary show. Actually, I was really upset that I didn't get an official invitation for that show. I may not have gone, but that's not the point. Phil Carson apparently felt that I wasn't healthy enough. I think Ahmet expected me to be there.

DANNY MARKUS (artist relations at Atlantic, subsequently comanager of Luther Vandross and others)   When Luther played his ten-night stand at Wembley Arena in 1988, Peter came down to see me. He looked like a dying man. He didn't smell good.

ED BICKNELL (former manager of Dire Straits)   Peter realized that if he didn't stop the drugs, he was going to kill himself. He locked himself in the bedroom for three or four days and flushed about three pounds of coke down the toilet. Ray Washburn apparently said, "If you'd told me, I'd have got you a refund."

HELEN GRANT (daughter of Peter Grant)   I remember I was with Dad one morning, and he woke up and just said, "I'm not gonna do this anymore. I'm gonna stop it now." And he did stop it, quite sort of abruptly. He never went into rehab. Never went anywhere like that.

SIMON KIRKE (drummer with Bad Company)   He got his act together and lost a ton of weight. "Si, I've lost an entire *person*," he told me when I met up with him. He also told me, when he sold Horselunges, that "the fuckin' VAT men stitched me up."

ED BICKNELL   Peter got into some financial difficulties. I'm pretty sure he was paying off a debt to the Revenue even then, and he sold Horselunges and moved into a flat in Meads in Eastbourne. I don't know how much money he had left. He'd certainly burned through a lot on the drugs. But the early Zeppelin royalties were not as high as you'd think. In fact, one of the biggest myths regurgitated about Led Zeppelin is that they had this great record deal.

JACK CALMES (Showco)   I talked to one of the Concerts West people, and they said that Peter got into serious habitual high-stakes gambling, and that that was what happened to his money.

ED BICKNELL   He came to see the Notting Hillbillies in Eastbourne. The door at the side of the stage opened, and this large guy shuffled in and plonked himself down on a flight case. When we'd finished rehearsing backstage, I went over to say hello, and he thanked me for some kind things I'd said about him.

I told Paul Crockford, the promoter, that Peter was my manager, and Peter immediately picked up on it and said he'd come down to count "the dead wood"—the ticket stubs. Paul, in a sort of panic, said, "But this is a council venue, it's all computerized." Peter didn't miss a beat and said, "Oh dear, I do hope we're not going to have a *problem*."

He once walked into my office and said, "Can I watch what you do?" After about three hours, he said, "I can't believe what you're doing. It's so *boring*." And I said, "You're absolutely right, Peter. It's become mind-numbingly boring." He said, "I couldn't do it now," and I said, "I can't imagine why you'd *want* to."

What Peter liked to do was to get on the bus with his band and go off and have a good time. He wasn't an office-bound manager, and he wasn't very interested in the minutiae of deals. He liked seeing the crowd go wild; it was a sort of pride by association.

HELEN GRANT When Dad moved to Eastbourne, I still saw things about him that the business hadn't taken away. Part of his persona was almost like bordering on very traditional and old-fashioned, not the big Svengali covered in turquoise and black hair and all this heavy stuff. Dad could really lack confidence and be very insecure around people.

He was scary, but if you didn't stand up to him, he'd be scarier. But the real Dad, the Dad I knew, was a very sensitive, normal person that liked to do normal things. You know, he used to wear pretty straight clothes, he liked his nice polished lace-up shoes. He wasn't this sort of *ogre*.

He would get cross with me if I wasn't there to see him. I'd just met somebody, and he had been so used to having me around. I used to come home, and when I opened the fridge, there'd be a note saying, "Clear this fucking flat up! Or else!" Spelled wrong, usually.

ED BICKNELL I remember when the second Zeppelin box set was being put together, Peter rang me at home and mentioned a royalty rate and asked what I thought, because he continued to represent Bonham's estate for Pat. And I said, "Peter, that's the kind of rate a new band would get now if only one record company was interested in it." And he went, "Well, that's what these cunts have agreed to."

Then he asked, "What's this packaging deduction on compact discs?" I said, "Well, it's 25 percent, and it's across the board, and you won't get any of the companies to break it." He said, "Well, it's outrageous." And what he did then was call Ahmet and get a proper deal that didn't need writing down. Because Ahmet came from that era when you could shake hands on it.

The other thing I remember is that Peter didn't like Steve Weiss very much. I think some iffy dealings went on there.

HARVEY LISBERG (manager of Herman's Hermits and other acts) There were murders going on between Led Zeppelin and Steve's office. It got very nasty, I think. They really didn't like Steve by the end.

ED BICKNELL   Peter once rang me at the office, and he was sobbing. I thought something awful must have happened, but he said, "This book's come out." It was the Bill Graham book. I asked Peter to fax through the pages about Oakland, and after I'd read them, I called him back and asked if it was true. He said, "Yes. But I don't want to be thought as a bad person." He was aware of the way he'd been, and I think he realized there were moments when he hadn't been very pleasant.

RICHARD COLE   I saw Peter with Jerry Greenberg in L.A. in 1989, and he was about to sell Horselunges. In the early '90s, when I'd come over from America, he would always come up to London to see me, and we'd have coffee at the Dome on the King's Road. The last time I saw him was about 1992.

ROBERT PLANT   I want to believe *Hammer of the Gods* [1986 Led Zeppelin biography by Stephen Davis], because it's done us huge favors, in terms of aura.

RICHARD COLE   I was excommunicated way before *Hammer of the Gods* came out. I got out of the nick [jail] after six months in 1981. When I got out, I called Bonzo's house, but I could only reach his daughter Zoe. Planty didn't answer my calls. I can't remember if I called Pagey or Jonesy. Peter answered my calls. He didn't give a fuck about *Hammer of the Gods*, either, probably because they'd already shat on him and fucked off with Phil Carson. I mean, wouldn't *you* feel hurt?

DAVID BATES (A&R man for Robert Plant and for Page and Plant in the '90s)   When Richard put out his *own* book [*Stairway to Heaven*], I can fucking tell you how angry they were. He was persona non grata, and anyone who *talked* in it was persona non grata.

JIMMY PAGE   It's totally inaccurate, and he's the sort of person who ought to know better, considering he's been in AA, and the whole thing about AA is that you keep things discreet. He went into AA as a chronic alcoholic and came out a chronic liar.

RICHARD COLE   He's a funny old sod, Percy. I saw him in 1991 in Wolverhampton, and he was quite happily talking about the old days.

I saw him at the beginning of 1993, and he said to my daughter, "Is Richard a good dad?" And she said yes. And he said, "Well, he was *my* dad for many years."

DAVE LEWIS Mick Hinton was very sore. At the end of it, he didn't come out of it very well. As I understand it, they gave a certain amount of money to all the roadies, and Mick had enough to set himself up with a little post office and blew it. I was doing an author tour for my Zeppelin book *A Celebration*, and I turned up at BBC Radio Nottingham, and I looked up and I thought, "That's Mick Hinton."

He said, "I've seen on the radio that you're talking about Zeppelin, and I wanna have my say." So we did a joint interview, and he was a good talker and knew the stories and he told good versions of them. He lived in this dreadful flat with a minder. He said, "Do you want a drink?" I said, "Yeah," and the Tennant's Extra came out. He had a crate of it. I started drinking, and Mick was great on the tape. He showed me his memorabilia, and he had lots of signed stuff, lots of tour materials. He said to me, "I could sell these, couldn't I?" I said, "You probably could."

He rang me up a couple of Saturdays before the Convention we had in 1992 and said, "I want to make a lot of money out of this." I said, "Look, I'm not an agent, I'm just organizing the Convention." I put him on to a couple of memorabilia guys, and he brought all his stuff along. We booked him in the hotel very foolishly and said we'd pay his expenses. He turned up on the Friday for the launch and was pissed when he got there. He proceeded to be sick in front of everyone when Debbie Bonham was on. It was all going pear-shaped.

The next morning, Mick turned up at about seven o'clock. He said, "I want a word with you. I need £500 now. I haven't come here to fuck about." He lost it a bit, and I lost it as well.

Eventually, he was sweet on the day and did a good job. Debbie got wind that he'd been nasty and made him apologize to me. In the end, it all calmed down. We then got a bill from the hotel for his bar bill, which was £200.

I know for a fact that Mick rang up Peter Grant and told him not to come. He said, "You don't want to be a part of this." Which was a fucker, because Peter was going to come.

. . .

ROBERT PLANT If anybody was to say to me, "Well, some of your career has been a bit patchy, and you've been a bit schizoid with the way it's danced around," I would say absolutely and merrily so.

There was stuff I could do that was so far away from the rock 'n' roll star persona or my contributing factors in Led Zep. It seemed just as likely to me to be working with a guy from some punk band in New York one week and then doing something more tasty for an Arthur Alexander tribute a year later.

PHIL JOHNSTONE (keyboard player and Plant collaborator, 1988–1993) He wanted to find some people to write some songs with . . . and he found what he was after. As a joke, one time when we were working on ["Tall Cool One"], we flew in some Led Zeppelin samples, thinking, "He'll laugh, but there's no way we'll get away with this." But no, he *embraced* it.

There were two pressures brought to bear, one by his songwriting partner—that is, me—and one by his manager, and it was, you know, "If we're gonna go for this—if you want to have solo success on a par with your previous success, and you want to play stadiums—then you're going to need to do Led Zeppelin."

ROBERT PLANT With *Now and Zen* we were looking for a hit, and that's what we got. We got three hits in America. That was the first time in about five or six years. It was a compromise at the time. When I look at it, with its techno splendor, more organically oriented singers might have said, "I'll never do that." But at the time I was thrilled with it, and it allowed me to work more with Toni Halliday. I loved her voice against mine.

AHMET ERTEGUN (head of Atlantic, speaking in 1988) Robert's album is a big hit, but you know what—there's still something missing from the music. I think he should do more stuff like that John Lee Hooker song he played—that was great. It began to sound like the old Zeppelin. You know what he's got to do? A little less adventuresome, less intellectual. Most intellectual rock is like bullshit, you know?

Because you know something, you have a few intellectual verses, and then you come to the middle part: "Rock me, mama, with the long green dress . . ." That's what gets it, right? The old blues thing.

DAVID BATES   I had an assistant named Lara, who would go home at weekends telling tales of madness and debauchery in the record business. Unbeknownst to me, her parents were best friends with Robert Plant, who was amused and intrigued by these stories. He was having a bit of a bad time with Atlantic U.K. His deal was coming up for renewal, and he wasn't sure what he wanted to do. And one day he just turned up in reception.

I said, "You'd better show him up." The double doors burst open, and in strolls the Viking with a great big grin on his face. All he wanted to talk about was records. All of a sudden, he started singing—blues songs, Moby Grape songs. I told him about the New Yardbirds gig I'd seen at Sheffield University. I said, "And now you're sitting here in my office, singing to me for free!" And then from that, he just suddenly sort of said, "I think I need a new home." He came to Fontana and signed with me, and that was that.

I asked him for some demos, and he looked at me sideways—like, "No one's ever asked me for *demos* before!" He brought some cassettes up, various recordings of him singing in the shower and singing in the car. It was Phil Johnstone on keyboards and Charlie Jones on bass, and they all seemed to be writing with Robert. That seemed to be very sacred.

ROBERT PLANT   [Charlie] is so adaptable, really into the Doors and that type of stuff, which means he can lay down an amazing groove, similar to "The End" or "Riders on the Storm." We can be led into beautiful crescendos, subtle waves of explosion.

DAVID BATES   I wasn't sure about all the songs, to be honest—especially after the previous two albums he'd done, where he'd strayed into computerized techno-rock stuff. Looking at my iPod, I see I only have three tracks from *Manic Nirvana*. After the first two albums, everything just seemed to noodle along, and nobody ever challenged Robert on what he was doing.

PHIL JOHNSTONE   Now, listening back to [*Now and Zen*] in the light of listening to the Felice Brothers or other bands like that—or even *Raising Sand*—it's horrible to listen to. It's 1988. It really *is* 1988. Robert definitely wanted more guitar on *Manic Nirvana*—less pop, more rock. And I think *Manic Nirvana* adequately reflects that change.

ROBERT PLANT   On *Manic Nirvana*, the personalities were so strong, Phil and Charlie especially. Everybody was up for writing the next *Sgt. Pepper*, so there was an energy level that was really good, and there was a faultless work ethic. Everybody was really going for it.

DAVID BATES   It struck me that people had got very comfortable around Robert, doing what they were doing without any great benefit to *him*. And I just wanted him to think about it: "What do you *really* want to do?" It was a slow process. *Fate of Nations* got pretty mixed reviews, but I think a lot of Robert's fans now think it's one of the best albums he's done.

In "I Believe," he addressed his feelings about the death of his son. I realized that this guy had been through a lot of pain. As a character, he's got a big heart and a big soul and a lot of feelings, and he fights hard to be a normal guy . . . to the point sometimes where he *over*-fights, I think. Behind the onstage Viking persona, there is a guy who is really fragile. I think that what happened around his son's death was never really dealt with at the time.

It was amazing that he wrote a song about his son, and that he wrote about other people in his life, including girlfriends. The girlfriend up until recently had been Alannah Myles, and that was now over; "29 Palms" was written about her. He wrote things about John Bonham ["Memory Song"] and other very personal subjects. He'd had an experience meeting the leader of one of the American Indian tribes and had a long conversation with him. It had had quite an effect on him, and he wrote about that.

The band evolved and changed at that point. And that period was amazingly creative for him. He was going off and doing things in Texas with Rainer Ptacek. We went to Paris and met with Martin Meissonnier and other people.

MARTIN MEISSONNIER (French world-music producer)   When Robert came to my studio, he came with the *Complete Recordings* box set of Zeppelin, but also with some of the Alan Lomax stuff that had been released. And he said that those prisoners' chants that Lomax recorded had really helped him find his voice at the start of his career. I think I already knew that Led Zeppelin were more interesting than a lot of other bands for those kinds of reasons. Basically, they never *were* about straight rock 'n' roll. When you listen to "Four Sticks," for instance, you have all this influence from the East. It's always something *more* than rock 'n' roll.

ROBERT PLANT   Maybe *Fate of Nations* was the time when I really did start putting my shoulders back and moving into another gear. By that time, I was working with all sorts of different people: Moya [Brennan] from Clannad, Nigel Eaton was playing the hurdy-gurdy; Nigel Kennedy was playing violin with me. I had string sections with sarod from south India playing on records. I was growing up. . . . I was really coming around.

PHIL JOHNSTONE   Robert was in a hurry, but I definitely felt that *Manic Nirvana* had been rushed, and this time he wanted it to be organic. The machines and the synthesizer noises and the bells and all that stuff should go and be replaced with proper organic music. Well, that was sort of fine, but, of course, I was still pulling toward the pop-song side of things, whereas he was much more, "Let's get the Indian orchestra in," and we *did*. Chris Hughes and I, we're poofy white soul pop boys, influenced primarily by the Beatles and the Beach Boys, so we couldn't realize it. We tried our best, and then he tried lots of other people . . . and when Robert was satisfied, it came out.

DAVID BATES   When *Fate of Nations* was finished, Robert and I had to fly on the Concorde to New York, because his deal was open for North America, and Polygram wanted a shot at getting him. And, of course, Atlantic wanted him to stay. So we went for lunch with all the Polygram people, and then we went to tea with Ahmet.

It was very interesting to see how Robert dealt with Ahmet. He clearly loved the man, and his respect for Ahmet was very evident.

And the way Ahmet dealt with Robert, it was like a father-and-son thing. Robert loved his dad to bits, but this was like having *another* dad. Polygram had put up a case, but when we went across the road to see Ahmet, Robert knew he wasn't leaving. The second he walked into Dad's study, he wasn't leaving home. God knows what Ahmet thought of the album.

• • •

PHIL CARLO   On the *Outrider* tour, with John Miles and Jason Bonham, Jimmy had a different manager by this time, Brian Goode.

GUY PRATT (bassist with Coverdale/Page)   Brian was the only man who ever called me to discuss business on a Sunday night because it's the cheapest time to make phone calls. I think he and Jimmy fell out because of something to do with him unveiling his master plan that he'd been working on for years, whereby he would get "Stairway to Heaven" to be the anthem for Club Med. It was like, "Here we are, Jimmy, it's all been leading up to this." Jimmy just said, "You're fired."

PHIL CARLO   On the first gig, Jim and I got to the hall, and Jason had his dad's symbol on the bass drum. I'd already seen it, so I said to Jim, "You'd better come out the front and have a look at this." We walked out the front, and he took one look and said, "Get fucking Cartoon"— meaning Carson—"to me here now!" So I went in and got Carson, and Jim absolutely tore him to bits. He said, "Anything for another fucking dollar, isn't it? He's not his dad. Get that fucking symbol off."

JIMMY PAGE   When I was writing material for Led Zeppelin, I knew *exactly* what the approach was going to be, and I was writing songs with Robert's voice in my head. I guess that's where *Outrider* might have been a little shaky.

JOHN KALODNER (A&R man who signed Coverdale/Page to Geffen Records, speaking in 1991)   Jimmy had really wanted to get Zeppelin back together, but when that fell through, he realized that he had a real urge to tour America and play that material for the kids here.

[He and David Coverdale] met in New York at the end of March and hit it off so well, they went right to Reno and started writing.

BRAD TOLINKSI (editor, *Guitar World*)   When Jimmy decides to do something, he believes it's the best thing. He doesn't necessarily speak about it in glowing terms, but he always talks about the actual project, the actual work, in positive terms. He seemed to really enjoy David Coverdale, who *is* a hilarious and charming guy. But I would say that Jimmy didn't have great personal energy at that time. I don't think he was doing drugs; it may have been alcohol.

I went back recently and listened to all the solo stuff and felt that *Coverdale/Page* was the culmination of a lot of things he'd been experimenting with. It's a very intricate record from a guitar perspective. In places, the album had eight or nine guitars on one track. At that point, he seemed super-positive and thought he had done good work.

JOHN KALODNER (speaking in 1991)   First off, David Coverdale is an improvement on Robert Plant. Once you hear David do a Led Zeppelin song, there won't be any debate about it. This is totally something Jimmy and David wanted to do for the music. This isn't a corporate decision, like an Eagles reunion tour. Jimmy Page couldn't *spend* all the money he has. It's hard to speak for Jimmy, but I think he wants to show he still has something to say. I think he wants to enjoy being Jimmy Page again.

GUY PRATT   Lionel Ward, Jimmy's guitar tech, called to say he had a gig for me. My manager nicknamed him Secret Squirrel because he wouldn't tell us who it was. He just rang up and said, "Do you want to do this tour?" I said, "Maybe. If it's Chris de Burgh, probably not." He said, "No, you'll like it." It was all top-secret and hush-hush until the day before my audition.

The vibe was very good, very funny. It was a world that was completely alien to me. I was a post-'80s London musician, and that world doesn't really register with you. It was like Spinal Tap, so I was very much a voyeur. I'd never played that full-on rock stuff, and it was actually really challenging. Obviously, Jimmy was a huge hero of mine and nowhere near as intimidating as I thought he'd be. He was quite overweight. He was drinking, but he wasn't doing anything *I* wasn't.

Coverdale would have a pop at Planty any chance he could. He was so unashamedly who he is. He said to me, "Guy, you either catch some dreadful disease, or they slap a lawsuit on you. Dark days indeed for a cocksman . . . " He and Jimmy got on pretty well. Whenever we had to learn Whitesnake songs, Jimmy was absolutely fantastic at picking them up. Of course, I'd forgotten that he was the ultimate old session dog. It was completely in his blood.

DAVID BATES   Jimmy tried with the Firm, with Coverdale, with *Outrider*—the worst album ever—and nothing worked. He clearly knew he had to get a singer in, and it had to be someone with a blues-rock voice. But where do you go after Robert?

JIMMY PAGE   David was really good to work with. It was very short-lived, but I enjoyed working with him, believe it or not. I was going to play in Japan with David—the only time we played live—and I had a call from Robert's management to pop in and see him in Boston on the way to L.A. to rehearse.

GUY PRATT   On the way back from Japan, Jimmy got me up in first class because he didn't want to be there on his own, and he had all these Japanese bootlegs. He said, "Right, four hours. Then let's go to sleep." So I had four hours of anorak heaven, with him telling me everything, about all the gigs and about the night Bonzo died. After four hours, he said, "Right, let's go to sleep." I said, "How do I do that?" He said, "Take this." I was actually wheel-chaired off the plane when we got to Heathrow. The New Orleans wife, Patricia, was at the airport when we arrived back in England. I have a feeling that was pretty much the end of the marriage.

PHIL CARLO   Patricia never got up in daylight. She thought England was going to be like being on tour: you'd be in the Plaza or the Beverly Hilton, you'd have strawberry daiquiris from the minute you opened your eyes, and you'd go to a concert every night and drive round in a limo. When she had to go down to the garden center, and it was freezing cold and there were no strawberry daiquiris, she didn't like it so much.

29

Mighty Rearrangements

"The song remains the same!"

"No, it doesn't, motherfucker!"

—Diamanda Galas responding to a fan on her
1994 tour with John Paul Jones

DAVID BATES (A&R man for Page & Plant) I had some history with Bill Curbishley before my involvement with Robert, because I was a massive Who fan as a kid. So here was Bill managing Robert, and we all got on very well.

JUNE HARRIS BARSALONA (wife of Premier Talent boss Frank Barsalona) Bill is a terrific manager, and I would think that he and Robert have a lot in common as they've both grown up. If Robert wants to work, he and Bill will talk it out and decide what they're going to do. And it'll be much easier, on a more adult level.

DAVID BATES We were talking one day, and Bill said, "What do you think about the idea of Robert and Jimmy getting back together?" I said, "It would be amazing, but there's a lot of problems with that." So

Page and Plant with Bill Curbishley at the Silver Clef Dinner and Auction, New York, November 13, 1996. (Evan Agostini/ Liaison/Getty Images)

he said, "There's a possibility that Jimmy might want to meet with Robert." So we discussed how we might bring this up with Robert, because that would have been a very prickly conversation.

Was John Paul even mentioned? I think the way Bill and I were looking at it was like, "Shall we just do one thing at a time?" Just getting Robert to talk to Jimmy was a big hurdle. There wasn't really a relationship at that point. There had *been* a relationship, of course, but there were also a lot of things that had been left *un*said and that hadn't been dealt with. I think that over the years, all that stuff builds up.

ROBERT PLANT   I realized that I missed Jimmy, missed his playing, so I was somehow going to have to deal with what was basically my own insistence on having nothing to do with any kind of Led Zeppelin rerun—which was pretty hypocritical at that stage, because I was doing Zeppelin songs with my own band.

DAVID BATES The meeting finally happened in Boston, at the end of Robert's tour. And that opened up possibilities of meeting again in England. Obviously, we knew all the stories of the various problems Jimmy had had. He'd dealt with his alcohol problem. He said to me, "I am now in control, and I'm okay."

Because of my relationship with Robert, Jimmy wanted to get to know *me*, so we spent quite a bit of time together. And once again, the common bond was playing records. I just thought it was quite bizarre, cruising around London in my car with Jimmy, listening to music. I had been assisting Don Was as a long-distance A&R consultant while he was doing *Voodoo Lounge*, and I'd gone out to the A&M studios to visit the Stones while they were trying to pare down twenty-eight songs to however many were on the record. So I had a very early copy of the album, and Jimmy and I drove around London playing it. He listened to it in *great* detail, zoned right in to what was going on.

ROBERT PLANT The thing to avoid was us being gotten into the wrong hands and manipulated into ending up like a sort of animated Pink Floyd, if you like: roll out the barrel, the same old shit. . . . Like a Rolling Stones situation, where the lads get back together, and it's like, "Well, I remember back in so-and-so, and they're still pretty good." Just being candy floss for some total retro occasion.

GLYN JOHNS (engineer on first Zeppelin album) The way Page and Plant treated John Paul in the '90s was disgraceful, disgusting. It's always the nicest ones who get it in the nuts. But he's happy enough, I think.

JOHN PAUL JONES I've never really understood why they did what they did. I remember one time when a journalist asked me, "What do you think about *No Quarter?*"—meaning Page and Plant's album title. And I said, "I always reckoned it was one of my best tunes."

BENJI LeFEVRE (Plant producer and collaborator in the '80s) Jonesy not being part of the *UnLedded* thing was probably nothing to do with Robert and more to do with Jimmy wanting to control everything.

VANESSA GILBERT (friend of Page and Plant) Every time I would see Jimmy or Robert after all that jazz, the first thing out of their mouths would be, "Have you heard from John Paul?" I did wonder why they'd left him out. I think it was just egos and fear. Easier not to deal with him.

ROBERT PLANT It reads as bad blood, but really it's just handbags. *Handbags with Jonesy*—it's a great name for the next solo album.

JOHN PAUL JONES [at the Rock and Roll Hall of Fame induction] I remember doing the sound check on my own—no sign of the others, so not much had changed in that department. There was a bit of fuss about Jason playing from some quarters yet again. I credited Peter Grant, because it was pretty stupid that he wasn't there.

ALAN CALLAN (former president of Swan Song in the U.K.) I used to invite Peter up to the golf tournaments. He'd come up to Gleneagles and stay for a week. At the Scottish Open, I used to put him in among all the golfers, Ian Woosnam and Nick Faldo, and he'd sit there and charm the pants off them. One night we're sitting there, and Ken Scofield says to me, "Who's your friend?" So I said, "He used to be the manager of Led Zeppelin." Norman MacFarlane goes, "Och, Ken, ya must know who Led Zeppelin were. Jimmy Page is mah favorite guitar player."

ED BICKNELL (former manager of Dire Straits) People would say to me, "How can you be friends with Peter Grant?" And I'd say, "Well, the person I know bears no relationship to the person I've read about." We would get together almost every week and go to the local gastropubs, where he would regale me with stories. Most of them were not about Led Zeppelin, though. They were about the Bo Diddleys and Little Richards of this world—probably because they were even bigger characters than the guys in Zeppelin.

Peter became this rather benign figure in the neighborhood. I like to think he was at peace with himself. I don't think he ever did a drug or had a drink again. He just used a little homeopathic dropper with some flower remedy in it, and he would go for a walk along Eastbourne front every day. He'd say, "I'm going to be down to X stone by my sixtieth birthday." He was completely inspired by his grandchildren. He was happy to stick his toe in the music business waters, but he didn't want to come back to it at all. He knew you couldn't repeat the experience.

WILLIE ROBERTSON (insurance broker for Zeppelin and Swan Song acts)   I had lunch with Peter at Morton's, and he was a totally changed man—lovely, quiet . . . lost all that "Fuck this and fuck that." And, of course, he'd lost a *lot* of weight.

AHMET ERTEGUN (head of Atlantic)   He came to see me in my hotel room, and when I saw him I couldn't believe it was the same man. He must have lost 250 pounds, and he was dressed in a very well-cut suit, a smart necktie . . . he looked like a *banker*. He was a thoroughly different person, but he still had that marvelous glint in his eye and that very warm smile.

ED BICKNELL   He used to do these chauffeuring jobs for weddings with a bloke called Lord John Gould. He would put on a cap and uniform, take the happy couple to the church in Hellingly or wherever, and then drive them off to the Grand Hotel in Eastbourne.

LORD JOHN GOULD (vintage car enthusiast and friend of Peter Grant)   I remember the first wedding, we were sitting outside munching a sandwich while they were getting married, and then we drove off. We were paid £30 each in cash, and I remember Peter saying to me, in his inimitable language, "Ah, fuckin' 'ell, John, first cash I've 'ad for years . . . *lovely!*"

ED BICKNELL   One night he'd been asked to judge a talent contest on the pier, and he asked if I fancied doing it with him. So a couple of weeks later, there's the managers of Led Zeppelin and Dire Straits judging these dreadful fucking bands at the end of Eastbourne pier.

I went up with Peter to the first "In the City" conference in Manchester. A group of managers had dinner at the Piccadilly Hotel, and we were all talking about how it was back then. At about one in the morning, Peter turned to Andy Dodd and Elliott Rashman and said, "I think you boys should go to bed and get your rest. You've got a big day tomorrow." And the two of them, rather sheeplike, toddled off to bed!

The next day, Paul Morley did this appalling interview with him. His whole line was that of a left-wing *NME* writer. He'd brought this kind of bouncer onstage to guard him, which was a joke that backfired completely.

A slimmed-down Peter Grant with Phil Carlo at the first "In the City" conference, Manchester, 1992. (Courtesy of Phil Carlo)

MARTIN MEISSONNIER (Paris-based world-music producer)   Malcolm McLaren wanted to make a film about Peter. Some people think that is strange, because they see Malcolm as the great punk inventor. But Malcolm never cared about punk; the only thing that interested him was creating hysteria and making himself famous through that moment. The thing that fascinated him about Led Zeppelin was the relationship between Peter Grant and organized crime, and he talked to Peter extensively about it.

MALCOLM McLAREN (former manager of the Sex Pistols)   Managers like myself were very conscious of the fear he used to inspire. When he entered a record company building, the silence was total. His stature created an air of menace, a catalyst encouraging acts of violence from his volatile entourage. . . . Grant needed the camaraderie of hard, dangerous men who gave him a sense of power. The harder they were, the tougher he felt, and only then was his desire for control satisfied.

DAVID DALTON (biographer of Janis Joplin and others) Tony Secunda asked if I'd be interested in ghosting Peter's autobiography, so I flew to Miami to meet Peter. He said, "Everyone always talks about the dark side of Led Zeppelin. I want to talk about the *happy* side." Before I left, I collected some shells for my son on Miami Beach, and he seemed very touched by that. He said, "You must be a good dad." I thought, "Here's this supposedly monstrous man who's touched by something so simple."

WARREN GRANT (son of Peter Grant) The fondest memory, I think, is when the kids were born. Seeing him with the grandchildren and how he was with them . . . this unselfish man who just wanted to please everyone else.

DESIREE KIRKE (ex-wife of Simon Kirke) Peter came to Miami on business in 1993. He'd lost a lot of weight, and his head was really in a good space. Then, at the end of 1994, I went to see him at the flat in Eastbourne. As we went to leave, Helen came running out and said, "Dad really misses you, can you come and see him again?" And I *couldn't* get to see him again, and it was very sad.

SIMON KIRKE (drummer with Bad Company) I last saw him at a Bad Company show in 1994. It was at the Mean Fiddler in Kentish Town. He came back to the hotel afterward and sipped on a club soda as we went down memory lane. I gave him a teary-eyed hug, told him I loved him, and went upstairs. And that was it, I never saw him again. He was the best manager I ever worked with.

ROBERT PLANT Backstage at London's Wembley Arena in 1995 [was] the last time I saw Peter, and he was a kind, warm, frail guy who invoked so many wonderful memories. He was a different person from the man I saw at the end of the '70s. He was clean, his vision was clean. He knew that he'd moved mountains, that he'd changed the world for artists.

HELEN GRANT (daughter of Peter Grant) It was just like they were so *pleased* to see each other all again. All the years had gone by, with all the crap and the not talking to each other.

ALAN CALLAN I was very touched when the family asked me to give the eulogy at Peter's funeral. I knew what I wanted to say, but as the church filled up, I started to feel terrified. I'm looking out, and there's Jimmy and Robert and Jeff Beck and Paul Rodgers, and I think, "How can I possibly express Peter's life to these people, some of whom had known him even longer than *I* had?"

Lord John Gould gets up and starts wittering on about life in Eastbourne, and I'm thinking, "Who *is* this guy?" And then comes the ultimate moment, when the coffin is picked up and on comes "We'll Meet Again." It transpires that Peter has organized the music in advance. It was brilliant. And then we all hared off to the reception, where Jeff Beck wandered around Peter's car collection, going, "Look at the engine on that . . ."

PHIL CARLO (assistant to Page in '80s and early '90s) I've never seen so many people with dyed hair. Beck, Jimmy, and the bloke from the

ST. PETER AND ST. PAUL
HELLINGLY

A SERVICE OF THANKSGIVING
FOR THE LIFE OF
PETER GRANT
1935 - 1995

MONDAY, 4th DECEMBER, 1995

Order of service for Grant's funeral, December 4, 1995. (Courtesy of Phil Carlo)

Pretty Things—a very strange man who wore black tights but had a big fat stomach and looked like someone out of a German porn film.

DESIREE KIRKE I actually went up to Gloria at Peter's funeral. Something compelled me to tell her that he'd really, really loved her. She just kind of looked at me, stunned. I don't know if she even knew who I was.

ED BICKNELL I think about him almost every day, and I don't know why. He almost became like a father figure to me. He was incredibly interesting, and not just about music. He would say things that were really on the nail. It's not often I'd say it of another man, but I loved Peter. And most of the people I know who knew him loved him, too.

• • •

DAVID BATES The first Page and Plant reunion I saw was April 7, 1994, in Buxton—the Alexis Korner thing. I'd just seen *Blow-Up* again, so I suggested "Train Kept a' Rollin'" as an encore. They just jammed it, and it was brilliant.

The Page-Plant project slowly evolved, and the next question obviously was, "Who's going to be in the band?" Charlie Jones was inked in straightaway, because his relationship with Robert was long and highly complex. He ended up going out with Robert's daughter Carmen and eventually married her. Charlie therefore at this point was Robert's bass player and Robert's son-in-law. He was also Robert's conscience, because Charlie and Carmen were two of life's beautiful people. Michael Lee wanted to be John Bonham and could do great Bonzo-type things. So that was the rhythm section.

ROSS HALFIN (photographer and friend of Page's) I never thought that much of either Michael or Charlie. Michael was an okay drummer, but he was just a thrasher with no real finesse. And Charlie was just there 'cause he was Plant's son-in-law. As for Porl Thompson from the Cure, there was just no point in him being there at all. Personally, I think Jimmy put up with a lot from that lot. There just wasn't a nice vibe around them. Maybe it's just because I was Jimmy's guy, but there were always two very firmly etched camps. Jimmy's camp was a very small camp, and Robert's was a very *large* camp.

DAVID BATES   The first rehearsals were at the King's Head at the end of the Fulham Road. Why? Because it was cheap. It was just the four of them. And nobody fucking knew they were in there. I remember going into the pub and thinking, "These people have absolutely no idea what's going on upstairs."

I was getting huge pressure from above—from Alain Levy and Roger Ames at Polygram—because they needed this album to be big. I ended up having a row with Robert and Jimmy about singles, because we needed something to sell this thing. And as we all know, singles are anathema to these guys. We all have those horrible moments that you look back on with regret, and that's one of mine, personally and professionally.

This thing came up with MTV, and, obviously, it was one of the biggest coups they could get. How fast does the word go out? How fast is the speed of light? Within days, Coca-Cola and Pepsi-Cola and Amex are queuing up outside Bill's office. I went to lots of meetings with Bill, but Robert was not keen on the sponsorship thing—because he *does* have integrity. The amount of money they *could* have made, had they gone down the sponsorship route, was millions upon millions. And that's partly because everyone's thinking the same thing: If a Led Zeppelin reunion ever happens, we want to get in on it.

Meanwhile, we're in a very fragile place here: we're trying to put two human beings back together again.

ROBERT PLANT   The offer from MTV really was so fortuitous. I'd started going to the Welsh mountains again, and reading the old books about mythology and Celtic history. . . . I missed the kind of thing that Jimmy and I had.

DAVID BATES   Jimmy and I stayed at the Ynyshir Hall hotel in Powys, and we would drive over to Robert's farm in the morning. One day Robert wanted to go out for a drive into the wilds. We went for a bit of a walk in these woods, and we got to this place with the most amazing view and with the most incredible sunset. At that moment, he started singing, *"There's a feeling I get when I look to the west . . ."* Then he went, "This is it." And I thought, "Fuck me, this is obviously the inspiration for it!" Then we got back in the car and drove off again. I was made for life.

JIMMY PAGE   Robert and I went into a real dark, dank rehearsal studio in the north part of London, and we just had the tape machine, some North African rhythm loops, and my guitar, and it was, "Let's see what you can do."

ROBERT PLANT   "Yallah" is a loop put together by Martin Meissonnier. He's married to Amina, the Tunisian singer, and he worked with Khaled and Youssou N'Dour and so on. I met him when I played in Paris, and I told him that Jimmy and I were thinking of working together, and could he come up with some drum loops from stuff that he'd recorded in Mauritania? I said, "Let's get some real slinky loops that are coming from an African or a desert sound."

MARTIN MEISSONNIER   He said they were looking for new ideas and rhythms, because they didn't want to do the old rock 'n' roll by itself. He said he would come back the next week, and he actually *came*. I had lots of loops I was using for Amina and for soundtracks, so I put about twenty together on a cassette for him. Some of them I had recorded in the desert. They ended up using four of the loops, and they invited me to see them recording in London. Jimmy was truly excited as well.

HOSSAM RAMZY (Egyptian arranger on *No Quarter* and the Page-Plant tour)   They wanted an Arabian, Middle Eastern feel, and the closest one that Robert, I believe, has been in touch with, of course, is the Moroccan side of things. Unfortunately, the kind of direction it was going in . . . was a full luscious Arabian flavor of sound . . . but it was just far too much falafel in the dish. The sound of Led Zeppelin is, in my mind, a combination of extreme richness with minimalistic kind of thrusts that combines various genres of music.

The idea was, "How do I put my style and the genre of music that I bring side by side in the same bed?" That was extremely difficult, and we had lots of rehearsals. [With "Friends"], Jimmy has a very particular tempo that he likes to play in, and to get that tempo right . . .

this took several weeks of rehearsals. [With "Four Sticks"], the difficulty was the counting. That's a tough one, especially for the Egyptian musicians and the Arabian musicians.

DAVID BATES   We went to Marrakech, and they just set up with the Gnaoua musicians in the Djemaa el Fna. They got changed in a bar across the road. Jimmy was incredibly nervous. We crossed over into the square; nobody knew who they were. Martin had prepared these tapes, and they played along to those. American tourists were doing a double take: "It's Led Zeppelin! What the fuck is going on?"

At some point during all this filming, Jimmy wanted to go back to the hotel. He was highly agitated. Now I had given up drugs, and I had even given up smoking. In fact, I had a no-smoking policy in my car. Jimmy got in and he was smoking away, and I said, "Jim, put the cigarette out." He fucking lost it, and I saw another side to Jimmy Page. It got very ugly. Because I have a reputation as well, and *I* lost it. I said, "Jimmy, if you're a friend, and if you're going to work with me, you have to fucking understand. Where's the respect in this? I'm not your fucking chauffeur."

I could have given in, but it probably would have happened in the future. The person who was in between us was Bill Curbishley, who wanted *one* of us to back down. And I wouldn't; I'd have fucking knocked him out. And it's something I regret, because you look at it on a piece of paper, and you think, "Why fall out over something like that?" But we did, and it was a huge shame. From that day on, it affected Jimmy as to how he talked to me or dealt with me. It was sad, odd, and weird.

MAT SNOW (former editor of *MOJO*)   There was still this whole thing about the unfinished business of the band: what Led Zeppelin *could* have been, which would have been a much more equal allocation and presentation of talents than had been the case before, where it had been very much Page's baby and something that caused Plant, in particular, to chafe. When the relationship picks up again, it's very much on Plant's terms because he seems to be getting better, whereas Page is floundering. Even though you couldn't say in 1994 that Plant had set the world on fire, at least he was getting an awful lot more kudos by trying things out and not just wanting to relive the myth.

BENJI LeFEVRE Robert came round for a cup of tea and said, "I don't know about this. . . . What am I going to *do*?" I said, "You owe it to yourself to find out, and you owe it to Karac to find out if you could ever make it work. But you have to make sure you can get out of it if you don't like it." Two weeks into the tour, he said, "It's insane. All I want to do is get up in the morning and play tennis, and Jimmy just wants to stay up all night."

JANINE SAFER (ex-Swan Song in the U.S.) A friend of mine did a bit of PR for them on the *Unledded* tour, and she said it was all she could do to stop them from clawing each other to death.

LORI MATTIX (former L.A. groupie) It was quite flattering when Jimmy met Jimena, and she looked exactly like me. She was nine months' pregnant with somebody else's kid. She had that baby and had him adopt it and popped out three more babies, and my girlfriend saw her in a club in London with a twenty-one-year-old boy.

PAMELA DES BARRES (former L.A. groupie) He got his heart broken, finally. It was the Brazilian. Apparently that was really devastating to him.

DAVID BATES Because it was Robert and Jimmy, which was the nearest thing many people had seen to Led Zeppelin, the fucking hoo-ha on that tour was incredible. My wife and I went to Philadelphia to see Jimmy and Robert play at the Spectrum, and Bill Curbishley ambled across to the side of the stage where we were and said, "Dave, when I say go, you go."

We go sailing out the back of the Spectrum with six outriders escorting us, and the convoy goes right from the Spectrum to a private airstrip on the outskirts of town. And we board a private jet that takes us to New York. We've gone from a nice quiet little tour with Robert to chaos and mayhem. So I know what it must have been like to travel with Led Zeppelin in the '70s.

RICHARD COLE When you consider that you could see Zeppelin in 1977 for $7, and now it was $125. . . . Frank Barsalona told me they made

$50 million on that tour. He said to me, "They've made more money on this tour than they did in the whole live career of Led Zeppelin."

HOSSAM RAMZY   On the tour itself, just to stand on the side of the stage and listen to the five notes that Jimmy plays as the introduction to "Since I've Been Loving You," that is worth all the musical experience in my life.

JIMMY PAGE   It was an incredible extravaganza to take rolling around the world, with these Egyptians who had no camaraderie among themselves whatsoever and who were all willing to stab each other in the back.

ROBERT PLANT   The Egyptians had their own internal power struggles, but we managed to sort ours out. Which is why, at the end, Jimmy and I were able to hug each other farewell, knowing there would be another time.

MARTIN MEISSONNIER   I thought they could have gone much further with the music than they did, and I think Robert was really looking for that. And then what happened later was that Robert started working with Justin Adams to go further in that direction.

JIMMY PAGE   The most obvious thing for us to do was to go back to the four-piece unit that we knew best and has always worked best for us.

ROBERT PLANT   It's daft, really, I suppose, going around looking at roadside buildings that have closed down in Banks, Mississippi, where Robert Johnson is supposed to have come in on a break between Son House and Bukka White, picked a guitar up after he'd been away for a year, and improved beyond all recognition. Clarksdale is a very sleepy town now, but it carries a history that had an amazing effect on both of us. . . . Being obsessed with that music, I wanted to go there. I guess I was just forty years too late.

JIMMY PAGE (speaking in 1998)   The greatest problem with a band that plays organically is someone to record it. We're fortunate with Steve Albini, because he really knows how to equalize using microphones, the old science of recording. Plus, it's been really wonderful working at Abbey Road in that great room.

STEVE ALBINI (producer of Nirvana and others)   *Walking into Clarksdale* was much more collaborative, I think, than Jimmy and Robert had been in Led Zeppelin. Zeppelin was Jimmy's band; he hired Robert to be the singer. And then in the intervening period, Robert had gone on to become quite successful on his own. I think Jimmy respected that. Now he was working with Robert as a peer and [a] comrade, rather than feeling responsible for the record as its auteur.

Both of them were very conscious, futilely, of not resuscitating the ghost of Zeppelin. But it was a shared experience they drew on quite naturally. Jimmy has enormously varied tastes, though. He kept talking about how much he liked the over-the-top aggression and adrenaline of the Prodigy.

DAVID BATES   By *Walking into Clarksdale*, I'd got clinical depression, so I was on gardening leave. To try and find someone who would produce the record and be honest, that was the issue. In theory, the honesty and purity of Albini's approach was perfect; in retrospect, it was not such a great solution, but there was nothing I could do about it.

MARTIN MEISSONNIER   It's funny how the follow-up to *No Quarter* is just a real *rock record*. I don't think Steve really understood Led Zeppelin. He applied loops, but he didn't know how to use them. But it's complicated when you add such huge egos into the mix.

ROBERT PLANT   Everything had become remote. I began to feel intimidated, committing myself to large parts of touring.

DAVID BATES   I believe Jim had got up to his old politics, in terms of the way he was treating band members. You see, there's a big elephant in the room, and no one talks about it. There are things from way back—some very heavy things that really hurt Robert that were never addressed. The issue of Jimmy not being at Karac's funeral is part of it, but it's not all of it. It gets even bigger than that, and when you start delving into it and you hear the stories, you sit there and go, "Are these people his mates? Do they not realize what this man is going through?"

I'm not a psychologist or a therapist, so if you think I'm going to be the one who goes, "There's the elephant, let's fucking deal with it," you're wrong. I'd just hope that Robert and Jimmy could sit down and talk about it. But you know what, the elephant is so fucking big now, I don't know if they ever will. It's okay when Jim is making overtures to Robert, but eventually the overtures stop, and then we're back to where we were before.

ROBERT PLANT   We were going 'round and 'round all those big gigs in Germany, where everything looks like a storeroom for some strange new flying machine, and you don't know where you are or what you are. I'd done it for years and years, and to prove what? I'd rather play a folk club in Birmingham and have a bit of fun with people.

ROY WILLIAMS (live engineer for Plant)   They did a gig for Amnesty International in Paris, and I think they were due to go to South America. And Robert just said, "No, I've had enough." Then he came back here and started talking with Kevyn Gammond.

30

What Was

> . . . the internal workings of the band are more complex than the Space Shuttle.
>
> —Kevin Shirley, *Sound & Vision*, April 2004

VANESSA GILBERT (friend of Page's and Plant's) I'm in the commercial business, so I asked Robert what Cadillac paid to use "Rock and Roll." He just looked at me and smiled. So I said, "Can I guess?" He said okay. I said, "Was it five million?" He shook his head. "*Seven* million?" "No." I said, "Not *ten million*?" And he nodded his head.

ABE HOCH (former president of Swan Song in the U.K.) The last time I saw Jimmy, I was managing Paula Abdul, and I ran into him on *Saturday Night Live*, because he was doing the *Godzilla* thing with Puff Daddy. He never wants to be pleasant in public so that people can see how close you are, so he's always pleasant in private—this is how life works with us. So I walked up and went, "Well, how are you?" He goes, "Naps. I have to take a lot of naps." I thought to myself, "This is the great god of rock 'n' roll, and he has to take a lot of naps."

ALAN CALLAN (former president of Swan Song in the U.K.) I was at the Grammys with Jeff Beck, and I saw Jimmy and said, "What are you up to?" And he said, "Not much." I said, "Why not?" He said, "Well, I did *DVD* three years ago, and I haven't really got a structure, and I don't really know what to do." And then I found out that he hadn't played the guitar for a year. I said, "What guitars have you got at home?" And he said, "I haven't." And when I got back to London, I badgered him and said, "Go and get your guitars."

• • •

DAVE PEGG (bassist with Fairport Convention) Robert phoned me up and left a message on my answering machine, saying, "All the times I've been up to your fucking festival and had to play all that bloody folk music shit, can you come and help us out? Our village hall needs rewiring, and we're having a benefit concert."

That's the way Robert thinks. He's obviously not hard up, but if the village hall is going to be rewired, he gets that gig together, and he didn't have to personally go, "Oh, of course, I'll do it." Which many people would conceive to be tight, but then if you just pay for it yourself, they just go, "Flash bastard, it's alright for him." It's a no-win scenario. He's been three or four times to the Fairports' Cropredy festival. One year we did about eight Zeppelin songs in the set when Dave Mattacks was the drummer, and that was fabulous.

ROY WILLIAMS (live engineer for Plant) Robert and Kevyn Gammond came up with the idea for Priory of Brion. It was a similar process to the original Honeydrippers, and he asked me if I'd book gigs for them. Except the remit this time was not to cross the A5. But while it was okay not to do Zeppelin songs when you had three hundred people in a little place, when you had three thousand in a bigger place, then there were more people who weren't so happy about it.

GEOFF GRIMES (former Atlantic song plugger and friend of Plant's) I saw Robert sitting outside a pub in Bishop's Castle with a lady friend, having a cup of coffee, so I went up and introduced myself. He didn't remember me. How could he? But he knew what I'd done at Atlantic. We became friends, and I was very pleased with that. He came by again and walked into this pub and said, "Where do you think I can try this new band out?" And they did the first gig here in a room in Bishop's Castle.

ROY WILLIAMS Robert had a kind of writer's block. With Priory of Brion, it was like, "Let's just do covers." I'd been bugging him for ages to listen to *Wrecking Ball* by Emmylou Harris. Eventually I played it to him, and he phoned me up and asked if I wanted to see Emmylou in Dublin. A day or so later, he said, "I've been having a think about this, let's shelve these gigs we're going to do"—the last one was at the Wulfrun Hall in Wolverhampton.

I'd worked with the Big Town Playboys for ten years, and they had Clive Deamer drumming with them, and I was always going on to Robert, "If you ever want a drummer that can really swing . . ." A few months later, he came back with what became the Strange Sensation—Clive, Charlie, Justin [Adams], and Porl [Thompson]—and I've been working with him ever since.

ROBERT PLANT With *Dreamland*, I think I sang better and more effectively and naturally than I have done since "The Rain Song."

ROY WILLIAMS As a unit, there was far more of a creative element. It was a band. They knew who the boss was, but he was very stimulated by their abilities, and he started writing again. I went over to the farm, and he said, "Have a listen to this." And I thought, "You've got a good one, too." *Mighty ReArranger* is probably not as recognized as it should have been, because it wasn't quite like anything anyone had heard. You had that African thing with Justin.

ROBERT PLANT With Justin, Skin, and myself, and my son Logan as cameraman, we went to Timbuktu and were exposed to some of the most vibrant music—basically, swordsmen with equipment and instruments. When they weren't prancing around, waving swords and cutlasses in the air, there was this amazing rhythm thing going down. It's John Lee Hooker's lost great-great-great uncle, and we took quite a lot of the rhythms from there and nicked them or superimposed them onto a rock 'n' roll structure, and it sounded good.

JUSTIN ADAMS (world-music guitarist and Plant sideman in the '90s)   I quickly began to realize that one of [Robert's] talents is setting atmospheres. Sometimes the most amazing music comes in a very short spurt of activity. Where has that come from? Yes, sometimes from hours of rehearsal, but sometimes from the feeling of camaraderie. Just living life together. That's one of the things Robert was doing with Strange Sensation. I've worked with musicians who think the idea of family is disgusting. But with Robert the whole thing is embraced.

• • •

JIMMY PAGE   I think *DVD* should just go out and have a life of its own. Then let all the dust settle and see where we're at. Led Zeppelin was important to me, but in a certain format. The idea of going out and being seen to be promoting material that you did thirty years ago seems quite comical, and I couldn't be part of that. It's not the way to present Led Zeppelin.

ROBERT PLANT   I don't think the song remains the same. As cute as it was in 1976 as a movie, it's a bit of a hoot now, and it needs tidying up, and if that was the last representation of Led Zeppelin, thank God this DVD did arrive.

HARVEY GOLDSMITH (British concert promoter)   Mica [Ertegun] asked if I would do something in London with all the British acts [on Atlantic]. So I set about with Phil Carson, Bill Curbishley, and Robert [to put] a show together. The original idea was to do two days and to reflect all of those British acts from the Rolling Stones to Phil Collins to Cream to Eric Clapton.

When I went to [Ahmet's] memorial service, I saw all three of the Zeps there. I went up to them, and I said, "You are the only guys who didn't perform at this." Then we got back and talked about it. Bill said it would be hard to get them together. I suddenly thought, "This is ridiculous. The one act that Ahmet adored was Led Zeppelin. He loved the Stones, and he loved other acts, but Led Zeppelin was his love." So I just dropped them all a note and said, "Forget about what everybody has said about touring and just do this one for Ahmet." All I asked them to do was to play for fifteen minutes or a half-hour. One after another, they came back immediately and said, "We should do this."

ROBERT PLANT They were great people, Ahmet and his widow, Mica. When she approached me, I told her I'd do anything for her, for Ahmet.

HARVEY GOLDSMITH A week later they called me up, and we had a meeting. Everybody was there. Jimmy came into the room and said, "Well, we tried it out, and we've thought about it. We decided"—and I'm thinking "Oh, no"—and he said, "We want to do the whole show." I just looked at him, aghast.

BENJI LeFEVRE (Plant's former producer and assistant) Once the news had been out in the public domain for a couple of months, Robert told me, "I can't fucking believe it, Benj, it's like going back to square one. We went for a meeting with Harvey at the O2, and Jimmy was just so rude to him and started shouting and screaming." He said, "I can't *ever* do this again. I'll do it for Ahmet, but I *already* feel like I don't want to do it."

MARTIN MEISSONNIER (French world-music producer) Robert called me and said, "You really have to come to this concert." I said, "Come on, Robert, you'll probably play in Paris next summer, and I'm quite busy at the moment." He said, "No, no, no, this will be the last one—the very last Zeppelin show."

JACK CALMES (Showco) I'm talking to Robert for a moment, and he's still the same Robert, and he says, "Why do we have to have all that shit up there? Why can't we just get on a stage and play?" I say, "Well, it never worked that way, Robert." Jimmy knew the value of it, and Peter Grant knew the value of it.

DAVID BATES (former Page & Plant A&R man; friend of Plant's) When I heard about the O2, to be honest, I thought, "Robert ain't gonna do that." And now we get to the nitty-gritty: it was *only* to do with Ahmet and the fact that the family had asked that he do it.

JOHN PAUL JONES [Robert] was the one who started all this, because he was a great friend of Ahmet's. Knowing Robert, he thought we'd get together, do a few songs, have a good time, go home and sink a few pints, and that would be it. That's how he is. He probably didn't anticipate 120 million hits on the website.

ED BICKNELL (former manager of Dire Straits) I think he got a bit ticked off that the fact it was an Ahmet Ertegun benefit got completely lost. And to me, he looked rather detached from the proceedings. It was perfectly performed and professional, and Jason Bonham did very well, but they couldn't possibly have lived up to the expectation.

JOHN PAUL JONES [Jason was] the star of the show, I thought. Not only did he pull it all off, he took chances—and that takes a lot of guts. He's a different drummer to his father, but there are certain elements that remind you of his father. So he's definitely got his dad's genes.

JASON BONHAM (son of John Bonham; drummer for the O2 show) All I was trying to impress on the day was the three guys on the stage. If I'd thought about who was there, I think it would have been more nerve-racking. Just to get a glance or a nod or a wink or a smile from any of one of them at any point made me feel like, "Yeah, this is okay, yeah?"

MAC POOLE (Midlands drummer and old friend of Bonzo's) Jason's had a tough ride, and I know for many years he did a lot of drinking. When you're the son of somebody like Bonzo, it's not easy. All over the world, it's, "Oh, you're Bonzo's son!"

HELEN GRANT (daughter of Peter Grant) Bonzo's mum was there at the O2. She was talking to Robert, and she said, "*You* haven't changed, you're still standing up there scratching your balls!"

ROBERT PLANT That was really the best Led Zeppelin gig since 1975, to me. But, of course, it *wasn't* Led Zeppelin. Let's not forget that.

ROSS HALFIN (photographer) I really didn't enjoy the O2 because I was having such a bad time there from the various camps. Because I'm seen as *Jimmy's guy*, the other two did not want me doing the pictures. But then they hated the pictures they *did* get. At the show, I was standing in the corridor about a minute before they went on, and I saw Plant and Jones talking. So I got Jason and Jimmy in and got a shot of them all laughing together—and that was the one group shot that everyone used.

BENJI LeFEVRE   Robert was very clear that it was only ever going to be about paying tribute to Ahmet, but Jimmy was hoping it would be the start of getting the whole thing rolling again. Robert told me that the minute they agreed to do the O2, one of the first things Jimmy was on about was the merchandising and how they were going to split the money.

JOHN PAUL JONES   I spoke to [Jimmy] just a few days afterward, and we both thought the same—that it felt like the first night of a tour. You think, "Oh, I could do that a bit better or change something in that song." And we didn't get a chance to do any more.

BRAD TOLINSKI (editor, *Guitar World*)   I think Page's feelings changed. He was very excited about the reunion and thought it was going to happen. And when it didn't, I think it was a disappointment. But I've talked to him a bunch of times, and he keeps his cards close to his chest. He was just upset that it was a lot of work to do for a one-off gig.

JIMMY PAGE   At the time of the run-up and rehearsals toward the show, I think we assumed that there were going to be more dates. It would have been nice to play more concerts. But even while I was going 'round doing Christmas shopping, people were still coming up and saying, "Is there a chance of a reunion?"

DAVID BATES   The amount of money they were offered to reunite was $240 million. It was obscene. And it *did not make any difference* to Robert. He does have an ego, and he does have pride, but he also has something called integrity, and that for him is worth more than two hundred and forty mil.

DENNY SOMACH (producer of "Get the Led Out" segments on U.S. classic rock radio)   There are two bands besides the Beatles and the Stones that have become cross-generational: Led Zeppelin and Pink Floyd. There's an outstanding offer of $3 million per show for Pink

Floyd, should they ever get back together and want to play. The offers that have been made to Led Zeppelin you've probably heard about; Live Nation offered $300 million plus. It's ridiculous money. And the people who would want to go wouldn't be kids. It would be people like me *bringing* their kids.

BRAD TOLINKSI   I don't really get what Robert has against reworking that unit. Maybe it's just what he's said on the surface of it, which is that Led Zeppelin was John Bonham. It's not a bad reason, it's pretty legitimate. But there seems to be something between Jimmy and Robert, and Robert doesn't want to go there, and Jimmy *certainly* won't go there. Robert is his own man now, and I think if it turned into a Zeppelin project, I don't know if he'd still be able to be his own man.

GYL CORRIGAN-DEVLIN (friend of Plant's and Page's)   They played well together, but they never *talked* well together. It's a strange relationship because they love each other, they really do, but they hate each other as well. People love to say it's about which one is the front man, but I never thought that's what it was. If they weren't both musicians, they wouldn't have anything in common at all.

BILL CURBISHLEY (manager of Robert Plant)   However much I still urge Page to call Robert, go have some lunch, just hang out, he can't do it. They're two different animals. Totally different animals.

CHRIS DREJA (former bassist in the Yardbirds)   Jimmy and John Paul booked the Ritz in Putney for three months, trying to find a replacement for Robert. They had all sorts of people there.

STEVEN TYLER (singer with Aerosmith)   I spoke to Jimmy Page's manager, Peter Mensch, who's been a good friend of mine forever. He said Robert wouldn't play with them again, and would I want to come over and jam with the guys? I went over and played. [But when] it came time for [Jimmy] to say, "You want to write a record with me?" I went, "No." I'm in Aerosmith. He's in the biggest band in the world, and I'm in a band like that.

HENRY SMITH (former Zeppelin roadie, subsequent roadie for Aerosmith)   What it came down to in the end was that Steven realized he's not Robert. It goes back to the three-legged table again: you can't replace somebody like that. Robert has his own unique way of presenting a song, and you can't expect any kid to go to a concert and hear "Stairway" sung by somebody else. And Steven didn't want to get in that position where maybe it will or won't work, while he already has a band that *does* work.

JOHN PAUL JONES   [Josh Homme and I] kind of met at Dave [Grohl]'s birthday party at Medieval Times, which was pretty strange. It was like a blind date with Josh, but [Dave] sat us together and watched us from the seats behind. And Josh was reasonably embarrassed about being there at all, I think. But it was fun, and we went into the studio the next day and just started jamming. And yeah, [Them Crooked Vultures] was quite immediate. We just realized, "Oh, actually there could be something here." I could have expected that there would be; I couldn't see how we could not happen. How we could not be great? Because I've always liked Queens of the Stone Age and always thought Josh was really interesting. Dave, you know, Dave is just great anyway. So I couldn't see how it could not be what it was.

JAAN UHELSZKI (writer for *MOJO, Harp,* and other publications)   Dave Grohl wants to collect all the right people. But dinner parties don't always work, even when you invite lots of cool people.

31

And What Should Never Be

My peers may flirt with cabaret, some fake the rebel yell/I'm
moving up to higher ground, I must escape their hell.
                                        —Robert Plant, "Tin Pan Valley" (2005)

ED BICKNELL (former Dire Straits manager) Right before the O2
show, I ran into Robert at Ronnie Scott's and he said something like,
"I'm going to go on tour with Alison Krauss, and if Jimmy doesn't like
it, he can fuck off." But he kind of grinned as he said it. In my recollection, he also said something like, "Jimmy wants to go out and play
the greatest hits, whereas I want to write some new songs and make a
new record." And that seemed to be the nub of the difference.

GYL CORRIGAN-DEVLIN (friend of Plant's) Robert is afraid of looking like
he doesn't have anything new to offer. And I hope that maybe now he's
proved himself in this area—and proved that he can sing and not just
yell—he might say, "Okay, let's go, I can do it." But he's also afraid of looking foolish. He thinks Mick Jagger looks silly when he's strutting around.

Robert is probably at his happiest traipsing around old churches and cemeteries. It's like an alter ego that goes onstage. He probably can't even remember who that Led Zeppelin guy *was*.

ALISON KRAUSS (Plant's partner on *Raising Sand*)   When I first met him at a Leadbelly tribute, I saw that big hairdo [and] I said, "Robert." He turns around, he's got these glasses on, and he goes, "There you are." And the first thing he starts talking about is Ralph Stanley. He's very passionate about music. We were riding around making the record, and he goes, "Do you think something's wrong with me? My kids say, 'We want a real dad, can't you be a normal dad?' and I'm like, 'They're going to be waiting a long time.'"

ROY WILLIAMS (sound engineer for Plant)   There was a guy who did a show called *Crossroads* for CMT, and they would invite two people from different genres. Alison was due to do something with Steven Tyler, but it had all fallen through. So the guy had sent this letter to Robert and asked if he might be interested. That brought them together. And then Alison brought T Bone Burnett into the frame.

ROBERT PLANT   With *Raising Sand*, I finally wanted to visit the America I've always loved musically. And I just had to believe I could do something I'd never tried before. That's the challenge, to go to a new land and be prepared to take the risk, be prepared to make a mistake. Be prepared for anything, really—Gene Clark's "Polly," for instance. When I first heard my vocal on that, I went, "My God, is that me?" It's such a beautiful song, and I'd never sung lyrics, I don't think, that are so poignant.

ROY WILLIAMS   Alison's expression on the first show was like a rabbit caught in the headlights. But then we realized that the fear of it being two audiences was unnecessary: most people were coming for *that album*. The fourth gig in, we realized, "There's an audience here for this." It became almost churchlike.

ROBERT PLANT   Alison is just a miracle. There was no real "Let's do it like this." The two of us step up to the microphone, and she's amazing, she can just follow my voice. She said, on "When the Levee Breaks," "If you want to go up, I'll come with you; just give me one split second . . ."

GYL CORRIGAN-DEVLIN Alison is like a petal, very sweet and delicate, everything very feminine. There was nothing rock chick about her, which I thought was very cool. Robert picks up the tambourine and starts banging it, and you could hear Alison whispering to him, "Tell me what to do." She was in awe of him, but he was in awe of *her*.

JAAN UHELSZKI (writer for *MOJO, Harp* and other publications) I saw Robert with Alison in Berkeley, and I thought, "He shouldn't be playing second fiddle to anyone. . . . This is subverting his power into some idyllic Americana dream that he has, and I think he's so much bigger than that." I was shocked that he was kind of making fun of Zeppelin, albeit in a very charming way. If it hadn't been him doing this kind of pastiche of Zeppelin songs, I'd have gone, "How *dare* you." It was very cute, but cute doesn't stand anywhere near monolithic.

ROBERT PLANT With everything I've done solo-wise, I've looked back and I've sort of mimicked and smiled at the Zeppelin thing a little impishly. But that's my prerogative.

ROY WILLIAMS I'm pleased for his success because it just came naturally, and no one expected it. I know that they got back together for a while with T Bone, and what I do know is that Alison said to Robert, "There's nothing wrong with killing the goose that laid the golden egg." They went to Nashville, and it wasn't quite working, and everyone else had their other schedules, so that's why nothing continued with Alison.

ROBERT PLANT It wasn't *Raising Sand*, it was *Raising Hell*. We had a few songs, but they weren't as immediate. Alison also wanted to do something more contemporary, so she went back to her band Union Station. Our record captured a moment, and I'm sure we'll have others.

JOHN OGDEN (former pop writer for the *Birmingham Express and Star*) Robert can walk 'round town, and nobody will bother him. He's got his mates, and if they go out on the town, they all pay the round. There's no superstar thing about it at all. If he ever intimidates people, it's only by his presence, not his attitude.

GYL CORRIGAN-DEVLIN   When you go and stay with him, everyone is like, "Morning, Planty!" It's like, "Don't be pulling your rock-god stuff *here*." When he goes to the pub, people go out of their way to ignore him.

ROY WILLIAMS   I think it's the nature of the Black Country that the people here are reasonably grounded. If Robert was stepping out of line, somebody would tell him. When he got his CBE, he was down the pub, and everybody was saluting him and calling him "My liege." It's the same when he goes down the Wolves. He's in the stands, and people are saying, "Still doin' a bit of singin', are we, Planty?"

DAVID BATES (former A&R man for Page and Plant; friend of Plant's)   I called Robert up to congratulate him just after he'd been made vice president or whatever it is of Wolves, because I knew how much that meant to him. He gets great pleasure and great pain from that club. And it always rankled with him, I think, that Wolves never really recognized him. The new owner, when he came in, realized that Robert in PR terms has done

Billy Wright Stand, Molineux, spring 2010. (Art Sperl)

an awful lot for them. I said to him, "Well done, but let's look at *you* and *Raising Sand* now. You've finally done it. You are no longer just 'Robert Plant, formerly of Led Zeppelin.'" I think he was touched by that.

MAC POOLE (drummer and old friend of Bonham's)   Robert was always smooth, always able to charm everybody. But he still had the Black Country manner. All the fame and fortune, it's all bollocks, and he knows that.

ROBERT PLANT   I'm still moving in the same space with the same people that I was forty-odd years ago. I'm able to go to a class reunion where everybody will take the piss out of me. I think my luck has been that I've always believed in the strength of family. There's nothing noble about that, but it's a better drug than anything you can buy.

KEVYN GAMMOND (former guitarist in the Band of Joy and Priory of Brion)   I don't think Robert likes the darker edge that I do. I remember asking if he wanted to come over and watch Lars von Trier's *Antichrist*, and he said no thank you very much. He likes happier things, I think because he's had a lot of sadness in his life.

GUY PRATT (bassist in Coverdale/Page)   Robert's arguments for not doing Zeppelin again stand up: it's a young man's job, and he says he can't get his shoulders back that far. On the stuff that he's doing, he sounds like a man who is very comfortable in his own skin. I feel sorry for Jimmy, and I'd do anything to see them together again.

JAAN UHELSZKI   I think Jimmy has one big move left, and I hope that he can get to it in time. I applaud Robert for going forward, but maybe in my time capsule I want to remember those guys in Valhalla. I feel like a child of divorce who's still hoping my parents will get back together.

UNITY MacLEAN (former manager of Swan Song office in the U.K.)   There *is* life after Led Zeppelin, according to Robert. Whereas Jimmy hasn't found it. It's ironic because *Jimmy* was always the one who loved to explore. Jimmy is stuck, and I think it's partly because he's a loner. He's always been alone in his room, instead of getting out there and socializing.

EDDIE KRAMER (engineer on *Led Zeppelin II* and *Houses of the Holy*) I just wish Jimmy would make something really significant today. I think he's living in the past. Robert is flexible, and Jimmy is not. Jimmy has one vision, and that's it. I admire Robert so much for having taken all those musical chances. Experimenting, trying different things. The thing that he did with Alison Krauss is bloody marvelous. You hear the Zeppelin influences very clearly, but it's different. It's *not* Led Zeppelin.

KEVYN GAMMOND Jimmy has kept the Zep flag flying. If you go into any W.H. Smith, there's always a magazine cover with him on it, whether it's *Record Collector* or a guitar mag. And in some ways it's kind of sad, because he was capable of going with someone like Scott Walker and doing some really interesting stuff—as opposed to working with Paul Rodgers or the Black Crowes or whoever it is.

JANE AYER (former press officer, Atlantic Records) When you look at Eric Clapton or Jeff Beck, who are always out there and touring and collaborating, you think, "Where's Jimmy?"

GUY PRATT For "Whole Lotta Love," we went into Olympic Studios 2, where they'd recorded the original, and they had all the original amps. And then Leona Lewis came in and sang it. My little joke is that it seems a bit shorter than the original, and I suddenly realized why. They had to leave the last verse out because nobody had the heart to tell Leona there is no female equivalent of a back door man.

I'm the bloke who accidentally leaked the name of the song to the press in my blog. I put a little footnote, saying, "Oh, by the way when Leona Lewis and Jimmy Page do 'Whole Lotta Love,' that's me playing bass on it." I was woken at six o' clock in the morning by a lawyer in Beijing. In the *Sun*, I was the appropriately named "Mr. Pratt."

Jimmy didn't want anything to do with me. When I saw him after that, about two years later, he said, "We're not talking to you." And he made me fucking tap-dance for about five minutes before he would speak to me. There's a certain type of pop star who just loves to be upset with people: "Just give me a reason to be upset."

Other than that, it was absolutely fine. I've done all sorts of stuff with Jimmy over the years and remain incredibly fond of him. He came to my book launch, and we had a very nice chat and he forgave me. He told me the terrible tale of Michael Lee, who spent the last fucking two years of his life homeless, alcoholic, and epileptic. Jimmy was saying he'd gone up to the funeral in Darlington. I thought it was very sweet of him to go.

LORI MATTIX (former L.A. groupie)   Jimmy did sell his soul. So many bad things happened, and I think Jimmy thought it was kind of his curse. In a way, his sobriety was making amends to himself, because he felt like a lot of it he brought on.

MARTIN STONE (guitarist and book dealer)   Jimmy today, clean and sober, doesn't seem like someone who would be drawing pentagrams. Recovery is about shedding the ego, whereas all that Crowley stuff seems to be about expanding and inflating it.

BRAD TOLINKSI   I just want to hear Jimmy play music and do something creative, and I think Robert's success has helped awaken some of those impulses.

MICHAEL DES BARRES (former lead singer of Silverhead and Detective)   Jimmy now has to capitulate to Robert's needs and wishes. Robert is a six-Grammy winner with three million sales who does not want to sing about squeezing lemons anymore. That being said, Jimmy is now sober, and I think he accepts what is going on. Is he sitting at home wishing he was playing at Madison Square Garden? Probably not. I think in the documentary with Jack White and the Edge, you can see that he's at peace.

JACK WHITE (singer-guitarist with the White Stripes and other bands)   Songwriting-wise, I was coming from the same places that Jimmy and Robert were—Robert Johnson, Tommy Johnson, Blind Willie McTell. We were feeding from the same trough. Like, "If you want this to be powerful *and* feed from these same influences, there are going to be moments where you sound like Led Zeppelin." So then it was, "Oh, well, maybe it *does* sound like that, but I know in my heart

I didn't sit down and try and copy Led Zeppelin. So what do we do? Do we leave them off the record?"

ROBERT PLANT   I love the way that Jack in his interviews says, "Robert Plant is the thing I *least* liked about Led Zeppelin." And I think, "Well, that's fine, boy, but if you're gonna play 'In My Time of Dying,' listen to the master . . . or even to 'Jesus Gonna Make Up My Dying Bed' from 1930. I tell you, there's no Blind Willie Johnson there. But you know, that sound hasn't really been heard in the contemporary world, in bedsit-college land, since 1970. So its sudden reemergence via the White Stripes was, like, "Hey, what's *that*?"

LORI MATTIX   Robert wanted to prove his success on his own, and he did it. Now that's out of the way, he might just go there, because he would like that adoration one more time. He'll never get that unless he does that coliseum shit again.

ROY WILLIAMS   From the physical point of view, Robert can keep on pursuing this musical adventure that he *has* got and know full well that he has control of his environment, rather than go back into that Zeppelin thing and not be in control because of the expectations.

ROBERT PLANT   I'd love to work with Jimmy and John Paul, but I don't see how we could give it anything constructive without falling back into the sort of general melée of everybody's expectations. It would be good to see what happened, but that means that you reinvoke that tired old harness. And I'm very, very happy where I am musically. I've reached that stage where the old guard has given up, and there's a new crowd out there that gives you far more energy and response when you play.

HENRY SMITH (former Zeppelin roadie)   Robert knows he can't do Zeppelin the way people would want it to be done. And that's no dis-respect to him; it's just what happens with age. You just can't hit those higher registers, and for a band like Zeppelin to take a song down a half-step, you lose the energy and feel of a song. And there's no way Robert would ever allow that to happen.

JACK CALMES (Showco)   There's all kinds of speculation on why Robert Plant won't do Zeppelin again. I think there's probably a little bit of the old "Something bad's going to happen if I do this again," but also a little bit of "I don't *need* to do it—I've got a good career going."

DANNY MARKUS (former artist relations man, Atlantic Records)   I've been on those One Show Too Many tours, and there's everything to lose and very little to gain. Led Zeppelin sell a million a year without ever doing *anything,* so why screw with that?

PHIL CARSON (former head of Atlantic Records in Europe)   It doesn't matter what Jimmy or Robert ever do in life separately or how successful it becomes. That magic when they're together takes it to a different level. And neither of them can get away from that fact.

· · ·

AUBREY POWELL (designer and cofounder of Hipgnosis)   Robert and Jimmy will always be joined at the hip by Zeppelin, but they will never embrace it again in the way they did.

BENJI LeFEVRE (former Zeppelin technician and producer of Robert Plant's)   It would be so interesting to have a candid conversation with the three of them sitting there and know that they were over it all and able to talk about it. Clearly, they aren't.

KIM FOWLEY (L.A. producer and scenester)   In the twenty-first century, there'll never be another Led Zeppelin, because there'll never be four geniuses in a band again. It's a different time and a different environment.

JIMMY PAGE   The music was never in fashion, in a way, and it was never *meant* to be in fashion. It was meant to be there, and it's still there, so that part of it is right and has triumphed. All the other things are relative to, "Oh, so-and-so did this in a hotel." But the bottom line of it is what the music is all about.

JOHN PAUL JONES   Listening to Zeppelin music now, it only dates because of the recording techniques—the *amount* of bass drum there is and so on. The music itself is timeless.

ROBERT PLANT   I was part of something magnificent that broke the *Guinness Book of Records*, but in the end, what are you going to get out of it? Who are you doing it for? You have to ask these questions: Who pays the piper, and what is valuable in this life? I don't want to scream "Immigrant Song" every night for the rest of my life, and I'm not sure I could.

DANNY GOLDBERG (former president of Swan Song in the U.S.)   My guess, and it's only a guess—again, I have no inside information—is that sometime in the next five years, Robert will call Jimmy and John Paul, and they'll do a tour. I think it's just as valuable to the market-place now as it would have been in 2009. It's still a billion-dollar tour. It's still an extraordinary opportunity.

AUTHOR INTERVIEWS

SAM AIZER   February 26, 2011, phone interview

KEITH ALTHAM   March 16, 2010, London

MIKE APPLETON   March 30, 2011, Cobham, England

JANE AYER   July 23, 2010, phone interview

JUNE HARRIS BARSALONA   November 20, 2010, phone interview

DAVID BATES   June 24, 2010, phone interview

MAGGIE BELL   March 23, 2010, London

ED BICKNELL   April 12, 2010, London

RODNEY BINGENHEIMER   July 23, 2010, Los Angeles

ROBBIE BLUNT   March 28, 2011, phone interview

BILL BONHAM   January 7, 2011, phone interview

CAROLINE BOUCHER   March 26, 2010, phone interview

LORAINE ALTERMAN BOYLE   July 12, 2010, New York City

BEBE BUELL   August 31, 2010, phone interview

ALAN CALLAN   December 23, 2010, phone interview, and February 17, 2011, London

JACK CALMES   May 11 and 18, 2010, phone interviews, and June 8, 2010, London

JULIE CARLO   May 21, 2010, Peacehaven, England

PHIL CARLO   April 20 and May 21, 2010, Peacehaven, England

GARY CARNES   April 28, 2010, phone interview

ROY CARR   September 3 and 9, 2010, phone interview

PHIL CARSON   November 4, 2010, London

CLEM CATTINI   January 11, 2011, phone interview

CHRIS CHARLESWORTH   November 9, 2010, phone interview

NICKY CHINN   December 10, 1997, London

PETER CLIFTON   January 31, 2011, phone interview

MARILYN COLE   March 4, 2010, London

RICHARD COLE   November 19, 2005, and March 1, 2011, London

JOHN COMBE   May 24, 2010, Kidderminster, England

GYL CORRIGAN-DEVLIN   January 19, 2011, London

JOHN CRUTCHLEY   May 24, 2010, Walsall, England

MICHAEL DES BARRES   May 5, 2010, phone interview

PAMELA DES BARRES   July 23, 2010, Los Angeles

MARIE DIXON   February 10, 2011, phone interview

CHRIS DREJA   April 23, 2010, London

MARK ELLEN   March 24, 2011, phone interview

BOB EMMER   February 7, 2011, phone interview

BP FALLON   July 11, 2010, New York City

MICK FARREN   July 23, 2011, Los Angeles

KIM FOWLEY   July 22, 2010, phone interview

MITCHELL FOX   June 25, 2010, phone interview

PAUL FRANCIS   May 14, 2011, phone interview

TONY FRANKLIN   May 31, 2011, e-mail interview

TOM FRY   November 2, 2010, London

KEVYN GAMMOND   April 15, 2010, Kidderminster, England

VANESSA GILBERT   February 21, 2011, phone interview

DANNY GOLDBERG   April 2, 2010, phone interview, and July 16, 2010, New York City

GLORIA GRANT   February 9, 2011, Eastbourne, England

HELEN GRANT   August 25, 2010, Eastbourne, England

JERRY GREENBERG   July 27, 2010, Los Angeles

GEOFF GRIMES   May 26, 2010, Bishop's Castle, Wales

ROSS HALFIN   January 11, 2011, Cheam, England

CONNIE HAMZY   June 7, 2010, phone interview

ROY HARPER   March 29, 2011, e-mail interview

BILL HARRY   May 5, 2010, London

ANDREW HEWKIN   April 2, 2010, London

DAVE HILL   April 14, 2010, Birmingham, England

ABE HOCH   July 27, 2010, Los Angeles

GLENN HUGHES   January 7, 2011, phone interview

ELIZABETH "BETTY" IANNACI   November 24 and December 3, 2010, phone interviews

TONY IOMMI   February 23, 2011, phone interview

ANNI IVIL   August 25, 2010, Brighton, England

ANDY JOHNS   July 20 and 23, 2010, Los Angeles

GLYN JOHNS   May 13, 2010, West Stoke, England

JOHN PAUL JONES   April 16, 2003, London

SHELLEY KAYE   September 22, 2010, phone interview

NICK KENT   May 14, 2011, Paris, France

DESIREE KIRKE   November 6, 2010, phone interview

SIMON KIRKE   May 5, 2010, e-mail interview

EDDIE KRAMER   July 22, 2010, Los Angeles

HARVEY KUBERNIK   July 27, 2010, Los Angeles

BENJI LeFEVRE   March 16, 2011, London

DAVE LEWIS   June 9, 2010, Bedford, England

HARVEY LISBERG   March 25, 2011, phone interview

PAUL LOCKEY   June 14, 2010, phone interview

MARK LONDON   May 10, 2011, phone interview

UNITY MacLEAN   November 11, 2010, phone interview

MIKEAL MAGLIERI   July 27, 2010, Los Angeles

TONY MANDICH   July 26, 2010, Los Angeles

TERRY MANNING   February 3, 2011, phone interview

DANNY MARKUS   July 28, 2010, Los Angeles

LORI "LIGHTNING" MATTIX   July 26, 2010, Los Angeles

MARIO MEDIOUS   April 26, 2010, phone interview

MARTIN MEISSONNIER   June 25, 2011, phone interview

JOHN MENDELSSOHN   July 13, 2010, phone interview

LAURENCE MYERS   February 21, 2011, phone interview

HOWARD MYLETT   June 3, 2010, Portslade, England

RON NEVISON   May 9, 2010, phone interview

DAVE NORTHOVER   January 17, 2011, phone interview

JEFF OCHELTREE   November 8, 2010, phone interview

JOHN OGDEN   May 25, 2010, Wolverhampton, England

JIMMY PAGE   April 17, 2003, London

DAVE PEGG   May 17, 2010, Banbury, England

ROBERT PLANT   April 15, 2003, Birmingham, England, and September 18, 2003, Machyllneth, Wales

MAC POOLE   June 10, 2010, London

IGGY POP   October 10, 1986, London

AUBREY POWELL   March 2, 2011, London

GUY PRATT   February 4, 2011, phone interview

PERRY PRESS   February 16, 2011, London

BARRY JAY REISS   January 25, 2011, phone interview

JAKE RIVIERA   February 28, 2011, London

WILLIE ROBERTSON   December 13, 2010, London

STEVEN ROSEN   April 28, 2010, e-mail interview

CYNTHIA SACH   February 3, 2011, phone interview

JANINE SAFER (WHITNEY)   July 13, 2010, New York City

ELLEN SANDER April 21, 2010, e-mail interview

RAT SCABIES February 11, 2011, phone interview

HARRY SHAPIRO March 4, 2011, e-mail interview

DENNIS SHEEHAN April 22, 2010, phone interview

JIM SIMPSON May 24, 2010, Birmingham, England

DIGBY SMITH September 12, 2010, Torquay, England

HENRY "THE HORSE" SMITH January 17, 2011, Skype interview

STEVE SMITH February 17, 2011, phone interview

BARNABY SNOW September 14, 2010, phone interview

MAT SNOW March 28, 2010, phone interview

DENNY SOMACH April 22, 2010, London

MARTIN STONE February 24, 2011, phone interview

BIG JIM SULLIVAN January 13, 2011, phone interview

BRAD TOLINSKI November 24, 2010, phone interview

JAAN UHELSZKI September 22, 2010, phone interview

JON WEALLEANS April 8, 2010, phone interview

CHRIS WELCH April 27, 2010, West Wickham, England

MORGANA WELCH January 14, 2011, phone interview

JERRY WEXLER March 30, 1993, Sarasota

JACK WHITE March 17, 2006, London, and August 18, 2009, Salt Lake City

RICHARD WILLIAMS May 19, 2011, phone interview

ROY WILLIAMS May 24, 2010, Bewdley, England

SALLY WILLIAMS November 16, 2010, phone interview

JOE "JAMMER" WRIGHT March 22, 2010, phone interview

OTHER SOURCES

JUSTIN ADAMS quote on p. 474 from interview by Keith Cameron in *MOJO*, September 2010, p. 86, used by kind permission of Keith Cameron.

STEVE ALBINI quote on p. 469 from interview by Nick Hasted on uncut. co.uk, January 2009, used by kind permission of Nick Hasted.

KENNETH ANGER quotes:

- (p. 309) Interview by Chris Salewicz, *New Musical Express*, 1977, used by kind permission of Chris Salewicz.
- (p. 308) Interview by Edward Helmore, April 2011, used by kind permission of Edward Helmore.

DICK ASHER quote on p. 108 from Chris Welch, *Peter Grant: The Man Who Led Zeppelin* (London: Omnibus Press, 2002), p. 67, used by kind permission of Chris Welch.

FRANK BARSALONA quote on pp. 75–76 from interview by David Beal for Steve Chapple and Reebee Garofalo, *Rock 'n' Roll Is Here to Pay: The History and Politics of the Music Industry* (Chicago: Nelson-Hall, 1977), pp. 124–125, used by kind permission of Steve Chapple.

PETER BARSOTTI quote on p. 374 from Bill Graham and Robert Greenfield, *Bill Graham Presents: My Life inside Rock and Out* (New York: Random House, 1993), p. 414, used by kind permission of Robert Greenfield.

LONG JOHN BALDRY quote on p. 13 from 1971 interview by John Pidgeon in his 2009 piece "Blues Incorporated: How British R&B Trashed Trad" on www.rocksbackpages.com, http://www.rocksbackpages.com/article.html?ArticleID=15485, used by kind permission of John Pidgeon.

JEFF BECK quotes:

- (first quote on p. 13 and pp. 64, 75, and 82) Interview by Stuart Grundy and John Tobler, *The Guitar Greats* (London: BBC Books, 1983), used by kind permission of Stuart Grundy and John Tobler.

- (second quote on p. 13) Interview by Will Nash in *Stu* (London: Out-Take, 2003).

- (pp. 10 and 63) Interview by Charles Shaar Murray, *MOJO*, August 2004, used by kind permission of Charles Shaar Murray.

- (p. 115) Interview by Dave Thompson, *Goldmine*, July 2007, used by kind permission of Dave Thompson.

- (p. 62) Interview by Alan DiPerna in *Guitar World*, March 2009, used by kind permission of Alan DiPerna.

JOHN "JB" BETTIE quotes on pp. 420 and 422 from interview in *Mr. Rock 'n' Roll*, VCTV documentary, 2000.

BEV BEVAN quotes:

- (pp. 42 and 52) Chris Welch and Geoff Nicholls, *John Bonham: A Thunder of Drums* (San Francisco: Backbeat Books, 2001), pp. 67 and 70, used by kind permission of Chris Welch.

- (p. 404) Mick Wall, *When Gods Walked the Earth: A Biography of Led Zeppelin* (London: Orion, 2008), p. 437, used by kind permission of Mick Wall.

CHRIS BLACKWELL quote on p. 108 from Robert Greenfield, *The Last Sultan: The Life and Times of Ahmet Ertegun* (New York: Simon & Schuster, 2011), pp. 217–218, used by kind permission of Robert Greenfield.

DEBBIE BONHAM quotes on pp. 40, 297, 387–388, and 410 from interview in *The John Bonham Story*, first broadcast on BBC Radio 2 on September 28, 2010.

JASON BONHAM quotes on pp. 49 and 476 from interview in *The John Bonham Story*, first broadcast on BBC Radio 2 on September 28, 2010.

JOHN BONHAM quotes:

- (p. 40) Interview in *Disc and Music Echo*, June 27, 1970.
- (pp. 41 and 179) Interview by Chris Welch, *Melody Maker*, June 21, 1975, used by kind permission of Chris Welch.
- (p. 137) *MOJO Classic: Led Zeppelin and the Story of 1969*.

MICK BONHAM quotes on pp. 40 and 49 from Mick Wall, *When Gods Walked the Earth: A Biography of Led Zeppelin* (London: Orion, 2008) pp. 32 and 88, used by kind permission of Mick Wall.

RUSTY BRUTSCHE quote on p. 399 from interview by Dave Lewis, *Tight But Loose*, February 2011, used by kind permission of Dave Lewis.

TREVOR BURTON quote on p. 32 from interview in BBC4 documentary *Steve Winwood: English Soul*, first broadcast in June 2010.

ALAN CALLAN quote on p. 405 from interview by Mick Brown, *Telegraph* magazine, January 20, 1996, used by kind permission of Mick Brown.

PHIL CARSON quote on p. 186 from interview by James McNair, *Q: 50 Years of Rock 'n' Roll* (2004), used by kind permission of James McNair.

ROBERT CHRISTGAU quote on p. 217 from "The Move into Rock," in *What'd I Say: The Atlantic Story* (New York: Welcome Rain, 2001), pp. 293–295, used by kind permission of Robert Christgau.

BILL COLE quote on p. 14 from *Goin' Home: The Uncompromising Life and Music of Ken Colyer* (London: Ken Colyer Foundation, 2010), used by kind permission of the Ken Colyer Foundation.

RICHARD COLE quotes:

- (p. 323) Chris Welch, *Peter Grant: The Man Who Led Zeppelin* (London: Omnibus Press, 2002), p. 212, used by kind permission of Chris Welch.
- (p. 222) Interview in *Classic Rock*, December 2007.

PHIL COLLINS quote on p. 442 from Chris Welch and Geoff Nicholls, *John Bonham: A Thunder of Drums* (San Francisco: Backbeat Books, 2001), p. 124, used by kind permission of Chris Welch.

CLIVE COULSON quote on pp. 155–156 from interview by Phil Sutcliffe, *MOJO*, April 2000, used by kind permission of Phil Sutcliffe.

CAMERON CROWE quote on pp. 231–232 from 2000 interview in *Almost Famous*, used by kind permission of Cameron Crowe.

BILL CURBISHLEY quotes on pp. 133, 197, 421, and 478 from Robert Greenfield, *The Last Sultan: The Life and Times of Ahmet Ertegun*

(New York: Simon & Schuster, 2011), pp. 219–222, used by kind permission of Robert Greenfield.

RAY DAVIES quote on p. 25 from *X-Ray: The Unauthorized Autobiography* by Ray Davies (London: Overlook Duckworth, 1994), pp. 186–187.

JACKIE DeSHANNON quote on p. 28 from sleeve notes to *Come and Get Me: The Complete Liberty and Imperial Singles* (Ace, 2011), used by kind permission of Jackie DeShannon.

MALCOLM DENT quote on p. 167 from interview by Calum Macleod, *Inverness Courier*, November 3, 2006.

DONOVAN quote on p. 417 from interview by Nick Hasted, uncut.co.uk, January 2009, used by kind permission of Nick Hasted.

DAVE EDMUNDS quote on p. 339 from interview by David Cavanagh, uncut.co.uk, January 2009, used by kind permission of David Cavanagh.

AHMET ERTEGUN quotes:

- (pp. 448–449) Interview by Eric Pooley, *New York*, June 20, 1988, used by kind permission of Eric Pooley.

- (first quote on p. 106) Jerry Wexler with David Ritz, *Rhythm and the Blues: A Life in American Music* (New York: Knopf, 1993), pp. 169–171.

- (second quote on p. 106, and p. 206) Speech inducting Led Zeppelin into the Rock and Roll Hall of Fame, 1995, used by kind permission of the Rock and Roll Hall of Fame.

- (pp. 107, 124, 371, and 419) Interview in *Billboard*, January 17, 1998.

- (p. 459) *Mr. Rock 'n' Roll*, VCTV documentary, 2000.

- (p. 8) Interview in *What'd I Say: The Atlantic Story* (New York: Welcome Rain, 2001), p. 281.

MARIANNE FAITHFULL quote on pp. 28–29 from Marianne Faithfull with David Dalton, *Faithfull* (London: Michael Joseph, 1994) pp. 45–46, used by kind permission of Marianne Faithfull and David Dalton.

BILL FORD quote on p. 41 from interview on Brum Beat website, http://www.brumbeat.net/senators.htm.

STEFAN GATES quote on p. 192 from *Stefan Gates' Cover Story*, Radio 4 documentary, first broadcast February 2010.

DANNY GOLDBERG quotes:

- (pp. 275–276) Danny Goldberg piece on Led Zeppelin in *Circus*, May 1975, used by kind permission of Danny Goldberg.
- (p. 270) Interview by Steven Rosen, *Guitar World*, July 1986, used by kind permission of Steven Rosen.
- (pp. 329–330) Danny Goldberg, *Bumping into Geniuses: My Life inside the Rock 'n' Roll Business* (New York: Gotham Books, 2008), pp. 88–89 and 90, used by kind permission of Danny Goldberg.
- (p. 489) Interview by Randy Patterson, *Perfect Sound Forever*, February 2010, http://www.furious.com/perfect/dannygoldberg.html, used by kind permission of Randy Patterson.

HARVEY GOLDSMITH quotes on pp. 81, 399, 474, and 475 from interview by Larry LeBlanc/Celebrity Access, June 2, 2010, used by kind permission of Larry LeBlanc.

LORD JOHN GOULD quote on p. 459 from interview in *Mr. Rock 'n' Roll*, VCTV documentary, 2000.

BILL GRAHAM quotes:

- (p. 130) *All You Need Is Love* documentary (1975), directed by Tony Palmer.
- (pp. 217 and 372–373) Bill Graham and Robert Greenfield, *Bill Graham Presents: My Life inside Rock and Out* (New York: Random House, 1993), p. 405, used by kind permission of Robert Greenfield.

BOBBY GRAHAM quote on p. 24 from unpublished interview by Kieron Tyler, 1999, used by kind permission of Kieron Tyler.

PETER GRANT quotes from:

- (p. 66) Interview by Michael Watts, *Melody Maker*, June 22, 1974, used by kind permission of Michael Watts.
- (pp. 65, 98, 112, 116, 124, 193, 212, third quote on p. 246, pp. 248, 403, and 405) Interview by Paul Henderson, *Kerrang!*, September 15, 1990, used by kind permission of Paul Henderson.
- (p. 125) 1995 TV interview used in *Mr. Rock 'n' Roll*, VCTV documentary, 2000.
- (pp. 88, 184, first and second quotes on p. 246, pp. 259, 279, 286, 321, 343, 380, 389, 396, 397, 413, 417, 419, and 443) Interview by Dave Lewis, *The Tight But Loose Files: Celebration II*

(London: Omnibus Press, 2003), pp. 89–100, used by kind permission of Dave Lewis.

- (pp. 161, 237, and 342) Chris Welch, *Peter Grant: The Man Who Led Zeppelin* (London: Omnibus Press, 2002), p. 92.

BOB HARRIS quote on pp. 260–261 from *The Whispering Years* (London: BBC Books, 2001).

ROY HARPER quotes from:

- (p. 236) Interview by Steve Lake, *Melody Maker*, February 9, 1974.
- (p. 431) Interview by Rob Hughes, uncut.co.uk, January 2009, used by kind permission of Rob Hughes.
- (p. 216) Interview by Allan Jones, *Uncut*, July 2011, used by kind permission of Allan Jones.

BILL HARVEY quote on p. 41 from *The John Bonham Story*, first broadcast on BBC Radio 2 on September 28, 2010.

MICK HINTON quote on p. 402 from Dave Lewis, *Led Zeppelin: Feather in the Wind—Over Europe 1980* (Bedford: Tight But Loose Publishing, 2011), used by kind permission of Dave Lewis.

CHRIS HUSTON quote on p. 140 from interview by Dave Lewis in *Classic Rock*, 2004, used by kind permission of Dave Lewis.

CATHERINE JAMES quote on p. 121 from Harvey Kubernik, *Canyon of Dreams: The Magic and the Music of Laurel Canyon* (New York/London: Sterling Publishing, 2009), p. 196, used by kind permission of Harvey Kubernik.

PHIL JOHNSTONE quotes on pp. 448, 450, and 451 from interview on *Robert Plant's Blue Note* (Sexy Intellectual DVD, 2011), used by kind permission of Elio España/Prism Films.

JOHN PAUL JONES quotes:

- (p. 11 and second quote on p. 22) Interview by Steven Rosen, *Guitar Player*, July 1977, used by kind permission of Steven Rosen.
- (p. 98, first quote on p. 124, pp. 246 and 361) Interview by Mat Snow, *Q*, December 1990, used by kind permission of Mat Snow.
- (pp. 104, 440, and 457) Interview by Steven P. Wheeler, *Happening* magazine, October 1999, used by kind permission of Steven P. Wheeler.
- (pp. 18, 21, and first quote on p. 22) Andrew Loog Oldham, *Stoned* (London: Secker and Warburg, 2000), pp. 79, 161, and 325, used by kind permission of Andrew Loog Oldham.

- (p. 190) Chris Welch and Geoff Nicholls, *John Bonham: A Thunder of Drums* (San Francisco: Backbeat Books, 2001), p. 97, used by kind permission of Chris Welch.

- (second quote on p. 124) Chris Welch, *Peter Grant: The Man Who Led Zeppelin* (London: Omnibus Press, 2002), pp. 63–64 and 161, used by kind permission of Chris Welch.

- (pp. 181, 196, 238, 246, 380, 403, 410, 441, and 458) Interview by Dave Lewis, *The Tight But Loose Files: Celebration II* (London: Omnibus Press, 2003), pp. 115–123, used by kind permission of Dave Lewis.

- (p. 476) Interview by Robert Sandall, *Q*, January 2008, used by kind permission of Anita Mackie Sandall.

- (pp. 12, 23, 25, 73, 154, 436, and 477) Interview by David Cavanagh, uncut.co.uk, January 2009, used by kind permission of David Cavanagh.

REG JONES quotes:

- (p. 50) Interview by Mick Bonham, October 30, 2001.

- (p. 113) Laurie Hornsby, *Brum Rocked On!* (Sutton Coldfield: GSM Bestsellers Ltd., 2003), p. 244.

JOHN KALODNER quotes on pp. 452–453 from interview by Patrick Goldstein, *Los Angeles Times*, June 16, 1991, used by kind permission of Patrick Goldstein.

ALEXIS KORNER quote on p. 14 from interview by John Pidgeon in his 2009 piece "Blues Incorporated: How British R&B Trashed Trad" on Rock's Backpages, http://www.rocksbackpages.com/article.html?Article ID=15485, used by kind permission of John Pidgeon.

ALISON KRAUSS quote on p. 481 from interview by Paul Sexton, *Daily Telegraph*, July 22, 2009, used by kind permission of Paul Sexton.

DENNY LAINE quote on p. 42 from Alan Clayson, *Led Zeppelin: The Origin of the Species* (New Malden: Chrome Dreams, 2006), p. 127, used by kind permission of Alan Clayson.

DON LAW quote on p. 127 from Fred Goodman, *The Mansion on the Hill: Dylan, Young, Geffen, Springsteen, and the Head-On Collision of Rock and Commerce* (New York: Times Books, 1997), p. 28, used by kind permission of Fred Goodman.

PAUL LOCKEY quote on p. 51 from interview on Achilles' Last Stand website, 1992.

LULU quote on pp. 223–224 from Mick Bonham, *John Bonham: The Powerhouse behind Led Zeppelin* (London: Southbank Publishing, 2005).

JOHN LYDON quote on p. 305 from interview by Kris Needs, *ZigZag*, June 1977, used by kind permission of Kris Needs.

STEVE MARRIOTT quotes on pp. 38 and 142 from Paolo Hewitt, *Small Faces: The Young Mods' Forgotten Story* (London: Acid Jazz Books, 1995), used by kind permission of Paolo Hewitt.

JOE MASSOT quotes on pp. 237 and 238 from interview by Samuel Mowbray, *Sounds*, November 6, 1976.

JIM MATZORKIS quotes on pp. 372–373 from Bill Graham with Robert Greenfield, *Bill Graham Presents: My Life inside Rock and Out* (New York: Random House, 1993), pp. 403 and 405, used by kind permission of Robert Greenfield.

MALCOLM McLAREN quotes:

- (p. 65) Interview by Mick Brown, *Telegraph* magazine, January 20, 1996, used by kind permission of Mick Brown.

- (pp. 66, 125, and 193) Interview in *Mr. Rock 'n' Roll*, VCTV documentary, 2000.

- (p. 460) Malcolm McLaren, "Peter Grant: The Great Rock 'n' Roll Manager," *Daily Telegraph*, September 18, 1999.

JONI MITCHELL quote on p. 160 from interview by Camilla Paglia, *Interview*, August 2005.

MICKIE MOST quotes:

- (pp. 26 and 82–83) Stuart Grundy and John Tobler, *The Record Producers* (London: BBC Books, 1982), used by kind permission of Stuart Grundy and John Tobler.

- (pp. 67, 69, 193, and 252) Chris Welch, *Peter Grant: The Man Who Led Zeppelin* (London: Omnibus Press, 2002), pp. 23, 83, 83–84, and 141, used by kind permission of Chris Welch.

- (pp. 64–65 and 83) Radio interview by Johnny Black, May 1997, on *Rock's Backpages Audio*, http://www.rocksbackpages.com/article.html?ArticleID=12391, used by kind permission of Johnny Black.

DON MURFET quotes on pp. 393 and 403 from Don Murfet, *Leave It to Me: A Life of Rock, Pop and Crime* (Great Britain: Anvil Publications, 2004), used by kind permission of Kevin Saunders.

CHARLES SHAAR MURRAY quotes on pp. 143 and 215–216 from *New Musical Express*, June 16, 1973, and April 10, 1976, used by kind permission of Charles Shaar Murray.

SIMON NAPIER-BELL quote on pp. 60–61 from interview by Jim Green in *Trouser Press*, October 1981, used by kind permission of Jim Green.

ANDREW LOOG OLDHAM quotes:

- (p. 22) Interview by Dave Thompson, *Goldmine*, November 24, 1995, used by kind permission of Dave Thompson.
- (p. 27) Interview by Rob Hughes, uncut.co.uk, January 2009, used by kind permission of Rob Hughes.

JIMMY PAGE quotes from:

- (pp. 5, 13, 15, 17, 19–20, 21, and 181) Interview by Stuart Grundy and John Tobler, *The Guitar Greats* (BBC Books, 1983), used by kind permission of Stuart Grundy and John Tobler.
- (p. 61) Interview by Keith Altham, *New Musical Express*, July 1966.
- (pp. 27–28, first quote on p. 30, pp. 62, 83, and 91) Interview by Pete Frame, *ZigZag*, 1972, used by kind permission of Pete Frame.
- (p. 179) Interview by Charles Shaar Murray, *New Musical Express*, June 16, 1973, used by kind permission of Charles Shaar Murray.
- (first quote on p. 16) Charles Shaar Murray, "All Hail the British Guitar Revolutionaries," *MOJO*, August 2004.
- (second quote on p. 16 and p. 20) Interview by Nick Kent, *New Musical Express*, September 1, 1973, used by kind permission of Nick Kent.
- (p. 130) Interview by Chris Welch, *Melody Maker*, March 23, 1974, used by kind permission of Chris Welch.
- (p. 245) Conversation with William Burroughs, *Crawdaddy* magazine, June 1975.
- (pp. 275, 300, and 323) Interview by Jonh Ingham, *Sounds*, March 13, 1976, used by kind permission of Jonh Ingham.
- (p. 295) Interview by Harry Doherty, *Melody Maker*, March 20, 1976, used by kind permission of Harry Doherty.
- (p. 25 and first quote on p. 63) Interview by Mick Houghton, *Circus*, October 12, 1976, used by kind permission of Mick Houghton.
- (first quote on p. 10) Interview by Chris Salewicz, *Gig*, May 1977, used by kind permission of Chris Salewicz.

- (second quote on p. 10, pp. 12, 19–20, second quote on p. 30, second quote on p. 63, pp. 99, 109, 168–169, 184, and 185–186) Interview by Steven Rosen, *Guitar Player*, July 1977, and *Guitar World*, May 1993, used by kind permission of Steven Rosen.
- (second quote on p. 16, pages 29, 64, 74, 162, and first quote on p. 298) Interview by Dave Schulps, *Trouser Press*, October 1977, used by kind permission of Dave Schulps.
- (p. 299) Interview by Chris Salewicz, *Creem*, November 1979, used by kind permission of Chris Salewicz.
- (second quote on p. 298, and pp. 430, 434, and 435) Interview by Chris Welch, *Creem*, April 1985, used by kind permission of Chris Welch.
- (pp. 143, 374) Interview by Charles M. Young, *Musician*, July 1988, used by kind permission of Charles M. Young.
- (p. 452) Interview by Timothy White in *Rock Lives: Profiles and Interviews* (New York: Henry Holt, 1990), p. 290.
- (p. 446 and third quote on p. 468) Interviews by Mat Snow, *MOJO*, December 1994, and *MOJO*, May 1998, used by kind permission of Mat Snow.
- (first quote on p. 468) Interview by Sylvie Simmons, *Rolling Stone*, April 1998, used by kind permission of Sylvie Simmons.
- (second quote on p. 468) Interview by H. P. Newquist for the National Guitar Museum, September 1998.
- (pp. 6–7, 7, 11, and 16) Interview by Charles Shaar Murray, *MOJO*, August 2004, used by kind permission of Charles Shaar Murray.
- (p. 477) Interview by James Jackson, *The Times*, January 8, 2010, used by kind permission of James Jackson.

ROBERT PLANT quotes from:

- (first quote on p. 92) Interview by Mark Williams, *International Times*, April 11, 1969, used by kind permission of Mark Williams.
- (pp. 36, 52, 53, and second quote on p. 92) Interview by Richard Williams, *Melody Maker*, September 12, 1970, used by kind permission of Richard Williams.
- (p. 57) Interview by Michael Wale, 1973, quoted in Howard Mylett, *Led Zeppelin* (London: Panther, 1976), p. 92.

- (p. 197) Interview by Caroline Boucher, *Disc and Music Echo*, April 21, 1973, used by kind permission of Caroline Boucher.

- (pp. 190–191) Interview by Loraine Alterman, *Melody Maker*, August 4, 1973, used by kind permission of Loraine Alterman Boyle.

- (pp. 245–246 and 247) Interview by Chris Charlesworth, *Melody Maker*, February 8, 1975, used by kind permission of Chris Charlesworth.

- (pp. 274–275) Interview by Danny Goldberg in *Circus*, May 1975, used by kind permission of Danny Goldberg.

- (p. 248) Onstage at Earl's Court, London, May 24, 1975.

- (pp. 122, 294–295, and 295) Interview by Chris Charlesworth, *Creem*, May 1976, used by kind permission of Chris Charlesworth.

- (first quote on p. 140) Interview in *Circus*, August 24, 1976.

- (p. 357) Interview by Jaan Uhelszki, *Creem*, July 1977, used by kind permission of Jaan Uhelszki.

- (p. 397) Interview by Mat Snow, *New Musical Express*, June 8, 1985, used by kind permission of Mat Snow.

- (p. 94) Joe Smith, *Off the Record: An Oral History of Popular Music* (New York: Warner Books, 1988), p. 339.

- (second quote on p. 98, first quote on p. 181, first quote on p. 406, second quote on p. 412, and pp. 434 and 442) Interview by Tom Hibbert, *Q*, March 1988, used by kind permission of Mark Ellen, trustee of Hibbert estate.

- (first quote on p. 182) Interview by Chuck Eddy, *Creem*, June 1988, used by kind permission of Chuck Eddy.

- (p. 39 and first quote on p. 59) Interview by Mat Snow, *Q*, May 1990, used by kind permission of Mat Snow.

- (p. 142) Interview by Charles M. Young, *Musician*, June 1990, used by kind permission of Charles M. Young.

- (first quote on p. 98, pp. 142–143, 162, 167, second quote on p. 181, pp. 218 and 268) Interview by Mat Snow, *Q*, December 1990, used by kind permission of Mat Snow.

- (pp. 446 and 465) Interview by Mat Snow, *MOJO*, December 1994.

- (pp. 119 and 464) Interview by Anthony DeCurtis, *Rolling Stone*, February 23, 1995, used by kind permission of Anthony DeCurtis.

- (p. 355) Interview by Mat Snow, *MOJO*, December 1997, used by kind permission of Mat Snow.

- (pp. 456 and 468) Interview by Sylvie Simmons, *Rolling Stone*, April1998, used by kind permission of Sylvie Simmons.

- (second quote on p. 406) Interview in *What'd I Say: The Atlantic Story* (New York: Welcome Rain, 2001), p. 385.

- (p. 402) Chris Welch and Geoff Nicholls, *John Bonham: A Thunder of Drums* (San Francisco: Backbeat Books, 2001), p. 121, used by kind permission of Chris Welch.

- (pp. 153, 155, 216, and 461) Interview by Adrian Deevoy, *Blender*, August 15, 2002, used by kind permission of Adrian Deevoy.

- (pp. 46, 362, 376, 458, and 474) Unpublished audio interview by Gavin Martin for the *Daily Mirror*, 2003, used by kind permission of Gavin Martin.

- (p. 120) G. Brown, *Colorado Rocks!: A Half-Century of Music in Colorado* (Boulder: Pruett Publishing, 2004).

- (second quote on p. 182) Interview by Nigel Williamson in *Uncut*, May 2005, used by kind permission of Nigel Williamson.

- (first quote on p. 481) Interview by Allan Jones in *Uncut*, November 2007, used by kind permission of Allan Jones.

- (second quote on p. 481) Interview by Sylvie Simmons, *The Guardian*, May 16, 2008, used by kind permission of Sylvie Simmons.

- (pp. 36 and 46) Anthony DeCurtis, ed., *Blues & Chaos: The Music Writing of Robert Palmer* (New York: Scribner, 2009), pp. 245–246 and 249, used by kind permission of Augusta Palmer.

- (first quote on p. 190, and pp. 459, 505, and 511) Interview by Keith Cameron, *MOJO*, September 2010, used by kind permission of Keith Cameron.

- (second quote on page 190) Loraine Alterman, *Melody Maker*, August 4, 1973.

- (p. 40) Interview on *The John Bonham Story*, first broadcast on BBC Radio 2 on September 28, 2010.

- (p. 31 and second quote on p. 482) Interview by Adrian Thrills, *Daily Mail*, October 8, 2010, used by kind permission of Adrian Thrills.

- (p. 489) Interview by Ed Vulliamy, *The Observer*, January 30, 2011, used by kind permission of Ed Vulliamy.

HOSSAM RAMZY quotes on pp. 465 and 468 from interview in *Robert Plant's Blue Note* (Sexy Intellectual DVD, 2011), used by kind permission of Elio España/Prism Films.

TERRY REID quotes on pp. 465 and 468 from unpublished transcript of interview by Mick Houghton, Autumn 2010, used by kind permission of Mick Houghton.

JOHN RENBOURN quote on p. 13 from Alan Clayson, *Led Zeppelin: The Origin of the Species* (New Malden: Chrome Dreams, 2006), p. 91, used by kind permission of Alan Clayson.

KEITH RICHARDS quote on p. 14 from *According to the Rolling Stones* (London: Weidenfeld and Nicolson, 2003), p. 34, used by kind permission of the Rolling Stones.

RICHARD RIEGEL quote on pp. 129–130 from interview by Chuck Eddy, *Creem*, June 1988, used by kind permission of Chuck Eddy.

LISA ROBINSON quotes:

- (pp. 202–203, 203, and 205) Paul Gorman, *In Their Own Write* (London: Sanctuary Books, 2001), used by kind permission of Paul Gorman.

- (p. 125) Robert Greenfield, *The Last Sultan: The Life and Times of Ahmet Ertegun* (New York: Simon & Schuster, 2011), p. 219, used by kind permission of Robert Greenfield.

PAUL RODGERS quotes on pp. 212 and 222 from *The John Bonham Story*, first broadcast on BBC Radio 2 on September 28, 2010.

TONY SECUNDA quotes on p. 39 from interview by Dave Thompson, *Goldmine*, April 2, 2004, used by kind permission of Dave Thompson.

BURKE SHELLEY quote on p. 139 from BBC4 documentary *Heavy Metal Britannia*, first broadcast in March 2010.

PAUL SIMONON quote on p. 304 from Chris Salewicz, *Creem*, November 1979, used by kind permission of Chris Salewicz.

SABLE STARR quote on p. 232 from interview by Nick Kent, *New Musical Express*, June 9, 1973, used by kind permission of Nick Kent.

ROD STEWART quote on p. 89 from interview by Bud Scoppa in *Circus*, July 1970, used by kind permission of Bud Scoppa.

RAY THOMAS quote on p. 34 from Pete Frame, *The Complete Rock Family Trees* (London: Omnibus Press, 1993), p. 13, used by kind permission of Pete Frame.

DAN TREACY quotes on pp. 304 and 336 from interview by David Cavanagh, uncut.co.uk, January 2009, used by kind permission of David Cavanagh.

STEVEN TYLER quote on p. 479 from radio interview by Howard Stern, January 18, 2011.

STEVE VAN ZANDT quote on p. 76 from speech inducting Frank Barsalona into the Rock and Roll Hall of Fame, January 2005, used by kind permission of the Rock and Roll Hall of Fame.

CHARLIE WATTS quote on p. 20 from *According to the Rolling Stones* (London: Weidenfeld and Nicolson, 2003), p. 43, used by kind permission of the Rolling Stones.

STEVE WEISS quote on p. 194 from John McDermott with Eddie Kramer, *Jimi Hendrix: Setting the Record Straight* (New York: Warner Books, 1992), p. 140, used by kind permission of John McDermott.

JERRY WEXLER quotes:

* (p. 108) Robert Greenfield, *The Last Sultan: The Life and Times of Ahmet Ertegun* (New York: Simon & Schuster, 2011), p. 218, used by kind permission of Robert Greenfield.

* (p. 106) Jerry Wexler with David Ritz, *Rhythm and the Blues: A Life in American Music* (New York: Knopf, 1993), pp. 169–71, used by kind permission of David Ritz.

DAVID WILLIAMS quotes on pp. 8, 9, and 10–11, and 21 from David Williams, *The First Time We Met the Blues* (York: Music Mentor Books, 2009), pp. 19, 22–23, and 101, used by kind permission of David Williams.

MICHAEL WINNER quote on p. 416 from interview by Stephen Dalton, uncut.co.uk, January 2008, used by kind permission of Stephen Dalton.

BILL WYMAN quote on p. 12 from *Stone Alone: The Story of a Rock 'n' Roll Band* (London: Viking, 1990), pp. 87 and 122.

ACKNOWLEDGMENTS

My gratitude to Robert Plant, Jimmy Page, and John Paul Jones for the interviews they have given me during the last decade.

My deepest thanks to the following musicians, engineers, roadies, groupies, security men, writers, relatives, employees, friends, enemies, partners-in-crime, and indirect acquaintances of Page, Plant, Jones, John Bonham, and Peter Grant, who spoke of their experiences with Led Zeppelin, the Yardbirds, and other bands:

Sam Aizer, Keith Altham, Mike Appleton, Jane Ayer, June Harris Barsalona, David Bates, Maggie Bell, Ed Bicknell, Rodney Bingenheimer, Robbie Blunt, Bill Bonham, Caroline Boucher, Loraine Alterman Boyle, Bebe Buell, Alan Callan, Jack Calmes, Julie Carlo, Phil Carlo, Gary Carnes, Roy Carr, Phil Carson, Clem Cattini, Chris Charlesworth, Peter Clifton, Marilyn Cole, Richard Cole, Gyl Corrigan-Devlin, John Crutchley, David Dalton, Michael Des Barres, Pamela Des Barres, Marie Dixon, Chris Dreja, Mark Ellen, Bob Emmer, BP Fallon, Mick Farren, Kim Fowley, Mitchell Fox, Paul Francis, Tony Franklin, Tom Fry, Kevyn Gammond, Vanessa Gilbert, Danny Goldberg, Gloria Grant, Helen Grant, Jerry Greenberg, Geoff Grimes, Ross Halfin, Connie Hamzy, Roy

Harper, Bill Harry, Andrew Hewkin, Dave Hill, Abe Hoch, Glenn Hughes, Elizabeth Iannaci, Tony Iommi, Anni Ivil, Andy Johns, Glyn Johns, Shelley Kaye, Nick Kent, Desiree Kirke, Simon Kirke, Eddie Kramer, Harvey Kubernik, Benji LeFevre, Dave Lewis, Harvey Lisberg, Paul Lockey, Mark London, Unity MacLean, Mikeal Maglieri, Tony Mandich, Terry Manning, Danny Markus, Lori Mattix, Mario Medious, Martin Meissonnier, John Mendelssohn, Laurence Myers, the late Howard Mylett, Ron Nevison, Dave Northover, Jeff Ocheltree, John Ogden, Dave Pegg, Mac Poole, Aubrey Powell, Guy Pratt, Perry Press, Barry Jay Reiss, Jake Riviera, the late Willie Robertson, Steven Rosen, Cynthia Sach, Janine Safer Whitney, Edward St. Aubyn, Ellen Sander, Rat Scabies, Dennis Sheehan, Jim Simpson, Digby Smith, Henry Smith, Steve Smith, Mat Snow, Denny Somach, Martin Stone, Big Jim Sullivan, Brad Tolinski, Jaan Uhelszki, Jon Wealleans, Chris Welch, Morgana Welch, Jack White, Richard Williams, Roy Williams, Sally Williams, and Joe "Jammer" Wright. I also drew on past interviews with Nicky Chinn, Iggy Pop, and the late Jerry Wexler.

I should also like to thank the following writers for generously granting permission to include quotes from their interviews and other published works:

In particular, Stuart Grundy, Dave Lewis, Steven Rosen, Mat Snow, John Tobler, and Chris Welch, but also Loraine Alterman Boyle, Keith Altham, Johnny Black, David Cavanagh, Chris Charlesworth, Robert Christgau, Alan Clayson, the Ken Colyer Foundation, Cameron Crowe, Stephen Dalton, Anthony DeCurtis, Adrian Deevoy, Alan DiPerna, Harry Doherty, Chuck Eddy, Marianne Faithfull, Pete Frame, Danny Goldberg, Patrick Goldstein, Fred Goodman, Paul Gorman, Jim Green, Robert Greenfield, Nick Hasted, Paul Henderson, Paolo Hewitt, Tom Hibbert, Mick Houghton, Rob Hughes, Jonh Ingham, James Jackson, Allan Jones, Nick Kent, Harvey Kubernik, Larry LeBlanc, Gavin Martin, John McDermott, Rick McGrath, Charles Shaar Murray, Andrew Loog Oldham, Paul Rambali, Randy Patterson, John Pidgeon, Eric Pooley, David Ritz,

Chris Salewicz, Paul Sexton, Adrian Thrills, Dave Schulps, Bud Scoppa, Sylvie Simmons, Phil Sutcliffe, Dave Thompson, Steve Turner, Kieron Tyler, Jaan Uhelszki, Ed Vulliamy, Mick Wall, Michael Watts, Steven P. Wheeler, David Williams, Richard Williams, Nigel Williamson, and Mark Williams. Thanks in addition to Mark Ellen, Jim Henke, and Augusta Palmer for granting permission on behalf of other writers.

I am especially indebted to Dave Lewis, Richard Cole, Phil Carlo, and the late Howard Mylett for their considerable kindness and help with this book.

Among those I interviewed, the following people provided me with additional assistance along the way:

Jane Ayer, Loraine Alterman Boyle, Ross Halfin, Dave Lewis, Unity MacLean, Don Snowden, Martin Stone, Chris Welch, and Roy Williams.

My thanks to the following people for granting permission to use photographs and other items from their personal collections:

Loraine Alterman Boyle, Phil Carlo, Gary Carnes, Peter Clifton, Richard Cole, John Crutchley, Chris Huston, Anni Ivil, Jas Kaur, Eddie Kramer, Tom Locke, Dave Pegg, and David Williams. Thanks to Jeff Schwartz for sourcing the Chuck Boyd images.

The following people also helped greatly in my research, and I thank them, too:

David Anderle, Ralph Baker, Lynden Barber, David Bickers, Hugo Brackenbury, Tracy Carns, Barbara Charone, Philip Dodd, Elio España, Andy Farquarson, Jan Favié, Jeff Gold, Carl Gottlieb, Nigel Grainge, George Groom-White, Nick de Grunwald, Noddy Holder, Jas Kaur, Tony Keys, Debbie Kruger, John Lewis, Dora Loewenstein, Gary Lucas, Rob Mady, Pete Makowski, Bob Mehr, Regine Moylett, Peter Noble, Joseph Pereira, Joel Peresman, Nicola Powell, Mark Pringle, Paul Rambali, Ira Robbins, Gilly Roswell, Len Sachs, Kevin Saunders, Jon Savage, Phil Sutcliffe, Rupert Wace, Alan Warner, Brian Wells, Peter Wilson, and Paul Yamada.

My thanks for sterling transcription services: Kat Johnson, Fred Hoskyns, Jake Hoskyns, and George Slater.

My deep gratitude to Lee Brackstone, Angus Cargill, and Dave Watkins at Faber for their unwavering belief in this book, and to Tom Miller, Jorge Amaral, John Simko, and Richard DeLorenzo at John Wiley & Sons. Thank you to my agents Jonny Geller and Sarah Lazin and others at Curtis Brown and Sarah Lazin Books who've gone out of their way to help.

Finally, for her love and unflagging support throughout: my adorable and gorgeous wife, Natalie.

NOTES

xv *"There is a point in your life"* Chuck Klosterman, *Killing Yourself to Live: 85% of a True Story* (New York: Scribner, 2005), pp. 197–200.

xvi *"Led Zeppelin always drew a difficult element"* Bill Graham and Robert Greenfield, *Bill Graham Presents: My Life Inside Rock and Out* (New York: Doubleday, 1990), p. 399.

xvi *"By 1975, ZoSo was painted or carved on every static thing"* Donna Gaines, "The Ascension of Led Zeppelin", in *Rolling Stone: The '70s* (New York: Little, Brown and Company, 1998), pp. 16–17.

xvii *"It's remarkable that we kept it going"* Steven Rosen, *Guitar World*, July 1986.

xx *"Pagey liked the idea"* Mat Snow, *New Musical Express*, 8 June 1985.

xxi *"The enjoyment that Led Zeppelin has given"* Erik Davis, *Led ZeppelinIV* (New York: Continuum Books), p. 152.

INDEX